All About Camping

All About

by Park

Camping

Ranger W. K. Merrill

Stackpole Books

ALL ABOUT CAMPING
Copyright © 1962, 1963 by W. K. Merrill

FIRST PRINTING in 1970 as
a STACKPOLE RUBICON BOOK

Published by
STACKPOLE BOOKS
Cameron and Kelker Streets
Harrisburg, Pa. 17105

Printed in U.S.A.

CONTENTS

1. Introduction to Camping   1

The variety of camping experience   /   Camping as family recreation /   Where to go and what to expect in state parks, national forests and parks, and trailer campgrounds   /   Camping organizations   / Advance planning

2. Information on National Parks, Forests, and Elsewhere   9

National and regional headquarters of the National Park Service   / Addresses of national parks   /   Locations and attractions of each national park   /   National and regional headquarters of the Forest Service   /   Locations and attractions of each national forest   / Where to write for information on game laws and travel in all the states and provinces and Mexico

3. Vacations—North or South   49

The Lake Superior Loop Trip   /   Canoeing, hunting, and fishing in the Quetico-Superior country   /   River and canyoneering trips   / The Trans-Canada and Alaska highways   /   Customs, firearms, and vehicle regulations for Americans traveling in Canada   /   Highway, rail, ferry, air, and steamship travel in Alaska   /   Hunting, fishing, and skiing in Alaska   /   Driving, hunting, and fishing in Mexico   / Restrictions on duty-free goods from Canada and Mexico

4. Automobile, Tent, and Trailer Camping   78

Semi-self-contained mobile outfits / Solving space and loading problems in station wagon camping / Bedding / Cooking and eating utensils / Keeping ice boxes cold and dry / Sizes and types of tents / How to erect tents and flies / Providing ventilation and shade for tents / Sheltering supplies from rain / Tent housekeeping / Waterproofing tents / Campsite selection / Protecting equipment and food from animals / Renting gear for a trial run / Dog care in camp / Folding tent-trailer outfits vs. travel trailers / Where to get camping equipment / Planning your trip / How to find and photograph nearly 200 birds / Predicting the weather / Preventing forest fires / What to do if lost / Suggested equipment for campers with autos and house trailers / How to stretch travel dollars / Things to check before you go / Disabled car distress signal / Avoiding poisonous plants and snakes / Safe mountain driving / Dangers of unexplored caves / Guidebooks for eating and lodging

5. Taking to the Water   138

Typical boating costs / Where to get boat handling instruction / Federal and state boating regulations / How to pick the boat you need / What to look for in buying a boat motor / Sturdy hitching arrangements for boat trailers / Tips on launching and operating boats / Where to get boating information / Safe ways of swimming, water skiing, scuba diving, and skin diving / What to take along on a boat cruise camping trip / Getting balky outboard motors to perform / How to prevent theft of boats and motors / Proper methods of loading and paddling canoes / Portages / Safe canoeing practices / Folboting

6. CB Radio Goes Camping   165

Federal licensing requirements for Citizens Band radio / Range and interference / How hunters, fishermen, and campers use CB radio / CB radio in Canada and Mexico / Where to get information / Conforming to FCC regulations / Observing the courtesy of the air waves

7. Desert Camping—All Seasons   177

Desert state parks and national monuments in the Southwest, Colorado, and Texas / Planning a desert trip / Four-wheel drive vehicles / Safety precautions / Equipment needed for jeep or power-wagon / Personal items to take along / Water supply / Avoiding flash floods, rattlesnakes, and scorpions

8. Snow Camping—Winter or Summer   182

Physical conditioning / Choosing your party / Clothing needed / Keeping clothing clean and dry / Building a lean-to / Tents / Bivouac sheet / Snow shelters / Sleeping bags and air mattresses / Tips on sleeping comfortably / Efficient ways to melt snow for drinking water / Lightweight food, cooking kits, and stoves / Rucksacks / Skis and ski maintenance / First-aid and repair kits / Avoiding avalanches / Loading sleds / Skiers' rules for safety and courtesy / Equipment check list

9. Knapsack Camping—Anywhere   202

Advantages in hiking / The Pacific Crest and Appalachian trails / Sources of trail information / Hikers' pointers on breaking in boots, foot care, and hitting a comfortable stride / Clothing, shelter, and bedding / Packs and packing for comfort / Food and cooking equipment / Trail guidebooks and backpacking manuals / Suggested equipment for single knapsackers and man-and-wife teams

10. Mountain Travel and Climbing Technique   217

Correct body balance / How to ascend and descend on hard ground, grassy slopes, scree slopes, and talus slopes / Safe climbing procedure / Using holds on steep slopes / Belaying, signaling, rappeling, and other rope-climbing techniques

11. Saddle and Pack-Outfit Camping   227

Services of professional packers / Costs / Hiking with rented burros / Pack outfit equipment check list

12. National Parks and National Forests   232

Services of forest and park rangers / How national parks differ from national forests in purpose and use / The "multiple use" management principle in national forests / Accommodations and guide service in national parks / Recreation available in national forests / Wilderness Areas in national forests / How to obtain a Forest Service summer home and maintain it safely

13. The Campfire   242

Campfire permit / Starting your campfire / Types of fire lays / Best woods for different cooking methods / Controlling and extinguishing fires / Fire pits and grates

14. Camp Cooking   252

Cooking with foil / Hearty outdoor recipes for coffee, tea, pancakes, biscuits, soups, stews, hashes, desserts, and many more / Cooking without utensils / Disposing of used foil

15. Camp Grub Lists and Emergency Rations   260

Food list for two persons on a 10-day trip / One week's menus for two persons / Food storage suggestions / Calculating quantities of food staples for 10-50 men on camping stays of any length

16. Dehydrated Food   265

Space- and weight-saving advantages / Directions for preparing / High-altitude cooking / Four-man and eight-man packaged daily menus / Suppliers of emergency rations and dehydrated foods

17. Wilderness Craftsmanship   272

How survival may depend on wilderness skills / Snares for trapping animals / Handling axes correctly and safely / Saws and knives

18. Pathfinding by Compass   280

Invention of the compass / Types of compasses / Meridians and magnetic declinations / Taking compass readings / Taking compass bearings from maps / Using landmarks with compasses / When to use the compass

19. Pathfinding with Maps   296

Map north and map scale / Geological Survey topographic maps / What the various lines on maps mean / How to stake a mining claim / Orienting a map / Pathfinding with a map but no compass / Finding direction without compass or map by the shadow, watch and sun, and Owendoff shadow-tip methods / Telling time with the Owendoff method / Finding direction by locating the North Star

20. Outdoor Measurement   307

Using your body measurements as an outdoor ruler / Measuring the length of your pace / How to measure the width of a stream or height of a tree / How to tell how soon the sun will set

21. Saddling and Packing   313

Horse nomenclature / Folding the blanket, placing the saddle, and tightening the cinch / Proper stirrup length / Mounting and dismounting / Saddling and loading a pack animal / Leading pack stock / Weight of load and mileage for horses, burros, and mules / Pack and saddle equipment / Pack hitches and knots / Lashings

22. Care of Saddle and Pack Animals and Sled Dogs   330

Gaining the animals' confidence / When and how much to feed and water stock / Shoeing / Symptoms and treatment for diseases of horses and mules / Grooming, resting, and preventive health care of stock / Buying a saddle horse / When and how much to feed sled dogs / Nutrition formula for sled dogs / Tips on handling sled dogs

23. Safety in the Outdoors   340

Avoiding common campground hazards / Treatment and prevention of mountain sickness, blisters, sun and wind burns, and snow blindness / How to purify water / Preventing cutting tool accidents / Ice and mountain rescues

24. Wilderness First-Aid   349

Shock / Wounds with severe bleeding / Snake bite / Stoppage of breathing / Heart stoppage / Heart attack / Burns / Fractures and dislocations / Minor wounds / Poisoning / Sprains / Prolonged exposure to cold / Fever and infections / Pneumonia and virus flu / Headaches / Abdominal injury / Medicinal uses of cold and hot packs, baking soda, mustard, sugar pine sugar, salt, grease, and vinegar / Medical supplies desirable

25. Survival   365

"Drownproofing" / Survival in cold and snow / Equipment needed for Arctic survival / Treatment for frost bite / Dangers of the deserts / Water, game, and edible plants in deserts / How to attract rescue in the desert or walk out under your own power / Coastal survival

Appendix I. Addresses of Outfitters   381
Appendix II. Bibliography   383
Index   389

ACKNOWLEDGMENTS

The production of this book would have been impossible without the kind assistance of many hands. The author wishes to acknowledge his deep appreciation to the many Rangers, State Highway and other officials who helped gather information from the traveling public throughout the United States, Canada and Mexico on what the outdoorsman wanted in a recreational handbook. Many thanks to the following dignitaries, officials, outdoor clubs, newspapers and outfitters for their material, comments, quotations, illustrations, and suggestions:

General Dwight D. Eisenhower, former President of the United States.

The Hon. Richard M. Nixon, former Vice President of the United States.

The Hon. Steward L. Udall, Secretary of the Interior.

The Hon. William A. Egan, Governor of the State of Alaska.

The Hon. Albert D. Rosellini, Governor of the State of Washington.

The Hon. Edmund G. Brown, Governor of the State of California.

The Hon. Nicholas Roosevelt, Author, Diplomat, Conservationist, Member of the California State Recreation Commission.

The Hon. Grant H. Pearson, Representative, 18th District of Alaska, former Chief Park Ranger and Superintendent of Mt. McKinley National Park, Alaska.

The Hon. Lawrence S. Rockefeller, Chairman, Outdoor Recreation Resources Review Commission and Conservationist.

The Hon. Jack W. Emmert, Member Consultant, ORRRC and former Superintendent of Idaho State Parks and Retired Superintendent, Glacier National Park, Montana.

Mrs. Anna Elinor Roosevelt, Author and Columnist, Hyde Park, New York.

The Bureau of Outdoors Recreation, Department of the Interior.

The Hon. Alan Field, Director, and staff, Canadian Government Travel Bureau, Ottawa, Canada.

The Hon. El Secretaria de Agricultura y Formento, Direccion Forestal y de Caza, Mexico, D. F.

El Jefe del Depto. de Parques Nacionales, Mexico, D. F.

The Hon. Sr. Roberto Garuno Garcia, Direccion General De Proteccion y Repolacion.

Admiral A. C. Richmond, former Commandant, United States Coast Guard.

Brigadier General J. B. Sweet, USA Ret., and his staff.

Colonel R. S. Gunderson, USAF, Ret.

Captain C. H. Roach, U. S. Coast Guard, Chief, Merchant Vessel Insp. Division.

Captain John S. Shaver, (MC)USN, Commanding Officer, Department of Cold Weather Medicine, U. S. Naval Medical School, National Naval Medical Center.

Conrad L. Wirth, Director, National Park Service, Department of the Interior.

Horace M. Albright, former Director, National Park Service, Member Advisory Council, ORRRC; Director-Consultant, U. S. Borax & Chemical Association, N. Y.

Eivin T. Scoyen, Associate Director, National Park Service, retired.

Daniel B. Beard, Assistant Director, National Park Service.

Lawrence F. Cook, Chief, Ranger Division & Activities, National Park Service.

John D. Coffman, Chief Forester, National Park Service, retired.

Carlos S. Whiting, Chief of Press Relations, National Park Service.

Jerry B. House, Lake Mead National Recreational Area, National Park Service.

Coleman C. Newman, Biologist, National Park Service, Washington, D.C.

Stanley McComas, Chief Park Ranger, Olympic National Park, Washington.

John B. Stratton, Superintendent, Haleakala National Park, Hawaii.

John C. Preston, Superintendent, Yosemite National Park, California.

Guy Hopping, Superintendent, General Grant National Park and Assistant Superintendent in charge, Kings Canyon National Park, Deceased.

Ernest P. Leavitt, Superintendent, Crater Lake National Park, Ret., Deceased.

Thomas Carpenter, Regional Landscape Engineer, National Park Service, Retired.

Edward P. Cliff, Chief, United States Forest Service, Department of Agriculture.

Dr. Richard E. McArdle, Chief, United States Forest Service, retired.

John Sieker, Director, Recreation and Land Uses, U. S. Forest Service.

Clint Davis, Director, Division of Information & Education, U. S. Forest Service.

The Regional Foresters and their staffs; Regions 1, 5, 6, 8, and 9, USFS.

The Forest Supervisor and his staff, Superior National Forest, Minnesota.

Harry D. Grace and his staff, Stanislaus National Forest, California.

Melville A. Walker, Forest Engineer, Forest Service, Retired.

Jesse R. Hall, Forest Supervisor, USFS, Retired.

Joe E. Elliott, Forest Supervisor, USFS, Retired.

Robert W. Ayres, Forest Supervisor, USFS, Retired.

DeWitt Nelson, Director, Department of Conservation, State of California; California State Contact Officer, ORRRC.

Charles DeTurk, Director, Parks and Recreation, Resources Agencies, California.

Edward F. Dolder, Chief, Division of Beaches & Parks, Resource Agencies, California.

Francis H. Raymond, State Forester, Department of Conservation, Calif.

Bert F. Williams, Information Officer, Department of Fish & Game, Calif.

William Overton, State Game Warden, San Diego County, California.

Vincent N. Dona, State Game Warden, Tuolumne County, California.

Clifford C. Presnall, Chief, P & R Control, Branch of Sports Fisheries, Fish & Wildlife Service, Department of the Interior.

Lewis D. Brown, Chief, Distribution Section, U. S. Geological Survey Service.

J. O. Kilmartin, Chief, Map Information Office, Geological Survey Service.
Richard S. MacCarteney, Chief, Reference Division, Library of Congress.
Jack B. Long, Traverse Engineer, Geophysical & Polar Research Center, University of Wisconsin.
William E. Long, Glacierologist, U. S. Antarctic Research Program, National Science Foundation, University of Ohio.
C. Frank Brockman, Professor of Forestry, University of Washington; former Chief Park Naturalist, Yosemite National Park; Member State Park Commission.
Archie Stevenot, President, Golden Chain Council, Mother Lode area, Conservationist.
Leslie Ivan Ferrell, Consultant, Anaheim, California.
Harry S. Hinkley, Tuolumne County Farm Advisor, University of Calif.
The late Luis Henderson, artist.
Richard Pargeter, Illustrator; Member Seattle Mountain Rescue Team.
Elinore Heiskell, Teacher, Critic and Advisor, Bakersfield, California.
Bruce E. MacKinnon, Illustrator, Ranger-Historian, Columbia State Park, California.
R. S. Owendoff, Author, Falls Church, Virginia.
Clay Blair, Jr., Director of Editorial Development, The Curtis Publishing Company, Saturday Evening Post and other Publications.
William B. Dover, Executive Story Director, Walt Disney Productions, Calif.
Robert I. Snajdr, Book Review Editor, Cleveland Plain Dealer, Cleveland, Ohio.
Cathrine E. McMullen, Managing Editor, Better Camping, Milwaukee, Wisc.
George Thompson, Department Editor, Family Camping, Philadelphia, Pa.
Richard S. Calhoun, Editor, Camping Trails, Whittier, California.
George & Iris Wells, Editors, Camping Guide, Canton, Ohio.
Charles Webster, Editor & Publisher, The Port Angeles Evening News, Wash.
Harvey McGee, Editor & Publisher, The Union Democrat, Tuolumne County, California.
The National Park Currier and Staff, Washington, D. C.
The Technical Editor, Ford Times, Ford Motor Company, Dearborn, Michigan.
Chevrolet Motor Division, General Motors Corporation, Detroit, Michigan.
The Buick Magazine, Editorial Department, Detroit, Michigan.
Every Woman's Family Circle Magazine, New York, N. Y.
Reader's Digest Association, Incorporated, Pleasantville, New York.
Alan Swallow, Publisher, The Swallow Press, Sage Books, Big Mountain Press.
The Stackpole Company, Publishers, Harrisburg, Pennsylvania.
Summy-Birchard Publishing Company, Evanston, Illinois.
Joseph J. Murphy, G. Shirmer, Incorporated, New York, New York.
The Sierra Club of California.
The Potomac Appalachian Trail Club, Washington, D. C.
The National Campers & Hikers Association, Orange, New Jersey.
The High Sierra Packers Association, Eastern & Western Units, California.
Dr. George A. Faris, M.D., Tuolumne County, California.

Chapter 1

INTRODUCTION TO CAMPING

IN ALL OF US at times there is an instinct to heed the CALL OF THE WILD. It has been bred into man since time began, when he had to live off the land under the most primitive conditions. Modern man often experiences this urge—stronger in some than others. He wants to get out and hunt and fish—go into the wilderness—get away from crowds—use his own initiative in feeding himself and his family away from civilization—and to have it quiet where he can think and relax for a time. Millions of people are following this urge by going camping each year.

THE JOYS OF CAMPING

We are indeed a fortunate country, for nowhere else in the world can there be found so many prepared campsites or so much forested land developed for camping. No other nation has so many state and national parks and forests where one may camp the year around. No other place contains such a variety of wonderland, ranging from 200 feet below sea level in Death Valley to 20,320 feet in elevation in the new state of Alaska.

There has been a tremendous upsurge in the past five years in the popularity of all types of camping. If the present trend continues, thousands of families will each year be making their first camping vacation expedition into the great outdoors.

It has not been too long ago that camping was looked upon as an experience for only the strong and hardy. A few of these rugged individuals are still encountered in remote wilderness areas; however, the trend is for family or group camping. The camping trip may be a three-weeks vacation or it may be for overnight.

People are beginning to find that getting away from the job and the stress of city life can be a refreshing experience for all members of the family.

Campers dress informally in comfortable clothes, and tend to

1

eat easily prepared and simple meals, for there is so much
fun waiting and perhaps the vacation time is short. Some like
to just plain rest and relax, others enjoy hunting, fishing,
hiking, boating, swimming, water-skiing, horseback riding,
picture taking, or other outdoor sports. Some, more experienced
and hardier, prefer "packing in" to more isolated regions with
a pack and saddle outfit. Some enjoy panning for gold in the
Mother Lode country, others enjoy the flowers and wildlife
of the lakes and streams, the valleys, the mountains, or even

(Drawing by Luis M. Henderson)

the deserts of this vast vacation land of America. Even the aged and infirm who prefer to stay close to camp can enjoy the beautiful scenery, listen to the bird and animal life or the babbling stream, or sniff the forest odors fragrant with the smell of pine and fir. And how good to start the day with the aroma of coffee and bacon cooking on the camp stove!

At night, under the starry heavens, or in your tent or perhaps your travel trailer—your home away from home—it is wonderful to just drift off to sleep, lulled by the whisper of the breeze sighing through the pines, the music of a mountain stream, the call of a night bird, or the song of a coyote.

Those of you who sleep out under the stars will sense the peace and mystery of the primitive outdoors, and feel much closer to Nature and to God.

WOMEN AND CHILDREN IN CAMPING TODAY

Women and children camp—of course! Sure they do, but it seems only a few years ago that the term "camper" meant to most a rather limited category of people—principally Scouts who hiked and camped, or hardy males who fished and hunted the rugged terrain of far places. Now the picture is changed. Women as much as men reserve camping fun, outdoor recreation, and some form of relaxation in the open air for their vacation schedules. Among the reasons camping has "boomed" and become so popular as a family recreation activity is that women have found they can participate with greater enjoyment than they might have ever dreamed. Some credit for this, no doubt, is due to the lightweight and better equipment designed especially for the comfort and convenience of both the small fry and the fairer sex.

But, not all the credit. Women and children's sport or play clothes are easily adaptable to most types of camping and casual outdoor wear. As a specialized activity, camping does not necessarily demand a completely new or expensive wardrobe although specialized clothing usually is required for the woman mountain climber, the skier, or the backpacker. Clothing and equipment for children is also more widely suitable for camping than ever before. There are even small sleeping bags, small air mattresses, and a wide variety of other work and play items for children resulting from camping's growing influence. Rainy-day duds and gear come in many colors and

types. Specialized foot wear for the whole family can be
secured at reasonable prices for hiking, canoeing, camping,
or mountain walking. There is a wide variety of tents in sizes
and types especially attractive to the youngsters. We may yet
lag behind the Europeans in variety of colored tents now available, but we have long since broken away from our old ideas
that tents necessarily must come only in unattractive white,
military brown, or dark green colors. For this welcome change
in tent color tradition we undoubtedly should credit the influence of woman's more imaginative ideas on color use.

But, regardless of the reasons, more women are heading for
outdoor vacations, shouldering their camping gear with their
mountain climbing husbands, or loading the car with the
family and the youngsters and leaving for some favorite campground.

Camping provides an opportunity for mother and father to
teach children good outdoor manners and sportsmanship.
Children are natural campers and enjoy the excitement and
adventure of something new and different. After the first camping trip they can hardly wait until the next. In no other way
will many of the younger generation find as good opportunity
to learn fishing, bird-watching, the names of wild flowers, facts
about animals, and other fascinating woods lore.

Surprisingly enough, there are more camping parties than
you might expect to find which are made up entirely of women,
or of women and children. The advantages of the small folding tent-trailers have not been overlooked by such campers
although many of them will be observed using conventional
tent outfits.

For most families, camping is the happy group venture
which during the usually limited vacation period allotted Dad,
can offer some new desirable form of activity to each family
member. Most everyone in the family enjoys some amount of
tourist travel. Dad and the boys may accent boating, fishing,
exploring, or taking pictures. Mother likes to meet new people,
have the family together, enjoy the sun, the scenery, and possibly the water sports. She finds the camping routine a
welcome change from the home routine. There is less housekeeping involved, and food preparation chores in camp take
on a new and novel character—a welcome change from home

routine, indeed. The girls enjoy the same and make a big adventure of it all. In later years when the children are grown there will be some wonderful memories of common family camping experiences to recall with wistful relish. Yes, women and children camp; more so now than ever before!

WHERE TO GO

Campers facing their first trip into vacation land want to know right away where to go camping. State, national forest, and national park campgrounds offer a large assortment of accessible sites, from very primitive areas in the back country to the latest, most modern campgrounds in the improved areas.

Most are within driving range of cities or towns. In the West, one can find developed camp sites in the rain forest of Washington, near the high waterfalls and in the big trees of Yosemite, or below sea level in Death Valley. Beach camps are abundant on both coasts of the United States, where coastal and deep-sea fishing may be enjoyed. Camping is not confined to the West for there are many fine state park camps and several national parks in the East.

Family campers can choose almost any type of outdoor recreation or a combination of vacation sports wherever they may decide to go. Many families flit from campground to campground—from the beach, to the desert, and on up into the mountains. Others go to the same camp spot each year because it holds some particular charm for them and their needs. In any event, expenses are kept at a minimum because camping is the most economical way of traveling.

Campers have learned that they can be comfortable and clean, thanks to the many new improvements that have been made recently, such as improved lightweight clothing and tents, and better sleeping bags, air mattresses, cots, camp stoves, lanterns, compact cooking utensils, and a growing list of packaged foods. Delicious, concentrated, dehydrated foods contain more nourishment and vitamins than ever before. They have been processed to make cooking a joy instead of a chore. New types of equipment and supplies appear in the market almost daily.

Getting ready to go camping can be almost as much fun as actually out on the trip; however, it does entail some organizing and planning. A lot depends on how many persons will be in your party, where you plan to go, and how long you will be gone. To the uninitiated the preparation can sometimes take on the aspects of a major expedition. But after a shake-down trip, you will know what to take, what to leave behind, and how to pack.

STATE PARK CAMPGROUNDS. Most state campgrounds are found in the lower elevations from sea level to 4,000 feet. They are usually located on a stream, lake, or along an ocean beach. Camping is permitted in most, only picnicking in others. A small fee is charged for camping and a nominal charge for fire wood, since in most parks it is prohibited to gather or cut wood.

NATIONAL FOREST CAMPGROUNDS. National forest campgrounds are located mostly in forested mountain country at elevations ranging from 2,000 feet to well above 10,000 feet. Recreation (and camping) is only one of the multiple uses of a national forest; therefore, only the simplest camping facilities are provided in regular forest camps, such as tables, benches, rock stoves and fire places, a water supply, and simple sanitary facilities of the pit-toilet type. In larger camps operated by a concessionaire, additional facilities and conveniences are provided at a nominal fee. Lodging, meals, and supplies may often be obtained along through roads in these forests. In the outlying primitive areas one may usually camp wherever it is safe. Here he will have to dig his own garbage and toilet pit, and build his own rock cooking stove. Nearby he will of course want a suitable water supply.

NATIONAL PARK CAMPGROUNDS. Campgrounds in the national parks may be found even below sea level, and range up to some very high elevations in some of the country's most spectacular scenery. Most camps are equipped with water, tables, grill stoves, and adequate rest rooms. Stores, curio shops, gas stations, post offices, resorts, and restaurants are available. Ranger-naturalist service is provided to explain the natural features and phenomena. Each park is outstanding, with its own special beauty.

TRAILER CAMPGROUNDS. Special trailer camps have been set aside for the enjoyment of those hauling tent and house trailers. It is wise to enter these camps afoot and scout around for a campsite, especially if the road should lead down a steep grade to a camp spot along a stream or lake. It can be very difficult to turn around in some of the smaller camps. Beware of sand and gravel. Keep off the beach for one can really get stuck with a car and trailer outfit, especially in the spring. Take along some flat boards to put under wheels if needed. When fording, watch out for wet grass, mud, snow, ice, rocks, and deep water.

CAMPING ORGANIZATIONS

Contrary to popular beliefs, camping is not a one-season activity reserved only for vacation months. If you would like to meet other campers, exchange views and information, and meet with others periodically to talk about camping activities there is an organization known as the National Campers and Hikers Association, Inc., which you may join. The address is Box 451, Orange, New Jersey. This Association is a member of the International Federation of Camping Clubs and is a nonprofit, volunteer organization dedicated to the camper and hiker. Chances are the Association has a Chapter organization in being, or soon to be, in your vicinity.

CAMPING SEASONS

The general camping season varies somewhat according to the geographical location and elevation. Camping is possible during most of the year in southwest regions. In the north and northwest areas, camping usually opens from May 1st to September 30th, depending on weather conditions. Camps at higher elevations can be very cold at night, with ice forming on water. Be certain that you have sufficient antifreeze in your car radiator. Information regarding opening and closing dates may be obtained from the Forest Supervisor of the national forest you are interested in or from the Park Superintendent of any particular national park. Information and details may also be secured from the Washington, D. C. office of the service concerned, their regional offices, and from the Ranger in the district in which you plan to camp. For addresses in writing for information, see chapters 2 and 3.

ADVANCE PLANNING

Advance planning is a must for any trip. An equipment and supply list should be prepared and whittled down to necessities which must be assembled and packed properly in the family car or in personal knapsacks.

If you plan on going into a primitive wilderness region with a saddle and pack outfit, you must carefully weigh and package all equipment and supplies in panniers or kyacks so that they may be balanced properly on the pack saddle. An unbalanced pannier will pull the pack saddle sidewise, causing a sore-backed animal.

Maps of the section of wilderness country you plan vacationing in must be obtained, and fire permits and hunting and fishing licenses must be secured if you plan on this type of activity. Be sure to check your car and house trailer and home insurance policies to note if they are still valid and have not lapsed.

Now you are about ready to start on one of the greatest adventures of your life—going on that long-anticipated camping trip.

Chapter 2

INFORMATION ON NATIONAL PARKS, FORESTS, AND ELSEWHERE

In addition to the information included in this chapter on individual national parks, national forests, national monuments, and wilderness areas, addresses are provided to whom the reader may write for further detailed information about specific areas. Most of this literature is free.

INFORMATION ON NATIONAL PARKS

NATIONAL PARK HEADQUARTERS: The Director, National Park Service, U. S. Department of the Interior, Washington 25, D. C.

REGIONAL HEADQUARTERS: Address *Regional Director, _____ Region,* National Park Service, U. S. Department of the Interior, at the location as shown below.

Southeast Region: Richmond, Virginia.
Midwest Region: Omaha, Nebraska.
Southwest Region: Santa Fe, New Mexico.
Western Region: San Francisco, California.
Northeast Region: Philadelphia, Pennsylvania.
National Capital Region: Washington 25, D. C.

NATIONAL PARKS.

ACADIA: Superintendent, Acadia National Park, Box 690, Bar Harbor, Maine.

Area: 47 square miles. Open all year. *Location:* On Mount Desert Island and the coast of Maine. *Highways:* U. S. 1, Maine 3, 103A, 198. *Attractions:* Rugged coastal area on Mount Desert Island, Isle au Haut, and nearby mainland. First French missionary colony established in America. *Facilities:* 545 camp and picnic sites. *Nearby towns:* Bar Harbor, Ellsworth, Winter Harbor, and South West Harbor.

BIG BEND: Superintendent, Big Bend National Park, Big Bend National Park, Texas.

Area: 1,106 square miles. Open all year. *Location:* Southwestern Texas. *Highways:* U.S. 90, 385, Texas 118. *Attractions:* Mountains and desert in the great bend of the Rio Grande; its south boundary is the International Boundary between the United States and Mexico. The scenery, fauna, and flora are more typical of Mexico. *Facilities:* 156 camp and picnic sites, cabins, and meal service. Limited supplies. Accommodations in nearby towns; Alpine, Sanderson, and Marfa.

10   *All About Camping*

BRYCE CANYON: Superintendent, Bryce Canyon National Park, Bryce Canyon, Utah.

Area: 56 square miles. Open all year. *Location:* Southern Utah. *Highways:* U.S. 89, Utah 12. *Attractions:* Box canyon filled with a countless array of myriads of colored pinnacles and spires carved by rain, snow, and frost. *Facilities:* Lodge open from mid-June to mid-October; camp and picnic sites. *Nearby towns:* Panguitch, Junction, and Mt. Carmel.

CARLSBAD CAVERNS: Superintendent, Carlsbad Caverns National Park, Box 111, Carlsbad, New Mexico.

Area: 77 square miles. Open all year. *Location:* Southeastern New Mexico. *Highways:* U.S. 62, 180, 285, New Mexico 54. *Attractions:* Largest underground chambers yet discovered; series of connected caverns with magnificent and curious formations. *Facilities:* Lunch room in caverns; lodging and meals in nearby towns of White City and Carlsbad, or Artesia.

CRATER LAKE: Superintendent, Crater Lake National Park, Box 672, Medford 4, Oregon.

Area: 250 square miles. Open all year. *Location:* Crest of the Cascade Range in southwestern Oregon. *Highways:* U.S. 97, 99, Oregon 62 and 230. *Attractions:* Crater Lake, deepest lake on North American continent (1,983 feet) and fifth deepest in the world, occupies the heart of a once gigantic volcanic peak, Mount Mazama. *Facilities:* Hotel, cabins, and meals, picnic sites, and 180 campsites. No fishing license required.

EVERGLADES: Superintendent, Everglades National Park, Box 275, Homestead, Florida.

Area: 2,341 square miles. Open all year. *Location:* Southwestern Florida. *Highways:* U.S. 1, 41, Florida 27. *Attractions:* Largest subtropical wilderness in the United States. Extensive fresh and salt water areas, mangrove forest, open grassy prairies; abundant wildlife including rare and colorful birds. *Facilities:* 115 campsites, picnic sites. Outside accommodations. *Nearby towns:* Homestead and Florida City.

GLACIER: Superintendent, Glacier National Park, West Glacier, Montana.

Area: 1,583 square miles. Open all year. Inquire locally after mid-September on road conditions. *Location:* In Rocky Mountains of Northwestern Montana. *Highways:* U.S. 2, 89, 93, Montana 17, 49. *Attractions:* Some of the country's finest mountain scenery, more than sixty glaciers, and over two hundred beautiful lakes. Abundant wildlife, black and grizzly bear, deer, elk, mountain goat, and big horn sheep. *Facilities:* Hotels, cabins, 255 campsites. *Nearby towns:* West Glacier, East Glacier, Babb, and Whitefish.

GRAND CANYON: Superintendent, Grand Canyon National Park, Grand Canyon, Arizona.

Area: 1,009 square miles. Open all year. *Location:* Northern Arizona. *Highways:* U.S. 66, 89, Arizona 64, 67. *Attractions:* One of the world's greatest spectacles—an immense chasm four to eighteen miles wide and a mile deep. A sea of flaming, changing colors that defy description. This great multicolored canyon was cut by the Colorado River millions of years ago. *Facilities:* Meals and lodging; 418 campsites. *Towns:* Williams, Flagstaff, Cameron, and Fredonia.

GRAND TETON: Superintendent, Grand Teton National Park, Moose, Wyoming.

Area: 484 square miles. Open from mid-May to late October. *Location:* Embraces most of the scenic portion of the Teton Range of Wyoming, and northern portion of Jackson Hole, a high mountain valley. *Highways:* U.S. 89, 287, 26, 187, Wyoming 22. *Attractions:* Sublime peaks, canyons, and valleys. Much of the mountainous section of the park is above timberline (10,500 feet), the Tetons rising to 13,766 feet. The park includes seven large lakes, glaciers, snow fields, and extensive evergreen forests. *Facilities:* 545 campsites; cabins, lodges, hotel, and dude ranches near the town of Jackson. *Nearby towns:* Jackson, Rexburg, Alpine, and Driggs.

GREAT SMOKY MOUNTAINS: Superintendent, Great Smoky Mountains National Park, Gatlinburg, Tennessee.

Area: 781 square miles. Open all year. *Highways:* U.S. 441, 129, 64; Tennessee: 68, 30, 71, 72, 73, and 75. *Location:* In Tennessee and North Carolina. *Attractions:* Astride the Tennessee-North Carolina border, the Great Smoky Mountains, a portion of the Appalachian Range, cast a spell of mystery and enchantment. Lush vegetation extends to the very tops of the lofty peaks. A tenuous mist rises into a deep blue haze from which the mountains receive their name. Over 200,000 acres of virgin forests remain within the park. There are over 1,200 species of plants and shrubs. *Accommodations:* Limited accommodations may be had. Most visitors obtain lodging and meals outside the park. *Facilities:* Campsites, Tennessee side: 538; North Carolina side: 282. *Nearby towns:* Gatlinburg, Parkerville, Benton, Madisonville, Maryville, Townsend, Pigeon Forage, Cosby, Tennessee; Smokemont, Cherokee, Topton, Murphy, Duck Town, and Isabella, North Carolina.

HALEAKALA: Superintendent, Haleakala National Park, Maui, Hawaii.

Area: 26 square miles. Kahului, Maui, Hawaii. Open all year. Reached by plane and boat from mainland, and scheduled flight daily from Honolulu to Kahului, Maui. Limited boat service. *Attractions:* Haleakala Crater—seven and one-half miles long, two and one-half miles wide, twenty-one miles in perimeter, and 3,000 feet deep; 30 miles of riding and hiking trails; famous Silversword plants. Meals and lodging at Silversword Inn, May 15 through September 15. *Nearby towns:* Kahului and Hana.

HAWAII: Superintendent, Hawaii Volcanoes National Park, Hawaii, Hawaii.

Area: 266 square miles. Open all year. Reached by plane and ship from mainland, and by scheduled flights from Honolulu and inter-island steamship. *Attractions:* Active volcanoes, exotic plants and bird life, hiking trails, and lookout points; meals and lodging nearby. *Nearby towns:* Hilo, Kamuela, Hawi, and Kailua.

HOT SPRINGS: Superintendent, Hot Springs National Park, Box 859, Hot Springs National Park, Arkansas.

Area: 1.6 square miles. Open all year. *Highways:* U.S. 70, 270, Arkansas 7, 5. *Location:* In the Ouachita Mountains in center section of Arkansas. *Attractions:* 47 hot springs said to possess healing properties. Many hotels and lodging houses capable of housing 25,000 people. *Nearby towns:* Hot Springs, Mountain Pine, and Mountain Valley.

ISLE ROYALE: Superintendent, Isle Royale National Park, 87 N. Ripley St., Houghton, Michigan.

Area: 209 square miles. Open May 15 to November 1. *Location:* Upper Lake Superior near the International Boundary, Canada and the United States. No roads in park; it is reached by plane and by boat only. *Attractions:* The island is 47 miles long and from 5 to 9 miles wide. It is distinguished by its island wilderness, remote character, and as a habitat of one of the largest single moose herds in North America. Travel is by foot trails and boat. *Accommodations:* Lodges and cabins at Rock Harbor and Windigo Inn. Campgrounds are located at 6 points on the shores of the main island. Boats available at Houghton and Copper Harbor, Michigan. *Nearby towns:* Grand Marais and Grand Portage, Minnesota.

KINGS CANYON: Superintendent, Kings Canyon National Park, Three Rivers, California.

Area: 710 square miles. Open all year. *Highways:* U.S. 99, California 65, 180, 198. *Location:* East-central California, in the heart of the Sierra Nevada Range. The former General Grant National Park and the famous Redwood Mountain Groves of Big Trees (sequoia gigantea) have been added to Kings Canyon National Park. The park contains the General Grant tree, second largest living tree. There are hundreds of miles of wilderness trails and streams to fish. Trails lead to many peaks over 13,000 to 14,000 feet in elevation. The Cedar Grove road leads to the South Fork of the Kings River, and trails lead on over to the Middle Fork of the Kings. Lodging may be obtained in the park and on private land at Wilsonia and Big Stump; also in nearby towns. *Nearby towns:* Fresno, Visalia, Miramonte, Badger, and Pinehurst.

LASSEN VOLCANIC: Superintendent, Lassen Volcanic National Park, Mineral, California.

Area: 165 square miles. The Park is never officially closed, however, roads may be closed from November to June due to snow. *Highways:* U.S. 99, 299, 395 via California 44, 89, 36. *Location:* Southern end of Cascade Range in northeastern California. Contains spectacular volcanic exhibits including Mount Lassen. The western section of park includes a profusion of volcanic peaks of the "dome" type, of which Mt. Lassen is the outstanding example. The peak, itself, rises 10,453 feet above sea level—its last eruptions were from 1914 till 1917. (*Caution:* Visitors to thermal areas should stay on the trails and avoid slippery or crusty places, as steam and water is dangerously hot. Surface may be thin.) *Accommodations:* The Park is primarily a campers park and contains 456 campsites. Lodging may be had at Manzanita Lake Lodge and at Drakesbad, with limited services at Juniper Lake. *Nearby towns:* Mineral, Redding, and Chester.

MAMMOTH CAVE: Superintendent, Mammoth Cave National Park, Mammoth Cave, Kentucky.

Area: 80 square miles. Open all year. *Location:* Southcentral Kentucky. *Highways:* U.S. 31W, 62, 68, Kentucky 62, 65. *Attractions:* Longest known caverns in the United States; discovered about 1799. Caverns furnished saltpeter for gunpowder in 1812. *Accommodations:* Lodging and meals in Park. *Facilities:* 37 campsites. *Nearby towns:* Cave City, Mammoth Cave, Bowling Green, and Glasgow.

MESA VERDE: Superintendent, Mesa Verde National Park, Mesa Verde National Park, Colorado.

Area: 80 square miles. Open all year. *Highways:* U.S. 160, 666, 550, Colorado 789. *Attractions:* The park is one of our major archeological preserves. It was created in 1906 to preserve the hundreds of prehistoric structures left by a tribe of Indians about 1,000 years ago; most of them were cliff-dwellers. Mesa Verde means "green table" in Spanish. Guided Ranger-Naturalist trips. (*Caution:* In several places inspection of ruins requires descent along precipitous cliff trails; steep ladder-climbing on return. Inquire re such hazards in the case of older persons and smaller children before inspecting particular sites.) *Facilities:* (Summer only.) Spruce Tree Lodge. A number of semipermanent tent cottages having cots and bedding, lights, and minimum furniture are maintained for rent; 170 campsites. *Nearby towns:* Durango, Cortex, Silverton, Colorado; Shiprock and Aztec, New Mexico.

MOUNT MCKINLEY: Superintendent, Mount McKinley National Park, McKinley Park, Alaska.

Area: 3,030 square miles. Open June to September 15. *Highways:* Park road network connects with the Denali Highway, Alaska 8, running from Paxson to Mount McKinley National Park. All sections of road are closed in wintertime. The Alaska Railroad provides transportation at Seward, the ocean terminus, at Anchorage or Fairbanks. The Park can also be reached by air. A 3,000 foot landing field is located close to the McKinley Park Hotel. *Attractions:* The Park is a vast mountain wilderness and contains the highest mountain (20,320 feet) in North America. All of the larger northward-flowing glaciers of the Alaska Range originate from the peaks in the Park. Unusual wildlife. The ascent of Mt. McKinley involves many hazards and should only be attempted by experienced climbers. *Permission* to undertake the ascent *must be obtained* from the park superintendent. *Nearby towns:* Windy, Carlo, Garner, Healy Fork, Richardson, Fairbanks, and Paxson.

MOUNT RAINIER: Superintendent, Mount Rainier National Park, Longmire, Washington.

Area: 377 square miles. Open all year. *Location:* In Cascade Range in southwestern Washington. *Highways:* U.S. 410, 99, Washington 5. During winter months make local inquiry, some roads closed by snow and slides. Road to Paradise Valley open all year. Mount Rainier rises 14,408 feet and is the eleventh highest mountain in the United States; its base covers 100 square miles. There are 26 active glaciers radiating from the summit and slopes. Outstanding in Alpine scenery. *Accommodations:* No overnight accommodations in winter. *Facilities:* 262 campsites, picnic sites. *Nearby towns:* Longmire, Ashfork, Packwood, American River, and Parkway.

OLYMPIC: Superintendent, Olympic National Park, 600 East Park Ave., Port Angeles, Washington.

Area: 1,406 square miles. Open all year. *Location:* Olympic Peninsula in northwestern Washington. *Highways:* U.S. 101. *Attractions:* A rugged mountain wilderness of glacier-clad peaks, rushing streams, and many Alpine lakes; a wild coastal strip. Alpine meadows and rain forests (average 144 to 160 inches of rain on west side). Famous Mount Olympus, 7,954 feet in elevation. Largest elk herds of famous Roosevelt Elk. *Facilities:* 503 campsites, picnic sites. *Nearby towns:* Port Angeles, Joyce, Forks, Sappho, La Push, Clearwater, Amanda Park, Quinualt, Hoodsport, and Sequim.

PETRIFIED FOREST: Superintendent, Petrified Forest National Park, Holbrook, Arizona.

Area: 146 square miles. Open all year. *Location:* Northeast section of Arizona. *Highways:* U.S. 66 and U.S. 260. Arizona 63 traverses park. *Attractions:* The park is the site of the largest and most colorful concentrations of petrified wood in the world. There are 6 "forests," with great logs of agate and jasper lying on the ground and countless broken sections, fragments, and smaller chips forming a varicolored ground cover. Prehistoric Indians used the petrified wood to build homes, the ruins of which may be seen in the park. In addition to the quantities of agate, jasper, and chalcedony clays that have weathered into a haunting painted desert landscape, there are many desert animals. *Facilities:* Refreshments, lunches, souvenirs, gasoline, and oil may be purchased at the Painted Desert Inn and Rainbow Lodge. No overnight accommodations; camping is not allowed. *Nearby towns:* Joseph City and Holbrook to the west; Navajo, Chambers, and Sanders, northeast; and Concho, to the south.

PLATT: Superintendent, Platt National Park, Box 379, Sulphur, Oklahoma.

Area: 1.42 square miles. Open all year. *Location:* Southern Oklahoma. *Highways:* U.S. 77, Oklahoma 7, 18. *Attractions:* Cold mineral springs with distinctive mineral properties. Most of the area is forested. Buffalo and Antelope Springs flow more than 5 million gallons of pure natural water per day. Overnight accommodations are available in towns. *Nearby towns:* Sulphur, Davis, Chickasaw, Springer, and Gene Autry.

ROCKY MOUNTAIN: Superintendent, Rocky Mountain National Park, Box 1086, Estes Park, Colorado.

Area: 405 square miles. Open all year. *Location:* Front Range of the Rocky Mountains in north-central Colorado. *Highways:* U.S. 34, Colorado 7, 16, 262, 278. Closed to trans-mountain travel by snow in winter. Season, late May to mid-September. *Attractions:* Little other scenery compares with this snow-capped group of mountains. Longs Peak rises at the head at an elevation of 14,225 feet. Here are found 65 named peaks with an altitude of over 10,000 feet, the legible record left by glaciers, a profusion of precipice-walled, multicolored canyons, beautiful Alpine lakes and streams, abundant wildlife, and beautiful forests and meadows of wild flowers. *Accommodations:* Meals and lodging in park during summer months; many dude ranches, lodges and motels outside of the park. *Nearby towns:* Estes Park, Allenspark, Glen Haven, Gould, Grand Lake, and Granby.

SEQUOIA: Superintendent, Sequoia National Park, Three Rivers, California.

Area: 604 square miles. Open all year. *Location:* Lies across the heart of the Sierra Nevada in eastern central California. Sequoia-Kings Canyon is administered from Ash Mountain, headquarters for both parks. *Highways:* U.S. 99, California 65, 198, 180, and the famous Generals Highway (inter-park). *Attractions:* Many groves of giant sequoias, including the General Sherman Tree, said to be the largest living thing in the world; vast primitive, high mountain wilderness areas (including Mount Whitney, elevation 14,496 feet, seventh highest peak in the United States), mighty gorges and canyons, rushing streams, and Alpine lakes. Famous inter-park Generals Highway to Cedar Grove. *Accommodations:* Lodging and meals at Giant Forest. *Facilities:* Campsites, 727; picnic grounds. *Nearby towns:* Three Rivers, Wood Lake, Badger, Pinehurst, Fresno, and Visalia.

SHENANDOAH: Superintendent, Shenandoah National Park, Luray, Virginia.

Area: 302 square miles. Open all year. *Location:* In the heart of the Blue Ridge Mountains of Virginia. *Highways:* U.S. 211, 522, 340, 33, Virginia 231, 276. *Attractions:* The Skyline Drive extends through the entire length of the park for over 105 miles. There is an abundance of superb mountain and valley scenery; peaks are of more than 4,000 feet. Surrounding country rich in historical association. The mountain parkway extends from Front Royal to Rockfish Gap. The Drive merges directly with the 468-mile Blue Ridge Parkway, and eventually to the Great Smoky Mountains. *Campsites are available* for both trailer and tent campers.

VIRGIN ISLANDS: Superintendent, Virgin Islands National Park, Box 1589, Charlotte Amalie, St. Thomas, Virgin Islands.

Area: Congress specified that the park not exceed 9,500 acres. *Location:* In the Virgin Island group in the Caribbean. It is 1,435 miles south and east of New York, 991 miles east and south of Miami, and 75 miles east of San Juan, Puerto Rico. *Accommodations:* On St. John; limited at present. Write for detailed information.

WIND CAVE: Superintendent, Wind Cave National Park, Hot Springs, South Dakota.

Area: 43 square miles. Open all year. *Location:* Black Hills in southwestern South Dakota. *Highways:* U.S. 16, 385, South Dakota 87, 36. *Attractions:* Limestone Caverns named because of strong winds that blow alternately in and out of mouth of cavern. Supports large herd of buffalo in native habitat as well as elk, deer, antelope, and other wildlife. Lodging and meals in outside towns. *Facilities:* Campsites, 12; picnic grounds. *Nearby towns:* Custer, Sanator, Hot Springs, Hermosa, and Keystone.

YELLOWSTONE: Superintendent, Yellowstone National Park, Wyoming.

Area: 3,472 square miles. *Location:* Southwestern Montana, northwestern Wyoming, and southeastern Idaho. *Highways:* U.S. 89, 20, 191, 287, 312, 14, and 20. *Attractions:* The park is larger than both the state of Delaware and Rhode Island combined. The park is a volcanic region, located in the high country of the middle Rockies. It is one of nature's wonderlands; its geysers are world famous for their size, power, and number. Yellowstone is also noted for its colored canyons, and it is a wildlife refuge. Buffalo and elk are numerous. The park contains both black and grizzly bear. Park season is from mid-June to mid-September; meals and lodging during open season. *Facilities:* 15 campgrounds; 1,642 campsites; picnic grounds. *Nearby towns:* West Yellowstone, Gallatin, Jardine, Mammoth Hot Springs, Silver Gate, and Red Lodge, Montana; Cody, Moran Junction, Wyoming; Ashton and Mack's Inn, Idaho.

YOSEMITE: Superintendent, Yosemite National Park, Box 577, Yosemite National Park, California.

Area: 1,189 square miles. Open all year. *Location:* On west slope of the Sierra Nevada Range; about 210 miles due east of San Francisco. A very mountainous region of unusual beauty. Its deep canyons, towering cliffs, and vast mountain wilderness with its world-famous Yosemite Valley containing El Capitan, Eagle Peak, Sentinel Dome, and Half Dome. The park's world-famous water falls and cataracts are among the highest. It contains three groves of big trees, The Tuolumne Grove, Merced Grove, and Mariposa Grove. *Accommodations:* Meals and lodging year around. *Facilities:* Campsites, 3,773; picnic grounds. *Nearby towns:* El Portal, Fish Camp, Course Gold, Mariposa, Groveland, Leevining, Fresno, and Merced.

ZION: Superintendent, Zion National Park, Springdale, Utah.

Area: 148 square miles. Open all year. *Location:* Southwestern Utah. *Highways:* U.S. 91, 89, Utah 14, 15. *Attractions:* Vividly colored Zion canyon; a magnificent gorge, depth from 1,500 to 3,500 feet, with precipitous walls of great beauty and scientific interest. Season, mid-May till mid-October. *Facilities:* 206 campsites; picnic grounds. *Nearby towns:* Parowan, Cedar City, Saint George, Mt. Carmel, and Kanab.

FOR INFORMATION ON NATIONAL FORESTS

NATIONAL FOREST HEADQUARTERS. Forest Service, U. S. Department of Agriculture, Washington 25, D. C.

FIELD OFFICES. To write to a national forest, simply address the Supervisor of the national forest at the headquarters location shown below.

Region 1, Northern Region

Headquarters, Federal Building, Missoula, Montana.

IDAHO

Clearwater National Forest, Orofino, Idaho.

Coeur d'Alene National Forest, Coeur d'Alene, Idaho.

Kaniksu National Forest, Sandpoint, Idaho.

Nezperce National Forest, Grangeville, Idaho.

St. Joe National Forest, St. Maries, Idaho.

FOREST DESCRIPTIONS

CLEARWATER. *Highways:* Idaho 9, 11. *Attractions:* Famous Lolo Trail, *Selway-Bitterroot Primitive Area.* Spring log drive on the Middle Fork and North Fork, Clearwater River; large stand of virgin white pine. Large timber operations. Trout and salmon fishing in back country. Hunting for elk, deer, bear, and other wild game. Scenic drives—North Fork, and Lewis and Clark Highway. *Facilities:* camp and picnic sites. Motels, cabins, and pack trip outfitters available. *Nearby towns:* Kooskia, Lewiston, Orofino, and Pierce, Idaho; Lolo Hot Springs, and Missoula, Montana.

COEUR D'ALENE. *Highways:* U.S. 10, 10A. *Attractions:* Lovely Coeur d'Alene Lake, 30 miles long with 104 miles of shoreline. Cataldo Mission, built in 1846. Coeur d'Alene River; fishing; hunting for elk and deer. Rich Coeur d'Alene mining district (zinc, lead, silver), several large sawmills. *Facilities:* 7 camp and picnic sites; two picnic only; Lookout Pass winter sports area; resorts, hotels and cabins. *Nearby towns:* Coeur d'Alene, Kellogg, Spirit Lake, and Wallace, Idaho; Spokane, Washington.

KANIKSU. *Highways:* U.S. 95, 195, 10A, 2, Washington 6. *Attractions:* Rugged back country, Selkirk Mountain Range. Massive Pend Oreille Lake (Loop Drive 107 miles); Priest Lake. Kullyspell House, Clark Fork River; Roosevelt Ancient Grove of Cedars; Chimney Rock; *Cabinet Mountains Wild Area.* Lake and stream fishing; big-game hunting. Scenic drives, boating. *Facilities:* 12 camp and picnic sites; 3 swimming sites; one winter sports area; resorts, hotels, lodges, cabins. *Nearby towns:* Bonners Ferry, Clark Fork, Priest River, and Sandpoint.

NEZPERCE. *Highways:* U.S. 95, Idaho 9, 13, 14. *Attractions: Selway-Bitterroot Primitive Area;* Seven Devils Range between Salmon and Snake Rivers; Hells Canyon on the Snake River; Red River Hot Springs; historic Elk City; wilderness big-game hunting: Elk, deer, and bear. Lake and stream fishing. Hiking and horse trails; wilderness pack trips. Scenic drives—Lochsa River, Salmon River, Selway River. *Facilities:* 6 camp and picnic sites; one picnic only; resorts, hotels, motels, cabins, pack trip outfitters. *Nearby towns:* Grangeville, Kamiah, Kooskia, and Riggins.

ST. JOE. *Highways:* U.S. 95A, Idaho 7, 8, 43. *Attractions:* Rugged Bitterroot Range of Idaho-Montana divide; St. Joe River drainage; St. Maries River Valley; canyon areas of Little North Fork of Clearwater River; Clearwater-St. Joe divide, Palouse River area; virgin stands of white pine. Large timber operations. Big-game hunting Elk, deer, bear, and mountain goat. Lake and stream fishing. Scenic drives along St. Joe River from source to mouth in Coeur d'Alene Lake. *Facilities:* 8 camp and picnic sites; one swimming site; north-south winter sports area. Dude ranch nearby. Cabins on St. Joe River. *Nearby towns:* Avery, Clarkia, Moscow, Potlatch, and St. Maries.

MONTANA

Beaverhead National Forest, Dillon, Montana.
Bitterroot National Forest, Hamilton, Montana.
Custer National Forest, Billings, Montana.
Deerlodge National Forest, Butte, Montana.
Flathead National Forest, Kalispell, Montana.
Gallatin National Forest, Bozeman, Montana.
Helena National Forest, Helena, Montana.
Kootenai National Forest, Libby, Montana.
Lewis and Clark National Forest, Great Falls, Montana.
Lolo National Forest, Missoula, Montana.

FOREST DESCRIPTIONS

BEAVERHEAD. *Highways:* U.S. 91, Montana 41, 34, 43, and 287. *Attractions:* Anaconda-Pintlar Primitive Area; Big Hole Battlefield Monument; Sacajawea Memorial Area; Bannack—the first capital of Montana. Tobacco Root, Madison, Ruby, Beaverhead, and Big Hole rivers; Alpine lakes. Fishing; hunting for deer, elk, moose, antelope, and bear. Hot springs, scenic drives, wilderness trips. *Facilities:* 28 camp and picnic sites; Rainy Mountain winter sports area. Resorts, hotels, cabins and dude ranches in and near the national forest. *Nearby towns:* Dillon, Ennis, Jackson, Lima, Sheridan, Virginia City, and Wisdom.

BITTERROOT. *Highways:* U.S. 93, Montana 43, 38. *Attractions:* Bitterroot Valley and spectacular Bitterroot Mountains; scores of mountain lakes and hot springs. Ancient Indian hieroglyphics, Saint Mary's Mission and Fort Owen. *Selway-Bitterroot Primitive Area; Anaconda-Pintlar Primitive Area.* Lake and stream fishing; hunting for elk, deer, and mountain goat. Bitterroot Valley scenic drives, riding trails, wilderness trips. *Facilities:* 11 camp and picnic sites; Lost Trail winter sports area. Resorts, hotels, cabins, and dude ranches. *Nearby towns:* Corvallis, Hamilton, Missoula, and Stevensville.

CUSTER. *Highways:* U.S. 10, 12, 85, Montana 8, 7, South Dakota 8. *Attractions:* Spectacular Red Lodge-Cooke City Highway; snow-clad peaks and Alpine plateaus; Granite Peak (12,962 feet) highest point in Montana; hundreds of lakes; Woodbine Falls, 900 feet high; glaciers and ice caverns; rich fossil beds, Indian hieroglyphics, and burial grounds. *Beartooth Primitive Area.* Trout fishing, big-game hunting, saddle and pack trips. *Facilities:* 13 camp and picnic sites; two, picnic only; Willow Creek winter sports area. Resorts, hotels, cabins, and dude ranches. *Nearby towns:* Absarokee, Ashland, Billings, Columbus, Hardin, Laurel, and Red Lodge.

DEERLODGE. *Highways:* U.S. 10, 10A, 91, Montana 38, 41. *Attractions:* Anaconda-Pintlar Primitive Area, Tobacco Root Mountains, Mount Powell and Flint Creek Range, numerous Alpine lakes. Lake and stream fishing; big-game hunting: Bear, deer, elk, and special moose seasons. Riding trails, wilderness trips. *Facilities:* 21 camp and picnic sites; five, picnic only. Cable Mountain and Pipestone Pass winter sports areas. Resorts, hotels, cabins, and dude ranches. *Nearby towns:* Anaconda, Boulder, Butte, Deer Lodge, Phillipsburg, and Whitehall.

FLATHEAD. *Highways:* U.S. 2, 93, Montana 35, 40. *Attractions:* Spectacular geological formations, including massive Chinese Wall and jagged Mission Mountains; hanging valleys; glaciers and scores of glacial lakes. Hungry Horse Dam and lake. *Mission Mountains Wild Area; Bob Marshall Wilderness Area.* Fishing; big-game hunting: Elk, deer, moose, bear, mountain sheep, and goats. Boating; canoeing; riding; scenic drives around Flathead Lake; wilderness trips. *Facilities:* 15 camp and picnic sites; one, picnic only; two swimming sites; Big Mountain winter sports area. Resorts, hotels, cabins, and dude ranches. *Nearby towns:* Belton, Bigfork, Columbia Falls, Coram, Kalispell, and Whitefish.

GALLATIN. *Highways:* U.S. 191, 20, 10, 89, Montana 19, 287. *Attractions:* Fertile Gallatin Valley; Crazy Mountains; snow-clad peaks; 11 outstanding waterfalls; more than 200 lakes and thousands of miles of trout streams. Madison River Canyon earthquake area. *Spanish Peaks and Absaroka Primitive Areas.* Lake and stream fishing; hunting: Bear, moose, elk, and deer. Scenic drives—Gallatin Canyon, Boulder Canyon, and Yankee Jim Canyon; trail riding and wilderness trips. *Facilities:* 33 camp and picnic sites; Bridger Bowl and Lionhead winter sports areas. Resorts, hotels, cabins, and dude ranches. *Nearby towns:* Big Timber, Bozeman, Gardiner, Livingston, and West Yellowstone.

HELENA. *Highways:* U.S. 12, 91, Montana 20. *Attractions:* Continental Divide; Big Belt and Elkhorn Mountain Ranges. Boat trip through *Gates of the Mountains Wild Area* on Missouri River; old Fort Logan original blockhouse; ghost towns: Diamond City, Marysville, Crow Creek Falls. Lake and stream fishing; hunting, deer and elk; scenic drives. Trout and Beaver Creek Canyons. Hiking and horse trails; wilderness trips. *Facilities:* 6 camp and picnic sites; two, picnic only; Grass Mountain winter sports area. Resorts, hotels, cabins, and dude ranches. *Nearby towns:* Helena, Lincoln, Townsend, and White Sulphur Springs.

KOOTENAI. *Highways:* U.S. 2, 93, Montana 37. *Attractions: Cabinet Mountains Primitive Area;* Yaak River, Kootenai Canyon, and Fisher River. Lake and stream fishing; hunting, black bear and deer. Scenic drives—Yaak River, Kootenai Canyon, Fisher River; riding trails. *Facilities:* 5 camp and picnic sites; Libby winter sports area. Hotels, cabins, and dude ranches. *Nearby towns:* Eureka, Libby, and Troy.

LEWIS AND CLARK. *Highways:* U.S. 12, 87, 89, 91, Montana 21, 287. *Attractions: Bob Marshall Wilderness Area.* Chinese Wall and Continental Divide; limestone canyons and rolling mountains with many open parks. Stream and lake fishing; hunting for deer, elk, antelope, grizzly, and black bear. Wilderness trips; riding trails; numerous scenic drives—Kings Hill, Judity River, Crystal Lake, Sun River, and Teton River. *Facilities:* 12 camp and picnic sites; *Kings Hill* winter sports area. Many resorts, cabins, and dude ranches. *Nearby towns:* Augusta, Chotear, Great Falls, Harlowton, Lewistown, and White Sulphur Springs.

LOLO. *Highways:* U.S. 10, 10A, 93, Montana 20, Idaho 9. *Attractions: Selway-Bitterroot Primitive Area;* Rattlesnake, Bitterroot, and Swan Ranges; Clark Fork and Blackfoot Rivers. Stream and lake fishing; hunting for native grouse, elk, deer, and bear. Wilderness pack trips; scenic drives; Lochsa River, Seeley Lake, Buffalo Park, Rock Creek. Mountain saddle trails, foot trails to a hundred lakes and peaks. *Facilities:* 18 camp and picnic sites; one, picnic only; one swimming site; Snow Park winter sports area. Resorts, dude ranches. *Nearby towns:* Alberton, Drummond, Ovando, Plains, St. Regis, Superior, Thompson Falls, and Missoula (Forest Service Regional Office—also Aerial Fire Depot and Smokejumper Headquarters).

WASHINGTON

Colville National Forest, Colville, Washington.

FOREST DESCRIPTION

COLVILLE. *Highways:* U.S. 395, Washington 22, 6, 4, 3P. *Attractions:* Roosevelt Lake, 151 miles long, 82,000 acres; Grand Coulee Dam, largest masonry structure in the world. Scenic drives. Old mission near Kettle Falls. Hunting in area noted for large mule deer, record weight of 440 pounds. Water transportation from Roosevelt Lake to Arrow Lakes in Canada. Huckleberries and mushrooms. Lake and stream fishing; Thomas, Swan, Sullivan Lakes, and others. *Facilities:* 16 camp and picnic sites; two swimming sites; Chewelah Peak winter sports area. Resorts and cabins. *Nearby towns:* Chewelah, Colville, and Republic, Washington; Grand Forts, British Columbia, Canada.

Region 2, Rocky Mountain Region

Headquarters, Federal Center, Building 85, Denver 7, Colorado.

COLORADO

Arapaho National Forest, Golden, Colorado.

Grand Mesa-Uncompahgre National Forest,* Delta, Colorado.

Gunnison National Forest, Gunnison, Colorado.

---

* Two separately proclaimed national forests under one supervisor.

Pike National Forest, Colorado Springs, Colorado.

Rio Grande National Forest, Monte Vista, Colorado.

Roosevelt National Forest, Fort Collins, Colorado.

Routt National Forest, Steamboat Springs, Colorado.

San Isabel National Forest, Pueblo, Colorado.

San Juan National Forest, Durango, Colorado.

White River National Forest, Glenwood Springs, Colorado.

FOREST DESCRIPTIONS

ARAPAHO. *Highways:* U.S. 6, 40. *Attractions:* Highest automobile road in U.S. to crest of Mount Evans, 14,260 feet. Gold, silver mining; ghost towns. *Gore Range Eagle Nest Primitive Area.* Moffat Tunnel, 6.2 miles long under Continental Divide. Lake and stream fishing. Big-game hunting for elk, deer, and bear; Loveland and Berthoud Passes, Peak to Peak Highway. Riding trails, wilderness trips. *Facilities:* 33 camp and picnic sites; 20 picnic only; four winter sports areas. Resorts, hotels, motels, cabin camps, and dude ranches. *Nearby towns:* Denver, Dillon, Golden, Granby, Grand Lake, Hot Sulphur Springs, Idaho Springs, and Kremmling.

GRAND MESA-UNCOMPAHGRE. *Highways:* U.S. 50, 550, 6. *Attractions:* Grand Mesa Plateau, 10,500 feet; 250 lakes and reservoirs; cliffs, canyons, waterfalls, wild flowers. Uncompahgre Plateau. *Uncompahgre and Wilson Primitive Areas:* Ouray and Telluride scenic areas. Lake and stream fishing. Deer, elk, bear, duck hunting. Scenic drives, saddle trips. *Facilities:* 31 camp and picnic sites, 6 picnic only; one winter sports area. Motels, resorts in and near the national forest. *Nearby towns:* Delta, Grand Junction, Montrose, Norwood, Ouray, and Telluride.

GUNNISON. *Highways:* U.S. 50, Colorado 135, 149. *Attractions:* Trout fishing streams, many high lakes. 27 mountain peaks more than 12,000 feet; Ruby Range. Taylor Park Reservoir and valley; ghost towns. *West Elk Wild Area.* Trout fishing. Hunting for elk, deer, mountain sheep, and bear. Saddle trips, wilderness trips. *Facilities:* 34 camp and picnic sites; one winter sports area. Commercial hotels, resorts, motels in and near the forest. *Nearby towns:* Gunnison, Lake City, Montrose, and Salida.

PIKE. *Highways:* U.S. 24, 85, 87, 285. *Attractions:* Pikes Peak with highway to summit, historic Cripple Creek and Alma gold camps, scenic Rampart Range Road. Devil's Head Forest Fire Lookout, Monument Forest Nursery, Platte and Arkansas River watersheds. Abyss Lake scenic area. Hunting and fishing; scenic drives. Mountain sheep and other wildlife. *Facilities:* 37 camp and picnic sites, 40, picnic only; one winter sports area. Commercial hotels, resorts, motels in and near the forest. *Nearby towns:* Colorado Springs, Cripple Creek, and Denver.

RIO GRANDE. *Highways:* U.S. 160, 285. *Attractions:* Mountain lakes and trout streams. Wolf Creek Pass, rugged high country. *Upper Rio Grande and La Garita—Sheep Mountain Primitive Areas.* Fishing; deer, elk, and duck hunting. Saddle and pack trips, scenic drives. *Facilities:* 31 camp and picnic sites; 5, picnic only; one winter sports area. Motels in and near the forest. *Nearby towns:* Alamosa, Antonito, Creede, Monte Vista, and Saguache.

ROOSEVELT. *Highways:* U.S. 34, 287, Colorado 14, 160. *Attractions:* Arapaho, Isabelle and South St. Vrain Glaciers; rugged Continental Divide with many Alpine lakes; Poudre, Big Thompson, St. Vrain, and Boulder Canyons. *Rawah Wild Area.* Boating; fishing; hunting for deer, elk, mountain sheep, bear, mountain lion, grouse, and water fowl. Saddle and pack trips; scenic drives. *Facilities:* 21 camp and picnic sites; 18, picnic only. Motels and dude ranches in and near the forest. *Nearby towns:* Boulder, Denver, Estes Park, Fort Collins, Longmont, and Loveland.

ROUTT. *Highway:* U.S. 40, Colorado 84, 131. *Attractions:* Continental Divide with perpetual ice and snow, trout streams and Alpine lakes. *Mount Zirkel—Dome Peak Wild Area, Big Creek Lakes Recreation Area.* Fishing; deer, elk, bear, grouse, and duck hunting. Saddle and pack trips; scenic drives. *Facilities:* 48 camp and picnic sites; 5, picnic only. Commercial cabins, motels near and in the forest. *Nearby towns:* Craig, Steamboat Springs, Walden, and Yampa.

SAN ISABEL. *Highways:* U.S. 24, 50, 85, 87, Colorado 69 and 165. *Attractions:* Highest average elevation of any national forest; Sangre de Cristo Range; twelve peaks more than 14,000 feet; Mount Elbert, second highest in the United States. More than 40 timberline lakes. Snow Angel on Mount Shavano;

molybdenum mines; *Lake Isabel Recreation Area.* Fishing; hunting for bear, deer, elk, mountain goat, grouse, and ducks. Scenic drives, saddle and pack outfits. *Facilities:* 26 camp and picnic sites; three winter sports areas. Motels and dude ranches in and near the forest. *Nearby towns:* Canon City, Leadville, Pueblo, Salida, and Walsenburg.

SAN JUAN. *Highways:* U.S. 160, 550, Colorado 145. *Attractions:* Alpine lakes; Mount Wilson, 14,250 feet; canyons, waterfalls, cataracts, peculiar geologic formations. Archeological ruins, historic mines. *San Juan Primitive Area; Wilson Mountain Primitive Area.* Fishing; hunting for deer, elk, bear, lion, grouse, and ducks. Scenic drives; saddle and pack trips. *Facilities:* 34 camp and picnic sites, 7, picnic only; one winter sports area. Motels and dude ranches in and near the forest. *Nearby towns:* Cortez, Durango, Pagosa Springs, and Silverton, Colorado; Farmington, New Mexico.

WHITE RIVER. *Highways:* U.S. 24, 6, Colorado 82, 132. *Attractions:* Spectacular Glenwood Canyon, Hanging Lake, Bridal Veil Falls, mineral hot springs, caves, Alpine lakes. Source of marble for Lincoln Memorial and Tomb of the Unknown Soldier. *Flat Tops Primitive Area; Gore Range-Eagle Nest Primitive Area; Maroon Bells-Snowmass Wild Area.* Fishing; elk, deer, bear, cougar hunting. Saddle and pack trails; scenic drives. *Facilities:* 58 camp and picnic sites; one, picnic only; one swimming site; three winter sports areas. Motels and dude ranches in and near forest. *Nearby towns:* Aspen, Craig, Eagle, Glenwood Springs, Gypsum, Leadville, Meeker, and Rifle.

NEBRASKA

Nebraska National Forest, Lincoln, Nebraska.

FOREST DESCRIPTION

NEBRASKA. *Highways:* U.S. 20, 83, Nebraska 2. *Attractions:* Bessey Nursery; extensive forest plantations on sand hills; entire forest in game refuge; mule deer; nesting ground of great blue heron, grouse, and prairie chicken. Fishing. *Facilities:* Three camp and picnic sites; two, picnic only; one swimming site. Hotel accommodations at Broken Bow, Valentine, and Halsey.

SOUTH DAKOTA

Black Hills National Forest, Custer, South Dakota.

FOREST DESCRIPTION

BLACK HILLS. *Highways:* U.S. 14, 16, 85, 385. *Attractions:* Spectacular canyons and waterfalls, crystal caves. Historic gold rush area where famous early-day characters lived and were buried, including Calamity Jane, Wild Bill Hickok, Deadwood Dick, and Preacher Smith; famous Homestake Mine; Harney Peak, highest east of Rocky Mountains. Mount Rushmore National Memorial. Lake and stream fishing; deer and elk hunting. Boating, saddle trips, and scenic drives. *Facilities:* 21 camp and picnic sites; 45, picnic only; two swimming sites, one winter sports area. Motels and dude ranches in and near the forest. *Nearby towns:* Belle Fourche, Custer, Deadwood, Edgemont, Hot Springs, and Rapid City, South Dakota; Newcastle and Sundance, Wyoming.

WYOMING

Bighorn National Forest, Sheridan, Wyoming.
Medicine Bow National Forest, Laramie, Wyoming.
Shoshone National Forest, Cody, Wyoming.

FOREST DESCRIPTIONS

BIGHORN. *Highways:* U.S. 14, 16, 87. *Attractions:* Bighorn Mountains, snow-capped peaks, glaciers; more than 300 lakes. Curious prehistoric Indian Medicine Wheel on Medicine Mountain; Indian battlefields. *Cloud Peak Primitive Area.* Fishing; elk, deer, bear, and duck hunting. Saddle and pack trips; scenic drives. *Facilities:* 60 camp and picnic sites; 14, picnic only. Motels and dude ranches in and near the forest. *Nearby towns:* Buffalo, Greybull, Lovell, Sheridan, and Worland.

MEDICINE BOW. *Highways:* U.S. 30, Wyoming 130, 230. *Attractions:* Medicine Bow, Sierra Madre, Laramie, and Pole Mountains. Many lakes and fishing streams; numerous beaver colonies. Fishing and deer hunting. Saddle and pack trips; scenic drives. *Facilities:* 23 camp and picnic sites; 25, picnic only; three winter sports areas. Motels and dude ranches in and near the forest. *Nearby towns:* Cheyenne, Encampment, and Laramie.

SHOSHONE. *Highways:* U.S. 14, 20, 12, 287. *Attractions:* Rugged Absaroka Mountains and Beartooth Plateau, Wind River Range with perpetual snow; Gannett Peak, 13,785 feet, highest in Wyoming; largest glaciers in Rocky Mountains; hundreds of lakes. Glacier, Stratified, and *North and South Absaroka Wilderness Areas; Popo Agie Primitive Area.* Fishing; hunting for mountain sheep, elk, moose, deer, antelope, black and grizzly bear, and game birds. Saddle and pack trips. Scenic drives: Red Lodge-Cooke City Highway, Sunlight Basin Road, Cody-Yellowstone Road, Togwotee Pass Road. *Facilities:* 34 camp and picnic sites; two, picnic only; one winter sports area. Motels and dude ranches in and near the forest. *Nearby towns:* Cody, Dubois, and Lander, Wyoming; Cooke City and Red Lodge, Montana.

Region 3, Southwestern Region

Headquarters, 510 2nd St., N.W., Albuquerque, New Mexico.

ARIZONA

Apache National Forest, Springerville, Arizona.

Coconino National Forest, Flagstaff, Arizona.

Coronado National Forest, Tucson, Arizona.

Kaibab National Forest, Williams, Arizona.

Prescott National Forest, Prescott, Arizona.

Sitgreaves National Forest, Holbrook, Arizona.

Tonto National Forest, Phoenix, Arizona.

FOREST DESCRIPTIONS

APACHE. *Highways:* U.S. 60, 260, 666. *Attractions:* Scenic Coronado Trail and other drives through spruce and mountain-meadow country. Prehistoric Blue River cliff dwellings, Big Lake, Crescent Lake, Luna Lake. *Blue Range Primitive Area; Mount Baldy Primitive Area.* Lake and stream trout fishing. Big-game hunting; elk, deer, bear, cougar, antelope, Mexican wild peccaries; also turkey and upland bird shooting. Horseback riding, pack trips, hiking. *Facilities:* 26 camp and picnic sites; one, picnic only; boats without motors for rent on Big and Luna Lakes. Resorts and motels. *Nearby towns:* Alpine, Greer, and Springerville, Arizona; Luna and Reserve, New Mexico.

COCONINO. *Highways:* U.S. 66, 89, 89A. *Attractions:* Graceful San Francisco Peaks, 12,611 feet, highest in Arizona; Oak Creek Canyon and the Red Rock country near Sedona offer exceptional scenic and photographic opportunities; *Sycamore Canyon Primitive Area* and Mogollon Rim. Scenic drives—Lake Mary-Long Valley Road; Mogollon Rim Road; Baker Butte Fire Lookout offering vast view of Arizona timber. Numerous national monuments nearby plus Lowell Astronomical Observatory, Museum of Northern Arizona, Flagstaff; Meteor Crater near Painted Desert. Boating on Lake Mary. Same kinds of hunting and fishing as Apache N.F. *Facilities:* 18 camp and picnic sites; 5, picnic only; Arizona Snow Bowl winter sports area. Resort hotels, dude ranches. *Nearby towns:* Camp Verde, Clarkdale, Cottonwood, Flagstaff, Sedona, and Winslow.

CORONADO. *Highways:* U.S. 80, 84, 89, 666, Arizona 82, 86. *Attractions:* Rugged mountains rising abruptly from surrounding deserts; cactus to fir trees, swimming to skiing in an hour's time—forty miles apart. *Santa Catalina Mountains Recreation Area* with Rose Canyon Lake, Sabino Canyon, and Mount Lemmon Snow Bowl, southern-most winter sports area in the Continental United States. Chiricahua Mountains with *Chiricahua Wild Area* and several small trout lakes. *Pinaleno Mountains Recreation Area* with Mount Graham, 10,713 feet; Riggs Flat Lake. Pena Blanca Lake, 52 acres of bass fishing, four miles from the boundary of Mexico. *Galiuro Wild Area.* Nearby are Arizona-Sonora Desert Museum, Colossal Cave State Park, Tucson Mountain Park. Hunting for deer, javelina, mountain lion, quail and dove. Scenic drives. Pack trips and hiking trails in rugged ranges of southern Arizona (*Caution:* carry adequate water.) Dude ranch and winter resort country. *Facilities:* 32 camp and picnic sites; 17, picnic only. *Nearby towns:* Benson, Bisbee; Mexican border towns of Douglas and Nogales; Fort Huachuca, Patagonia, Safford, San Simon, Tombstone, Tucson, and Wilcox.

KAIBAB. *Highways:* U.S. 66, 89, 64, 67. *Attractions:* Grand Canyon National Game Preserve with famous North Kaibab deer herd, wild buffalo herd, and the only habitat of the Kaibab squirrel. Access to both the north and south rims of the Grand Canyon and Supai Indian village in Havasu Canyon. Other points of interest are beautiful North Kaibab high country; pines, spruce, and aspen forests with open meadows; *East Rim, North Canyon, Bill Williams Mountain, Whitehorse Lake, Cataract Lake, and Sycamore Canyon Wild Areas.* Wildlife the same as in the Coronado Forest. *Facilities:* Six camp and picnic sites. Motels and resorts, guest ranches. Hunting camps with groceries in season. *Nearby towns:* Ashfork, Cottonwood, Flagstaff, Fredonia, Grand Canyon, and Williams, Arizona; Kanab, Utah.

PRESCOTT. *Highways:* U.S. 89. *Attractions:* Ideal year around climate. Rugged back country, many roads primitive. Granite Basin Lake near Granite Mountain, Hassayampa Lake. Limited trout fishing. *Sycamore Canyon and Pine Mountain Primitive Areas.* Jerome, the largest U.S. ghost town. Deer, antelope, dove, quail, and general hunting of coyotes and javelina. Many horse trails; scenic drives. *Facilities:* 8 camp and picnic sites; 8, picnic only. Resorts, dude ranches and motels. *Nearby towns:* Clarkdale, Cottonwood, Jerome, Mayer, and Prescott.

SITGREAVES. *Highways:* U.S. 66, Arizona 77, 173. *Attractions:* Scenic Mogollon Rim Drive; pueblo ruins, elk herd. Woods Canyon Lake. Hunting of deer, antelope, bear, and turkey. Saddle and pack trips. *Facilities:* Public golf and swimming at White Mountain Country Club. Four camp and picnic sites; numerous resorts, hotels, summer homes, guest ranches. *Nearby towns:* Holbrook, Lakeside, Pinetop, Show Low, Snowflake, and Winslow.

TONTO. *Highways:* U.S. 60, 70, 80, 89. *Attractions:* Semi-desert to pine-fir forests, elevations 1,500 to 7,300 feet. The lakes in the low country form an all-year haven in the desert; the cool pine forests along the Mogollon Rim are very popular in summer. Famous *Superstition Mountains, Tonto Basin, Bloody Basin, Mazatzal and Superstituion Wilderness Areas, Pine Mountain Primitive Area; Sierra Ancha Wild Area;* 30,000 acres of man-made lakes including Roosevelt, Apache, Canyon, and Saguaro Lakes on the Salt River; Bartlett and Horseshoe Lakes on the Verde River. Popular for boating, swimming, skin diving, water skiing, bass fishing. Public boat ramps at most lakes. Boats and tackle also for rent. Limited trout fishing in high country. Hunting for deer, elk, bear, javelina, turkey, quail, and mountain lion. Saddle and pack trips into high country. Scenic drives—Apache Trail, Beeline Highway, Payson-Mogollon Rim drive. *Facilities:* 16 camp and picnic sites; 12, picnic only. Resorts, dude ranches. *Nearby towns:* Globe, Mesa, Miami, Payson, Phoenix, Pine, Superior, and Young.

NEW MEXICO

Carson National Forest, Taos, New Mexico.

Cibola National Forest, Albuquerque, New Mexico.

Gila National Forest, Silver City, New Mexico.

Lincoln National Forest, Alamogordo, New Mexico.

Santa Fe National Forest, Santa Fe, New Mexico.

FOREST DESCRIPTIONS

CARSON. *Highways:* U.S. 64, New Mexico 3, 75, 38. *Attractions:* Massive timbered Sangre de Cristo mountains and other ranges flanking the upper Rio Grande Valley. Wheeler Peak, 13,151 feet, highest in New Mexico. *Pecos Wilderness Area; Wheeler Peak Wild Area;* Alpine lakes and timberline country. Trout streams, 12,000 to 13,000-foot peaks. High green valleys with Spanish-speaking villages. Scenic drives, Taos-Questa-Red River-Eagle Nest Loop. Tres Piedras-Lagunitas lake country. Santa Barbara Canyon near Penasco. Taos: Home and burial place of Kit Carson; well-known art colony. *Nearby towns:* Taos and Tierra Amarilla, New Mexico; Alamosa and Pagosa Springs, Colorado.

CIBOLA. *Highways:* U.S. 85, 66, 60. *Attractions:* Magdalena, Manzano, Sandia, San Mateo, and Zuni Mountain Ranges. Mount Taylor, 11,389 feet, and Sandia Crest, 10,700 feet, accessible by car. Deer and antelope hunting; bighorn sheep often visible at Sandia Crest in summer. Nearby are Pueblo Indian villages, prehistoric ruins, ancient "sky city" of Acoma. Limited fishing at Bluewater and McGaffey Lakes. Scenic drives. *Facilities:* 15 camp and picnic sites; 15, picnic only; La Madera winter sports area in Sandia Mountains. Motels, hotels, dude ranches. *Nearby towns:* Albuquerque, Bernalillo, Gallup, Grants, Magdalena, Mountainair, Socorro.

GILA. *Highways:* U.S. 60, 70, 80, 85, 260, New Mexico 61, 25, 78. *Attractions:* Semi-desert to Alpine country, most of it very remote and undeveloped. Elevation. 4,500 to 10,700 feet. Pack trips into the large *Gila and Black Range Primitive Areas.* Mogollon Rim; many prehistoric ruins. Lake fishing in Wall Lake and Bear Canyon Reservoir. Stream fishing in the three forks of the Gila, other streams; most of it "packing in" to little-used streams. Abundant game; uncrowded big-game hunting; black bear, mule deer, white-tailed deer, antelope, mountain lion, turkey. Scenic drives—Outer Loop, Inner Loop; ghost town of Mogollon. Riding and hiking trails. *Facilities:* 12 camp and picnic sites; three, picnic only. Some hotels, resorts, dude ranches. *Nearby towns:* Deming, Las Cruces, Lordsburg, Reserve, Silver City, and Truth or Consequences, New Mexico; Clifton and Springeville, Arizona.

LINCOLN. *Highways:* U.S. 54, 70, 380, New Mexico 83, 24, 37, 48. *Attractions:* White Mountain, 12,000 feet (summit is in Mescalero Apache Indian Reservation) with beautiful scenery, hiking trails. *White Mountain Wild Area.* Sacramento, Capitan, and Guadalupe Mountain Ranges with extensive ponderosa pine and fir stands. Resort cities of Cloudcroft, Ruidoso. Fishing, big-game hunting. Limited winter sports; scenic drives; saddle and pack trips. Golfing at Ruidoso (7,000 feet) and at Cloudcroft (9,000 feet). *Facilities:* 10 camp and picnic sites; two, picnic only; one winter sports area. Resorts, hotels, dude ranches, organization camps. *Nearby towns:* Alamogordo, Artesia, Capitan ("Birthplace of Smokey Bear"), Carlsbad, and Roswell, New Mexico; El Paso, Texas.

SANTA FE. *Highways:* U.S. 285, 85, 64, 84, New Mexico 4, 126, 96, 63. *Attractions:* Southern Sangre de Cristo Range including 13,000-foot Truchas Peaks; across Rio Grande to the west, Jemez and San Pedro Ranges, 10,000-12,000 feet. Headwaters Pecos, Jemez, and Gallinas Rivers; mountain streams and lakes; *Pecos Wilderness Area; San Pedro Parks Wild Area.* Wilderness pack trips, saddle trails. A dozen living Indian Pueblos nearby, great vistas, ancient ruins, Spanish missions, cliff dwellings. Turkey, elk, deer, and bear hunting. *Facilities:* 29 camp and picnic sites; 9, picnic only. Winter sports at Santa Fe Basin; scenic double-chair lift to 11,600 feet, operates summer by appointment (inquire Santa Fe). Resorts, hotels, guest ranches on Pecos River up as far as Cowles, and Jemez River near Jemez Springs. *Nearby towns:* Albuquerque, Bernalillo, Cuba, Espanola, Las Vegas, Pecos, and Santa Fe.

Region 4, Intermountain Region

Headquarters, Forest Service Building, Ogden, Utah.

IDAHO

Boise National Forest, Boise, Idaho.

Caribou National Forest, Pocatello, Idaho.

Challis National Forest, Challis, Idaho.

Payette National Forest, McCall, Idaho.

Salmon National Forest, Salmon, Idaho.

Sawtooth National Forest, Twin Falls, Idaho.

Targhee National Forest, St. Anthony, Idaho.

FOREST DESCRIPTIONS

BOISE. *Highways:* U.S. 20, 30, 95, Idaho 15, 16, 17, 21, 52, 68. *Attractions:* Rugged back country including portions of *Sawtooth Primitive Area.* Abandoned mines and ghost towns. Scenes of early Indian camps and massacres. Virgin stands of ponderosa pine. Arrowrock, Anderson Ranch, Cascade, Deadwood, and Lucky Peak Reservoirs; other lakes; included headwaters of Boise, Payette, and Salmon Rivers. Lake and stream fishing for trout and salmon. Hunting for bear, elk, and deer. Spectacular scenic drives in Payette and Boise River Canyons, along Boise Ridge, and edge of *Sawtooth Primitive Area. Facilities:* 121 camp and picnic sites; 22 picnic only; one swimming site; Bogus Basin winter sports area. Resorts, motels, dude ranches with horses, boats, and other facilities. *Nearby towns:* Boise, Cascade, Emmett, Horseshoe Bend, Idaho City, and Mountain Home.

CARIBOU. *Highways:* U.S. 91, 191, 30N. *Attractions:* High country; towering mountain ranges divided by beautiful valleys. Historic markers and trails, natural soda springs, rushing streams, and waterfalls. Stream fishing; game bird, deer, and bear hunting. Scenic drives—Mink Creek to Scout Mountain, Skyland Road, Snake River-McCoy Road along south bank of South Fork of Snake River, Georgetown Canyon-Diamond Creek and Snowslide-Crow Creek roads. Numerous riding trails into wilderness country. *Facilities:* 16 camp and picnic sites; 6, picnic only; two winter sports areas. Resorts and motels. *Nearby towns:* Idaho Falls, Malad City, Montpelier, Pocatello, Soda Springs, and Swan Valley, Idaho; Afton, Wyoming.

CHALLIS. *Highways:* U.S. 20, 93, 93A. *Attractions:* Lost River Range with Mount Borah, 12,655 feet, highest peak in Idaho. Lemhi, Lost River, and White Cloud Peaks; Salmon River and White Knob Mountain Ranges, head-waters of the Salmon River. Majestic *Sawtooth Primitive Area and Stanley Basin;* Middle Fork of the Salmon River in the *Idaho Wilderness Area.* Stream and lake trout, salmon fishing. Hunting for deer, elk, mountain goat, mountain sheep, antelope, bear, and small game. Stanley Basin scenic drive, riding and hiking trails, wilderness boating and pack trips. *Facilities:* 19 camp and picnic sites. Resorts, hotels, cabins, and dude ranches; commercial packers and guides. *Nearby towns:* Challis, Mackay, Salmon, and Standley.

PAYETTE. *Highways:* U.S. 95, Idaho 15. *Attractions:* Idaho Primitive Area. Hells Canyon of Snake River, 5,500 to 7,900 feet, deepest gorge in the United States; *Payette Lakes Recreational Area,* Seven Devils Mountains. Fishing for trout and salmon, 154 fishing lakes, 1,530 miles of fishing streams. Big-game hunting for deer, elk, mountain goat, bighorn sheep, and bear. Scenic drives; wilderness trips. *Facilities:* 31 camp and picnic sites; Payette winter sports area. Dude ranches. *Nearby towns:* Cascades, Council, McCall, New Meadows, and Weiser.

SALMON. *Highways:* U.S. 93, Idaho 28. *Attractions: Idaho Primitive Area,* Big Horn Crags, historic Lewis and Clark Trail, Salmon River Canyon. Fishing; big-game hunting, including deer, elk, bighorn sheep, mountain goat, bear, cougar, and antelope. Salmon River and Panther Creek forest roads; boat trips on "River of No Return" and Middlefork. *Facilities:* 5 camp and picnic sites; two, picnic only. Dude ranches. *Nearby towns:* Leadore and Salmon.

SAWTOOTH. *Highways:* U.S. 30N, 30S, 93. *Attractions:* Panoramic views of Snake River Valley. *Sawtooth Primitive Area.* Colorful mountains and lakes, developed hot springs. Sun Valley with four-season opportunities for outdoor sports. "Silent City of Rocks," fantastic formations worn by wind and water. Fishing; swimming; big-game and grouse hunting in season; saddle and pack trips; scenic drives. *Facilities:* 57 camping and picnic sites; 15, picnic only; one swimming site; five winter sports areas including Magic Mountain, Mount Harrison, Soldier Creek, and Sun Valley. Numerous dude ranches, camps, and motels. *Nearby towns:* Burley, Gooding, Sun Valley, and Twin Falls.

TARGHEE. *Highways:* U.S. 20, 26, 89, 91, 191, Idaho 22, 28, 31, 32, 47. *Attractions:* Island Park Reservoir, Grand Canyon of Snake River, Teton and Snake Ranges, Big Falls, North Fork of Snake River, Cave Falls, Falls River, Palisades Dam. Lake and stream fishing; hunting for bear, deer, elk, and moose. Many riding and hiking trails into remote country. Scenic drives. *Facilities:* 16 camp and picnic sites; 7 picnic only; Bear Gulch, Moose Creek, and Pine Basin winter sports areas. Resorts, motels, dude ranches, boating facilities, pack outfits for hunting parties, fishing camps. *Nearby towns:* Ashton, Driggs, Dubois, Idaho Falls, Rexburg, St. Anthony and Victor, Idaho; Afton and Jackson, Wyoming.

NEVADA

Humboldt National Forest, Elko, Nevada.
Toiyabe National Forest, Reno, Nevada.

FOREST DESCRIPTIONS

HUMBOLDT. *Highways:* U.S. 40, 93, 95, Nevada 43, 46. *Attractions:* Wildhorse Reservoir; Owyhee River Canyon; Humboldt, Independence, Ruby, and Santa Rosa Mountains. Spectacular canyons, colorful cliffs, old historic mining camps, *Jarbidge Wild Area.* Fishing in streams and Wildhorse Reservoir;

All About Camping

deer hunting, saddle and pack trips. *Facilities:* 24 camp and picnic sites; three, picnic only; Ward Mountain winter sports area. Resort and dude ranch at Wildhorse Reservoir; hotels. *Nearby towns:* Ely, Elko, Mountain City, Wells, and Winnemucca.

TOIYABE. *Highways:* U.S. 395, 6, 50, 95, California 4, 108, Nevada 8A, 52, 39, 31, 28, 27, 22. *Attractions:* Lake Tahoe; Nevada Beach Forest Camp; historic ghost towns; rugged High Sierra country. Many beautiful lakes and streams. Notable trout fishing. *Hoover Wild Area.* Big-game hunting, saddle and pack trips. Scenic drives—Mt. Rose, Lake Tahoe, Ebbets and Sonora Passes; wilderness trips. *Facilities:* 33 camp and picnic sites; one swimming site; Kyle Canyon, Lee Canyon, and Reno Ski Bowl winter sports areas. Motels, resorts, dude ranches. *Nearby towns:* Austin, Carson City, Minden, Reno, and Tonopah.

UTAH

Ashley National Forest, Vernal, Utah.

Cache National Forest, Logan, Utah.

Dixie National Forest, Cedar City, Utah.

Fishlake National Forest, Richfield, Utah.

Manti-La Sal National Forest, Price, Utah.

Uinta National Forest, Provo, Utah.

Wasatch National Forest, Salt Lake City, Utah.

FOREST DESCRIPTIONS

ASHLEY. *Highways:* U.S. 30, 40, Utah 44. *Attractions:* East half of Uinta Range, Kings Peak (13,498 feet) highest point in Utah; Red Gorge of the Green River, 1,500 feet deep; exposed geological formations a billion years old; site of Flaming Gorge Dam. *High Uintas Primitive Area,* mostly above 10,000 feet; numerous scenic gorges, natural erosion formations. Lake and stream fishing; big-game hunting including deer, elk, and antelope. Riding trails, wilderness pack trips. *Facilities:* 33 camp and picnic sites; three, picnic only; one winter sports site. Resorts, motels, dude ranches. *Nearby towns:* Green River and Rock Springs, Wyoming; Duchesne, Manila, Roosevelt, and Vernal, Utah.

CACHE. *Highways:* U.S. 30S, 89, 91, Utah 39. *Attractions:* Rugged mountains, Bear River and Wasatch Ranges, Minnetonka Cave, Logan and Ogden Canyons, Monte Cristo Mountain. Bear Lake nearby. Fishing; deer and elk hunting. Scenic drives, riding and hiking trails. *Facilities:* 46 camp and picnic sites; 17, picnic only; Beaver Mountain and Snow Basin winter sports areas. *Nearby towns:* Brigham Logan, and Ogden, Utah; Montpelier, Preston, and Soda Springs, Idaho.

DIXIE. *Highways:* U.S. 91, 89, Utah 14, 18, 24. *Attractions:* Red Canyon, Panguitch and Navajo Lakes, Pine Valley Mountains. Boulder Top Plateau, and its many lakes not accessible by road. Table Cliff Point with vista into four States (Colorado, Arizona, Nevada, and Utah). Spectacularly colored cliffs. Deer, elk, and cougar hunting; lake and stream fishing. *Facilities:* 13 camp and picnic sites; 8 picnic only; Cedar Canyon winter sports area. Resorts, motels, dude ranches. *Nearby towns:* Cedar City, Enterprise, Escalante, Panguitch, Parowan, and St. George, Utah; Las Vegas, Nevada.

FISHLAKE. *Highways:* U.S. 50—6, 89, 91, Utah 10, 13, 24. *Attractions:* Beaver Mountains, Thousand Lake Mountain Scenic Area. Fish Lake, Petrified Wood Scenic Area. Lake and stream fishing; big-game hunting, including deer and elk. Scenic drives—Beaver Canyon, Wayne Wonderland, Fish Lake-Salina, Marysvale-Belknap, and others. *Facilities:* 24 camping and picnic sites; 5, picnic only. Resorts, hotels, and motels. *Nearby towns:* Beaver, Delta, Fillmore, Kanosh, Loa, Monroe, Richfield, and Salina.

MANTI-LA SAL. *Highways:* U.S. 50—6, 89, 160, Utah 46, 47. *Attractions:* This forest offers much spectacular desert and mountain scenery in several areas, not all adjoining. A part of the forest extends over the Colorado line. Along the east side of U.S. 89, the main part of Manti-La Sal offers attractions quite similar to the Uninta N.F. which it adjoins at its north end, and from which it extends mostly in a southerly direction. At the southeast corner of Utah and west of Monticello, the forest includes Horse, Shay, Linnaeus, and the Abajo (Blue) Mountains. Abajo Peak is 11,357 feet tall. Natural Bridges National Monument is outside the southwest corner of this part of the forest but since the Monument is so close, travelers usually visit both areas. Farther north and to the east of U.S. 160 not far from Moab, another portion of Manti-La Sal N.F. includes Mt. Waas (12,586 feet), Mt. Peale (13,089 feet), and La Sal Mountain area. The scenic Arches National Monument north of Moab, though not within the forest, is also often combined in visitors' itineraries. Mountain fishing; big-game hunting; many other attractions. *Facilities:* At least 15 camp and picnic sites; 4, picnic sites only; one winter sports area. Facilities vary somewhat depending on the particular forest area visited. Motels and restaurants along main routes. *Nearby towns:* Price, Moab, and Monticello.

UINTA. *Highways:* U.S. 40, 50, 89, 91, and 189. *Attractions:* Cool high mountains rising out of desert. Near Provo, deep canyons with spectacular waterfalls cutting through upthrust Wasatch limestone. Timpanogos Cave; Alpine Scenic Highway around Mount Timpanogos; Nebo Scenic Loop Road; maple, aspen, and oak make brilliant color landscapes in fall. Fishing in mountain streams; deer and elk hunting; 6-mile hiking trail to top of 12,000-foot Mount Timpanogos. *Facilities:* 42 camp and picnic sites; 6, picnic only; two winter sports areas; four valley view overlook points. Hotels, motels. *Nearby towns:* American Fork, Heber, Nephi, Provo, and Spanish Fork.

WASATCH. *Highways:* U.S. 30S, 40, 89, 91, 189, Utah 35, 150, 152, 210, 65, 36. *Attractions:* Big cool mountains on the doorstep of Salt Lake City; rugged back country; Wasatch, Uinta, Stansbury, Onaqui Mountain Ranges. *High Uintas Primitive Area,* with 12,000 to 13,000-foot peaks. Mirror Lake; Grandaddy Lakes; Bridger Lake; many others. Picnic sites in Mill Creek and Big Cottonwood Canyons. Lake and stream fishing, deer and elk hunting. Boating, swimming, riding and hiking trails, wilderness trips, outstanding skiing, skating, and mountain climbing. *Facilities:* 51 camp and picnic sites; 20, picnic only; four winter sports areas including the famous developments at Alta and Brighton. Numerous resorts, motels, and dude ranches. *Nearby towns:* Heber, Kamas, Murray, Ogden, Provo, and Salt Lake City, Utah; Evanston, Wyoming.

WYOMING

Bridger National Forest, Kemmerer, Wyoming.

Teton National Forest, Jackson, Wyoming.

FOREST DESCRIPTIONS

BRIDGER. *Highways:* U.S. 26, 89, 189, 187, 30N. *Attractions:* Salt River, Wyoming, and Wind River Mountain Ranges, live glaciers, *Bridger Wilderness Area;* Gannett Peak, highest in Wyoming at 13,785 feet. Lots of remote country. Lake and stream fishing; hunting for bear, moose, elk, mountain sheep, and deer. Scenic drives—Pinedale Skyline Drive, Greys River Road. Wilderness trips. *Facilities:* 24 camp and picnic sites; two, picnic only; one swimming site. Divide and Surveyor Park winter sports areas. Resorts, hotels, cabins, and dude ranches. *Nearby towns:* Afton and Pinedale.

TETON. *Highways:* U.S. 89, 187, 26, 287, Wyoming 22, 1. *Attractions:* Unspoiled scenic back country famous for big-game herds. Gros Ventre Slide; Gros Ventre, - Teton, and Wind River Ranges; Continental Divide. *Teton Wilderness Area;* famous Jackson Hole country. Outstanding skiing; stream, lake fishing; big-game hunting, moose, elk, deer, mountain sheep, grizzly bear. Scenic drives—Hoback Canyon, Snake River Canyon, Wild River Highway. *Facilities:* Four camp and picnic sites; seven, picnic only; one swimming site; three winter sports areas including Jackson and Teton Pass Ski Runs. Resorts, dude ranches, cabins. *Nearby towns:* Dubois and Jackson, Wyoming; Rexburg, Idaho.

Region 5, California Region

Headquarters, 630 Sansome St., San Francisco 11, California.

CALIFORNIA

Angeles National Forest, Pasadena, California.

Cleveland National Forest, San Diego, California.

Eldorado National Forest, Placerville, California.

Inyo National Forest, Bishop, California.

Klamath National Forest, Yreka, California.

Lassen National Forest, Susanville, California.

Los Padres National Forest, Santa Barbara, California.

Mendocino National Forest, Willows, California.

Modoc National Forest, Alturas, California.

Plumas National Forest, Quincy, California.

San Bernardino National Forest, San Bernardino, California.

Sequoia National Forest, Porterville, California.

Shasta-Trinity National Forest,* Redding, California.

Sierra National Forest, Fresno, California.

Six Rivers National Forest, Eureka, California.

Stanislaus National Forest, Sonora, California.

Tahoe National Forest, Nevada City, California.

FOREST DESCRIPTIONS

ANGELES. *Highways:* U.S. 6, 66, 99, California 2, 39. *Attractions:* Steep rugged mountains adjoining Los Angeles metropolitan area; Old Baldy, 10,000 feet. Chiefly a chaparral forest, that serves as a watershed for the Los Angeles area and as an easily reached mountain playground for the area in the timbered regions at the higher elevations. *Devil Canyon-Bear Canyon Primitive Area.* Scenic drives with wonderful views, especially of the city lights at night. Riding and hiking trails, skiing in season, fishing and hunting, some swimming and boating. *Facilities:* 82 camp and picnic sites; 11, picnic only. (Because of extreme fire danger in southern California, open campfires are not permitted in this forest.) Two swimming sites; six winter sports areas with ski lifts and other facilities. Resorts, cabins, pack and riding stables. Hotels and motels in Los Angeles and foothill towns.

CLEVELAND. *Highways:* U.S. 101, 395, 80, California 78, 79, 71, 74. *Attractions:* Primarily a watershed forest with an unusually mild climate between the desert and the sea. *Agua Tibia Primitive Area.* The world's largest telescope at Palomar Observatory on Mount Palomar. Camping; warm water fishing and duck hunting on the impounded lakes of the water systems. Deer hunting is very popular with a necessarily short season; pigeon, dove and quail hunting. The Mexico-to-Oregon Trail (Pacific Crest Trail) starts here. *Facilities:* 22 camp and picnic sites; four, picnic only. No open fires are permitted. Dude ranches, resorts, motels. *Nearby towns:* El Centro, Los Angeles Oceanside, and San Diego.

ELDORADO. *Highways:* U.S. 50, California 88. *Attractions:* Rugged mountains in the Sierra Nevada. Hundreds of mountain lakes; including south shore of spectacular Lake Tahoe, 23 miles long, 13 miles wide, elevation 6,225 feet. California Gold Rush country, famous Mother Lode mining communities including site of Sutter's Mill. *Desolation Valley Primitive Area.* Lake and stream fishing, deer and bear hunting. Scenic drives—Highway 50 to Lake Tahoe, Carson Pass Highway 88 (route of Fremont expedition of 1844); Georgetown to Wentworth Springs. Riding trails, wilderness trips. *Facilities:* 28 camp and picnic sites; three, picnic only; two swimming sites; seven developed winter sports areas. Resorts, motels, and dude ranches. *Nearby towns:* Placerville, and Sacramento, California; Carson City and Reno, Nevada.

INYO. *Highways:* U.S. 395, 6, California 168. *Attractions: High Sierra Primitive Area; Hoover Wild Area; Mount Dana-Minarets Primitive Area; and the Mammoth-High Sierra Recreation Area.* Palisade Glacier, southernmost glacier in the United States. Ancient Bristlecone Pine Forest Botanical Area with many 4,000 year old trees—the oldest living things on earth. Many wild and rugged granite peaks 12,000 to more than 14,000 feet in elevation. Mount Whitney, 14,496 feet, is the seventh highest in the United States. Lake and stream fishing, deer and bear hunting, wilderness trips. Dozens of natural

---

* Two separately proclaimed national forests under one supervisor.

lakes, some accessible by paved road; elevations up to 9,700 feet. *Mammoth and Reversed Creek Recreation Areas. Facilities:* 61 camp and picnic sites; four, picnic only; two swimming sites; six winter sports areas. Resorts, motels. *Nearby towns:* Big Pine, Bishop, Independence, Leevining, and Lone Pine.

KLAMATH. *Highways:* U.S. 99, California 96, 97. *Attractions:* Big timber forest. Klamath River and tributaries, famous for salmon and steelhead. *Marble Mountain Wilderness Area and Salmon-Trinity Alps Primitive Areas.* High mountain lakes and streams. Great scenic beauty in wild setting. Steelhead and salmon fishing; deer and bear hunting. Hiking, riding, pack trips. *Facilities:* 28 camps and picnic sites; two, picnic only; one swimming site; two winter sports areas. Motels, resorts, and dude ranches. *Nearby towns:* Eureka, Mount Shasta, and Yreka, California; Medford, Oregon.

LASSEN. *Highways:* U.S. 395, California 36, 89. *Attractions: Caribou and Thousand Lakes Wild Areas.* Many lakes; southern end of Cascade Wonderland; volcanic lava flow tubes, hot springs, mud pots. Indian pictographs and hieroglyphics, old emigrant trails. Lake and stream fishing for rainbow, Lochleven, and steelhead trout; deer and bear hunting; riding and hiking trails. *Facilities:* 59 camp and picnic sites; 5, picnic only; one swimming site; four winter sports areas. Privately owned resorts, hotels, motels, and cabins. *Nearby towns:* Chester, Chico, Mill Creek, Red Bluff, and Redding.

LOS PADRES. *Highways:* U.S. 101, 99, 399, California 1, 166, 150, 178. *Attractions:* Undeveloped, rugged country, varying from lonely coast to semi-desert, from brush and oak country to pine timber; elevations from near sea level to almost 9,000 feet; home of the rare California condor. *Ventana and San Rafael Primitive Areas;* snowcapped peaks in winter. Quail, dove, and pigeon hunting; some deer and wild boar hunting; trout fishing. Scenic drives, oceanside camping, wilderness trips. *Facilities:* 286 camp and picnic sites, 7, picnic only. (Because of extreme fire danger in southern California, no open campfires are permitted in this forest.) Three swimming sites, two winter sports areas including Kern County Ski Lodge. Hotels, motels, cabins, and a few dude ranches. *Nearby towns:* Atascadero, Carmel, King City, Monterey, Ojai, Paso Robles, Taft, San Luis Obispo, Santa Barbara, Santa Maria, and Ventura.

MENDOCINO. *Highways:* U.S. 99W, 101, California 20. *Attractions:* Coast Range of California about 100 miles north of San Francisco. Peaks up to 8,600 feet. Beautiful lake country. *Yolla Bolly-Middle Eel Wilderness Area.* Columbian black-tailed deer. Hunting, fishing, saddle and pack trips. *Facilities:* 49 camp and picnic sites. Dude ranches, motels. *Nearby towns:* Corning, Laytonville, Sacramento, Ukiah, Willits, and Willow.

MODOC. *Highways:* U.S. 299, 395, California 139. *Attractions:* Remote northeast corner of California. Scenic rides, wilderness trips on trails such as the summit trail through *South Warner Primitive Area.* Glass Mountain lava flows, scene of Modoc Indian wars. Winter range of interstate deer herd. Clear Lake Reservoir migratory bird refuge. Stream and lake fishing; mule deer and water-fowl hunting. *Facilities:* 25 camp and picnic sites; two, picnic only; one swimming site; two winter sports areas. Hotels, cabins, hunter's camps during deer season. *Nearby towns:* Adin, Alturas, Canby, Cedarville, and Tulelake.

PLUMAS. *Highways:* U.S. 40A, 395, California 89, 24. *Attractions:* Beautiful Feather River country; Feather Falls, one of the highest and most picturesque waterfalls in the United States. Historic gold mining areas of La Porte, Johnsville, and Rich Bar; extensive hydorelectric developments. Limestone caves; large beautiful mountain valleys, such as Indian, American, Mohawk, and Sierra Valleys. Lake and stream fishing; hunting for mule and black-tailed deer, bear, ducks, geese. quail, and dove. Scenic drives include Feather River Canyon, Bucks Lake, Bald Rock Canyon, Quincy-La Porte and Lakes Basin Recreational Areas, and Little Last Chance Creek. Pacific Crest Trail. *Facilities:* 27 camps and picnic sites; two, picnic only. Resorts, hotels, and cabins. *Nearby towns:* Chico, Greenville, Marysville, Oroville, Quincy, Sacramento, and Sierraville.

SAN BERNARDINO. *Highways:* U.S. 60, 70, 99, 66, 395, California 2, 18, 74. *Attractions:* Highest mountains in southern California. San Gorgonio, 11,485 feet; six others more than 10,000 feet. *San Jacinto, San Gorgonio, and Cucamonga Wild Areas.* Historic landmarks; Big Bear and Arrowhead Lakes; Mt. San Jacinto. Lake and stream fishing, deer hunting. Life zones from desert to Alpine within few miles. Camping and pack trips, winter sports. *Facilities:* 41 camp and picnic sites; 10, picnic only. (Because of extreme fire danger in southern California, no open campfires are permitted in this forest). Two swimming sites; nine winter sports sites. Resorts, hotels, motels, cabins at Lake Arrowhead, Big Bear Lake, Idyllwild. *Nearby towns:* Banning, Indio, Palm Springs, Riverside, and San Bernardino, California.

SEQUOIA. *Highways:* U.S. 395, California 190. *Attractions:* Giant sequoia trees, Hume Lake, Boydens Cave, *High Sierra Primitive Area.* Mineral King Game Refuge. High mountain lakes and stream fishing, home of the golden trout. Big-game hunting, mule deer and bear. Scenic drives—Kern River Canyon, Kings River Canyon. Wilderness hiking and riding trails; swimming and boating. *Facilities:* 45 camp and picnic sites; 8, picnic only; 8 swimming sites; three winter sports areas. Motels, resorts, lodges. *Nearby towns:* Bakersfield, Fresno, Porterville, and Visalia.

SHASTA-TRINITY. *Highways:* U.S. 99, 299, California 44, 96, 89. *Attractions:* Beautiful Mount Shasta (14,162 feet) with eternal snow, five living glaciers. Shasta and Trinity Lakes with outstanding boating. Lava beds, Glass Mountain, and Castle Crags. *Salmon-Trinity Alps Primitive Area and Yolla Bolly-Middle Eel Wilderness Area.* Lake and stream fishing, home of Dolly Varden trout. Waterfowl, upland birds, deer, bear, small game hunting. Limestone caves, lava caves, and chimneys. Riding trails in the wilderness. Skiing. Scenic drives. *Facilities:* 64 camp and picnic sites; 5, picnic only; 8 swimming sites; two winter sports areas. Resorts, hotels, motels, cabins, and guest ranches. *Nearby towns:* Callahan, Dunsmuir, McCloud, Mount Shasta, Redding, Weaverville, and Weed.

SIERRA. *Highways:* U.S. 99, California 168, 180, 41. *Attractions:* Huntington Lake, Florence Lake, Shaver Lake, Dinkey Creek, and Bass Lake Recreation Areas. Nelder and McKinley Groves of big trees (sequoia giantea); Central Sierra section of the John Muir Trail. *High Sierra Primitive Area; Mount Dana-Minerets Primitive Area.* Rainbow Falls in the Reds Meadows area. Lake and stream fishing; deer, bear, and quail hunting. Boating, mountain climbing, pack and saddle trips, winter sports. *Facilities:* 79 camp and picnic sites; 19, picnic only, 12 swimming sites; one winter sports area. Hotels, resorts, dude ranches. *Nearby towns:* Fresno and North Fork.

SIX RIVERS. *Highways:* U.S. 101, 299, California 36, 96. *Attractions:* Giant Coast Redwood and fir forests stretching 135 miles south from the Oregon line. Klamath, Smith, Eel, and Mad Rivers. Mild, cool climate year long in redwoods; rugged backcountry. Trout fishing, spring and summer; steel-head and salmon fishing fall and winter in six rivers; deer and bear hunting; riding trails; scenic drives. *Facilities:* 33 camp and picnic sites; one, picnic only; two swimming sites; one winter sports area. Resorts, motels, and hotels, cabins. *Nearby towns:* Arcata, Crescent City, Eureka, Fortuna, Klamath, Orick, and Orleans.

STANISLAUS. *Highways:* U.S. 99, 395, California 4, 108, 120. *Attractions:* Nearest high mountain country to San Francisco Bay region and portion of San Joaquin Valley; elevations 1,100 to 11,575 feet. Deep canyons cut by Merced, Tuolumne, Stanislaus, and Mokelumne Rivers; fine timber stands; *Emigrant Basin Primitive Area.* Gold rush country (Mother Lode) with many a tall tale. Routes of pioneers, Sonora and Ebbets Passes. (Calaveras Big Tree State Park and Calaveras Big Trees National Forest.) Fishing in lakes and 715 miles of streams; hunting for deer, bear, quail, dove, coyote. Scenic drives, saddle and pack trips, winter sports. *Facilities:* 55 camp and picnic sites; two swimming sites; three winter sports areas. Resorts, cabins, stores, boating, packer stations. *Nearby towns:* Angels Camp, Columbia State Park, Groveland, Jamestown, San Andrews, and Sonora.

TAHOE. *Highways:* U.S. 40, California 20, 49, 89. *Attractions:* Squaw Valley, site of the 1960 Winter Olympics and now a state park. Outstanding conditions and facilities for winter sports; adjacent valleys being developed. Lakes and streams, including northwest shore of beautiful Lake Tahoe. Historic Donner Pass Emigrant Trail; Gold Rush country. Lake and stream fishing, hunting for deer and bear. Hiking and riding trails, scenic drives through historic gold mining towns. *Facilities:* 54 camps and picnic sites; two, picnic only; three swimming sites; six winter sports areas. Summer resorts, cabins, motels, and hotels. *Nearby towns:* Downieville, Grass Valley, Nevada City, Sierra City, Sierraville, and Truckee, California; Carson City and Reno, Nevada.

Region 6, Pacific Northwest Region

Headquarters, 729 N.E. Oregon St., Portland 8, Oregon.

OREGON

Deschutes National Forest, Bend, Oregon.

Fremont National Forest, Lakeview, Oregon.

Malheur National Forest, John Day, Oregon.
Mount Hood National Forest, Portland, Oregon.
Ochoco National Forest, Prineville, Oregon.
Rogue River National Forest, Medford, Oregon.
Siskiyou National Forest, Grants Pass, Oregon.
Siuslaw National Forest, Corvallis, Oregon.
Umatilla National Forest, Pendleton, Oregon.
Umpqua National Forest, Roseburg, Oregon.
Wallowa-Whitman National Forest,* Baker, Oregon.
Willamette National Forest, Eugene, Oregon.
Winema National Forest, Klamath, Oregon.

FOREST DESCRIPTIONS

DESCHUTES. *Highways:* U.S. 126, 97, 26, 20. *Attractions:* Beautiful southern Cascade Range. Snow-clad peaks, ice caves, waterfalls, and over three hundred lakes; lava caves; Deschutes River; Newberry Crater; scenic Century Drive; Bend Forest Service Nursery; historic Williamette Military Road; *Mount Jefferson Wild Area and Three Sisters Wilderness Area.* Sections of Oregon Skyline Trail from Mount Jefferson to Mount Thielsen. *Mount Washington and Diamond Peak Wild Areas,* and *Lava Cast Forest Geological Area* in a ponderosa pine setting. Rainbow trout fishing, deer hunting. Scenic drives, saddle and pack trips, skiing. *Facilities:* 76 camp and picnic sites; 11, picnic only; 7 swimming sites; one winter sports area. Dude ranches, motels, and resorts. *Nearby towns:* Bend, Chemult, Redmond, and Sisters.

FREMONT. *Highways:* U.S. 395, Oregon 66, 31. *Attractions:* Indian paintings and writings. Protected herds of antelope; Oregon Desert; *Gearhart Mountain Wild Area.* Drier inland forests. Deer and bird hunting, winter sports. Abert geologic fault east of Lake Abert, second largest vertical fault in world. *Facilities:* 21 camp and picnic sites; one winter sports area. Motels. *Nearby towns:* Bly, Chemult, Klamath Falls, Lakeview, and Paisley.

MALHEUR. *Highways:* U.S. 26, 395. *Attractions:* Mountains, fishing streams, archers' hunting reserve, fossil beds of prehistoric plants and animals, extensive stands of ponderosa pine. *Strawberry Mountain Wild Area.* Steelhead and rainbow trout fishing; elk and deer hunting. Cabin of Joaquin Miller. Scenic drives, saddle and pack trips. *Facilities:* 39 camp and picnic sites; two winter sports areas. Motels; cabins in and near the forest. *Nearby towns:* Burns, Dayville, John Day, and Prairie City.

MOUNT HOOD. *Highways:* U.S. 30, 99E, 26. *Attractions:* Beautiful Mount Hood with Timberline Lodge; Multnomah Falls, glaciers, lakes, hot springs, and flower-filled Alpine meadows. *Mount Hood Wild Area and Mount Jefferson Primitive Areas.* Mount Hood Loop and Columbia Gorge scenic drives; Oregon Trail route. North end of Oregon Skyline Trail, a segment of the Pacific Crest Trail system. Stream and lake fishing, swimming, saddle and pack trips, huckleberry picking, winter sports areas. Timberline Lodge, Multnomah Falls Lodge, and other resorts in and near the forest. *Nearby towns:* Gresham, Hood River, Maupin, Oregon City, and Portland.

OCHOCO. *Highways:* U.S. 26, 126, 97, 20. *Attractions:* Parkline ponderosa pine forest; many beaver colonies. Fort Watson and Camp Maury, frontier-day Army posts; scenes of early-day range wars. Steins Pillar, geological landmark. Trout fishing, elk and deer hunting, scenic drives. *Facilities:* 28 camp and picnic sites. Motels, cabins. *Nearby towns:* Bend, Burns, and Prineville.

ROGUE RIVER. *Highways:* U.S. 99, 199, Oregon 62, 66. *Attractions:* Beautiful Rogue River, lakes, trout streams, and waterfalls; extensive sugar pine and Douglas-fir forests; mammoth sugar pine roadside specimen. Table Rock, site of bloody war with Rogue River Indians. Rainbow and steelhead trout fishing; deer and migratory bird hunting. Oregon Skyline Trail extends through the forest from Crater Lake almost to the California line. Scenic drives, saddle and pack trips, skiing. *Facilities:* 47 camp and picnic sites; three, picnic only; one swimming site; Onion Creek and Tomahawk winter

---

* Two separately proclaimed national forests under one supervisor.

sports areas. Resorts, motels, cabins. *Nearby towns:* Ashland, Grants Pass, Klamath Falls, and Medford.

SISKIYOU. *Highways:* U.S. 99, 101, 199. *Attractions:* Beautiful Oregon coast, famous salmon fishing in lower Rogue River Gorge; early-day gold camps. Home of rare species, including Port Orford-cedar, "Oregon myrtle," rock rhododendron, Brewer weeping spruce, and Saddler oak. Profuse growth of wild lilac, rhododendron, azaleas, and pitcher plants. *Kalmiopsis Wild Area.* Cutthroat and steelhead trout and salmon fishing. Deer, bear, and cougar hunting. Boat trips up the pristine Rouge; saddle and pack trips, scenic drives. *Facilities:* 18 camp and picnic sites; two, picnic only. Resorts, outfitters, and cabins in and near the forest. *Nearby towns:* Brookings, Gold Beach, Grants Pass, Port Orford, and Powers.

SIUSLAW. *Highways:* U.S. 20, 99, 101, Oregon 34. *Attractions:* Heavy stands of Sitka spruce, western hemlock, cedar, and Douglas fir; pitcher plants, rhododendron, azaleas. Bordered by Pacific Ocean; 34 miles of public beach, shoreline, and sand dunes including Cape Perpetua Overlook, Mary's Peak, highest in the Coast Range, with road to campsites near summit. Ocean, lake, and stream fishing; deer, bear, cougar, and migratory bird hunting. Swimming, boating, clam digging, Scuba diving, scenic drives. *Facilities:* 23 camp and picnic sites; four, picnic only. Resorts, motels. *Nearby towns:* Corvallis, Eugene, Florence, Mapleton, Reedsport, Tillamook, and Waldport.

UMATILLA. *Highways:* U.S. 30, 395, 410, Oregon 11. *Attractions:* Skyline trip along summit of Blue Mountains on the Kendall-Skyline Forest Road. Spectacular views of Touchet and Wenaha River Canyons. Extensive stands of ponderosa pine. Oregon Trail route; hot sulfur springs. Stream fishing for steelhead and rainbow trout; elk, deer, pheasant (and other bird) hunting. Saddle and pack trips, scenic drives, skiing. *Facilities:* 44 camp and picnic sites; Tollgate-Spout Springs winter sports area. Hotels, resorts, dude ranches. *Nearby towns:* La Grande and Pendleton, Oregon; Clarkston, Pomeroy, Waitsburg, and Walla Walla, Washington.

UMPQUA. *Highways:* U.S. 99, Oregon 42. *Attractions:* Spectacular North Umpqua cataracts, Steamboat and Watson Falls, Umpqua River; a little Matterhorn, Mount Thielsen, rising above beautiful Diamond Lake. Unique stands of incense-cedar. Steelhead and rainbow trout fishing; deer, bear, cougar hunting. Oregon Skyline Trail from Windigo Pass to Crater Lake. Scenic drives, saddle and pack trips, skiing. *Facilities:* 39 camp and picnic sites; one, picnic only; four swimming sites; Taft Mountain winter sports area. Resorts, dude ranches, motels. *Nearby towns:* Canyonville, Cottage Grove, and Roseburg.

WALLOWA-WHITMAN. *Highways:* U.S. 26, 30, Oregon 7, 86, 82. These are two forests. *Attractions:* Snowcapped peaks; Wallowa and many other lakes; glaciers; Alpine meadows and rare wild flowers; Minam River, famous fishing stream. Grand spectacle of Snake River and Imnaha Canyons from Grizzly Ridge Road and Hat Point. Blue and Wallowa Mountains, Anthony Lakes, *Eagle Cap Wilderness Area.* Stream and lake trout fishing; elk, deer, bear hunting. Saddle and pack trips, scenic drives. *Facilities:* 40 camp and picnic sites; two, picnic only; Little Alps winter sports area. Resorts, dude ranches, motels. *Nearby towns:* Baker, Enterprise, Halfway, La Grande, and Union.

WILLIAMETTE. *Highways:* U.S. 126, 99, 20, Oregon 58, 22. *Attractions:* Most heavily timbered national forest in the United States. Snowcapped peaks, lakes, waterfalls, and hot springs; McKenzie Pass Highway and lava beds. Historic Williamette Military Road. *Three Sisters Wilderness Area* including numerous volcanic formations; *Mount Jefferson Primitive Area, Mount Washington, and Diamond Peak Wild Areas.* Sections of Oregon Skyline Trail from Mount Jefferson south to Maiden Peak. Stream and lake fishing, deer and bear hunting. Scenic drives, saddle and pack trips, winter sports. *Facilities:* 69 camp and picnic sites; two winter sports areas. Motels, cabins, pack trip outfitters. *Nearby towns:* Albany, Eugene, Lebanon, and Salem.

WINEMA. *Highways:* U.S. 97, Oregon 66 and 31, with side roads branching off state highways entering this new forest. *Attractions:* This relatively new national forest consists of a large portion of the Klamath Indian Reservation and former parts of Fremont, Deschutes, and Rogue River national forests. Its lower southwest boundaries edge the Upper Klamath Lake. The western boundary joins with the east boundary of Crater Lake National Park. It contains the Klamath Forest National Wildlife Refuge located in what is known as Klamath Marsh, near the center of the forest. The famous *Lake of the Woods Recreation Area* is now within the forest boundary; and *Mountain Lakes Wild Area.* Scenic drives; hunting, fishing, picnicking, and camping. *Nearby towns:* Chiloquin, Pine Ridge, Sand Creek, Kirk, Crescent, Silver Lake, Paisley, Fort Klamath, and Klamath Falls.

WASHINGTON

Okanogan National Forest, Okanogan, Washington.
Gifford Pinchot National Forest, Vancouver, Washington.
Mount Baker National Forest, Bellingham, Washington.
Olympic National Forest, Olympia, Washington.
Snoqualmie National Forest, Seattle, Washington.
Wenatchee National Forest, Wenatchee, Washington.

FOREST DESCRIPTIONS

OKANOGAN. *Highways:* U.S. 97, Washington 16. *Attractions:* Alpine meadows, snow peaks, and glaciers. Cascade Crest Trail, a segment of the Pacific Crest Trail System, originates at Canadian boundary and extends southward to Harts Pass. *North Cascade Primitive Area.* Lake and stream fishing, boating; saddle and pack trips, mountain climbing, winter sports. *Facilities:* 52 camp and picnic sites; one, picnic only, two swimming sites; Loup winter sports area. Dude ranches, motels. *Nearby towns:* Brewster, Okanogan, Tonasket, and Twisp.

GIFFORD PINCHOT. *Highways:* U.S. 99, 830. *Attractions:* Mount Adams, 12,300 feet, reached by scenic Evergreen Highway; Spirit Lake, many other lakes; snowcapped peaks; Mineral Springs. Wind River Forest Nursery. *Goat Rocks and Mount Adams Wild Areas.* Lake and stream trout fishing; Cascade Crest Trail extends through the forest. Spectacular auto tours, saddle and pack trips, mountain climbing, winter sports. *Facilities:* 54 camp and picnic sites; two, picnic only; one swimming site. Resorts, motels, cabins. *Nearby towns:* Castle Rock, Morton, Stevenson, Vancouver, and White Salmon.

MOUNT BAKER. *Highways:* U.S. 99, Washington 1, 17A. *Attractions:* Superb mountain scenery; snowcapped peaks, including *Glacier Peak Wilderness Area;* numerous glaciers; Alpine lakes; heavy stands of Douglas fir up to 200 feet in height. *North Cascade Wilderness Area. Mount Baker Recreation Area* featuring both summer and winter recreation. Segments of Cascade Crest Trail from Harts Pass to Glacier Peak. Steelhead and rainbow trout fishing; deer and bear hunting, skiing, saddle and pack trips, mountain climbing. *Facilities:* 51 camp and picnic sites; three, picnic only; Mount Baker and Mount Pilchuck winter sports areas. Hotels, resorts; experienced guides. *Nearby towns:* Bellingham, Darrington, Everett, and Granite Falls.

OLYMPIC. *Highways:* U.S. 99, 410, 101. *Attractions:* Dense rain forests, big trees, spectacular snow peaks, scores of lakes and streams. Fishing includes salmon and steelhead trout; hunting for deer, bear, cougar, and elk. Scenic drives; saddle and pack trips. *Facilities:* 14 camp and picnic sites; two, picnic only; two swimming sites. Resorts, motels, dude ranches. *Nearby towns:* Aberdeen, Olympia, Port Angeles, Quilcene, and Shelton.

SNOQUALMIE. *Highways:* U.S. 99, 10, 410, 2. *Attractions:* Snoqualmie Falls, 250-feet high; scenic Chinook and White Pass Highways; giant Douglas firs; snow peaks, lakes, fishing streams. Sections of Cascade Crest Trail from Cady Pass to Goat Rocks. Mather Memorial Parkway, *Goat Rocks Wild Area.* Stream and lake fishing, including salmon and steelhead trout; hunting black-tailed and mule deer, bear, and elk. Scenic drives, saddle and pack trips, skiing. *Facilities:* 100 camp and picnic sites; Snoqualmie Pass and White Pass winter sports areas. Motels and outfitters locally available. *Nearby towns:* Cle Elum, Everett, Seattle, Tacoma, and Yakima.

WENATCHEE. *Highways:* U.S. 10, 2, 97. *Attractions:* Lake Chelan, 55 miles long between precipitous mountain ranges; lake bottom 389 feet below sea level. Snowcapped peaks, lakes, Alpine meadows, rare wild flowers in Tumwater Botanical Area; fishing streams; Lake Wenatchee. Stream and trout fishing; deer and bear hunting. Cascade Crest Trail between Rainy Pass and Blowout Mountain. Scenic drives. Lake Chelan boat trip, saddle and pack trips, winter sports. *Facilities:* 93 camp and picnic sites; four, picnic only; six winter sports areas. Motels and dude ranches. *Nearby towns:* Cashmere, Chelan, Cle Elum, Ellensburg, Leavenworth, and Wenatchee.

Region 7, Eastern Region

Headquarters, 6816 Market St., Upper Darby, Pennsylvania.

KENTUCKY
Cumberland National Forest, Winchester, Kentucky.

FOREST DESCRIPTION

CUMBERLAND. *Highways:* U.S. 25, 27, 60, 421, and 460. *Attractions:* Western rim of Cumberland Plateau, sandstone cliffs 100 feet high, Red River Gorge, natural rock arches, numerous limestone caves and mineral springs. Cumberland Falls and Natural Bridge State Parks within this forest. Bass and pike fishing in larger streams. Lake Cumberland created by Wolf Creek Dam provides 250 miles of forest shoreline. About 500 miles of fishing streams. Hunting for squirrel, deer, cottontails, and upland game birds. *Facilities:* Four camp and picnic sites; 8, picnic only. Swimming sites at Cumberland Falls and Natural Bridge State Parks; also hotels and cabins. Motels and cottages at the boat docks on Lake Cumberland at confluence of Laurel and Rockcastle Rivers. *Nearby towns:* Boonesboro, Corbin, Lexington.

NEW HAMPSHIRE
White Mountain National Forest, Laconia, New Hampshire.

FOREST DESCRIPTION

WHITE MOUNTAIN. *Highways:* U.S. 2, 3, and 302, New Hampshire 16. *Attractions:* Very popular mountains and forest including a major part of the White Mountains. Mount Washington, 6,288 feet, highest point in New England; Presidential Range; *Great Gulf Wild Area;* Glen Ellis Falls; Tuckerman Ravine; the *Dolly Copp Recreation Area.* Some 650 miles of streams, 39 lakes and ponds, provide brook trout fishing. Deer, bear, and small-game hunting. Scenic drives through famous notches and over mountain highways. Outstanding skiing with spring skiing often lasting into June. Rock climbing; 1,000 miles of foot trails; swimming. *Facilities:* 14 camp and picnic sites; 6, picnic only; 26 shelters and high-country cabins for hikers; one swimming area; Wildcat, Tuckermans Ravine, Waterville Valley winter sports areas. Cabins, motels, hotels. *Nearby towns:* Berlin, Conway, Gorham, Lancaster, Littleton, Pinkham Notch.

PENNSYLVANIA
Allegheny National Forest, Warren, Pennsylvania.

FOREST DESCRIPTION

ALLEGHENY. *Highways:* U.S. 6, 62, 219. *Attractions:* Allegheny Plateau country; Hearts Content and Tionesta virgin timber stands; 260 miles of trout streams, 85 miles of bass fishing in Allegheny and Clarion Rivers; 32 acres of lake fishing in Twin Lakes and Beaver Meadows Pond; hunting for deer, turkey and bear; scenic drives. *Facilities:* 7 camp and picnic sites; four, picnic only; 27 roadside tables; three swimming sites. Hotels nearby; cabins in Cook Forest and Allegheny State Parks. *Nearby towns:* Bradford, Kane, Ridgway, Sheffield, Tionesta, and Warren.

VERMONT
Green Mountain National Forest, Rutland, Vermont.

FOREST DESCRIPTION

GREEN MOUNTAIN. *Highways:* U.S. 2, 4, Vt. 12, 100, 103, 108. *Attractions:* Picturesque 4,000-foot New England mountains in western Vermont offering hiking, fishing, scenic drives, and many varied outdoor activities. Smugglers Notch, between Jeffersonville and Stowe. *Facilities:* 8 camp and picnic sites; two, picnic only; swimming site; two winter sports areas. Resorts, hotels, motels, and restaurants along routes approaching area. *Nearby towns:* Waterbury, Montpelier, Rutland, Burlington.

VIRGINIA
George Washington National Forest, Harrisonburg, Virginia.

Jefferson National Forest, Roanoke, Virginia.

FOREST DESCRIPTIONS

GEORGE WASHINGTON. *Highways:* U.S. 50, 11, 220, 211, 33, 60, 29, Virginia 42, 259. *Attractions:* Rugged mountainous terrain with elevations up to 4,500 feet; Blue Ridge, Shenandoah, Allegheny, and Massanutten Ranges. Outstanding scenery; Crabtree Falls, limestone caverns, Lost River sinks, Devils Garden, Trout Run sinks, and other unusual geological sites. Duncan, Bald, High, Reddish, and Elliott Knobs; Shenandoah and Warm Springs Valleys. Civil War iron furnaces. Sherando Lake campsite, with 20-acre swimming and fishing lake. Trout and bass fishing, 208 miles of cold water fishing streams. Hunting, including black bear, deer, turkey, grouse, and squirrel. Panoramic views, scenic drives; Blue Ridge Parkway and 391 miles of foot trails. *Facilities:* 9 camp and picnic sites; 7, picnic only; two swimming sites. Hotels, resorts, and small cabins available. Many secondary roads. *Nearby towns:* Luray, Harrisonburg, Staunton, and Winchester, Virginia; Franklin and Moorefield, West Virginia. About 90 miles from Washington, D.C.

JEFFERSON. *Highways:* U.S. 220, 11, 21, 52, 23, 58. *Attractions:* Blue Ridge Mountains; Mount Rogers, 5,719 feet, highest in Virginia. Transitional zone between northern and southern flora; rhododendrons. Glenwood and Roaring Run Civil War iron furnaces; Appalachian Trail; Blue Ridge Parkway. More than 200 miles of fishing streams, three fishing lakes. Four camp and picnic sites; 60, picnic only; two swimming sites. Resorts, hotels, and cabins. Network of good secondary roads. *Nearby towns:* Bristol, Bluefield, Lexington, Marion, Radford, Roanoke, and Wytheville.

WEST VIRGINIA

Monongahela National Forest, Elkins, West Virginia.

FOREST DESCRIPTION

MONONGAHELA. *Highways:* U.S. 33, 60, 219, 220, and 250. *Attractions:* Appalachian and Allegheny Mountains; Spruce Knob, 4,860 feet, highest in West Virginia; Blackwater Canyon and 60-foot falls; spectacular Seneca Rocks on historic Seneca Indian Trail. Botanically curious Cranberry Glades; rhododendrons in early July; unexplored limestone caves; beaver colonies. Parsons Forest Nursery, Smoke Hole rugged mountain scenery. Some 1,900 miles of trout and bass fishing streams; hunting for deer, turkey, squirrel, bear, grouse, and other game. Swimming, horseback riding, scenic drives. Man-made lakes at Spruce Knob, Summit, and Sherwood offer trout and bass fishing with good campsites nearby. *Facilities:* 21 camp and picnic sites; 15, picnic only; six swimming sites. Tourist homes and motels. *Nearby towns:* Charleston, Elkins, Lewisburg, Petersburg.

Region 8, Southern Region
Headquarters, 50 Seventh St., N.E., Atlanta 23, Georgia.

ALABAMA

(Supervisor's Address: 401 Federal Building, Montgomery, Alabama.)

William B. Bankhead National Forest
Conecuh National Forest
Talladega National Forest
Tuskegee National Forest

FOREST DESCRIPTIONS

WILLIAM B. BANKHEAD. *Highways:* U.S. 31, 78, 278, Alabama 5, 74, 195. *Attractions:* Limestone gorges, Lewis Smith Reservoir, two natural bridges, wildlife refuge and management area. Deer, turkey, and squirrel hunting. Bass and bream fishing in Brushy Lake. *Facilities:* One camp and picnic site; three, picnic only; one swimming site. *Nearby towns:* Cullum, Decatur, Haleyville, Jasper, and Russellville.

Conecuh. *Highways:* U.S. 29, Alabama 137. *Attractions:* Large, clear ponds. Bass and bream fishing. Deer, turkey, and small-game hunting. *Facilities:* One picnicking, one camping, and one swimming site. *Nearby town:* Andalusia.

Talladega. *Highways:* U.S. 78, 231, Alabama 5, 6. *Attractions:* Payne Lake Wildlife Management Area; Skyway scenic drive; Mount Cheaha, 2,407 feet, highest point in Alabama; Lake Cinnabee. Deer, turkey, duck, and squirrel hunting; bass, bream, and perch fishing; swimming at Cheaha State Park. *Facilities:* Four camp and picnic sites; 7, picnic only; one swimming site. Resort, hotel, and cabins at Cheaha State Park. *Nearby towns:* Anniston, Centreville, Heflin, Marion, Selma, Syacauga, Talladega, and Tuscaloosa.

Tuskegee. *Highways:* U.S. 29, 80, Alabama 81. *Attractions:* Pine plantation of advanced size. Bream fishing in streams. *Facilities:* Two picnicking sites. *Nearby towns:* Auburn and Tuskegee.

ARKANSAS

Ouachita National Forest, Hot Springs National Park, Arkansas.
Ozark National Forest, Russellville, Arkansas.
St. Francis National Forest, Russellville, Arkansas.

FOREST DESCRIPTIONS

Ouachita. *Highways:* U.S. 59, 70, 71, 270, 271, Arkansas 7, 10, 21, 27. *Attractions:* Ouachita, Kiamichi, and Winding Stair Mountains; eight major and numerous smaller artificial lakes in or near the forest. Caddo Gap, where De Soto fought Indians; land explored by La Salle and De Tonti, accounting for the many French names. Crystal Cave, Little Missouri Falls, four game refuges, medicinal springs. Bass fishing, deer, quail, and squirrel hunting; scenic drives, hiking and swimming. *Facilities:* 8 camp and picnic sites; 17, picnic only; 11 swimming sites. Hotels, resorts, and cabin camps. *Nearby towns:* Booneville, Hot Springs, and Mena, Arkansas; Heavener and Poteau, Oklahoma.

Ozark—St. Francis. *Highways:* U.S. 64, 71, Arkansas 7, 22, 23. *Attractions:* Inviting summer climate, oak forest, rock cliffs and pools, scenic drives, five game refuges. Three recreational lakes; Mount Magazine. Stream and lake fishing, deer and small game hunting; two large reservoirs. *Facilities:* Ten camp and picnic sites; seven swimming sites. Mount Magazine Lodge and cabins. White Rock Mountain cabins, others nearby. *Nearby towns:* Clarksville, Fayetteville, Fort Smith, Harrison, Ozark, Paris, and Russellville.

FLORIDA

(Supervisor's Address: 303 Petroleum Bldg., Tallahassee, Florida.)
Apalachicola National Forest
Ocala National Forest
Osceola National Forest

FOREST DESCRIPTIONS

Apalachicola. *Highways:* U.S. 98, 319, Florida 20, 65, 369. *Attractions:* Pine-hardwood forests, Coastal Plain type. Natural sinks, bottom land hardwood swamps along large rivers with trees typically found far to the north. Old Fort Gadsen; old river landings. Three rivers and their tributaries with many miles of fishing waters—bass, bream, perch. Quail, deer, and bear hunting. Numerous lakes, sinks, and ponds provide boating and swimming. *Facilities:* Four camp and picnic sites; ten, picnic only; four swimming sites. Hotels not far away. *Nearby towns:* Apalachicola, Blountstown, Bristol, and Tallahassee.

Ocala. *Highways:* U.S. 17, 301, Florida 19, 40, 42, 314. *Attractions:* Juniper Springs and Alexander Springs; large clear-flowing streams through subtropical wilderness; botanical lore, palms, hardwoods, and pine. Hundreds of clear lakes. The Big Scrub, characterized by vast stands of sand pine, is unique. Wildlife management area, annual deer and bear hunts. Silver Springs is nearby. Numerous lakes, streams, and ponds with fishing and camping sites. *Facilities:* 12 camp and picnic sites; 10, picnic only; four swimming sites. Hunting, camps; commercial accommodations near the forest. *Nearby towns:* DeLand, Eustis, Leesburg, Mount Dora, Ocala, and Palatka.

OSCEOLA. *Highways:* U.S. 41, 90, 441, Florida 100. *Attractions:* Flat country, dotted with numerous ponds, sinks, and cypress swamps. State game breeding ground. Bass, perch, and bream fishing; deer, turkey, quail, and dove hunting. Swimming and boating at Ocean Pond. *Facilities:* One camp and picnic site; three, picnic only; two swimming sites; opportunities for aquatic sports. *Nearby towns:* Jacksonville, and Lake City.

GEORGIA

Chattahoochee National Forest, Gainesville, Georgia.
Oconee National Forest, Gainesville, Georgia.

FOREST DESCRIPTIONS

CHATTAHOOCHEE. *Highways:* U.S. 19, 23, 27, 41, 76, 123, 129, 441, Georgia 5, 60, 75. *Attractions:* Brasstown Bald, 4,784 feet, highest point in the State of Georgia; Blue Ridge Mountains; lakes; Tallulah Gorge; waterfalls; southern end of Appalachian Trail. Deer and small-game hunting, archery hunting for deer; trout and bass fishing. Swimming, boating, hiking. *Facilities:* Ten camp and picnic sites; 23, picnic only; 6 swimming sites. *Nearby towns:* Atlanta, Blue Ridge, Clarkesville, Clayton, Dahlonega, Dalton, and Toccoa, Georgia; Chattanooga, Tennessee.

OCONEE. *Highways:* U.S. 278, 129, Georgia 15, 44, 77. *Attractions:* Heavily forested Piedmont hills, archeological remains, Rock Eagle Lake, effigy of Eagle, Mammoth 4-H Center, Piedmont Wildlife Refuge; deer and small game hunting, bass and bream fishing. *Facilities:* Two picnic sites. *Nearby towns:* Eatonton, Greensboro, and Madison.

LOUISIANA

Kisatchie National Forest, Alexandria, Louisiana.

FOREST DESCRIPTION

KISATCHIE. *Highways:* U.S. 71, 165, 167, 84, Louisiana 19, 21, 28. *Attractions:* Colonial homes; Natchitoches, oldest town in Louisiana on Old San Antonio Trail; Stuart Forest Service Nursery, one of the largest pine nurseries in the world. Extensive plantations of longleaf, loblolly, and splash pines. Many bayous and lakes screened by Spanish moss. Fishing in lakes and bayous; hunting for deer, quail, and migratory birds; boating, camping, and scenic drives. *Facilities:* Two camp and picnic sites; 6, picnic only; four swimming sites. Hotels. *Nearby towns:* Alexandria, Leesville, Minden, and Winnfield.

MISSISSIPPI

(Supervisor's Address: P. O. Box 1144, Jackson, Mississippi.)
Bienville National Forest
Delta National Forest
De Soto National Forest
Holly Springs National Forest
Homochitto National Forest
Tombigbee National Forest

FOREST DESCRIPTIONS

BIENVILLE. *Highways:* U.S. 80, Miss. 35. *Attractions:* Coastal Plain second-growth pine and hardwood forest; numerous forest management demonstration areas. Eighty acres of virgin loblolly pine surrounding Bienville Ranger Station. Quail hunting; fishing. *Facilities:* Two camp and picnic sites; three, picnic only; one swimming site. *Nearby towns:* Jackson and Meridian.

DELTA. *Highways:* U.S. 61, 80, 49. *Attractions:* Camping, picnicking, hunting outside in season. *Nearby towns:* Rolling Fork, Vicksburg, Greenville, and Jackson.

DE SOTO. *Highways:* U.S. 11, 49, 90, Miss. 26. *Attractions:* Site of South Mississippi Gun and Dog Club field trials. Quail hunting, fishing, boating. Ashe Forest Service Nursery. *Facilities:* Three camp and picnic sites; 8, picnic only; three swimming sites. Gulf coast resorts. *Nearby towns:* Biloxi, Gulfport, Hattiesburg, Laurel, and Wiggins.

HOLLY SPRINGS. *Highways:* U.S. 72, 78, Miss. 7, 15. *Attractions:* Intensive erosion control projects. Annual bird dog field trials at Holly Springs. Quail and small-game hunting. No improved recreation sites. *Nearby towns:* Holly Springs, New Albany, and Oxford.

HOMOCHITTO. *Highways:* U.S. 61, 84, Miss. 33. *Attractions:* One of the finest natural timber growing sites in the United States; numerous forest management demonstration areas. Picturesque eroded loess country near Natchez. Fishing, swimming. *Facilities:* Three picnicking, one camping, and one swimming site. Trailer spaces at Clear Springs Recreation Area. *Nearby towns:* Brookhaven, Gloster, Neadville, and Natchez.

TOMBIGBEE. *Highways:* U.S. 82, Miss. 8. 15. Natchez Trace Parkway. *Attractions:* Upper Coastal Plain pine and hardwood forests, Indian mounds, Davis and Choctaw Lakes, Natchez Trace Parkway. Deer and quail hunting, fishing, boating. *Facilities:* Two picnicking, one camping, and two swimming sites. Resort lodge and cabins at Choctaw Lake. *Nearby towns:* Ackerman, Houston, Kosciusko, and Tupelo.

NORTH CAROLINA

(Supervisor's Address: 42 N. French Broad Ave., Asheville, North Carolina.)

Croatan National Forest

Nantahala National Forest

Pisgah National Forest

Uwharrie National Forest

FOREST DESCRIPTIONS

CROATAN. *Highways:* U.S. 17, 70, N.C. 24, 58. *Attractions:* Historic New Bern, founded 1710; Civil War breastworks. Five large lakes; pine and swamp hardwoods, three miles from Atlantic Ocean, Neuse River Estuary. Deer, bear, turkey, quail and migratory bird hunting; fishing, boating, swimming. *Facilities:* Two picnic and two swimming sites. Resorts and motels. *Nearby towns:* Goldsboro, Morehead City, New Bern, and Wilmington.

NANTAHALA. *Highways:* U.S. 19, 23, 64, 129, N.C. 28, 107. *Attractions:* Fontana, Hiwassee, Santeetlah, Nantahala, Cheoha, Glenville, and Apalachia Lakes; Fontana Dam, Cullasaja, White Water River, Bridal Veil, Toxaway, and Dry Falls. Joyce Kilmer Memorial Forest; sixty miles of Appalachian Trail. Annual big-game hunts; European wild boar, deer; also turkey and bird hunting. Southern Appalachian Mountains, famous for azaleas and rhododendrons. Lake and stream fishing for bass and trout. Hiking, swimming, and boating. Scenic drives. *Facilities:* Ten camp and picnic sites; 15, picnic only; three swimming sites. Tourist and cabin accommodations available. Eight resorts. *Nearby towns:* Bryson City, Franklin, Hayesville, Highlands, Murphy, and Robbinsville.

PISGAH. *Highways:* U.S. 19, 23, 25, 64, 70, 221, 276, 321, and Blue Ridge Parkway. *Attractions:* Mount Mitchell, 6,684 feet, highest point east of the Mississippi; Linville Falls and Gorge. Pisgah National Game Preserve and five other cooperative wildlife management areas with annual hunts for deer, bear; also small-game hunting. Craggy Gardens and Roan Mountain, famous for purple rhododendron; Appalachian Trail. Trout, bass, and perch fishing. Hiking, horseback riding, swimming. Scenic roads and trails. *Facilities:* 28 camp and picnic sites; 23, picnic only; nine swimming sites. Resorts and cabins available. *Nearby towns:* Brevard, Burnsville, Canton, Hot Springs, Lenoir, Marion, and Waynesville.

UWHARRIE. *Highways:* U.S. 220, N.C. 27 and 109. *Attractions:* Scenic views; Uwharrie Mountains in the Piedmont Plateau, Badin Lake. Deer, quail, and squirrel hunting. Wild turkeys still are protected. Accommodations in nearby towns. Candor, Biscoe, and Seagrove are communities within the forest boundaries. Recreation facilities are not yet fully developed.

SOUTH CAROLINA

(Supervisor's Address: 901 Sumter St., Columbia 1, South Carolina.)

Francis Marion National Forest

Sumter National Forest

FOREST DESCRIPTIONS

FRANCIS MARION. *Highways:* U.S. 17, 52, S.C. 41, 45. *Attractions:* Ruins and remnants of early colonial settlements and plantations. Many "Carolina bays," small lakes, believed to be caused by meteors; picturesque moss-hung oaks, flowering yucca, dogwood, redbud, and holly. Bass and other fishing; alligator, deer, turkey, and quail hunting. Boating. *Facilities:* Three camp and picnic sites; ten, picnic only. Hotels and motels near the forest. *Nearby towns:* Charleston, Georgetown, McClellanville, and Moncks Corner.

SUMTER. *Highways:* U.S. 25, 76, 123, 176, 221, 378, S.C. 28, 72, 107. *Attractions:* Piedmont and Blue Ridge Mountains, rank growth of rhododendron and other flowering shrubs; Walhalla Trout Hatchery. Trout and some bass fishing, quail hunting, scenic drives. *Facilities:* 20 picnicking, two camp and picnic sites, two swimming sites. Hotels and motels near the forest. *Nearby towns:* Abbeville, Clinton, Edgefield, Greenwood, Newberry, Union, and Walhalla.

TENNESSEE

Cherokee National Forest, Cleveland, Tennessee.

FOREST DESCRIPTION

CHEROKEE. *Highways:* U.S. 411, 11, 421, 19E, 19W, 25, 64, State 68, 67, 70. *Attractions:* Rugged mountain country cut by river gorges. Beautiful scenery, mountains of rhododendron and laurel blooming in season. Lake and stream fishing, rainbow and brook trout. Hunting for small and big game, including wild boar. Hiking, boating, swimming. Ducktown Copper Basin, one of the nation's worst cases of deforestation through air pollution, with consequent erosion. *Facilities:* 17 camp and picnic sites; 27, picnic only; 9 swimming sites. Hotels, and tourist cabins in nearby towns. *Nearby towns:* Cleveland, Erwin, Etowah, Greeneville, Johnson City, Madisonville, Mountain City, Newport, Parksville, and Tellico Plains.

TEXAS

(Supervisor's Address: McFadden Bldg., P. O. Box 380, Lufkin, Texas.)

Angelina National Forest

Davy Crockett National Forest

Sabine National Forest

Sam Houston National Forest

FOREST DESCRIPTIONS

ANGELINA. *Highways.* U.S. 59, 69; Texas 147. *Attractions:* Flat to rolling sandy hills with longleaf pine-hardwood forest along river bottom. Angelina River and many overflow lakes, Boykin Lake. Bass and cat fishing in rivers and lakes; quail and dove hunting. *Facilities:* Two camp and picnic sites; three, picnic only; one swimming site. *Nearby towns:* Jasper, Lufkin, and San Augustine.

DAVY CROCKETT. *Highways:* U.S. 287, Texas 7, 94, 103. *Attractions:* Flat, short-leaf-loblolly pine woods; hardwoods in bottoms; timber management demonstration area at Ratcliff Lake. Bass and cat fishing in rivers and lakes; some deer hunting. *Facilities:* Two camp and picnic sites; three, picnic only; one swimming site. *Nearby towns:* Alto, Crockett, Groveton, and Lufkin.

SABINE. *Highways:* U.S. 96, Texas 21, 87. *Attractions:* Southern pine and hardwood forest, Sabine River and overflow lakes, Boles Field Fox Hunt Area. Bass and cat fishing in river and lakes; fox hunting. *Facilities:* Two camp and picnic sites; three, picnic only; one swimming site. *Nearby towns:* Center, Hemphill, Jasper, and San Augustine.

SAM HOUSTON. *Highways:* U.S. 59, 75, 190, Texas 105, 150. *Attractions:* Flat, shortleaf-loblolly pine woods, hardwoods in bottoms, numerous lakes and small streams; part of "Big Thicket" area. Bass and cat fishing in rivers and lakes. *Facilities:* Two camp and picnic sites; three, picnic only; one swimming site. *Nearby towns:* Cleveland, Conroe, and Huntsville.

Region 9, North Central Region

Headquarters, 710 N. 6th St., Milwaukee 3, Wisconsin.

ILLINOIS

Shawnee National Forest, Harrisburg, Illinois.

FOREST DESCRIPTION

SHAWNEE. *Highways:* U.S. 45, 51, Illinois 1, 3, 34, 127, 144-146, 151. *Attractions:* Prehistoric stone forts and Indian mounds; interesting rock formations. Much of the Illinois shore of the Ohio River and some of the Mississippi; their confluence nearby at Cairo, Illinois. Stream and river fishing; hunting for quail, migratory waterfowl, squirrel, rabbit, fox, and raccoon. Artificial lakes in and adjacent to the forest provide fishing, boating, and swimming. *Facilities:* One camp and picnic site; 24, picnic only; two swimming sites. Hotels and cabins. *Nearby towns:* Anna, Cairo, Carbondale, Harrisburg, Marion, Metropolis, and Murphyboro, Illinois; Paducah, Kentucky, and St. Louis, Mo.

INDIANA

Hoosier National Forest, Bedford, Indiana.

FOREST DESCRIPTION

HOOSIER. *Highways:* U.S. 50, 150, Indiana 37, 46, 62, 64. *Attractions:* Pioneer Mothers Memorial Forest containing nation's outstanding specimens of black walnut. Final outlet of Lost River; Ten o'clock Indian Boundary Line crosses the forest. Old trail of migrating buffalo between Western Plains and French Lick. Squirrel, fox, and quail hunting; fishing in the East Fork of the White River, Salt Creek, and the Ohio, Lost, and Patoka Rivers for catfish, bass, and bluegill. Scenic drives among spring flowers (dogwood and redbud) and fall coloring. *Facilities:* One camp and picnic site; two, picnic only; one swimming site. Hotels and motels. *Nearby towns:* Bedford, Bloomington, Evansville, Jasper, Paoli, and Tell City.

MICHIGAN

Ottawa National Forest, Ironwood, Michigan.

Lower Michigan National Forests (Huron National Forest and Manistee National Forest), Cadillac, Michigan.

Upper Michigan National Forests (Hiawatha National Forest), Post Office Building, Escanaba, Michigan.

FOREST DESCRIPTIONS

OTTAWA. *Highways:* U.S. 2, 45, Michigan 28, 35, 64, 73. *Attractions:* Numerous accessible lakes and streams; Bond, Agate, Sturgeon, Conglomerate, Gorge, Sandstone, and Rainbow Falls. Victoria Dam, James Toumey Forest Service Nursery, State Fish Hatchery, forest plantations, Porcupine Mt. State Park. Lake and stream fishing, deep-water trolling in Lake Superior. Deer and bear hunting. Several winter sports areas nearby. Many scenic drives. *Facilities:* 13 camp and picnic sites; 10, picnic only; 7 swimming sites. Numerous hotels and cabins. *Nearby towns:* Bessemer, Iron River, Ironwood, Ontonagon, Trout Creek, Wakefield, and Watersmeet, Michigan; Duluth, Minnesota.

HURON. *Highways:* U.S. 23, 27, Michigan 33, 65, 72, 144, 171. *Attractions:* Lumberman's Monument. A forest easily reached from heavily populated southern Michigan, northern Ohio, Indiana, and Illinois. Trout fishing in the Au Sable River and smaller streams; deer, small-game, and bird hunting. At edge, Lake Huron with excellent beaches. *Facilities:* 9 camp and picnic sites;

8, picnic only; two swimming sites; Au Sable and Silver Valley winter sports areas. Many resorts, hotels, and cabins. *Nearby towns:* Grayling, Harrisville, Mio, Oscoda, and Tawas City.

MANISTEE. *Highways:* U.S. 10, 31, 131, Michigan 20, 37, 46, 55, 63, 82. *Attractions:* Another forest less than a day's drive from Chicago, South Bend, Detroit, Toledo, and Cleveland. Lake and stream fishing; deer and small-game hunting. Good skiing on northern part of the forest. Many of the lakes, including Lake Michigan, have fine beaches for swimming. Canoeing. *Facilities:* 12 camp and picnic sites; 17, picnic only; one swimming site; Caberfae and Manistee winter sports areas. Many resorts, hotels and cabins. *Nearby towns:* Big Rapids, Cadillac, Ludington, Manistee, Muskegon, and Reed City.

HIAWATHA. *Highways:* 2, 41, Michigan 28, 94, 48, 123. *Attractions:* Lake Huron, Lake Michigan and Lake Superior; some shoreline within the area. Many smaller lakes among mixed evergreen and hardwood forests. Pictured Rocks on Lake Superior; Mackinac Island country; scenic drives; waterfalls. Lake and stream fishing for trout, bass, northern and walleye pike, perch; smelt dipping; deer, black bear, ruffed and sharptailed grouse hunting. Canoeing. *Facilities:* 18 camp and picnic sites; 16, picnic only; three swimming sites; Gladstone winter sports area. Resorts, hotels, many cabins. Nearby well-equipped State Parks. *Nearby towns:* Escanaba, Gladstone, Manistique, Munising, Rapid River, Saint Ignace, Sault Sainte Marie, and Trout Lake.

MINNESOTA

Chippewa National Forest, Cass Lake, Minnesota.
Superior National Forest, Duluth, Minnesota.

FOREST DESCRIPTIONS

CHIPPEWA. *Highways:* U.S. 2, 71, 371, Minn. 6, 34, 38, 46. *Attractions:* Headwaters of the Mississippi River; Leech Lake, Lake Winnibigoshish, Cass Lake, and hundreds of smaller lakes; stands of virgin red pine. Home, and present headquarters of the Chippewa Indians. Lake fishing for walleyes, northern pike, and pan fish; waterfowl and upland game bird hunting; big-game hunting for deer and black bear. Hundreds of miles of good roads and scenic drives; swimming, boating, and water sports. Winter sports including skiing, tobogganing, snowshoeing, and ice fishing. *Facilities:* 21 camp and picnic sites; 33, picnic only; four swimming sites; Shingobee winter sports area. Three hundred resorts in and adjacent to the forest. Hotels, cabins. *Nearby towns:* Bemidji, Blackduck, Cass Lake, Deer River, Grand Rapids, Remer, and Walker.

SUPERIOR. *Highways:* U.S. 53, 61, Minn. 1, 35, 73, 169. *Attractions:* 5,000 lakes, rugged shorelines, picturesque islands, sand beaches. More than a million acres of virgin forest. The *Boundary Waters Canoe Area* is a part of the National Forest Primitive System. It has four divisions: Superior, Little Indian, Sioux, and Caribou—finest canoe country in the United States. Land of the French voyageurs—their historic water route to the Northwest. Sixteen unusual canoe routes in wilderness country. Adjacent Quetico Provincial Park in Canada also maintains a canoe-wilderness character over a large area. Lake and stream fishing, deer hunting. Two ski areas nearby. Scenic drives—Honeymoon and Ely Buyck Roads; Gunflint and Sawbill Trails. *Facilities:* 185 canoe campsites; 29 camp and picnic sites; 12, picnic only. Resorts, hotels, cabins outside the wilderness area. *Nearby towns:* Duluth, Ely, Grand Marais, International Falls, Two Harbors, and Virginia, Minnesota. Port Arthur and Winnipeg, Canada.

MISSOURI

Missouri National Forests (Clark National Forest and Mark Twain National Forest), Rolla, Missouri.

FOREST DESCRIPTIONS

CLARK. *Highways:* U.S. 60, 61, 67, 160, Missouri 19, 21, 32, 49, 72. *Attractions:* Big springs; clear, fast-flowing streams, Ozark Mountains covered with oak and pine forests; spring bloom of redbud and dogwood; brilliant fall coloring. Smallmouth bass and other fishing; squirrel, coon, and fox hunting. Current and Eleven Point Rivers and others provide hundreds of miles of streams for "John-boat" float trips; riverbank campsites in numerous places. Several large lakes. *Facilities:* Three camp and picnic sites; 6, picnic only. *Nearby towns:* Doniphan, Piedmont, Potosi, Poplar Bluff, St. Louis, and Van Buren.

MARK TWAIN. *Highways:* U.S. 60, 63, 66, 160, Missouri 32, 17, 14, 76, 125, 39, 86. *Attractions:* Ozark Mountains; numerous caves, rock cairns, and springs. Clear streams with fishing for pan fish, bass, and walleye; quail hunting. Scenic drives. Several State parks. *Facilities:* 8 camp and picnic sites; 14, picnic only; 5 swimming sites. Resorts and hotels. *Nearby towns:* Branson, Forsyth, Rolla, Springfield, and Willow Springs.

OHIO

Wayne National Forest, *Bedford, Indiana.*

FOREST DESCRIPTION

WAYNE. *Highways:* U.S. 21, 23, 33, 35, 50, 52, Ohio 75, 141, 124, 7, 37. *Attractions:* Particularly beautiful fall coloring of hardwoods. Nearby are historic Marietta, Gallipolis, Blennerhasset's Island, and Amesville "Coonskin Library." Old charcoal furnaces. Small-game hunting, fishing on numerous streams and lakes. Horseback riding, auto tours, scenic lookout points. *Facilities:* One camp and picnic site; three, picnic only; one swimming site. Overnight accommodations at numerous motels, tourist homes, and hotels along the main highways and at the larger towns. *Nearby towns:* Athens, Ironton, Jackson, Marietta.

WISCONSIN

Chequamegon National Forest, Park Falls, Wisconsin.
Nicolet National Forest, Rhinelander, Wisconsin.

FOREST DESCRIPTIONS

CHEQUAMEGON. *Highways:* U.S. 2, 8, 63, Wisconsin 13, 64, 70, 77, 182. *Attractions:* Hundreds of large and small lakes. Pine, spruce, and balsam forests; extensive jack pine plantations. Lake and stream fishing, particularly for muskellunge; hunting for deer and small game. Canoe travel on Flambeau and Chippewa Rivers; skiing. *Facilities:* 9 camp and picnic sites; 14, picnic only; five swimming sites; one winter sports area. Resorts and cabins. *Nearby towns:* Ashland, Eau Claire, Hayward, Medford, Park Falls, Superior, and Washburn.

NICOLET. *Highways:* U.S. 8, 45, Wisconsin 32, 52, 55, 70, 64, 139. *Attractions:* Northern Wisconsin lake region, trout streams and scenic rivers. Pine, spruce-balsam, hardwood, and cedar-spruce swamp forests. Lake and stream fishing for muskellunge, pike, bass, and trout. Deer, bear, grouse, and duck hunting. Swimming, boating, canoe trips, snowshoeing, and skiing. *Facilities:* 19 camp and picnic sites; 14, picnic only; 7 swimming sites. Sheltered Valley Ski Area. Numerous resorts and private cabins on private lands within or near the forest. *Nearby towns:* Eagle River, Green Bay, Marinette, and Rhinelander.

Region 10, Alaska Region
Headquarters, Federal & Territorial Bldg., P. O. Box 1631, Juneau, Alaska.

ALASKA

Chugach National Forest, Anchorage, Alaska.
North Tongass National Forest, Juneau, Alaska.
South Tongass National Forest, Ketchikan, Alaska.

FOREST DESCRIPTIONS

CHUGACH. *Highway:* To Anchorage and Seward. Most travel by sea or air. Rail service from Anchorage to Seward. *Attractions:* Tidewater, Hanging, and Piedmont Glaciers. Remote Aleut villages. Picturesque old Russian churches; native bidarkis (boats). Shrimp, crab, clam, and salmon canneries. Kenai Mountains with road down Kenai Peninsula; fiords of Port Wells. Unexcelled scenery. Trout and salt-water fishing. Hunting for moose, sheep, mountain goats, and Alaska brown bear; also for ducks, geese, grouse, and ptarmigan. Scenic trails and roads. *Facilities:* 5 camp and picnic sites; 16, picnic only. One swimming site; three winter sports areas. Plane service to these. *Nearby towns:* Anchorage, Cordova, Kodiak, Seward, Valdez, and Whittier.

NORTH TONGASS. *Routes:* Alaska Highway to Haines with road and ferry to Juneau, June 1-November 1; also direct plane service from Juneau. *Attractions:* Rugged Alaska coast; hundreds of islands, fiords, snowcapped mountains above the sea; totems; territorial museum and Indian villages. Salmon canneries. Gateway to Canadian hinterland and Yukon, Trail of '98 gold mines. Glaciers; "Ice Cap" back of Juneau; fiords of Tracy Arm. Admiralty Island, Trout fishing, also salt-water fishing for salmon and halibut. Hunting for Alaska brown and grizzly bear, mountain goat, and deer. Boating on lakes and inland waterways. Scenic wilderness trails; mountain climbing. *Facilities:* Five picnic sites, one swimming site; two winter sports areas. Hotel accommodations in all southeastern Alaska towns such as Juneau, Petersburg, Sitka, and Skagway. All of these are served by plane.

SOUTH TONGASS. *Routes:* Direct plane service from Ketchikan. *Attractions:* Fiords of Walker Cove and Rudyerd Bay of the Behm Canal and Portland Canal. Same game as in North Tongass including black bear. Canneries and pulpmills. *Facilities:* Two camp and picnic sites; one, picnic only; one swimming site; one winter sports site. All Alaska towns served by plane.

PUERTO RICO

Caribbean National Forest, Rio Piedras, Puerto Rico.

(Write for full details.)

FOR INFORMATION ON GAME LAWS, TRAVEL, AND PLACES OF INTEREST

UNITED STATES.

ALABAMA: Dept. of Conservation, 711 High St., Montgomery 4, Alabama.

ALASKA: Fish and Wildlife Service, Bureau of Sports Fisheries & Wildlife, Box 2021, Juneau, Alaska.

Div. of Econ. & Tour. Development, Dept. of Natural Resources, 310 Alaska Office Bldg., Juneau, Alaska.

ARIZONA: Game & Fish Dept., 105 Arizona State Bldg., Phoenix, Arizona; Development Board, 1521 W. Jefferson St., Phoenix, Arizona.

ARKANSAS: Game & Fish Commission, Game & Fish Bldg., State Capitol Grounds, Little Rock, Arkansas.

Arkansas Pub. & Parks Comm., State Capitol Bldg., Little Rock, Arkansas.

CALIFORNIA: Dept. of Fish & Game, 722 Capitol Ave., Sacramento 14, California.

Dept. of Natural Resources, Division of Beaches & Parks, P. O. Box 2390, Sacramento 11, California.

California State Cham. of Comm., 250 Bush Street, San Francisco 4, California.

All-Year Club of S. California, 628 W. 6th St., Los Angeles 17, California.

Redwood Empire Association, 46 Kearny St., San Francisco 8, California.

California Mission Trails Assn., 6912 Hollywood Blvd., Los Angeles 28, California.

Californians, Inc., 703 Market St., San Francisco, California.

Sierra Club, 1050 Mills Tower, San Francisco 4, California.

COLORADO: Dept. of Game & Fish, 1530 Sherman St., Denver 3, Colorado.

Dept. of Public Relations, State Capitol, Denver 2, Colorado.

CONNECTICUT: State Development Commission, State Office Bldg., Hartford 15, Connecticut.

DELAWARE: Delaware State Development Dept., Dover, Delaware.

DISTRICT OF COLUMBIA: Washington Con. & Vis. Bureau, 1616 K St., N.W., Washington 6, D. C.

National Parks Association, 1300 New Hampshire Ave. N.W., Washington 6, D. C.

National Capital Parks, Washington 25, D. C.

FLORIDA: Game & Fresh Water Fish Commission, Tallahassee, Florida.

Tourist Services Div., Florida Devel. Comm., Carlton Bldg., East Wing, Tallahassee, Florida.

Florida Park Service, Tallahassee, Florida.

GEORGIA: State Game & Fish Commission, 412 State Capitol, Atlanta, Georgia.

Georgia Dept. of Commerce, State Capitol, Atlanta, Georgia.

Dept. of State Parks, State Capitol, Atlanta 3, Georgia.

HAWAII: Hawaii Visitors Bureau, 2051 Kalakaua Ave., Honolulu, Hawaii.

IDAHO: Dept. of Fish & Game, 518 Front St., Boise, Idaho.

State Dept. of Comm. & Devel., Boise, Idaho.

ILLINOIS: Dept. of Conservation, Division of Law Enforcement, 102 State Office Bldg., Springfield, Illinois.

Illinois Dept. Info. Service, 406 State Capitol, Springfield, Illinois.

INDIANA: Dept. of Conservation, Division of Publicity, 311 W. Washington St., Indianapolis, Indiana.

Dept. of Comm. & Pub. Rel., 333 State House, Indianapolis 4, Indiana.

IOWA: State Conservation Commission, 7th and Court, Des Moines 9, Iowa.

Iowa Development Comm., 200 Jewett Bldg., Des Moines 9. Iowa.

KANSAS: Kansas Indus. Devel. Comm., State Office Bldg., Topeka, Kansas.

Forestry, Fish & Game Commission, Box 581, Pratt, Kansas.

KENTUCKY: Kentucky Dept. of Pub. Rel., New Capitol Annex, Frankfort, Kentucky.

Kentucky Tourist & Travel Commission, Room 66, Capitol Annex, Frankfort, Kentucky.

Dept. of Fish & Wildlife Resources, Frankfort, Kentucky.

LOUISIANA: Wildlife & Fisheries Commission, 126 Civil Courts Bldg., New Orleans 16, Louisiana.

Dept. of Commerce & Industry, Tourist Bureau, P. O. Box 4291, Baton Rouge, Louisiana.

MAINE: Dept. of Inland Fisheries & Game, State House, Augusta, Maine.

Maine Publicity Bureau Gateway Circle, Portland 4, Maine.

MARYLAND: Director, Game & Inland Fish Commission, Annapolis, Maryland.

Department of Information, State Office Bldg., Annapolis, Maryland.

MASSACHUSETTS: Division of Fisheries & Game, 73 Tremont St., Boston 8, Massachusetts.

Department of Commerce, 150 Causeway Street, Boston 14, Massachusetts.

MICHIGAN: Michigan Tourist Council, Lansing 1, Michigan.

Dept. of Conservation, Lansing, Michigan.

MINNESOTA: Div. of Promotion & Publ., Dept. of Business Development, 213 State Office Bldg., St. Paul 2, Minnesota.

State Parks Division, Conservation Department, State Office Building, St. Paul, Minnesota.

Division of Game & Fish, Room 337, State Office Bldg., St. Paul, Minnesota.

MISSISSIPPI: Game & Fish Commission, P. O. Box 451, Jackson, Mississippi.

Mississippi Park Commission, 1104 Woolfolk State Office Bldg., Jackson, Mississippi.

Mississippi State Parks, P. O. Box 649, Jackson, Mississippi.

Mississippi Agric. & Indus. Bd., 1504 State Office Bldg., Jackson, Mississippi.

MISSOURI: Missouri Div. of Res. & Devel., State Office Bldg., Jefferson City, Missouri.

MONTANA: I. & E. Division, Montana State Fish and Game Dept., Helena, Montana.

State Highway Commission, Helena, Montana.

Advertising Director, Montana State High. Comm., Helena, Montana.

NEBRASKA: Nebraska Game, Forestation & Parks Commission, State Capitol, 9th Floor, Lincoln 9, Nebraska.

NEVADA: Nevada Dept. of Econ. Devel., Capitol Building, Carson City, Nevada.

Fish & Game Commission, Box 678, Reno, Nevada.

NEW HAMPSHIRE: Fish & Game Dept., 34 Bridge St., Concord, New Hampshire.

New Hampshire State Plan. & Devel. Comm., Concord, New Hampshire.

NEW JERSEY: Division of Fish & Game, 230 W. State St., Trenton 25, New Jersey.

Div. of Planning & Devel., Dept. of Conservation & Economic Development, 520 E. State St., Trenton, New Jersey.

National Campers & Hikers Assn. Inc., Box 451, Orange, New Jersey.

NEW MEXICO: Dept. of Game & Fish, Box 2060, Santa Fe, New Mexico.

New Mexico Dept. of Devel., P. O. Box 1716, Santa Fe, New Mexico.

NEW YORK: State Dept. of Commerce, 112 State St., Albany, New York.

Camping Council, Inc., 17 East 48th Street, N. Y. 17, New York.

NORTH CAROLINA: Wildlife Resources Commission, Box 2919, Raleigh, North Carolina.

Advertising Division, Dept. of Conservation & Development, Raleigh, North Carolina.

NORTH DAKOTA: State Game & Fish Dept., Capitol Bldg., Bismarck, North Dakota.

N. D. State Highway Comm., Bismarck, North Dakota.

State Historical Society, Bismarck, North Dakota.

OHIO: Dept. of National Resources, 1500 Dublin Rd., Columbus 12, Ohio.

Ohio Develop. & Pub. Comm., 21 W. Broad St., Columbus 15, Ohio.

OKLAHOMA: Dept. of Wildlife Conservation, Oklahoma City 5, Oklahoma.

Div. of Publ. & Tour. Information, Oklahoma Plan. & Res. Board, 533 State Capitol, Oklahoma City 5, Oklahoma.

OREGON: State Game Commission, 1634 S. W. Alder, Portland 8, Oregon.

Travel Information Division, State Highway Dept., Salem, Oregon.

PENNSYLVANIA: State Dept. of Forests & Waters, Harrisburg, Pennsylvania.

Bureau of Travel Devel., Pennsylvania Dept. of Comm., 129 Capitol Bldg., Harrisburg, Pennsylvania.

RHODE ISLAND: Division of Fish & Game, Veteran's Memorial Bldg., 83 Park Street, Providence, Rhode Island.

Information Division, Development Council, State House, Providence 3, Rhode Island.

Publicity & Recreation Div., Rhode Island Devel. Council, Roger Williams Building, Providence 8, Rhode Island.

SOUTH CAROLINA: South Carolina Devel. Board, Columbia, South Carolina.

Director, Wildlife Resources Dept., Division of Game, Box 360, Columbia, South Carolina.

SOUTH DAKOTA: Dept. of Game, Fish & Parks, Pierre, South Dakota.

Publicity Director, State Highway Comm., Pierre, South Dakota.

TENNESSEE: Div. of State Information, Dept. of Conservation, Nashville, Tennessee.

Game & Fish Commission, I. & E. Section, Cordell Hull Bldg., 6th Ave. N., Nashville, Tennessee.

Division of State Parks, 203 Cordell Hull Bldg., Nashville 3, Tennessee.

TEXAS: Information Service, Texas Hwy. Dept., Austin, Texas.

State Parks Board, Drawer E., Capitol Station, Austin, Texas.
Game & Fish Commission, Director of Law Enforcement, Walton Bldg., Austin 14, Texas.

UTAH: Utah Tour. & Pub. Council, 327 State Capitol Bldg., Salt Lake City, Utah.
Dept. of Fish & Game, 1596 West North Temple, Salt Lake City, Utah.
Tourist & Publicity Council, 327 State Capitol Bldg., Salt Lake City, Utah.

VERMONT: Vermont Devel. Comm., Montpelier, Vermont.
Department of Forest & Parks, Montpelier, Vermont.

VIRGINIA: Div. of Public Rel. & Adv., Virginia Dept. of Con. & Dev., 315 State Office Bldg., Richmond, Virginia.
Division of Parks, Conservation Commission, Richmond 19, Virginia.

WASHINGTON: Wash. State Dept. of Comm., State Capitol, Olympia, Washington.
Dept. of Game, 600 N. Capitol Way, Olympia, Washington.
State Resort Assn., 2100 Fifth Ave., Seattle, Washington.
Tourist Promotion Division, Department of Commerce and Economic Dev., General Administration Bldg., Olympia, Washington.

WEST VIRGINIA: W. Va. Indus. & Pub. Comm., State Capitol, Charleston 5, West Virginia.
Conservation Commission, Div. of Education, Room 663, State Office Bldg., Charleston, West Virginia.

WISCONSIN: Recreational Pub. Section, Wisconsin Conserv. Dept., 830 State Office Bldg., Madison, Wisconsin.
Conservation Department, P.O. Box 450, Madison 1, Wisconsin.

WYOMING: Wyoming Travel Commission, Capitol Bldg., Cheyenne, Wyoming.
Game & Fish Commission, Box 378, Cheyenne, Wyoming.

PUERTO RICO: Puerto Rico Visitors Bureau, San Juan, Puerto Rico; *and* Puerto Rico Visitors Bureau, 666 Fifth Avenue, New York, New York.

VIRGIN ISLANDS: Tourist Development Board, St. Thomas, Virgin Islands.
Virgin Islands National Park, P. O. Box 1589, Charlotte Amalie, St. Thomas, Virgin Islands.

CANADA.

CANADA: Canadian Government Travel Bureau, Ottawa, Ontario, Canada. (Also write here for information on the Yukon and Northwest territories.)

ALBERTA: Travel Bureau, Legislative Bldg., Edmonton, Alberta, Canada.

BRITISH COLUMBIA: Office of the Game Commission, 567 Burrard St., Vancouver 1, British Columbia, Canada.
The Commissioner, Government Travel Bureau, Dept. of Recreation and Conservation, Victoria, British Columbia, Canada.

MANITOBA: Bureau of Travel and Publicity, 254 Legislative Bldg., Winnipeg 1, Manitoba, Canada.

NEW BRUNSWICK: Travel Bureau, P. O. Box 1030, Fredericton, New Brunswick, Canada.

NEWFOUNDLAND: Wildlife Division, Dept. of Mines and Resources, St. John's, Newfoundland, Canada.
Tourist Development Office, Fort Townshend, St. John's Newfoundland, Canada.

NORTHWEST TERRITORIES: Dept. of Northern Affairs and National Resources, Ottawa, Ontario, Canada.

NOVA SCOTIA: Bureau of Information, Provincial Bldg., Halifax, Nova Scotia, Canada.

ONTARIO: Conservation Information, Dept. of Lands & Forests, Parliament Bldg., Toronto, Ontario, Canada.
Information Branch, Dept. of Travel & Publicity, 67 College St., Toronto, Ontario, Canada.

PRINCE EDWARD ISLAND: Dept. of Industry and Natural Resources, P. E. I. Travel Bureau, Charlottetown, Prince Edward Island, Canada.

QUEBEC: Provincial Publicity Bureau, 106 Grande-Allee, Quebec, Canada.

SASKATCHEWAN: Tourist Branch, Legislative Annex, Regina, Saskatchewan, Canada.

YUKON TERRITORY: Director, Territorial Game Dept., Box 2029, Whitehorse, Yukon Territory, Canada.
Supervisor of Fisheries, c/o R. C. M. Police, Box 1129, Whitehorse, Yukon Territory, Canada.

MEXICO.

Secretaria de Agricultura y Fomento, Direccion Forestal y de Caza, Ingnacio Mariscal No. 11, Mexico, D. F.

Chapter 3

VACATIONS—NORTH OR SOUTH

THE LAKE SUPERIOR LOOP

The new road around Lake Superior is now paved and completed, and is the first highway along the north shore of Lake Superior. It opens up the Ontario wilderness country that has been isolated for generations. From this new highway one can observe wildlife such as moose, deer, and bear deep in the forests.

(Courtesy **Better Camping**, © 1962 Kalmbach Publishing Co.)

You can now make the 654-mile circle trip around Lake Superior in comfort, and find campgrounds within driving range throughout the trip. Starting from Duluth you can take U. S. 2, U. S. 41 and Michigan 28 on the south or lower section to Sault Ste. Marie or vice versa. From Duluth you can take U. S. 61 and Ontario 61 and 17 to Sault Ste. Marie. No matter where you start your trip on this loop route it will be scenic all the way.

Travelers can reach the highway from Canada via Ontario No. 17 from Sault Ste. Marie or from Duluth, Minnesota in the States. The road stretches west from Sault Ste. Marie 475 miles to Port Arthur and hugs the Superior shore for much of

49

the distance. While there are a number of modern cabins, fishing lodges, and motels along the route, accommodations are still limited. Vacationists should be prepared to camp. Extensive campgrounds are available. They range from sites that will only accommodate one or two tents, to larger camping sites along broad beaches. In Lake Superior Provincial Park, a 600-square mile area that is preserved in a primitive state; facilities are provided for tents and trailers only. There are no hotels or motels in this park.

These newly-opened roads lead to outstanding scenic regions where both Americans and Canadians can enjoy camping at its best. Better still, it is close to the millions of people living in the Great Lakes Region's vast industrial areas.

CANOEING IN THE QUETICO-SUPERIOR COUNTRY

In several of the water boundary areas in canoeing country, prepared campgrounds equipped with fireplaces and sanitary facilities may be encountered. However, this is not true everywhere. You can still explore country where there are no campgrounds nor marked portages. One of the least crowded is the land of the *voyageur* in the Quetico-Superior Area, which is now part of the Boundary Water Canoe Area on the Canadian border. Here you can travel many streams and thousands of lakes connected by well-marked portages without crossing your trail.

In this section you can really get away from the everyday cares of civilization. Planes are not allowed to fly low over this primitive country nor land on any of its lakes. There are no poisonous snakes and the water is safe to drink from lakes or streams. Even the inexperienced can now make safe and successful voyages into this marvelous country.

This wonderland lying astride the American-Canadian border includes the roadless areas of the Superior National Forest and Ontario, Canada's Quetico Provincial Park, 14,500 square miles set aside solely for the use of canoeists. It stands today exactly as it stood since the dawn of our age when huge glaciers carved and filled its numberless deep, clear lakes, linked with bubbling, murmuring, singing streams and rapids. Primeval forests of balsam fir, pine, spruce, and birch guard its shores and give shelter to many species of wildlife. Over

(Drawing by Luis M. Henderson)

three hundred years have passed since the first *voyageurs* explored and threaded their way through these winding and twisting waterways by birchbark canoe.

Although the songs of the voyageurs are heard no more, the laughter of loons still ricochets off the rocks painted with mysterious symbols by the red men of long ago. The water, the forest, the sky are still there. Thousands of Americans and Canadians who have visited the Area are grateful that the primitive flavor has been retained.

Civilization has approached the very door of this primitive region, but no further. Good roads lead to its boundaries, but all roads stop there. It is today, as it has always been, a canoeist's, fisherman's, and camper's paradise.

The thousands of lakes frequently merge into one another, and hundreds of them are separated only by narrow necks of land. Some of the lakes are merely wide places in slow-moving streams; others are so large that it is easy to lose one's bearings, and strong winds can develop upon them without warning. Many loop trips are possible; other trips can be made one-way affairs by arranging for pickup of gear at the conclusion of the trip.

The land areas are almost completely forested. The principal conifers are the pines, jack, white, and red. But white spruce, black spruce, balsam fir, northern white-cedar, and tamarack are also present. The principal broadleaf trees are quaking aspen, paper birch, yellow birch, sugar maple, red maple, willow, green ash, mountain ash, cottonwood, choke-cherry, pin-cherry, and service-berry. While much of the area has been logged in the old days, there are still fine stands of timber that have never been touched. Forest fires burned over much of the region in the early days following logging. These areas can usually now be identified by the predominance of aspen, paper birch, and pin-cherry.

Common plants are trailing arbutus, wintergreen, Labrador tea, dwarf kalmia, twinflower, and spring beauty. Leather-leaf is common in the muskegs. Rocks in heavily shaded places are frequently covered a foot deep with Spaghnum moss. Thimbleberries, raspberries, and huckleberries are abundant. Wild rice grows at edges of streams or lakes in the western part of the area.

WILDLIFE. The region is the home of wildlife in interesting variety. The most common big-game animals are the white-tailed deer, moose, and black bear. The canoeist is likely to see beaver, muskrat, snowshoe hare, porcupine, red squirrel, and chipmunk. Other mammals present are red fox, timber wolf, coyote, fisher, otter, weasel, skunk, and mink. Some of the more interesting birds are spruce grouse, or "fool's hen," ruffed grouse or "partridge," eagle, raven, pileated woodpecker, (Canada jay, commonly called "camp robber" or "whiskey jack"), and various hawks and owls. Among the waterfowl are loon, blue heron, golden eye, merganser, and mallard.

(Drawing by Luis M. Henderson)

The principal native game fish in the Boundary Water Canoe Area are walleye, northern pike, and lake trout. Most canoeists fish for walleye and "northerns," since lake trout go deep in summer. Some lakes have smallmouth bass, and a few have largemouth bass. Bluegills, perch, and crappies are occasionally taken, but are not widely distributed. Rainbow and brook trout have been stocked in a few lakes. In general, lake trout and northern pike predominate in the deep, cold lakes; northerns and walleyes in warmer waters. Bass and panfish are likely to be found in the shallow, warm lakes.

Fishing tackle should be limited and kept simple. Guns are a nuisance and might cause an accident. They should be left at home. Firearms are not allowed in Canada except under special hunting regulations through Customs.

BEST SEASONS. The lakes are usually ice-free from about May 10 to November 1. Following "ice-out," fishing for lake trout is usually fast for the short period they are near the surface. Fishing for walleyes and northerns is usually better in May, early June, and early October. When the water is warm it is necessary to fish deep for lake trout. But for bass fishing, warm water means a better season. Northerns tend to strike regardless of season.

The best season for canoeing is between July 15 and October 1. Spring weather is chilly, and in October the days are short and apt to be cold. Rain and wind may be expected any time of the year. Mosquitoes and black flies are at their worst in June, becoming less troublesome as the season advances. Autumn foliage is most colorful for the camera fan from September 10 to October 10.

POINTS OF ENTRY. The major entry points are Ely, Winton, and Grand Marais. Access is also possible directly from Crane Lake and Tower, by the Sawbill Trail, and from Tofte and by the Arrowhead Trail from Hovland. The most popular starting points by car are from the Gunflint Trail out of Grand Marais, the Fernberg Road east of Ely, and the Ely-Buyck Road north and west of Ely.

Ely is accessible by train from Duluth, by bus from Virginia, and by unscheduled plane from Hibbing. Grand Marais is accessible by bus and unscheduled plane from Duluth.

Outfitters and resorts are numerous along the upper portion of the Gunflint Trail and on roads in all directions from Ely. The towns offer many hotels and motels. Food and other supplies can be purchased in all access towns, and most outfitters carry small stocks.

Cars may be left parked in the parking areas at developed

public campgrounds, along bordering roads and, with permission, at resorts and outfitters. Among the campgrounds most useful to canoeist are: East Bearskin Lake, Flour Lake, Lake One, Moose Lake, Portage River, Sawbill Lake, Sioux River, South Kawishiwi River, and Trails End.

MAPS. W. A. Fisher Company of Virginia, Minnesota publishes a series of maps covering the entire Boundary Waters Canoe Area and adjoining country in the United States and Canada. The series may be obtained in a bound volume on plain paper, and each of the fifteen maps is also individually available on water-resistant parchment paper. Portages are indicated with distances; rapids and similar features are shown. Most outfitters stock these maps or they can be ordered directly from the publisher.

Detailed timber-survey maps may be obtained from the Regional Forester, United States Forest Service, Milwaukee, Wisconsin. These are on a scale of two inches per mile. Each map covers a township of thirty-six square miles. The price is twenty-five cents each in minimum orders of $1.00. In ordering describe the particular area you are interested in. These maps show lakes, timber types, portages, swamps, etc., and are accurate. But they are detailed and require more study than the Fisher maps. Maps for Canadian territory may be obtained from the Department of Lands and Forests, Toronto, Ontario.

EQUIPMENT NEEDED. The Forest Service recommends that you include in your personal outfit a complete change of clothing from the skin out. Woolens are recommended, including a heavy shirt and windbreaker jacket, slicker, strong shoes or boots, moccasins or tennis shoes for camp, extra socks, and *a good compass, and map,* waterproof match-box, heavy pocket knife, flashlight, toilet articles, and (if you use them) smokes. There is no real "best" outfit, for each individual has his own ideas on what is best for him. But, for the novice, the following information may be of help.

Tents should be light-weight. A good size for two persons is either 7 x 7 or 7 x 9 feet. It is usually difficult to find level sites for larger ones, and they are heavy. A tent should have a sewn-in mosquito screen and sod cloth. Nested cooking kits are common. But campfires are hot and the heat uneven; many people object to cups of metal, preferring to put together their own combination. Sleeping bags are in order. Three woolen blankets with a double one of cotton to sleep between are satisfactory as a substitute. Most campers use an air mattress; the kind with a rubber-fabric cover will serve well whereas plastic demands continual repair. A small belt-axe is all right for driving stakes but, for chopping, something with a 2½ to 3-pound head with a 28 to 36-inch handle is needed. There should be a sheath for the blade, either leather or of canvas.

You will want some matches (kept in a watertight container); some for your packs or to be carried on your person. The matches should be waterproofed. A good compass with an adjustable declination and sighting-line, the best map you can secure of the region, candles, insect repellent, insect spray, pocket and sheath knife, soap, sharpening stone, rope (50 feet of ⅜-inch manila rope for "tracking" canoe, etc.), flashlight with extra batteries and bulbs, small sewing kit, first-aid kit, pair of work gloves, canvas duffel bags, and a packsack for each member to use in portaging.

CLOTHING NEEDED. Trousers should be of tough material. For chilly weather, quilted down or dacron is excellent in either under or outer garments. These seem to be more popular now than heavier woolens. Rainwear is essential, and should cover the knees when the wearer is seated in the canoe. The parka-type long rain shirt is excellent. Avoid thin plastic—it tears too readily. Rubberized material is stronger.

Ankle-high leather shoes with non-skid leather soles are serviceable—boots aren't a necessity. Oxfords or gym shoes are all right for canoe or camp, but are dangerous on portages and in rocks. Socks of light wool mixture or spun nylon are desirable.

CAMPING SITES AND CAMPGROUNDS. Nearly two hundred campsites along canoe routes inside the Boundary Waters Canoe Area have been provided with very simple facilities. Mainly the facilities consist of a level cleared spot, a place to beach the canoe, rocks for a fireplace, and sometimes a crude table and simple toilet facilities. Tent poles left by previous campers are frequently on hand. But remember these are not highly developed camp sites, and some may be difficult to locate on the larger waters.

CAMPSITES NEAR BOUNDARY WATERS CANOE AREA

Name of Development	Location	Camp Sites	Water Source
GRAND MARAIS—GUNFLINT TRAIL AREA			
†Pike Lake Picnic Area	14 mi. W Gr. Marais	..	Pump
Cascade River Campground	16 mi. NW " "	2	River
*Brule Lake Campground	30 mi. NW " "	2	Lake
†Devil'strack Lake Campground	11 mi. NW " "	6	Pump
†Kimball Lake Campground	14 mi. NE " "	3	Pump
*East Bearskin Lake	30 mi. N " "	11	Pump
*Flour Lake Campground	31 mi. NW " "	9	Pump
Iron Lake Campground	40 mi. NW " "	6	Pump
*Trails End Campground	55 mi. NW " "	10	Lake
TOFTE—SAWBILL TRAIL AREA			
			Nearby
Ox-Bow Campground	6 mi. N. Tofte	5	Spring
Temperance River Campground	12 mi. N. Tofte	3	......
*†Sawbill Lake Campground	24 mi. N. Tofte	12	Pump
ISABELLA AREA			
Isabella River Campground	4 mi. W. Isabella	4	Pump
Dumbell Lake Campground	5 mi. E. "	3	Pump
ELY AREA—STATE HIGHWAY NO. 1 AND 35 AREA			
*Birch Lake Campground	32 mi. SE Ely	3	Lake
*†South Kawishiwi River Campground	12 mi. SE Ely	12	Pump
*Birch Dam Campground	9 mi. SE Ely	4	River
ELY-FERNBERG TRAIL AREA			
*Moose Lake Campground	18 mi. NE Ely	6	Lake
*Lake One Campground	21 mi. NE Ely	5	Lake
ELY-ECHO TRAIL AREA			
*†Fenske Lake Campground	12 mi. N Ely	12	Pump
*Portage River Campground	26 mi. NW Ely	3	River
Meander Lake Campground	31 mi. NW Ely	3	Lake
*Sioux River Campground	36 mi. NW Ely	2	River
Jeanette Lake Campground	42 mi. NW Ely	6	Lake
VIRGINIA-TOWER AREA—STATE HIGHWAY NO. 53 AND 169			
†Lake Leander Picnic Area	19 mi. NW Virginia	..	Pump
†Phleffer Lake Campground	11 mi. SW Tower	5	Pump

Simple swimming facilities will be found at several of the above developments, but none offer lifeguard protection. As this country is characterized by deep, cold waters with rocky shorelines, extreme care should be taken in selecting a place to swim.

Due to the rough character of the country, it is inadvisable to pull large house trailers into some of these recreation areas. Inquire at some local source before taking your house trailer to these campgrounds.

GUIDES. One should have some experience in camping before starting an extended canoe trip. There is no good substitute for firsthand knowledge of the problems of primitive living, sleeping on the ground, starting a fire with wet wood,

---

* Starting locations for canoe trips.
† Areas which have swimming beaches.

and all the rest a wilderness trek entails. However, never having been in a canoe should not be a deterrent. Although guides are required in certain back areas in Maine, guides are not absolutely necessary in the Boundary Water Canoe Area. Any neophyte can negotiate these waterways if good judgment is used.

Guides are available, if desired; their wages are $20.00 per day, plus $6.00 per day for the guide's outfitting and food.

CANOE OUTFIT. Outfitters at Ely, Winton, and other Minnesota and Canadian towns will provide everything you will need for a canoe trip for an average of $6.00 per person per day. If you furnish your own provisions, the rate is only $4.00 per person per day.

A complete outfit includes an aluminum canoe, paddles, yoke, tent (with sewn-in floor and mosquito netting), large packsack, blankets or sleeping bag, axe, cooking and eating utensils, insect bomb, candles, and an excellent supply of food. Part outfits may be rented. Canoes alone are available, as well as portable aluminum boats. Canoes with square sterns may be obtained with little difficulty for motors as large as 5.5 h.p. Canoes and boats rent for $3.50 per day. Outboard motors up to 5 h.p. rent for $3.00. Fishing license: non-resident Canadian $6.50, outboard motor license for Canada $2.00, Minnesota non-resident license $4.00. It is not necessary for you to purchase both Minnesota and Canadian licenses unless you plan to fish on both sides of the border. License fees are subject to change.

WHERE TO GET INFORMATION.

Border Lakes Outfitting Company, Ely, Minnesota.

Chamber of Commerce, Ely, Minnesota.

Chamber of Commerce, Grand Marais, Minnesota.

Canoe Country Outfitters, Ely, Minnesota.

Commercial Club, Crane Lake, Minnesota.

Fishermen's Headquarters & Canoe Outfitters, Ely, Minn.

Gunflint Northwoods Outfitters, Grand Marais, Minn.

Handberg's Quetico-Superior Outfitters, Ely, Minn.

Minnesota Arrowhead Association, Duluth, Minn.

CANOE CAMPING CHECK LIST—TWO PERSONS

	Lbs.	Oz.		Lbs.	Oz.
2 Air mattresses	4	0	1 Folding camp saw	2	4
1 Aluminum fire grate	1	0	2 Insect repellents	0	6
1 Aluminum griddle	3	0	2 Knives, BSA type	0	6
1 Axe, single-bit	3	0	1 Map, large scale	0	2
1 Axe sheath	0	6	1 Waterprf. matches	0	2
1 Bottle water purifying tab-			2 Match-safes	0	2
lets (50)	0	1	1 Notebook & pencil	0	4
1 Bucket, plastic	0	8	2 Ponchos	2	8
1 Bug bomb	0	8	1 Reflector oven	2	0
1 Camp kitchen kit	2	0	2 Sets extra clothes	4	0
6 Candles	0	6	2 Sets moccasins (or tennis		
1 Canteen, 1 gal. (filled)	8	0	shoes for camp)	2	4
1 Compass w/sighting line ...	0	4	2 Sets, dinnerware	0	8
1 Cook kit, nesting type	6	0	1 Shovel, "0" size	3	0
4 Duffel bags, canvas	6	0	2 Sleeping bags	8	0
2 Fishing rods and gear	3	0	2 Sun glasses	0	2
1 First-aid kit and snake kit .	1	0	1 Tarpaulin, 10'x10'	6	0
2 Flashlights, pen type	0	6	1 Tent (optional)	6	0
1 Flashlight, 2-cell type (ex-			2 Toilet kits	2	0
tra batteries & bulbs)	1	0			
1 Rope, ⅜", nylon, 100 feet ..	1	8			

Total: 81 pounds, 15 ounces. Add cne pound of dehydrated food a **day per** person. If in portage country, canoe weight will add another 65 to 85 **pounds** to be transported overland. Take mosquito netting as appropriate.

RIVERS AND CANYONEERING

Were it not for the fact that a good many campers are genuinely interested in the explorations possible only via river routes, the commercial river guide and outfitting concerns would have to turn to other lines of endeavor. But often the sportsman finds a river route the only way to real rewarding hunting and fishing spots. And groups of all kinds, including enrollees from summer camps and summer schools, and many family groups have learned that a river or canyoneering trip offers a vacation highlight of unusual interest and enjoyment. If you would like a change in your vacation camping routine, start assembling information on some of the various river trips available. Here is a list which can only be but representative of the many such trips available. Likewise, costs and routes will vary with time. Write to get more complete information.

WHERE TO WRITE

L. L. Anderson, Challis, Idaho. Middle Fork of the Salmon River. 4-day trip, $325, 6-days, $425, 7-days, $500.

Elmer Briggs, 719 South West Laurel Street, Grants Pass, Oregon. 1-day scenic trips covering 25 miles of the roaring Rogue River; $30 for two people, $33 for three persons.

Frost Expeditions, 710 Catalina, Artesia, New Mexico. San Juan-Glen Canyon of the Colorado; trips, 8 to 10 days, $200. Special attention given to archaeology and geology enroute.

Art Greene, Cliff Dwellers Lodge, Via Cameron, Arizona. Glen Canyon of the Colorado River, 9-days, $200. Up Glen Canyon by motorboat from Lee's Ferry to Rainbow Bridge and return, 3-days, $110. Shorter trips available.

Harris-Brennan River Expeditions, 2500 East 48 South, Salt Lake City, Utah. Motorboats, Glen Canyon, 7-days, $150. Yampa and Green Rivers through Dinosaur National Monument, 3-days, $75. Grand Canyon of the Colorado, 12-days, $400. Desolation Canyon of the Green River, 2-days, $75. Hell's Canyon, 7-days, $250. Middle Fork of Salmon, 9-days, $250.

Hatch River Expeditions, 411 East 2nd North, Bernal, Utah. Rubber boats on Yampa and Green rivers through the incomparable bottomlands of Dinosaur. Weekly special; 4-days leaving Thursday, $60 each. One to six-day trips, $18.70 to $122 (per person rate goes down with each addition to party). Middle Fork of Salmon, 7-days, $220. Middle Fork and main Salmon, 10-days, $300. Grand Canyon, 10 days, $300.

Price E. Helfrich & Sons, Vida, Oregon. McKenzie, Deschutes, John Day, Owyhee, Rogue Rivers in Oregon; Middle Salmon, Idaho. Rates on request.

Inland Navigation Company, Snake River Route, Lewiston, Idaho. Every Wednesday at 6 a.m., the 52-foot diesel-powered Wenaha heads up-stream from Lewiston for an overnight round trip. Write for information. Two weeks' notice on all reservations.

Kriley Brothers, Shoup, Idaho. Middle Fork of Salmon, 10-days; also 200-mile run on main Salmon. Dude ranch at Shoup.

Larabee and Aleson Western River Tours, Richfield, Utah. Glen Canyon, 14-days, $250. San Juan River, 9-days, $200. Grand Canyon, 18-days, $750; McKenzie River in Canada, 1,025-miles north to the Arctic, 21-days, $850. (Flight north to the Pole optional.)

Lewiston Navigation Company, c/o Global Travel Service, Lewis & Clark Hotel, Lewiston, Idaho. One-day or overnight trips up the Snake from Lewiston. Minimum of four passengers.

McKenzie River Guides, McKenzie River, Oregon (P. O. Vida, Oregon). Variety of McKenzie trips.

Mexican Hat expeditions, Blanding, Utah. Successors to Norman Nevills, pioneer Colorado River runner. Deluxe versions of historic expeditions. San Juan, 6-days, $200. Glen Canyon, 7-days, $200. One, two, and 4-day trips on San Juan. Grand Canyon, 10-days, $1,000; upper (6-days), $500, or lower (12-days), $600.

Moki-Mac River Expeditions, 968 James Court, Salt Lake City, Utah. Specialty is guiding young people's groups (Explorer Scouts, YMCA, etc.) who take their own camping gear and food. Glen Canyon, 8-days, $50. San Juan, 10-days, $40. Yampa and Green Rivers, 4-days, $27.50. Also trips in Lodore, Grand, and Desolation canyons. Canoe trips through Glen Canyon, $45.

Bob Pruitt, 715 N. E. A Street, Grants Pass, Oregon. Rogue River from Grants Pass to Gold Beach. July-August 20 (scenic), 4-days, $160, 5-days, $175; August 20-November 30 (steelhead fishing), 4-days, $175, 5-days,. $200. Also trips on Owyhee, Deschutes, and Middle Fork of Salmon.

Sid Pyle, 2319 Jerome Prairie Road, Grants Pass, Oregon. Rogue River from Grants Pass to Gold Beach. Summer, 5-days, $175. Fall (beginning August 16), $200. (No camping out—nights at riverside lodges.)

Reynolds Canyon Expeditions, Red Canyon Lodge, Green's Lake, Utah (P. O. Box 129, Bernal, Utah). Galloway-type rowboats through the canyons of the Yampa, Green, and Colorado; The Firehole, Red Canyon, Flaming Gorge, Lodore Canyon, Echo Park, Whirlpool Canyon, Split Mountain. Trips of any length arranged.

Rogue River Boat service, Gold Beach, Oregon. By U. S. mailboat 32 miles up Rogue to Agness and return the same day, $4. Special rates for children.

Kenneth I. Ross, Southwest Explorations, Mancos, Colorado. Cataract Canyon, 8-days, $175. Also 11-day San Juan-Glen Canyon run for high school boys as part of summer camping-exploring program.

Don L. Smith, North Fork, Idaho. Salmon River in roomy, high-and-dry sweep-steered scow, 6-days, $250 to $400. Special fall hunting trip $400. Middle Fork of Salmon, rubber boats, 6-days, $250 to $400 depending on size of the party. Longer trips, up to 10-days, available.

Blain Stubblefield, Weiser, Idaho. Famed Hell's Canyon of the Snake River. One to five-hour trips to Ox-Bow and Kinney Creek, $4.50 to $22.50. Homestead, Oregon, to Lewiston, Idaho, 5-day minimum, charter trips, rates on request.

Ed Thurston, 240 Idaho Street, Bend, Oregon, McKenzie, Rogue, Salmon, and Deschutes rivers. (Write for details.)

Georgie and J. R. White, 435 West Laconia Blvd., Los Angeles 61, California. Grand Canyon, 19-21 days, $300. San Juan and Glen Canyons, 9-day each, $100. Green River and Cataract, $100. Middle Fork of the Salmon, $100. River of No Return, $100. Hell's Canyon of the Snake, $100.

Glen Wooldridge, 413 West H Street, Grants Pass, Oregon. Pioneer builder of the Rogue River roughwater boats. April-July; 2-day scenic trips on Rogue River, $75 (includes meals and lodging).

TRANS-CANADA HIGHWAY

The new Trans-Canada Highway beginning at Victoria, British Columbia, ends 5,000 miles nearly due east at St. John's, Newfoundland. Generally speaking, the Highway follows the shortest practical route across Canada consistent with the needs of the provinces and the interest of Canada as a whole. It provides North American motorists with one of the finest scenic touring routes in the world. The Highway extends northward from Victoria, British Columbia to Nanaimo where ferries connect it to the mainland at Vancouver; from there it passes through distinctive towns and villages and famous cities as it makes its way eastward. Most of the cities it touches are familiar to North American motorists. The road is paved across the continent. Gravel roads will tie in with this and others of Canada's federal road system.

CANADA AND THE ALASKA HIGHWAY

A unique and thrilling vacation for the traveler with a taste for adventure is a trip along the famous Alaska Highway. If you are enthusiastic about camping, hunting, fishing, or journeying through a wild and beautiful country, this is the holiday for you!

The Alaska Highway . . . "the Big One" . . . leading through friendly, hospitable Canada to the 49th and largest state in the Union provides an unforgettable trip, as pleasant as it is long.

THE ALASKA HIGHWAY.

ROUTES. You can head north via Highway #1 from Vancouver to Cache Creek, then on north via #2 and #97 to Dawson Creek—distance 764 miles. From the south near Glacier National Park, Montana, you can cross the border and take Highway #2 up to Calgary and Edmonton and then Highway #43 to Dawson Creek. Dawson Creek is the terminal point of the Northern Alberta Railway, 475 railway miles northwest of Edmonton. Should you have the time for it, the loop route between Calgary and Edmonton via Highways 1, 1A, and 16 through Jasper and Banff National Parks would be well worthwhile.

Edmonton, for many, is the starting point of the trip, though the Alaska Highway, proper, begins at Dawson Creek, terminal point of the Northern Alberta Railway, 475 railway miles from Edmonton. From Dawson Creek, British Columbia, the highway, a graveled, all-weather road, runs 1,523 miles to Fairbanks, Alaska—1,221 miles of which is in Canada, and 302 miles in Alaska.

Pushing back the last frontiers of the north, the highway traverses a tremendous region of unbroken forest, rivers, lakes, and mountains. After crossing the lush and rolling Peace River Basin, the road soon begins to penetrate a wilderness almost untouched by the hand of man. Through the densely forested Rocky Mountain region and deep into the spruce, birch, and aspen-clad river valleys of the interior there is little sign of habitation except for infrequent small outposts, or the occasional mining project and highway construction camp. It is a lonely land—rugged, wild, and austerely beautiful. In the deep silences of these virgin forests civilization seems far away indeed.

Here is where you will rub shoulders with the men who are taming the frontier. Trappers, Indians, bush pilots, missionaries, fur traders, prospectors, government agents, and the world famous Mounties—you meet them all! And, wherever you go, there's the helping hand and true hospitality that characterizes the north country. These north country people are jolly but reserved. Never forget that you are a guest passing through their fair land, and conduct yourself as you would in your own land.

The Alaskan portion of the route features pavement starting at the Alaska-Canadian border and extending all the way to Fairbanks. Additionally, paved surfaces connect the cities of Anchorage, Valdes, Fairbanks, and Seward. Alaska's highway system totals approximately 4,000 miles of which 1,000 miles are paved or blacktopped. The rest are dirt or gravel. Of this system, about 2,000 miles are maintained the year long. There are hundreds of miles of trails in this vast land, making it one of the world's best camping, hunting, fishing, and mountain climbing frontiers.

TRAVEL SEASONS. The best season for traveling the Alaska Highway is between May 15 and October 15. In other seasons extreme winter cold or early spring thaw can make driving uncomfortable and difficult as a pleasure trip, although the road is open all winter. Some experienced travelers prefer the winter journey, driving on compact snow rather than the sometimes dusty graveled road. But common sense rules must apply when making the trip in December, January, and February. As he would when driving open highways in any of the northern states during such months, the prudent traveler insures his comfort and safety with a properly winterized vehicle in good mechanical condition, warm clothing, a good car heating system, chains, shovel, axe, towrope or cable, and a small supply of sand.

During the summer dust and mosquitoes are quite bad in some areas but if you are properly prepared this will not mar your trip. A good insect repellent or spray-bomb is recommended. It is well to remember that in the mountain areas nights are cold, even in mid-summer. And when planning your journey, take advantage of the fact that you will have 16 to 20 hours of daylight in this country. If there are more than one in the party, it is safer to change drivers every 50 miles if you plan on long distances each day. With such rotations no one becomes too tired from driving or tempted to fall asleep at the wheel.

CAR AND TRAILER. Be sure that your car and trailer are in excellent mechanical condition, and have been serviced correctly for the long trip. It is smart to carry spare items such as fan belt, points, spark-plugs, coil, and condenser; sometimes it is good insurance to carry an extra carburetor since such equipment for all makes of vehicles is not always to be found in towns and garages enroute. Should you not use these spare articles you probably can return them for a refund from your home dealer after the trip. Since there are over a thousand miles of graveled roads in the Canadian section of the Big Road, the use of six-ply tires is desirable. Don't forget the basic car tool kit and a good flashlight. Reflector road flares may come in handy if you have a breakdown and cannot get the vehicle off the road at night. Be sure that your car battery is in good condition and not too old. An axe, shovel, chains, and tow cable should be taken along on any trip of this kind. Pack them where they will be handy so that you don't have to unload the car too much to get to them.

Protect your gas tank from flying stones by covering it with a rubber floor mat or other material that will break stone shock. Rubber undercoating helps considerably. Don't let your gas tank get below the half-way point; never below one-third, for gas stations are not close together. Remember the Imperial gasoline gallon is one-fifth larger than the American gallon. You will find gasoline prices higher in British Columbia, the Yukon, and Alaska than in the States. This is because northern fuel stocking involves a long haul and stiff transportation expense.

Protect trailer water lines by sheathing them with rubber hosing. This keeps them from being pounded by flying gravel. Some drivers protect their car finish along the left side through use of masking tape. To protect the front of the trailer and its windows fasten a piece of plywood or masonite across the entire front of the unit, from the A-frame to up over the windows. You can also tape cardboard across the front and any wide windows on the left side as protection for traveling. Such pieces are easily removed when you camp at night.

If you have an older type of trailer, it is wise to turn off the gas tank at night. Leaking canned or cylinder gas can be dangerous if your stove or gas lights leak during the night while you are asleep. Always be sure to have some ventilation at all times when using gas appliances, especially in the case of gas heaters. This also applies when cooking or heating with charcoal grills in a tent or trailer. For safety reasons, all gasoline lanterns and stoves should be filled outside your tent or trailer.

You will find that food is more expensive the farther north you travel. Take as much canned and dehydrated goods as Canadian Customs will allow.

CAMPING EQUIPMENT. Tent campers should use a light, insect-proof tent, warm sleeping bags or blankets. They will need a cooking outfit, camp axe, and first-aid kit. If you expect to tent camp along this route, plan to wear the same clothing as you might for traveling in the northern United States with the addition of an extra warm sweater or coat for cool nights.

Camera film is often difficult to obtain enroute, so plan to carry or purchase a sufficient amount in advance of the trip.

ACCOMMODATIONS. Campgrounds with adequate cooking facilities have been prepared along the route for the use of travelers who are equipped for camping and carry their own supplies. Roadside accommodations—hotels, motels, stores, meals, gas, oil, and car repairs—are available along the entire route. A list of these facilities may be obtained from the Canadian Government Travel Bureau, Ottawa, Ontario, Canada. The traveler should think ahead about stops and plan carefully for he is not entitled to help in the matter of food, shelter, or automotive repairs from personnel of the Northwest Highway System maintenance camps. Arrangements for overnight accommodations should, if possible, always be made in advance.

HUNTING. Hunting and fishing laws are very strictly enforced throughout the territory traversed by the Alaska Highway. Information about seasons and licenses should be obtained before making the trip. The northern regions of Alberta and British Columbia offer the sportsman the finest variety of fish and game on the continent. You can bag mule deer, moose, caribou, sheep mountain goat, black and grizzly bear, ducks, geese, and grouse in season.

The surest way for the sportsman who does not know Canada to find game is to go to one of the lodges that cater to sportsmen. The hunter will be provided with a guide who knows the runs where the tracks are biggest, the flyways where the honkers and the big ducks move, the fields where the sharptails feed, and the ridges where the ruffed grouse drum. The guide may even unlimber his birchbark horn and tease the evening air with the grunt of the mating moose thus bringing that elusive trophy rack into the crosshairs of the hunter's scope. Elk, too, are found in this wild land.

The cost per person for a big game hunting license in British Columbia will run about $25 for the American hunter. But license costs elsewhere depend upon the Province involved so write in advance to learn the cost and license details.

FISHING. The angler may stop along the way for giant rainbow trout, land-locked steelhead, Arctic grayling, northern pike, pickerel, lake trout, Dolly Varden, and the southeastern Alaska cutthroat. Salmon is abundant along the coasts! Canada's sport fishing usually peaks in mid-May. Until the end of June, the fish will not have dispersed or gone deep. The ice is off all but the northern waters by May. At this time the lake trout are near the surface and other species are less difficult to find than later in the year when they go deep. June is regarded as the most generous month for Canadian fishermen.

The American fisherman should write in advance to learn the cost of fishing licenses in the particular area he wishes to fish. Licensing is regulated by the individual Provinces and costs as well as limits allowed will fluctuate from place to place and time to time. In some locales the fee may be as low as $2 to $3, but in many other parts of Canada a fee of at least $15 is not unusual.

ENTERING CANADA. American citizens do not require passports to enter Canada. However, citizens should carry papers establishing their citizenship, and permanent resident aliens should carry their Alien Registration Receipt Card (U. S. Form 1-151). Necessary wearing apparel and personal effects are duty-free, along with fishing tackle, sporting, and camping equipment. Check on firearms regulations before departing on a trip to determine which rifles and shotguns are allowed (no revolvers or pistols). Car registration must be carried, and non-owner drivers must have written permission of owner to drive in Canada.

To take a pet into Canada you must show Canadian Customs a certificate of proof that the pet has received recent rabies shots.

Visitors traveling in Canada by car and trailer should carry the official Non-Resident Motor Vehicle Liability Insurance Card for each province in which they plan to motor. Get the full details from your insurance agent. He can supply you with the proper insurance cards for Canada. While it's not compulsory that you have these cards, they can save you much time and embarrassment should you become involved in an accident. If your agent doesn't have the cards, he may secure them from the Superintendent of Insurance, Legislative Building of each provincial capital through which you expect to travel.

Cars may be used in Canada with your own state's plates for six months without payment of any duty or fee. If you are driving a truck camper, you will have to pay a special fee in some Provinces ($20—Ontario). Your valid operator's license is also honored in Canada. Motorcycles and bikes are under the same regulations. No separate permit is needed for trailers, but a list of removable items in the trailer (radios, TV, typewriter, etc.) will speed you through Customs.

The visitor may take into Canada one or two days' food supply, gasoline and oil for 300 miles by car, and 50 rounds of ammunition duty-free. Excess is subject to duty. A list of the serial numbers of your cameras, guns, outboard motors, typewriters, etc., will save you time at the border. When departure time arrives, it is your responsibility to satisfy U. S. Immigration authorities of your right to re-enter the United States. If you have complied with regulations admitting you to Canada, return to the United States is normally routine.

ALASKA

Alaska, with far less than 1 percent of the total national population, contains 31 percent of the lands in the national park system, 65 percent of the wildlife refuge lands, 64 percent of the public domain, and 11 percent of the national forest acreage. Alaska is BIG!

This is the place to head for when you and your family get fed up with the everyday business of earning a living, bucking traffic, and meeting all the responsibilities of urban life. Your family will enjoy it and it will be a real change for you!

Alaska is so large it is difficult to grasp its bigness. Its differences in climate, people, geography, and economy are almost as great as those between the Rocky Mountain region and the Middle West, or between Massachusetts and California. Alaska is as large as Texas, California, and Montana together—a total of 586,000 square miles, with a coastline longer than all of the first 48 states. It is interesting to know that Juneau is farther from Dutch Harbor than New York is from San Francisco. Also, it is almost as far from Juneau to northernmost Point Barrow as it is from Seattle to the Mexican border.

Alaska's magnificent and fabulous geography, its extremely varied climates, its wide and sparkling vistas of scenic beauty, and its wild life and fish demand in themselves separate volumes to touch upon their depth and scope. Thus we can hope to cover here only some aspects of pertinent interest to the potential camping or sportsman visitor. The first of these is transportation, since this has always been of unique and critical importance in Alaska's widely diversified and rugged terrain.

THE ALASKA HIGHWAY. The Alaska Highway extends 2,350 miles from the United States border to Fairbanks, Alaska. Minimum travel time is eight days, and will cost the average couple about $235; for further information, refer to the section on Canada.

THE ALASKA RAILROAD. Rail service to Interior Alaska from Seward, on the Gulf of Alaska, is provided by the Alaska Railroad, which is owned and operated by the Federal Government. It is 470 miles long and has a short branch into the Matanuska coal fields. Mount McKinley National Park is accessible by this route. Mt. McKinley (20,320 ft.) is the highest peak on the North American continent.

WHITE PASS AND YUKON RAILWAY. This 111-mile route was constructed from Skagway, Alaska to Whitehorse, Yukon Territory, Canada at the turn of the century. At Whitehorse it connects with the Alaska Highway.

ALASKA STATE FERRY SYSTEM. This system serves as a marine highway to southeastern and south-central Alaska. The service areas of the system lie along coastal regions of the State. The system permits the movement of tourist and auto traffic through these areas and provides a "loop" for automotive traffic using the Alaska Highway and its connecting links, both rail and highway.

Three ships operate on through-run schedules to serve southeastern Alaska. The southern terminus is Prince Rupert, where highway and railroad facilities connecting Canada and the lower 48 States are available. Terminal facilities are located at Ketchikan, Wrangell, Petersburg, Sitka, Juneau, Haines, and Skagway. The Haines Highway from the city of the same name connects with the Alaska Highway at Haines Junction, 96 miles west of Whitehorse. Skagway, Alaska, northern terminus of the system, connects with Whitehorse via the White Pass and Yukon Railway. Ships on this run have a capacity of 100 cars and 500 passengers. They make the run from Prince Rupert to Skagway in 36 hours direct, or 42 hours via Sitka.

HAINES-SKAGWAY-JUNEAU FERRY. Juneau, the capitol of Alaska, may be reached by using the state-operated Haines-Skagway-Juneau Ferry during the summer months.

OTHER TRANSPORTATION. Alaska's vast size and its sketchy highway system have made air transportation of paramount importance. Service to the first 48 States is available on a daily basis. The interstate air systems are well developed and patronized. Steamship freight service by sea is provided from west coast ports. Passenger service is available during the tourist season from Vancouver, British Columbia.

HUNTING AND FISHING. Alaska provides unrivaled hunting grounds for brown, black, grizzly, and polar bear. Walrus, seal, and Beluga whale abound in iceberged seas. Moose, reindeer, caribou, elk, buffalo, deer, and wolverine rove the plains and forests. Wolves, too, are plentiful. Mountain goat and the convolute-horned mountain sheep flourish in high craggy homes. Grouse, ptarmigan, geese, and scores of other game birds are plentiful. Throughout Alaska, experienced guides are on hand to transport you by boat, canoe, seaplane or airplane to magnificent, remote areas whose vast, lonely, untrammeled grandeur offers in itself a thrilling adventure! Alaska hunting may be as brief or as extensive as you wish. You may camp for days in wild, virtually inaccessible spots— or you may return at the end of the day's hunt to the bright lights of a frontier town. Whichever you choose, once you have bagged your trophy from the Big Land of the Arctic, your hunting experiences of earlier years will seem tame in comparison.

Fishing in Alaska's cold, clear lakes, and swift-running mountain streams is one challenge and thrill followed by another for Alaska is a fisherman's dream come true! Prize-quality king salmon, silver salmon, rainbow trout, steelhead, cutthroat, and Dolly Varden run thick. Great Northern pike, arctic char, grayling, and shee fish abound. Fishing areas are too numerous to be counted. You'll find an abundance of fishing camps with comfortable quarters, boats, and experienced fishing guides for hire. Or, if you prefer to fish alone, almost any Alaskan you will meet will be happy to give you a choice of a dozen excellent fishing spots where you may make your own camp and fish in solitary contentment. Fishing in Alaska is an unforgetable experience.

March through November is generally considered the open season for most fish and game. There are exceptions, and full details may be obtained by writing to the Alaska Department of Fish and Game, Subport Building, Juneau, Alaska. Experienced guides are available, and throughout Alaska are found stores that can supply you with all types of outdoor clothing, fishing, hunting, and camping gear.

HUNTING—FISHING—TRAPPING LICENSES. The license period is from January 1 to December 31 inclusive, in any calendar year. Licenses may be obtained from designated agents in Alaska, or by mail from the Commissioner, Alaska Department of Fish and Game, at Juneau. No sport fishing license is required for persons under the age of sixteen. Non-resident license fees:

Visitors 10-day Sport Fishing Permit ....$ 5.00
Non-resident Sport Fishing Permit ....$ 10.00
Non-resident Hunting ....$ 10.00
Non-resident Hunting and Fishing ....$ 20.00
Non-resident Hunting and Trapping (two trophies) $100.00

State tags must be procured for each animal in addition to the proper license for hunting big game.

SKIING. There are three major ski areas now under development—slopes near Anchorage, Fairbanks, and Juneau—with modern lift or convenient rope-tow facilities either in existence, or planned for the near future.

WHERE TO WRITE. A free list of the state parks and Federal waysides in Alaska is available from the Alaska Division of Lands, 344 Sixth Avenue, Anchorage. Fire permits are not required for camping in state campground waysides. Though most of the wayside camps can accommodate trailers, no trailer utility "hook-ups" are available. An illustrated map of the 49th State is available free from the Alaska Highway Department in Juneau. There are also two booklets of special interest to potential Alaskan visitors who plan to travel the overland route from the States; write to the Canadian Governmen Travel Bureau, Ottawa, Canada for "Alaska Highway," and "Adventure Along The Trans-Canada Highway." Of these, the first is especially a pertinent reference to the camping traveler since it contains a complete listing of accommodations along the way—inclusive of campgrounds. A free listing of 22 Yukon campgrounds and 10 Territorial lunch stops is also available from the Department of Travel and Publicity, Box 939, Whitehorse, Yukon.

MEXICO

If you really want a different kind of vacation for you and your family, something new, try Old Mexico! It is the southern-most country of North America. Its language and food are different. The first is soft liquid Spanish-Mexican and the latter is tasty and spicy. Over 36,676,982 people live in Mexico's thirty states, two federal territories, and one federal district. Less than a million Mexicans are pure Spanish; about half the population is pure Indian, and the rest are a mixture of Spanish and Indian. In the more isolated regions the natives still speak only their Indian tongues.

THE COUNTRY. Mexico is a land of sharp contrasts. Its towering mountains with broad plateaus and scenic highlands give way to unexplored tropical jungles. Its 758,259 square miles lie both in the temperate and torrid zones. The country is roughly triangular in shape with two jutting peninsulas—Lower California and the Yucatan.

Mexico's coastline along the Pacific Ocean totals 4,438 miles, as compared to 1,774 miles along the Gulf of Mexico and the Caribbean Sea. A low, sandy coastline characterizes the western section of the country, with the plateau rising steeply behind it. Rainfall is heavy along the Gulf coast section, while irrigation is needed on the Pacific slope and in the interior.

In the state of Oaxaca, from Nudo de Zempoaltepetl, the Sierra Madre is divided into two great mountain ranges northward, the Sierra Madre Oriental in the east, and the Sierra Madre Occidental in the west, forming the eastern and western edges of the great plateau country. The highest peak, an 18,851 foot volcano, is called Orizaba, or just plain Citlalepetl. Popocatepetl volcano is 17,761 feet and Ixtaccihuatl is 17,343 feet high. There are hundreds of other volcanic peaks in Mexico.

LAND OF CONTRASTS. The mountain heights are enhanced in the interior by the deep valleys and canyons, some being more than 1,000 feet below the general level of the plateau. In these valleys the characteristics of the tropics are found in the luxurious vegetation and climate. The plateau above the valleys is for the most part fairly level, sloping gradually from about 3,400 feet at the United States border near El Paso, to over 8,000 feet in the states of Mexico and Puebla. Mexico City lies in a great basin completely surrounded by mountains. Its elevation is slightly over 7,000 feet. Many lakes are found throughout Mexico's mountain areas and fishing is excellent in most.

The river system of this beautiful land is neither varied nor extensive. Very few rivers are navigable for any distance. The main rivers are the Rio Grande del Norte, much of which lies in the United States; Coatzacoalcos, in the isthmus region; the Grijalva, whose headwaters are in the mountains of Guatemala; and the Balsas, which rises in the state of Tlaxcala, Mexico.

Because of the varying altitudes, the climate of Mexico ranges from tropical in the low-lands to cold in the high mountains. The seacoast areas and the lower altitudes of the interior are generally intensely hot, and in this area are the swamps and tropical jungles. Rain falls throughout the country between May and October, however, continual rainfall is rare during the summer months. It seldom rains during the remaining months.

ENTERING MEXICO. As a guest and tourist, you should be ever mindful of the fact that you are an alien in a foreign country and that you are expected to follow the laws of Mexico while in that country. Familiarity with the customs of the Mexican people will help to make your trip harmonious and pleasant. Mexico, its roots grounded in ancient civilization, is so rich in charm and abundant in attractions that it could not help but appeal to everyone. A careless diplomat (tourist), given to a feeling of superiority, could harm the prestige of our country by an ostentatious display of money, accompanied by rudeness and loudness in manner.

To enter Mexico, American citizens must have proof of citizenship, tourist card, and a recent (three years) smallpox vaccination certificate. In addition, permanent resident aliens should have a visaed passport and two passport-size photos, and

should check with their respective consulates. Single entry
tourist cards cost about $3.00 (six-month multiple entry cards
are $5.00 and require two front-view passport-size photos) and
can be obtained at any Mexican consul or from the Mexican
Immigration Office at the point of entry. Tourist cards are not
required for visits to border towns not exceeding 72 hours, or
for minors under 15 years of age. Clothing and personal effects
up to 100 pounds may be carried duty free, and one camera per
tourist, with 12 rolls of film per camera.

TRAILERING. In most cases, the use of house or camping
trailers for touring Mexico should be confined to the main highways. The Central Highway from El Paso, Texas to Mexico
City, and the Saltillo route to Mexico City are two of the
easier routes. Traveling the Pan-American Highway is not
discouraged despite the 120 miles of winding mountain roads.
The same regulations apply to trailers that apply to automo-
biles. Happily, there is no charge for taking your trailer across
the border.

Before you start on a long trip into any foreign area you
should be sure that your car is in A-1 mechanical condition. It
is well to have 6-ply tires if you plan to travel side or gravel
roads. Check your brakes, battery, lights, and have a good
basic tool kit aboard. A shovel, axe, and tow rope or tow cable
may come in handy. Extra spark plugs, fuses, and an extra fan
belt is advisable. There are capable mechanics in most of the
larger cities, but not in all the small towns. There are two
grades of gasoline—use the best grade. Carry the latest AAA
or similar maps and information booklets in your glove com-
partment for ready reference. If you run into trouble, become
sick or need help, contact your American Consular office immediately!

TRAFFIC. Road signs along Mexican highways are in Spanish. If you do not understand them, slow your speed in an-
ticipation of something ahead that will require your attention.
Play safe—you are a long way from home! Be careful when approaching bridges. These are marked Puente Angosto and are
narrow, one-way bridges. When two cars approach from opposite directions, the one that flicks his lights first has the
right of way. Keep bags and valuables locked in your car trunk.

The maximum speed limit in Mexico is 100 kilometers, or

approximately 62 miles per hour, unless posted otherwise. In most towns and villages the limit is 30 kilometers or 18 miles per hour. The cities have many one-way streets. Signs on each corner indicate traffic direction by an arrow; two-way streets display an arrow with two points.

CAR PERMITS. These must be obtained at the Port of Entry. They are free and good for 90 days. Proof of car ownership must be displayed. The initial car permit may also be renewed for an additional 90 days; should you fail to have an expired permit renewed on time, you may be fined three times the duty payable on your car; this is usually the total value of the vehicle! To renew a car permit, the tourist should apply at the Internal Revenue Office *(Oficina Federal de Hacienda)* at least seven days before the initial permit expires. Permits must be kept and returned for cancellation upon leaving the country.

Be sure that your insurance is valid in Mexico. If not, short-term policies can be obtained from Mexican insurance companies to cover your visit.

If you store your car in Mexico, your tourist permit or card is stamped *Con Automovil* (with car), and you may not leave Mexico without the vehicle unless through special arrangement with the Mexican Customs Service.

HUNTING. The outdoorsman can find excellent hunting in this land of sunshine. Mexico's primeval forests and mountains abound in game such as black and silver-tipped bear, deer, Mexican peccary (or wild pig), panther, lynx, badger, fox, coyote, turkey, ducks, geese, snipe, quail, doves, and pheasant.

Outdoorsmen may be admitted to Mexico for hunting by complying with requirements additional to those established for the issuance of regular tourist cards. Some outfitters handle much of the detail for their clients.

LETTER FROM SHERIFF. You must secure a letter from your county sheriff addressed to a Mexican Consul to present when you apply for the necessary papers and documents to hunt. This letter serves to identify and recommend you as a law-abiding citizen who will not abuse the privileges accorded hunters by the Mexican government. The document must carry a front view, passport-sized photograph for identification purposes. The applicant must write his name across his photograph; four additional photographs besides the original must be furnished by the applicant.

The Mexican Consul will issue the applicant a certificate of identity which also carries a description of the firearms the hunter is taking into Mexico. A maximum of four firearms and 100 rounds of ammunition for each gun will be permitted duty-free. Instead of his allotted rounds of ammunition, the hunter may bring two pounds of powder for each firearm. The fee for certificate is $16.00, plus the $3.00 fee for a tourist card.

HUNTING LICENSE. Upon arrival at the Mexican Port of Entry, the hunter must apply at the game warden's office *(Delegado Forestal y de Caza)*, where a hunting license will be issued after he has presented his consular certificate. The license is good in one state and its bordering states only. The fee is $19.20 in U. S. currency or coin. It is recommended that the hunter check at a Mexican government office before hiring a guide to insure that he will get competent guide service.

After receiving the hunting license, the sportsman proceeds to the office of the commander of the military garrison to obtain approval for the arms listed on his certificate. From there he must return to the Custom office again for final clearance.

The game warden should provide a list of the open and closed seasons, and the amount of each species of game which may be taken home. The regulations are strictly enforced.

On returning to the United States, the hunter must again stop at the office of the military commander to have his firearms checked; then, another stop must be made at the Customs post on the Mexican side of the border for the same purpose.

FISHING IN MEXICO. The Mexican rivers and lakes contain many varieties of fish, most common of which are trout, black bass, and catfish, while deep-sea fishing for marlin, tarpon, shark, and sailfish is said to be unexcelled. During the late winter months, storms in the Gulf of Mexico may make fishing difficult during the rainy season. When an area is closed to fishing, signs are posted to that effect.

A license obtainable from the local game and fish warden or from authorities at principal resorts and seaports is the only requirement for fishing in Mexican waters. The charge for a license varies from six pesos for a three-day license, to fifty pesos for one year.

HOW MUCH DUTY-FREE?

If your traveling should bring you into Canada or Mexico, the law allows you to bring home duty free $100.00 worth of purchases after a period of 48 hours (24 at California-Mexico border—no time limit at Texas, Arizona or New Mexico border). This must not include more than one gallon of alcoholic beverages (check your own state restrictions) or more than 100 cigars. Each member of the family is entitled to one exception, and these may be pooled. This must not be claimed more than once every 31 days. Articles intended to be gifts may be included on your account, but articles intended for sale or the accommodation of others are not exempt.*

* Courtesy: **General Motors, Buick Division;** American Automobile Association; Texas Highway Department; and Mexican and U. S. Customs Service.

Chapter 4

AUTOMOBILE, TENT, AND TRAILER CAMPING

UNDER THE TENSIONS of the past decade the American public has been seeking a way to relieve the pressure of high-powered living and the feeling of being hemmed in by the restrictions and demands of the modern business world. The industrialization and urbanization of present-day life has whetted man's desire to get away for a while from his busy treadmill and man-made gadgets and do something different. Especially he wants to enjoy the fun of the great outdoors and the almost forgotten beauties of Nature. He gets a primitive urge for the simple life. He wants to head for the shore or the hills and go "native."

FAMILY CAMPING

In the United States a new way of satisfying this latent urge for recreation and adventure has swept the nation. The new craving is to go camping, to get closer to nature. The trend is to go family camping—to the seashore, a lake, the desert, or the mountains. The family may camp overnight at a nearby state or county campsite. Some families, with more time available and a craving to see new places, like to visit different camp areas and engage in new forms of recreation, some going entirely across the country.

GETTING BACK TO NATURE. Why this mass exodus to the tall timber and wide-open spaces? Because more people have more cars and trailers; because there are more improved highways and freeways, bringing the parks and forests, the lakes and streams, the mountains and seashore ever closer—within minutes, where it once took hours, and hours where it once took days; because incomes have gone up, with more dollars available to buy camping equipment, cars, trailers, boats, and even saddle and pack horses; because of fewer working hours and more leisure time today than a decade ago. Why do people like to prepare and eat meals in camp and to live out of doors? Because they are tired of eating at the same lunch counter and don't

78

(Drawing by Luis M. Henderson)

want to spend hard-earned money at expensive restaurants, motels, and hotels; because they want a change; because automobile camping provides an inexpensive way to vacation, where you and your family can dress informally, relax and have fun, and just be yourselves for a change.

In an auto or trailer camp you will meet people from all walks of life. Camp touring people are usually jolly and carefree. Sometimes you meet people you especially like and your friendship grows with the years.

You have a restful vacation outdoors and you can come home

physically fit. Perhaps we Americans have been getting soft by too much food and too much nerve strain, and too little exercise and relaxation. Note that the President of the United States is asking the nation's people to get out into the open country and harden up under his new physical fitness program.

Have you ever tried a vacation in a wilderness area? More people do every year. In fact, there are "Wilderness" bills before the Congress to set aside *more* wilderness areas in our national parks and forests for the present 187,000,000 citizens and for future generations. Usually you can drive to or near the edge of these wilderness regions, but from there on the hunter, fisherman, and others who wish to enjoy primeval sections will have to do it by saddle and pack outfit, or on good old "shanks-mare."

A trip of this sort will give the whole family a chance to really get acquainted with each other again, and the cost will not be much more than if they stayed at home, whether they go camping in their car for a week, two weeks, or for a month or more. The extra expense involved would usually be for gas and oil and curios purchased en route.

MOTOR CAMPING. Car and trailer camping offers practically limitless possibilities for fun so long as the driver sticks to passable roads. He and his family can camp overnight in a nearby state or county campsite, or he can range throughout the national parks and forests of the United States, head north into Canada, or south to old Mexico. The length of the trip will, of course, depend on the amount of leisure time and the family finances.

For those hardier individuals who like to roam off the beaten path and enjoy the side roads of desert or mountain, the 4-wheel drive 4-speed jeep or similar type of vehicle is a "must." (See chapter 7 on desert camping for off-road trips.) If you want to travel through the swamps of the deep South or the Everglades of Florida to hunt and fish, you will need a "swamp-buggy" type of vehicle. In areas where vehicles are allowed to travel certain mountain trails, there is the new "Tote-Goat" or "Pack Burro" motorscooter that hunters are now using. In national parks and in some national forests, motor vehicles are forbidden on trails, and for cogent reason. Saddle and pack train outfits have met with serious accidents when one of the snorting "go-devils" suddenly came around a zig-zag or bend in the trail. In several areas, however, the Forest Service has set aside territories where "jeepsters" and members of jeep clubs may roam and camp in out-of-the-way wild areas.

Motor camping has become a major national pastime, and the number of campsites has jumped from 3,000 to over 33,000 in the past decade. These campground figures are for camps that furnish water, rock stoves or grills, tables and benches, and sanitary facilities. Most of these campgrounds are in the 30 national parks and 155 national forests; over 2,000 are in state parks and forests throughout the country. However, thousands of primitive back-country wilderness camps are still in the "raw" and have no modern conveniences. You can motor to the road or trail end and then hike or pack in with horses or burros. In these out-of-the-way camps you can have the fun and adventure of providing your own shelter, building your own rock camp stove, and digging your own latrine and kitchen waste facilities. In this manner you soon become self-sufficient.

The mobile camper will have a wider choice of food and equipment than his hiking brother, since he can haul them by car or pack saddle instead of having to carry them in a knapsack on his back. The car camper can cover a far greater area, as he can be several hundred miles away in a day where the hiker will have covered only a few miles.

SEMI-SELF-CONTAINED MOBILE OUTFITS

Two classifications of compact, mobile, and mostly self-contained camping outfits are becoming more popular. One class is typified by the Volkswagen "Microbus" and the Chevrolet Corvair "Greenbriar." Ford's "Falcon" also has a somewhat similar "bus" type body in its line. A small family can rig these up pretty much to suit themselves: you can sleep in them; you can cook, dress, and keep gear in them. If you dislike the thought of a woods animal poking about your tent at night or the thought of possible tenting discomforts in rain or storm, these little "buses" will have definite appeal. Usually you can equip them with a small icebox or ice chest. Your lighting problems, and often your heating problems are also minimized because the interior car lights answer most needs, and the heater can be operated occasionally to remove the chill when necessary. Some have small closets for clothing and other ingenious features copied from the trailer industry.

Not all of these models are adequately powered; not all of them are offered with entirely desirable choices of transmission. Some do have a built-in wash bowl or basin. Not all of them have an ideally flat, level, and roomy interior floor. On the highway, driving them is mostly a two-handed job at all times, especially in windy weather. Here again you are confronted with a degree of compromise.

If these oufits appeal to you, give them very careful study, especially consider how you would arrange your sleeping accommodations, how to arrange them for meal preparation, and so on. Get in one and stand up; move around, practice or try to get an idea how you would make your bed, where you would dress and undress, and so on. Headroom is quite limited and if you are tall this could be a decided problem. To minimize this problem in the Chevrolet and Falcon the Travel Equipment Corporation offers an unusual and very special top. It is called "Travel Top." This top is permanently mounted on the roof of the "Greenbriar" after a special cut-out has been made in the roof. When traveling, the new top is folded down flat; when you make camp, the top unfolds upwards very quickly. When it is up, it provides a glassed skylight as well as headroom over the center portion of the vehicle's interior. Special fittings also enable you

CHEVROLET'S CORVAIR HOME CRUISER WITH TRAVEL TOP BY CALTHORPE.

to mount an extra canvas bunk which will sleep one person towards the top.

The second group of mostly self-contained outfits is currently represented by the house-trailer body, modified and mounted on the back of a pick-up truck. Sometimes these are called "slip-on" units. The numerous ways in which such an outfit can be bought include buying the truck from an automobile dealer who will arrange to have the coach fitted on, or buying from the coach dealer who will get the truck per your specifications from the truck dealer. Ford offers several body options for camping in their "Falcon" line.

When you travel, you may remark upon the great and growing popularity of this general classification of slip-on mobile rigs in the West where you will see a remarkable assortment on the summer highways. In Colorado such rigs are cometimes called "Tote Goats" although national advertising identifies to the hunting and fishing fraternity a stripped down motor scooter for wilderness use as a "Tote Goat."

On the asset side, there is little question but what some of the larger pick-up trucks with travel coach bodies approach the ultimate for deluxe vacationing travel. Good coach bodies can be had for less, but to get one with most of the features you will want entails an outlay of about $1100 and up.

With these rigs we again encounter compromise. The boat owner must plan to transport his boat by means of a trailer behind the vehicle because there is little or no space for a boat over the truck cab.

If you acquire one, use care when going around curves. A number have tipped over on curves through improper weight distribution within the coach or because of excessive speed. Take a lesson from the trailer designers and try to keep your heaviest loading as low as possible and along the inside left where it will be as close as possible to the crown of the highway.

One other feature deserves comment. Theoretically, the coach body can be easily removed for storage thus enabling you to use the pick-up truck as a more or less multi-purpose vehicle. Many owners do just that but the task of removing the coach body and later re-installing it can prove quite a chore for some. Consequently, many owners justify frequent week-end outings by leaving the coach body on more or less permanently.

STATION WAGON CAMPING

While perhaps impractical for larger families, you may, if you already own a station wagon, use this in your first camping trips at considerable economy. Then later on you can use the benefits of your experience to decide more precisely the camping rig best for your use.

A small family can have a very enjoyable vacation without a tent simply by putting their station wagon to multiple use as combination sleeping quarters, snack bar, and storage facility. The long top provides an excellent base for carrying gear in a roomy car-top carrier.

Special, easily removable window screens can be had for the car doors thus allowing the windows to be down or partially down for night ventilation without disturbance from mosquitoes or other insects while occupants are asleep.

When you camp, you will see all sorts of platforms, boxes, and car-top racks on station wagons, some of which open into car-top tents and provide sleeping room for two persons. A small folding stair-ladder is used with this clever arrangement.

But this is not all. A number of tents today are deliberately made to be erected behind a station wagon with a special tent wall opening and canvas shroud extending over and fastening around the rear of the wagon. Passage between the interiors of the station wagon and the tent is thus conveniently arranged. The tent provides space for dressing for those who will sleep in the wagon, and the interior of the wagon provides sleeping space for those who cannot be accommodated in the tent interior, or who wish to sleep well up off the ground.

Even without this extra attaching tent, more camping space can be squeezed out of the station wagon by lowering the tail-gate and covering the entire back opening with a special screened and zippered canvas shroud made for such use. This way two people can sleep with their heads toward the front of the car and their feet comfortably out on the lowered tail-gate area, leaving considerable space between their heads and the front seat for storage space.

Station wagon camping offers so many different possible combinations of wagon alone, wagon with folding sleeping tent on top, wagon with rear shroud, wagon with tent attached on rear,

wagon and separate tents, and so on, that one automobile manufacturer finally published a booklet on it.

One of the wonderful things about station wagon camping is
that your imagination and "do it yourself" capabilities are the
only factors which limit the kind of outfit you can have. Many
station wagon fans devote much hobby time during the winter
months devising and making newer and more ingenious storage
boxes, racks, folding tables, partitions, portable kitchens, and
other self-contained units for improving their outfits.

A plywood shelf large enough for two people to sleep on in the
back of the station wagon is usually the first of such projects.
Mounted about a foot above the floor level, it thus permits both
storage boxes and luggage to be conveniently accessible, yet out
of the way underneath the sleeping space when not needed.

GMC, Chevrolet, International Harvester, and others manu-
facture an oversize station wagon referred to by such terms as
"Carry-all," "Suburban," and so on. These vehicles offer more
space, especially in vertical dimensions; while they ride fairly
well and cruise at quite adequate speeds, many people consider
them too suggestive of a truck for all around use. At the other
end of the station wagon totem-pole we note the smaller, so called
"compacts" which range from the small Hillman "Minx" up to
the roomier dimensions afforded by the Rambler line. Because
of their smaller usable space they are less preferable although
many use them.

If you favor the station wagon as your family car or as one
of your family cars and expect it to be extensively used in camping, be sure the interior is of generous size. In camping with
a station wagon every inch of space counts; the wagon should
excel in such measurements as interior length and width. Often
overlooked but equally critical to your camping comfort are the
interior vertical dimensions—the distance between the floor of
the flat bed space and the ceiling. This dimension is of real importance to your comfort because when you get an air mattress
or pad on the floor of the wagon, and over that a sleeping bag,
you still want enough vertical space left so you can sit up.
Ability to do some dressing in at least a sitting position is most
desirable. Some of the higher priced and more deluxe station
wagons have extremely poor inside vertical dimensions; beware!

An old duck hunter taught me something else about station

wagon living, as it is popularly called. He said the standard sized two-door station wagon was his first and his last; now he only uses the standard four-door. Why?

About eleven o'clock at night and in the midst of a heavy period of cold, rain, and bad weather, he and his hunting partner joined the line of cars waiting to get into a State hunting area the following morning. In the two-door wagon there was the inconvenience of crawling over the back of the front seat to fix up their sleeping bag beds for the night. Worse than that, they had several occasions to put on their long rubber boots, leave the car and return during the heavy downpour.

"From now on," he said, "I'll have only the four-door station wagon so that I can open a back door, swing my feet around to the door sill, put my boots on, and get in and out easily. My wet, muddy boots won't slop up the inside of the wagon and we'll both get in and out without breaking our backs!"

Before we leave the topic of station wagons, one other factor is of importance to your safety. Families using such a vehicle for camping tend to overload their vehicles; when this happens the rear end goes down and the car performs sluggishly on most secondary roads—broken springs often result. The wise station wagon camper should add a set of overload springs to the vehicle before camping use. The cost of such springs and their installation is not high; it is the best insurance I know of against unnecessary car repair during a station wagon vacation.

EQUIPMENT FOR THE MOTOR CAMPER

For the car camper who enjoys a comfortable camp and sound sleeping, air mattresses, sleeping bags, folding cots, chairs, and tables will add to his well-being. A gasoline or bottled gas stove and lantern, nesting cooking utensils, and tableware are also necessary. A good insulated ice box will keep perishables for about four days by placing wrapped dry ice in the bottom and "wet" ice on top. *Caution:* Be very careful when handling dry ice. The fumes can be injurious and you can burn your hands if you are careless in handling it. The more experienced camper uses three or four "freeze cans" in the bottom of his "cold box." In this manner the bottom of the container is not messed up with melted ice. These cans can be purchased commercially and contain a chemical that will freeze rapidly when placed in the home refrigerator. Some campers use new empty one-quart cans and fill them with water to within one and a half inches from the top to allow for expansion. Screw the covers down tight and place in the home freezer over night so that the homemade units are frozen and ready for the trip the next day. These "ice-cans" will last for several days if the box lid isn't opened too many times. Setting the ice box in a dry well dug in the ground, in the shade, or the shallow water of a creek will make the "ice" last longer. Be sure to put a rock on top of the box so that it can't float away if kept in a stream. Milk cartons may also be used for freezing ice.

If you prefer cold water or ice-water to drink during the heat of the day, you can take one of the new type non-breakable plastic one-gallon water jugs and fill it to within two inches of the top with water and freeze it in the refrigerator over night. This will work on the same principle as the "freeze cans," but it will only last during the day since it is not insulated. In three or four days you will have to make arrangements while en route to have the "freeze cans" refrozen at some store or resort.

Since motor camping has become a national pastime, some people are beginning to regard this nomad mode of life as fun the year around. They buy various types and makes of cars and trailers to suit their needs. On the highways and side roads you will see one and two-wheel tent trailers, utility trailers in which to haul camping equipment, and station wagons equipped for sleeping. There are many types of tent slip-on living quarter units, car-top tents, and tents that attach to the back end of a station wagon. And there are just plain tents of many colors, sizes, and shapes that can be tossed into the trunk of the car or packed into the rear seat.

YOUR CAMP TENT

For the mobile camper, shelter and privacy are insured in the public campgrounds to those who use some sort of tent. Long six-foot wide canvas tarpaulins will add to your camping pleasure by keeping the wind from blowing loose material through your forest home, or when used as a canopy over the camp table as a shelter from the hot sun or the rain. These lightweight windbreaks are indispensable when camping on the beach or along a coast.

Webster describes a tent as a portable shelter of skins, coarse cloth, or canvas, supported by one or more poles, and usually extended by ropes fastened to pegs in the ground. No doubt this explanation hits the nail on the head. Some nomad tribes are still roaming Asia and Africa with crude skin shelters.

Over the years, modern man has improved on this portable shelter, making it more or less snag, wind, mildew, and moisture-proof, and fire-repellent. He has made tents in many sizes and shapes, and for many types of use.

SIZES AND TYPES

For automobile camping where considerable equipment may be carried in the car, and where trips involve setting up the tent camp only once or twice for a week's stay at a time, you will be glad to have more room in the tent than that required if you move your tent camp frequently. A figure of 40 square feet per occupant should be about right for calculating desirable total tent size for the longer stays. Smaller children, of course, will need less floor space, particularly if individual cots will not be used. Aluminum camping cots are now available in the double decking arrangement; with the cottage type tents and others having high, straight walls, this could reduce the total square feet of floor space otherwise required.

Where it is imperative to plan camping with light packs use a figure of about 18 square feet for each person in arriving at the tent size to use. If a person plans to pack in by himself and carry everything on his back, a tent or shelter-fly weighing not

Left: HIMALAYAN HIGH ALTITUDE TWO-MAN TENT. Right: UMBRELLA TENT.

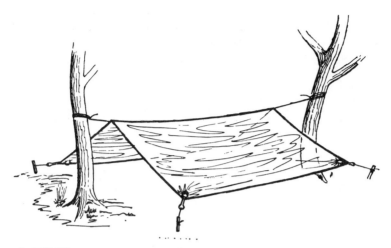

A POLYETHYLENE CLOTH OR TARPAULIN. A simple, light, back-country shelter.

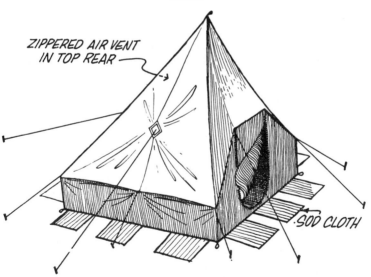

MT. LOGAN HIGH ALTITUDE THREE-MAN TENT.

over five or six pounds is the best answer. Two persons making camping trips by canoe, however, can handle a larger tent. If their outfit is held to a total of 130 pounds or less, they can take along a tent weighing up to 18 or 20 pounds. Larger ones will use up a disproportionate amount of room and take up unnecessary weight in their outfit.

A lightweight tent has been found to be a satisfactory shelter for all types of camping, whether it is used for winter ski-mountaineering at high elevations, or in the desert or deep jungles of the tropics. High altitude tents, such as the Himalayan or the Mt. Logan, have a sod cloth to help, in a high wind, keep the tent on the ground.

The type of tent you purchase will depend upon what kind of camping you plan on doing, the location, the time of year, and your budget. For back-packing or traveling by canoe or plane, you will need one of the lightweight tents. For family automobile and trailer camping, you will need one of the umbrella or high-walled tents. For travel into the back country by saddle and pack train, the wall or Baker tent is used. Some prefer using just a tarpaulin. Whatever type you decide on, buy the best you can afford, for it will last you longer.

The automobile umbrella tent and side-room umbrella, and various types of high-walled cabin models, are the most popular, and come in varying sizes. Whatever kind of tent you choose, be sure that it is large enough to accommodate the whole family. If the family is large, two people could sleep in the station wagon or in two "jungle" hammocks. This would cut down on the size and bulk of a large tent and save weight. When the

(Drawing by Luis M. Henderson)

WALL TENT.

weather is fair, some campers enjoy sleeping on a cot out under the stars. The jungle type hammock has a rain canopy over the top with mosquito netting around the sides, so neither rain nor crawling things can get inside.

HOW TO ERECT TENTS

UMBRELLA TENTS.

1. Be sure that ground is fairly level and clear of all rough ground litter and overhead obstructions.

2. Next, stake out all four corners of the tent.

3. Insert the center pole from the inside through the opening on top of the tent; place on reinforced area provided by the manufacturer. Frames that have the automatic lock-type ring need no tightening. Other frames must be tightened by the wingnut to secure the center pole.

4. Holding the center pole in hand, raise tent by pushing up pole. Set base of pole in center of tent floor. (*Note:* Use a piece of board about 10x10-inches square and about 1-inch thick as a plate. It should be well smoothed with sand paper, especially along the edges. Place the bottom of the pole on the plate so as not to damage the canvas floor. The whole weight of the tent will push down in this area and if the ground is soft, it could easily push through the fabric.)

5. Insert arms of the umbrella frame assembly in the corner grommets of the tent. Where the automatic lock-type ring is used, pull down on the assembly until tent is taut. In other type frames, push up and tighten the wing bolt securely.

6. Stake out the bottom of the wall where loops are provided. Stretch awning and insert poles. Hook on guy lines at an angle so as to draw the extension awning evenly. Do not pull the awning too tight as this exerts a great deal of strain on the wall of the tent.

7. If your umbrella tent frame has no center pole, erection is the same except that you use one of the corner poles temporarily as a center pole to hold up the tent while you fit the other three poles, each in a corner. The tent will stand by itself on the three poles in the corners while you remove the center pole and insert it in the slot provided in the remaining corner. Adjust each corner to desired tautness.

WALL TENTS.

1. Lay the tent out flat on the ground. Square out the four corners and stake them down.

2. Temporarily guy out the four corners.

3. Install one upright in grommet at the front of the tent to provide yourself initial headroom. Step inside the tent with the remaining upright and ridgepole.

4. Place one end of the ridgepole over the second upright and insert the pin through the grommet in the ridge at the rear of the tent. Adjust the front upright as necessary.

5. Tighten all guy lines and complete staking out the tent.

CABIN—COTTAGE—HI-WALL TENTS.

1. Lay the tent out flat. Square out all the lower corners and stake them down.

2. Insert the four corner poles on the outside of the tent and guy them out loosely.

3. With two upright poles and the ridgepole, step inside the tent. Place one end of the ridgepole over the spike of one of the uprights and insert through the grommet in the peak of the tent. Repeat the same for the other end and guy out front and rear loosely.

4. Where there is an awning, insert awning poles and guy it loosely.

5. Insert and guy out remaining poles.

6. Complete staking out tent; adjust poles and guy lines on entire tent, tightening to proper tensions.

EMPLORER TENTS.

1. Stake down all four corners. Connect the jointed pole to the short ridgepole and place upright inside the tent. This will hold the tent erect while you continue.

2. Guy out the front of the tent and stake out all four sides. The sides may be guyed out for extra space. If your tent does not have a canvas floor, make it bug-tight by weighting down the sod cloth all around.

ARMY ARCTIC OR MOUNTAINEER TENTS.

1. Stake down all corners. Begin with the top rear guy rope; stake it out loosely. Connect the two rear side jointed poles and insert the eye loop at the top of one pole over the eye loop

of the other. Next, place the rear top loop of the tent over the top of the eye in the jointed poles. Insert the bottom spike of one pole in the bottom loop on the right side of tent along the outside. Repeat the same for the left side. Now pull the top guy rope taut and stake out.

2. Repeat the same operation with the front section of the tent. Guy out the front rope. Tighten rear guy.

3. Stake out (guy) the sides of the tent to provide more inside room.

4. Tie ventilators at each end of tent to front and rear guy lines.

5. These tents usually come with two colors; green outside, and white inside. By turning the tent wrong-side out, the color can be changed. The white side will reflect heat to better advantage.

LEAN-TO OR BAKER TENTS.

1. Lay tent out flat. Square out the four corners and stake them down. Place rear rope stakes about three feet out from each corner following a diagonal line through the corner. Adjust rear corner ropes and attach ends to stakes.

2. Place front rope stakes about six feet from corners on a diagonal. Adjust ropes and attach to stakes.

3. Place the upright jointed wood or aluminum poles in each front corner. Erect first one and then the other, looping the rope over the pin and tightening the rope.

4. Trim all rope, and stake-down loops around the bottom of tent. Extend the awning over car, poles, or a tree. Awning can be tied down in case of a storm.

ERECTION OF TENT OR DINING FLIES AND TAR-PAULINS.

1. To erect a fly over a tent, pull the fly over the top of the tent. Next, set fly grommets over the projecting spikes of tent uprights. Top of fly should be held away from ridgepole canvas. Guy out fly so there is air space all the way between tent and fly. Tighten securely, making certain that the fly extends at least six inches over the eaves of the tent.

2. To erect a tarpaulin or a fly for a dining area, place canvas tarp or tent-fly over ridgepole with grommets mated over

one or more of the spikes which protrude through the ridge-pole.

3. Guy out loosely until an even strain is placed on all ropes, then tighten evenly. If you use side poles, slope them at an angle toward the center until the fly is secured at all points. Then to tighten, just straighten the upright side poles to desired height and this will automatically tighten the fly to desired tautness.

PUP TENTS.

1. Stake down all four corners and rear extension on pup tents.

2. Join one pole, insert and erect in rear; then join, insert, and erect front pole. Guy out front of tent.

3. Stake down all floor loops.

TIPS FOR THE TENT CAMPER

Some of the many different kinds of tents available have already been referred to. The kind of tent you select will, in the end, depend upon the kind of camping you do most. The family desiring to spend a week or more at one place each year will want a different outfit than the two men who plan to team up on desert rock hunting expeditions, or who will move every day or so during their trip.

For the larger family, a good solution is a separate tent for Mom and Dad, and one or more smaller ones for the rest of the family. All can use the larger one for dressing, changing to and from swimming attire, etc.

There is hardly anything more oppressively hot than a tent in the summer sun which has poor ventilation. While extra windows or screened sidewalls add to the cost, they are definitely desirable for the summer camper.

Many families are well satisfied with the umbrella tent; it is a very good compromise tent—easy to erect and easy to take down. It withstands stiff winds and the better ones have several windows, properly screened and protected with storm flaps so that whether it be hot and sultry or rainy the camper can adjust his tent to suit the occasion. Most of the umbrella tents come with a canvas marquee or awning which extends out from above the entrance and is supported by two tall poles and guy lines.

The idea is that in warm and sunny weather this awning will provide shade; in bad weather this awning should be let down and thus provide insurance against wind or rain entering the doorway. From another point of view, however, this awning is of dubious merit. It is really too small to enable you to use the space underneath for anything except storage; if you use it for this in bad weather you need the set of side curtains, usually thus adding to the cost. Unfortunately, if the awning is left up during rainy weather it usually collects water rapidly and you may find yourself busy pushing up from underneath to dump the water all too frequently. I have seen these awnings as full of water as a bathtub, and sagging down nearly two feet in the center. Watch for this little problem if you use an umbrella tent in rainy weather.

Another problem which plagues the umbrella tent user is how to rig the tarp or roof fly so you will have canvas over you all the way from the inside of the tent to the adjacent picnic table. Many campers like the idea of having a roof fly or large tarp over their food preparation area; in rainy weather they can still get around underneath the tarp or fly and fix their meals, then retreat inside the tent until the weather lets up. No doubt ingenious campers, using a large enough fly, can figure out a really good way of rigging this up with an umbrella tent but I haven't seen any that really looked as solid and secure as that often seen in front of the regular "A" shaped wall tent. Unfortunately, the latter tent tends to be a bit heavy and difficult to erect for many families. Certainly the larger ones cannot be recommended for those making short stays and doing much traveling.

A number of ingenious stoves have been devised for heating tents. The better ones always employ a small diameter stove pipe and the top of this emerges through an insulated collar piece mounted in either the side or the top of the tent. This arrangement is very satisfactory in the "A" shaped wall tent and such heating set-ups are common among those camping during the fall hunting season and in cold weather. Such an arrangement should also work in an umbrella tent, though the stove would probably have to occupy a place near the center of the floor or near the entrance door in order to permit successful stove pipe rigging. If you expect to use a stove and stovepipe arrangement in your tent, look for the diamond-shaped collar now available for fitting the canvas where your stove pipe passes through. There was a time when you had to cut a hole in your canvas to mount your stove pipe fitting properly but this method is now old-fashioned. With the diamond-shaped collar (two-piece) all you need to do is carefully loosen the threads in a seam near the point where your piping must pass through the canvas, then insert your diamond-shaped plate within this line—the canvas will give but still fully enclose the fitting. With the outside plate tightened firmly against the canvas, and in turn the inside plate held tight against it by thumb screws, you can finish mounting your piping without further worry about either tent leakage or fire hazard in the fitting.

Why not use your gasoline lantern to heat your tent—or a portable kerosene heater, or a charcoal stove? The reason simply is because they can't be recommended as safe! One of the first symptoms of carbon monoxide poisoning is drowsiness; presently good intentions of turning off the lantern or stove are forgotten. The fabrics used in today's tents are quite tight; zippered doors and windows rule out the leaky ventilation common to the flappy windowed tents of years ago. Don't take chances! Better to do your warming up outside around the campfire or cook stove, or out under your fly. And this brings up the matter of tent-fly and tarps.

Some campers use at least two large pieces of canvas, usually square or oblong, as a regular part of their outfit. One piece is mounted across the top of the tent but on a separate line or ridgepole about five or six inches above the regular tent roof and guyed out at the sides to retain this spacing at all times. This is your tent-fly. The air is free to circulate between your tent roof and the fly. It provides at least two worthwhile advantages and is certainly recommended if you have room to carry such extra canvas in your car. One advantage is that in wet weather you need not worry about rain getting inside your tent. Even if it is windy the fly is not likely to blow away if properly guyed down. A number of servicemen used such an arrangement over wall tents during World War II and no doubt as far back as Civil War days, or before, when they had the horses or wagons to carry them. Even in the Okinawa typhoons with winds frequently exceeding 100 miles an hour such canvas flies were maintained in place over the roofs of many tents throughout storms.

The second advantage of a tent roof fly is that it provides the best possible insulation from hot summer, beach, or desert sun. If you want your tent to offer a relatively cool place for a comfortable nap away from the outdoor sun, be sure it has a fly rigged over the top and good ventilation. You will appreciate what the fly can do for you as soon as you enter your tent on a real hot day.

As a practical economy, you can get by with just one tarp or tent-fly, as many campers do. Usually this is rigged over the

(Drawing by Luis M. Henderson)

TARP USED AS EMERGENCY SHELTER.

picnic table or eating area. In the case of campers using the "A" wall tent, the tarp is usually out directly in front and over the tent entrance. When needed as a fly over the tent, the canvas is simply pulled back farther. Those who have two large flies usually leave one over their tent roof all the time, the other is used over the eating or cooking area. In this way you have a great place to lounge around in during the evening, and shade as well, often welcome even during the breakfast hour.

Very useful to campers, especially in rainy weather, are sheets
of polyethylene plastic. At a cost ranging from 99 cents to about
$1.30, you can buy a sheet of transparent plastic roughly six
feet wide and nine to fifteen feet long. Hardware, auto supply,
and sporting goods stores usually have them. They serve the
camper in many ways—as handy covers over collections of cooking and other gear and even to keep the dew off supplies overnight. When properly guyed with small rubber balls and Vis-
klamps at the corners and sides, they can serve even as temporary tent flies. Do not depend upon clothespins to hold them long
as they tear with such fastenings, then quickly go to pieces.

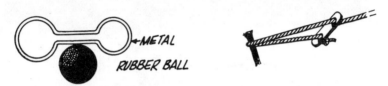

Left: VISKLAMP. For attaching a rope to polyethylene or other fabric. Right:
TENT GUY-LINE TIGHTENER.

One of the leading manufacturers of tenting equipment makes
a tarp called a "Para-Wing." This is a very well made multi-
purpose tarp distinctive because of its broad bands of white
alternated with one other color such as red, yellow, etc. The
"Para-Wing" actually consists of a fly approximately twelve feet
square. Good sized grommets are mounted for heavy duty service
in each corner. A lot of people were somewhat mystified about
the true shape of the "Para-Wing" when it was first marketed
because in ads the "Para-Wing" was usually shown with the
two opposite diagonal corners mounted on poles thus forming a
rather unique shape when the other corners were well guyed
out. Stripped of its mystery, the "Para-Wing" is actually a
large square, 12 feet by 12 feet, made up of several pieces of
good canvas. It can be used in many ways. In the diagonal
mounting it makes a fine shelter over a picnic table and can
be strung from trees or your car if both poles are not handy.
Many imitations of the "Para-Wing" have appeared.

As with the "Para-Wing," most any similar sized and shaped
piece of strong canvas can be mounted in many different ways,
ranging from simple use as a tent-fly to folded and suspended as

a satisfactory wind break. Keep in mind that every tarp or fly you bring along should have its own designated line fastenings—or rope.

One of my friends carries a long piece of ½-inch rope with him on every camping trip. There are also two shorter lengths, about eighteen feet in each piece, which ride along in his gear. These pieces plus some hanks of ¼-inch sash cord comprise all the line equipment he has ever needed.

The long single heavy strand is used to support his fly; it is used in place of a ridge pole for the fly over his cooking and eating area. It often serves as a clothesline. It took a bit longer, however, before I learned what the two shorter pieces of heavy line were for, but one pleasant afternoon he brought them out and mounted a hammock in the shade between two friendly trees. After many summers spent in camping all around the United States, he recommends the hammock as a "must" item; it takes very little room and greatly increases the charm of camping. Again the question is, how much space do you have for the multitude of things you feel you would like to take?

For example, shall we or shall we not take camp cots?

In cold weather, a camper will sleep warmer if he sleeps on the ground without a cot. Once settled down for the night there is no space for a draft to pass under the bed and chill the lower side. In summer you may find that the underneath air space provided by cots will be advantageous in hot weather. Even though cots may add to comfort, the basic question is usually—do we have room for them along with the other gear? The canvas, itself, is not heavy—it's the framework or legs for the cot that take up the room and add weight. In either case you will want to put a ground cloth under your sleeping bag; in fact, it should go under your air mattress to insure a dry bed. Rubberized fabric, sometimes even a plastic raincoat, serves efficiently here.

If you would like to use cots be sure your tent is roomy enough. With your beds raised roughly about eleven inches from the floor on cots, you must reckon with the sloping walls of most tents. To allow for this, the inner edge of your cots must be pulled in toward the center of the tent thus narrowing the usable floor space. Usable floor space is at a premium in most tents; the lack of reasonable space can be quite an annoyance to everyone in the party and especially to those who find they must get up at night to visit the half-mooned house thoughtfully provided (practically always) by an understanding park management.

It is well to have your flashlight handy for such excursions, though in many instances you will find latrine facilities quite adequately marked and lighted. How good are such places and how well are they maintained?

This is a good time to be conservative, especially in planning the items or supplies which you will need to take along. As a general rule you don't need to include toilet paper unless you are really going off the beaten path. In spite of this, many families do take some, at least a small supply. In some parks the facilities are quite modern; they usually feature plain concrete floors but good ventilation. In Mesa Verde National Park, for example, a man can plan to shave with his electric razor. On the other hand, some of the parks in the Adirondacks are a bit more primitive; latrine facilities are given a thorough hosing down each morning and disinfectants mingle their odor with the mist arising from the wet floors. But then the good camper must expect some minor irksome circumstances; the irritations usually turn out to be of short duration. But some can be a bit chronic, for example, the daily trip out of camp to get ice and other supplies; irksome, perhaps, because this requires time some campers feel should more suitably be spent in fishing, boating, or in just resting.

With a good ice chest you may get by for two or three days without refilling but this can depend, oddly enough, on when you are camping. If you camp in August and find yourself dependent upon a local ice house that stocks river or lake ice which is all that is available to refill your ice chest, you will probably have to go after ice oftener than if you were camping around the end of June. When ice cutting begins, some of the first ice arriving at the local ice house goes to the bottom of the supply and is known as "slush" ice. As cutting progresses, better ice is obtained but stacked upward by layers by the local supplier. When camping begins in June, the early campers get the best ice when they come in to fill their ice chests, since the ice cakes are usually worked out of the ice house from the top. Supply diminishes with astonishing rapidity during July, and presently the dealer has little left except the lower several layers of "slush" ice. Nothing to worry about though, really—it just doesn't seem to last quite as long as you think it should, and of course the hotter weather in August influences this, too.

Small old rugs can play a useful part in your tent camping. If space permits, take along a couple; one just inside your tent door can be removed each day to shake out the sand, dirt, etc., that tends to otherwise accrue on the tent floor. If the other one is not used inside the tent, put it just outside the entrance and use as an entrance mat. It is amazing how this simple arrangement lightens housekeeping chores in camp.

THE NEW TENT

Apart from erecting your new tent in the back yard or somewhere close to home for the first time, and thus becoming familiar with how to set it up and being sure you have all the poles, line, and pegs needed, some manufacturers recommend that a new tent be well sprinkled with a garden hose and then thoroughly dried before extensively used on a trip. They assert new tents can shrink as much as up to one inch per square foot of fabric, especially canvas.

In any case, this is a good way to check for leaks since sometimes though there may be no leaks in the roof or walls, some may appear in seams around the windows, the door, or at the base. If you find any, they can quickly and easily be remedied by rubbing the leaky areas with candle wax, softened beeswax, or even spruce gum (in an emergency).

WATERPROOFING TENTS

Before attempting to waterproof a tent for the first time after having bought it new and given it some use, be sure to find out what kind of waterproofing was used by the manufacturer. For example, if it was originally waterproofed with paraffin and you try to renew this through a solution of alum and lead, it may not work out successfully since this solution is unlikely to penetrate the fabric deep enough. On the other hand, no matter what the manufacturer used, you can use a paraffin solution over most any tent fabric successfully. Remember that the paraffin solution must be treated with respect because it is flammable; your tent must also be considered in that category even though most of them are treated to be fire *resistant*.

To waterproof a tent, pitch it outside where it will get plenty of sun and air. When it is thoroughly dry and well aired, apply your solution by spray or brush. Instructions will accompany most of the spray solutions available. A good paraffin solution may be evolved from blocks of paraffin bought at the grocery store or through a filling station. Let the blocks melt in a can dipped in hot water not exposed to an open flame. When melted, mix in some turpentine; you may heat the turpentine first in hot water (keep away from intense heat or flame), and melt the paraffin in the warm turpentine. For every 3 quarts of turpentine use about ¾ pounds of paraffin. Two coats will usually do the job. The tent will be ready to use as soon as the turpentine odor has left following the second coat. If you are pressed for time, one coat may do the job, however, the floor and all seams are likely to need a minimum of two coats.

CAMPSITE SELECTION

All too often it is not possible for the camping family to choose the exact site where they would like to camp. With most of our parks and forests rather crowded during the vacation season, it frequently is a matter of slipping into the first site that you find vacant. When the season is at its height—July usually—you may have a longer wait than you would like. You might therefore do well to give some careful thought to the matter of timing your arrival at your camping area in such a way as will minimize site-finding problems.

A lot of the people who camp are not just there for an overnight stay. By the time you get your camp set up to your liking and then take it down a few times you will understand why most campers plan on staying several days, especially in attractive surroundings. What can be done to get a good site?

First of all, consider that most families will try to arrive at a camping area as soon as they can reach it after the husband has finished his last day's work before vacation. Usually that will be on a Friday afternoon. As a result, there tends to be a much greater turnover among campsite users on Saturdays and Sundays. People tend to leave at the last minute that will still permit the head of the household to be back at work the first thing Monday. If they don't live far away, they tend to linger until perhaps even three or four o'clock on Sunday afternoon, though most depart shortly after the noon hour. Some of them, of course, must plan to leave camp late Friday night, or as early as possible on Saturday or Sunday to allow time for their trip home.

If your trip is planned for late June, July, or early August, and if you know the area you wish to visit is a pretty popular place, try to time your arrival so you get there about the time this turnover starts. It is hard to tell exactly when this will be best at your particular destination; as a general rule I think an arrival around eleven a.m. on a Saturday or a Sunday would give you time to look the situation over and line up a definite site by evening.

A rather common habit has come to my attention regarding some campers. It seems to be a sort of unwritten law that a vacant campsite may be securely claimed by leaving a person from the party there or even by leaving an article there. I once saw an attractive site claimed simply through a rolled-up umbrella laid diagonally across the park table.

In one instance I heard of a party coming to a campground from a town nearby and putting up an old, bedraggled, and quite empty tent on a very desirable site. He did this on a Wednesday, then returned to town and actually did not show up in this otherwise crowded area to set up a much better tent camp until a full ten days later. For some reason or another, none of the many incoming campers who paused to examine the otherwise abandoned looking site ever went up to the Ranger to question its availability; however, they should have. The rules are not always uniform concerning how long an area such as this can be held without occupancy; in many places at least twelve to twenty-four hours are permissible.

But, let us suppose you have found quite a few good-looking sites available, what should you consider in making a choice?

Presumably, if you have a boat, you would like to locate where you can leave it in the water, motor attached, and ready for use at your whim throughout your stay. In such cases, the camp site choice is usually made primarily with regard to convenient access to the water.

A lot of other considerations are, of course, important to camp site selection, some of them quite obvious. No one would want a site which forms a basin for rainwater; no one enjoys finding himself enveloped in heavy fog in the morning; and no one wants a tree, boulder, or large branch likely to tumble on his location any time.

Beach camping poses a general problem in that the soft sand requires the use of sand stakes rather than ordinary tent pegs to hold the tent down securely. Sand stakes are longer than the average stake and usually have flanges or other features which will hold securely in soft sand. Some campers pre-cut some small boards, attach lines and rings, and bury these deep in the sand with the rings exposed for tie-down purposes. Others skip the rings and tie directly to the boards, which are then buried deeply.

Most desirable, the campsite should face the east or southeast so you will have the benefit of morning sun, assuming the weather is good, when you arise. This quickly dispels dew, dries your canvas or cloth-covered articles, and is a great blessing in getting rid of any dampness from the night.

Hollows sometime attract insects more than the higher areas of ground, as well as cold air and mists. But on the crests you may be plagued with winds, and find yourself too exposed in case of lightning; also it may be a longer walk down to the stream or lake from such a site. Then, too, you will need to consider the distance involved in getting firewood and water. The usual practice in most of our parks is to provide water through taps and spigots located about three feet above the ground and at intervals affording convenience to several campsites. Even so, you may have to lug water in a pail or fill your water cans, then carry them a distance of perhaps one block. Usually, it's less.

In canyons, those on the west side enjoy morning sun and more protection from the noon sun and heat than those on the east side.

Wind will usually blow off a lake and travel up toward higher ground during the daytime; at night, winds move toward the water. This may help you in calculating your best campfire or cooking arrangement and heighten your enjoyment while sitting around the evening campfire without getting smoke in your eyes.

Usually, you will find there is most wind from two to four or five p.m. There can be exceptions to this, however, on high peaks, near the coast, or in large, deep, straight valleys.

CAMPSITE CHECK LIST

(1.) Health and safety come first. Never camp under large tall trees which may attract lightning, or where wind or the elements may cause limbs or trees to fall on you or your camp. These are called "widow makers" by woodsmen.

(2.) Never camp in tall dry grass nor near heavy brush fields or swamps, for there is a fire hazard ever present in the former, and there are mosquito pests in the latter. Black flies and gnats hold forth in heavy brush, and midges or "no-see-ums," as the Indians call them, are constantly near water.

(3.) Don't ever camp in a gully or canyon where a flash flood, beginning miles away, may wash you and your camp away.

(4.) Camp well above high tide on the coast; never camp under an overhanging cliff or bluff where a rock slide or avalanche may endanger you.

(5.) Needless to say, keep your camp away from poison oak, ivy, and sumac.

(6.) Pure water is essential to your health. Never take it for granted that wilderness water is pure. Boil or treat it chemically to purify it.

(7.) The camp should be located, if possible, on higher ground away from lake, beach or stream edge, out of the way of high winds, but so that some breeze will keep insects away.

(8.) Pitch your tent on a level knoll or slight slope so that the ground will drain properly away from the front of your canvas. Keep away from marshy or clay soils where mud puddles and rain will collect.

(9.) The tent should be pitched to take advantage of favorable exposures. Face it towards the southeast to get the morning sun, but place it so that you will get some shade during the afternoon, and remember to protect it against high winds.

(10.) Most campers like to have their tent faced away from other tents, or the highway, if they are camping in a public campground. Don't pitch your camp so close to the public washroom that pedestrian traffic will disturb you.

(11.) Be sure that all rocks, sharp sticks, and other hard objects are removed from the spot you pitch your tent. Sharp objects can puncture the tent floor and air mattress.

(12.) Keep the prevailing winds in mind so smoke and sparks from your campfire won't damage your equipment nor become bothersome.

(13.) If you are in a public camp area and have pets and children, be considerate. Keep your children and pets out of other people's camps unless invited.

(14.) When you have chosen your campsite and pitched your tent, assign each member of your party some specific camp chore.

(15.) When breaking camp—strike your tent as soon as the dew has dried away from the canvas—get packed and on your way so that you can reach your next campsite at least two hours before dark. This affords you a better chance to pick a more desirable site and have camp set up before dark.

ANIMAL PESTS

Be sure your tent has a sewed-in floor, screened windows and a screened zippered door for ventilation. This is a "must" if you are going to keep out crawling and flying pests. It will also keep out the friendly "pets" like playful field mice, chipmunks, skunks and squirrels. Little "Oscar the Skunk" may feel that you are intruding on his territory and may protect himself

(Drawing by Luis M. Henderson)

because you won't welcome him in for a night's lodging and a free meal. Should—Heaven forbid!—a skunk spray you, there is only one way that you can deodorize your clothes and bedding and decontaminate your surrounding quarters. This "Ol' Ranger" has tried everything and finds the best method is to spray the surroundings with vinegar or household ammonia. Your clothes will have to be washed in a solution of one or the other. Heating the liquid will make it more effective and a liquid or fly sprayer will help disperse it. If you fail to get rid of the skunk odor, you will find that you are not very popular with your nearby camper friends when you try to borrow the "makin's" in the middle of the night. Normally it is a foregone conclusion that once the camp is awakened, no one is going to go back to sleep. Next morning most of the neighbors will be wearing sun-glasses and giving you the "glassy-eye."

Don't forget that another over-friendly little visitor may come around—a "sticky" little chap, Mr. Porky the porcupine. If you happen to be in his territory, don't leave your ax, canoe paddle, oars, gloves, saddle bags, or other sweaty or salty articles unprotected at night, for this little "wood-eating rat" can make them look as if his cousin the beaver had made a meal on them.

Do not leave food in your tent, car or on your camp table if you leave camp for any length of time. Jays, "camp robbers," squirrels, and deer will take over the table contents with glee.

(Drawing by Luis M. Henderson)

A hungry bear can make a shambles of your tent. Tent doors are easy pickings, and irresistible if there is a nice fat hunk of bacon or ham inside. Mr. Yogi enjoys fish, too! He will leave by a different way than he entered, usually right through the side of your nice new tent. He will at times wrench open a car door and help himself to that box of candy that you forgot to

(Drawing by Luis M. Henderson)

remove. If you're camped pretty much by yourself, be sure that your food cache-box is hoisted high and hung from a limb of a tree far enough away from the tree trunk so that a bear cannot reach out and pull the box to him nor chew through the rope while you are out swimming or fishing. Find out if you happen to be in "bear country." Ask the local game warden or ranger what the situation is and what precautions to take.

PARK ANIMALS. Feeding the birds, chipmunks, and squirrels is not frowned on by the rangers, but do not feed the bear, deer, elk, or buffalo. Human food and cigarettes are not good for deer. If you leave the animals alone they will not harm you. Deer can do considerable damage to you if they strike out with their sharp hoofs. Don't think that you can always run up close to a bear or other wild animal and snap a camera in its face. You might get away with it once or twice and again you might not. Several park visitors have been bitten and mauled, especially when they got between the female bear and her young. The few accidents that have occurred in the national parks usually have taken place near a "warning" sign. The few people that do not heed these safety signs for their protection probably do not read or obey traffic signs either.

In some areas and campgrounds, dogs and cats are not allowed to enter because they may disturb visitors or wildlife and for sanitary reasons.

Make it a habit when you leave your camp to be certain that your fire is absolutely out, unless you have a camper friend to watch it for you. If not, *it must be out!*

RENT TO TEST

Camping gear may be rented. For the novice car camper or trailer "gypsy," it is suggested that you rent all your gear and give it a trial run. In this manner you can find out what you need when you decide to invest in your own outfit. Most cities have stores where you can rent all types of camping equipment for a nominal fee.

Even if you do not own a car nor have a friend with one, this need not stop you from giving this wonderful recreational sport a trial. You can rent a car for as little as $8.00 to $10.00 per day, plus 8 to 10 cents per mile, depending on the size and type of vehicle you wish to drive. House trailers rent for around $25.00 per week end. The rental price is also based on size, type, and accommodations furnished inside. The outfitter usually furnishes a trailer hitch that will fit your car.

YOUR DOG IN CAMPING

Dogs probably love to go camping as much as their owners. A springer spaniel we know of recently returned from a three-week canoe camping trip in one of the more primitive and remote lake regions of Canada. Because his owner had checked with the veterinarian in planning the trip, his papers and the proper special tag were ready for inspection at the border checkpoint and there was no inconvenient delay.

At night, their campsites were successively in regions strangely silent except for the lapping of waves and the far away but infrequent crying of wolves. Much of the time it rained; the dog slept inside the tent with his owners and made no disturbances whatsoever.

Standing on the bow of the canoe in his eagerness to be the first ashore, he sometimes lost his balance and received an untimely drenching. On every portage he made at least 10 round-trips to his owner's one. He encountered no porcupines (fortunately), nor did he get sick. Deer and elk seen at some distance from the canoe were new to him but his response was purest apathy. Wisely, his owners kept him on leash when other parties were sighted; though not hostile, he was indisposed to fraternize with the occasional stranger met along trails or portages. His only extended absences from the party occurred on vigorous but disappointing forays after grouse, some of which he tracked and ultimately flushed. In general, his owners wouldn't want to go camping without him.

But consider very carefully before you decide whether or not you should let *your* dog accompany you on your camping trip. In most of our Parks and Forests some regulation of pets has become mandatory. Note the accompanying list of regulations concerning state parks which appears through the courtesy of *Better Camping* magazine. A lot, of course, depends upon your destination, how you will travel, your dog's disposition, etc.

Write beforehand and learn of any special restrictions aplying to dogs at your destination. Consult your veterinarian; he has made himself familiar with most regulations and laws which might pose problems. You may need health certificates and special tags. Also be sure your dog will carry the proper identification tag so that if he becomes lost the finder can get in touch with you. Incidentally, it is wise to carry along some extra recent snapshots of your dog; if he should become lost, these could prove very helpful in his recovery.

REGULATIONS ON DOGS IN STATE PARKS*

State Parks   *Restrictions*

Alabama—Dogs must be leashed and are not permitted in cabins.

Alaska—Owners must show proof of rabies vaccination.

Arizona—Pets are invited but must be leashed in public use areas.

Arkansas—Dogs must be kept leashed and must not be permitted to create disturbances.

California—Dogs must be leashed during the day and are not permitted in camping or other public use areas overnight.

Colorado—No state park campgrounds.

Connecticut—Dogs must be leashed and are not permitted on beaches. Number is restricted to one pet per campsite.

Delaware—NO DOGS ALLOWED.

Florida—Dogs must be leashed (maximum 6 ft.) and are not permitted to remain in camping or other public use areas overnight.

Hawaii—Dogs entering Hawaii must be quarantined at owner's expense for 120 days. They must be kept leashed and are not permitted on beaches.

Maryland—NO DOGS ALLOWED.

Massachusetts—Dogs must be leashed and are not permitted on beaches.

Michigan—Dogs must be leashed (maximum 6 ft.) and are not permitted on beaches.

Minnesota—Dogs must be leashed (maximum 6 ft.) and are not permitted in public buildings.

Nevada—No information given.

New Hampshire—Dogs must be leashed and are not permitted on beaches.

New Jersey—No information given.

New Mexico—Dogs must be leashed and must be kept quiet.

New York—Dogs must be leashed and are not permitted in bathing or picnic areas.

Ohio—NO DOGS ALLOWED.

Pennsylvania—NO DOGS ALLOWED.

Rhode Island—No information given.

South Carolina—Dogs must be leashed and are not permitted in cabins.

Utah—Dogs must be kept under control.

Vermont—Dogs must be leashed (maximum 7 ft.).

Washington—Dogs must be leashed and are not permitted on trails nor in swimming or dining areas.

* "Should You Take Your Dog?" Pat Larmoyeux, *Better Camping* (© 1962 Kalmbach Publishing Co.), May-June, 1962. (By Permission.)

Wisconsin—Dogs must be leashed (maximum 8 ft.).; never allowed in swimming areas.

Wyoming—Dogs must be leashed; never allowed on trails or in boats.

In the rest of the states, dogs must be leashed.

Regulations differ slightly in detail, but in general dogs are permitted in camp grounds in national parks, forests and monuments if kept leashed.

Dogs entering Mexico and Canada must have a health certificate and proof of recent rabies vaccination. Dogs must be kept leashed in Canadian national parks, and require individual licenses which can be obtained at park entrance.

There are two special hazards which you should always be prepared for when camping with your dog. One of these is poisoning.

Poisoning: Some dogs just can't pass up the chance for a free meal here and there along your trip. In many cases, you may never establish what they ate or where they found it. Assuming you consulted your veterinarian before starting your trip, you will be prepared to treat any case of poisoning promptly and effectively. Remember, a poisoned dog requires *instant* treatment. Don't waste precious time looking for a veterinarian; instead administer the treatment your veterinarian has already recommended. In general, you must take "immediate action" to empty the dog's stomach.

One way to do this is to use hydrogen peroxide. Mix the regular drug store strength (3%) with water 50-50 and pour it down the dog's throat. Use at least a tablespoonful to each 10 pounds of dog. It turns into oxygen and water and is harmless. He will vomit in about two minutes. After the stomach settles, give some Epsom salts—about a teaspoonful in a little water—to empty the intestine. Hydrogen peroxide is an antidote for the phosphorus so often used in rat poisons; Epsom salts is an antidote for lead poisoning. After you have completed the "immediate action" phase of treatment, consult a veterinarian.

Porcupines: If you expect to be in or near porcupine country, try to control your dog against the porcupine hazard. Prevention is by far preferable to a dog's first and probably unfortunate experience with the quills. Certainly you should never encourage an unleashed and inexperienced dog to attack one of these menaces! Porcupines are a very real hazard to the family pet who has never previously encountered one. A porcupine does not shoot his quills but instead employs his tail to lash a dog attacking him. Usually the quills will penetrate the dog's mouth, tongue, chest, shoulders, and legs. Then, unfortunately, most dogs will roll over and paw themselves. This, of course, makes matters worse.

Once a dog receives a dose of quills there just isn't any fast way of removing them. It is likely to be an ordeal painful to both you and the dog. You will need a pair of pliers with tight fitting jaws; this item should be among your camping tools anyhow.

You will have to be very businesslike about holding him securely and using the pliers. Get the quills out of the mouth and eyes first, then any behind the ribs. Those in the legs may be most troublesome, especially if they are in the wrist joints.

Quills look like thistles but have countless little scales—their points protruding backward. The least painful method of removing quills is to yank them out rather than subject the dog to slower extractions. Remove them as cleanly as possible lest stubs remain to further irritate the tissue. Some quills are best removed by pushing them through tissue and pulling them out from the other side because of their construction.

Check with a veterinarian for alternate and less barbaric ways of removing porcupine quills. It has been claimed that when snipped off and the embedded ends soaked with a liquid they may be easily loosened and more humanely removed.

Apart from poisoning and porcupines there are other hazards familiar to most dog owners and which require little comment covering camping since such hazards attend dogs in almost every other environment. A dog should never be left in a car unless the car affords him complete shade, and unless the windows are opened for an adequate degree of ventilation. The sun beating down on the roof of a standing car causes the interior to heat rapidly; fresh oxygen-laden air cannot enter unless the windows are well open. Hence, the danger of suffocation; it can happen even on humid days when the sun is behind clouds. Always keep this hazard in mind when traveling with a dog.

TRAILER CAMPING

Trailer camping is growing in popularity. Many enjoy the very deluxe camping available with a house trailer. Others swear by the trailer tent that can be erected in a few minutes.

Tent trailer outfits are seen more everywhere. Apache, Heilite, and Nimrod are leading examples, to name but a few. Even these have models now considerably improved over their originals, but many serious campers find it difficult to decide between this kind of attractive *folding* outfit and the small, solid house—or travel trailers—some of which sell for less than $200 to $300 additional.

For a lot of families the compact, folding tent-trailer outfits are hard to beat, especially those who camp mainly in the summer when interior heating requirements are unimportant. Furthermore, in one stroke they thus usually solve the problem of where to load camping paraphernalia otherwise carried in the car; and the camper benefits through more comfortable space inside the car with often the top of the car left free as well for extra luggage or for transporting a boat. The tent-trailer outfit can be adequately heated for fall or winter excursions, but to do so safely and satisfactorily you will first have to investigate carefully the small under-floor and other heaters available through trailer supply houses.

Though many campers honestly feel their outfits, whether tenting, trailer, or mobile rigs, are ideal in meeting their needs, thoughtful campers should realize that there are limitations in achieving one really completely ideal outfit. As you gain camping experience you will find that some compromises are inevitable. If you have a trailer, or a tent-trailer, you may all too often find that the areas reserved for such outfits are completely full in some of our parks and forests, and you will have to look elsewhere for a place to stay overnight. In some parks and forests, rules do not permit vehicles to be parked in other than designated automobile parking areas. Often these rules are enforced with barriers so placed that even if you wished to unhook your folding tent-trailer from your car and push it off the macadam automobile parking lot to some much more desirable surrounding, it simply can't be done. In this situation the purely tenting outfit has obvious advantages over any other.

The house trailer has the advantage over the tent in that it has closet space; some have toilets and many other conveniences. It is more comfortable, especially in wet weather. Folding and packing a wet tent can be somewhat annoying.

House trailers range from the compact 13-foot Scotty

Sportsman aluminum trailer that sleeps three people and will negotiate most back country roads to 55-foot monster trailers that require a truck to pull them.

The larger house trailers or mobile homes, are fine for living in but difficult to move. They take up a lot of space in a campground. Don't hold up traffic with your trailer outfit. If traffic starts to line up in back of you be courteous and pull over at the first turnout and let the faster traffic pass. If you do not do so and there is a ranger or traffic officer present you may receive a ticket.

If you are pulling a house trailer or a small utility trailer, be sure to check ahead and obtain information as to grades and road conditions. Watch out for high-centered roads. The smaller travel trailers not over 15 feet in length are more easily handled, especially in woods and camps. Trailers longer than 18 feet are difficult to haul over steep winding roads and mountain passes, and will make your car motor eat up much more gas. Should your motor over-heat and form a "vapor lock," pour cold water on the fuel pump or hold a cold cloth on the pump until the gas returns to liquid form. If you have stopped on a curve in the road, be sure that someone is flagging traffic both ways for you so that you don't cause an accident.

WHERE TO GET CAMPING EQUIPMENT

For the large family on a budget, there are many types of tents that will serve them well. There is the economical army type 5-man tent, 8 feet high at its center, with 2-foot side walls and 13 feet in diameter; it sells new at most large surplus stores for $34.95. This and other army type tents are advertised in *Field & Stream, Outdoor Life, Sports Afield,* and other outdoor and equipment magazines. Palley's of 2263 East Vernon Avenue, Los Angeles 58, California, is one of the larger surplus stores in the West. Morsan Tents, Incorporated, is another large camp equipment store that sells surplus army tents. They have a fair selection of many types of new camping equipment; their address is 10-37 50th Avenue, Long Island City 1, New York. Goldberg's of 202 Market Street, Philadelphia 6, Pennsylvania, is well equipped to fill the needs of the outdoorsman. They have two excellent catalogs, one for camping and one for marine supplies for the seagoing camp cruiser. Corcoran, Inc. of

Stoughton, Mass. has an excellent catalog. L. L. Bean of Free-port, Maine, is another outfitter from whom you may get a catalog.

Most of the sporting goods and larger hardware stores now handle camping equipment. So do the larger department stores. Montgomery Ward and Company lists a wide selection of outdoor camping and boating supplies in their "Outdoor Equipment" catalog. Sears, Roebuck, and Company has a complete line of all types of outdoor clothing, camping, and boating equipment. Both of these nation-wide mail-order companies have numerous retail stores across the country.

It is advantageous to be a member of a state or national automobile club. Most clubs furnish the latest information on road and weather conditions, and on motels and restaurants. They also have good road maps and best of all, excellent recre-ational maps and campsite directories for the United States, Canada, and parts of Mexico. They perform many other helpful services for the motoring public and are exceptionally helpful to the automobile and trailer camper since this outdoor sport has become big business.

If you have decided against renting your equipment for a trial run and wish to purchase your own camping equipment, it is suggested that you write for the Potomac-Appalachian Trail Club's Hiking, Camping, and Mountaineering Equipment catalog, priced at 50 cents. Their address is The Potomac Appalachian Trail Club, 1916 Sunderland Place, N.W., Washington 6, D.C. This little "gem" names types of articles, description, weight, supplier, and price of most camping, mountaineering, and out-door equipment of companies in the United States and several other countries.

PLANNING YOUR TRIP

A good idea after you have purchased all your "gear" is to pitch your new tent in the back yard and turn the lawn sprinkler on it for an hour or so, then check for leaks. Try sleeping in it a night or two and make certain that your air mattress is in good shape. In fact, try out all your equipment so that you can become acquainted with it and know that it will work before you haul it miles away and then perhaps find that the tent or air mattress leaks, or the gas lantern will only sputter. You

should become familiar enough with your outfit before you head
for the tall timber so that you can pitch or strike camp in the
dark if it ever becomes necessary to do so. Next, after everything is found working satisfactorily, take a week end off and
drive to your nearest state park or forest for a shake-down
breaking-in trip. You might have a friend who is an expert
outdoorsman who would go along and give you a few pointers.
If you are not an experienced camper it is suggested that you
study chapter 17, "Wilderness Craftsmanship" of this "guide"
before you head for the hills.

You should protect your tent, air mattresses, and other fragile
equipment by placing them in canvas bags or by wrapping them
in sheets of canvas or a tarpaulin so that they will not be
bruised, punctured, or damaged by axes, tent stakes, or other
sharp articles in the car or in camp. Your investment in your
camp equipment can be further protected and kept ready to go
at the so-called drop of a hat if, on return home, you check it
over, make any necessary repairs, and see that it is properly
stored. A mouse-proof storage place is advisable.

Normally your outfit shouldn't run over $150.00 for two people,
or about $200.00 for a family of four. Of course if finances don't
enter the picture, the sky is the limit. You can get a tent for
over $1,200. Even an inexpensive tent—this home away from
home you plan on buying if you don't already possess one—
should, with care, last you for years.

Now that you have all your gear together, get a good road
map and a Geological Survey contour map of the area in which
you plan to camp. For your first shake-down trek take not over
a 100-mile trip; a 50-mile trip is better. Take a compass divider
(you can buy one at Woolworths for 15 cents) and note the
mileage scale on your road map. Mark off 50 miles with your
dividers. Next place one leg of the compass on your town as
a pivot or hub and draw a circle with the other end. You will be
surprised at the number of swimming, boating, hunting, fishing,
camping, and picnicking areas you will find in this 50-mile circle.
Reach out farther and draw a 100-mile circle and another at
150 miles. Normally you will find a county or state park or
forest or even a national forest within this 150-mile circle. There
might even be a national park; it all depends on the section of
the country in which you live. Within this area of 150 miles

there may be lakes and streams as well as reservoirs where camping and water sports are allowed.

If you can get away for only a day at a time, there is no reason why you can't find excellent picnic spots where you can swim, fish, or loaf for the day in the 50-mile circle without being tired out from driving too far. If you can get away only on week ends, look over the recreational features and campsites that are to be found within the 100 or 150-mile radius. You should find many beautiful locations within this circle. Recreational areas can even be found near a city the size of New York.

To help speed you on your way, make up lunches* and cook some extra food the day before and place it in your refrigerator and have it ready to go with your camp outfit in the morning. If you get a fairly early start you will arrive early and have more time to play and relax the next two days. In the summer you should be able to leave right after work Friday and have your car tent or trailer camp set up and supper over with before dark. Late Sunday afternoon strike camp and head for home so that you don't arrive late and all tired out. You should get home in time for a good night's rest and be refreshed for the job Monday morning. During the week you can start planning and getting the outfit ready to roll for the next week's trip. Try a new location next time and see more country and new scenery.

With a little foresight and planning you should be able to cram all your gear into the family chariot, and still leave room for the passengers to be comfortable. After a trip or two a system will work itself out to everyone's satisfaction. You might even decide to add a car-top rack in order to get everything aboard. However, after a few trips you will start discarding the unnecessary items that you at first thought you couldn't get along without, but found that you seldom used on the whole trip.

If you have trouble loading all your camping gear in the family car, you might keep in mind the possibility of removing the back seat of the car to accommodate more gear. This space-gaining measure might avoid the expense of a car-top carrier or small trailer otherwise needed.

---

* A word of advice on lunches. Don't take food that will spoil quickly in warm weather; food poisoning can result. Ham sandwiches, potato salads, and cream puffs are not recommended. Cheese, peanut butter, roast beef, egg, and jelly sandwiches are safer. Make the sandwiches just before you eat them, meanwhile keeping the food items separated in their containers. Fresh fruit is fine for dessert.

Be sure that the spare tire, jack, tools, axe, shovel, water, and bucket are readily available, and not buried deep under a lot of camp gear. The last things to come out of the car should be the first to be stowed inside. Its quite a job to unload or reload a car if you have buried the jack or other needed equipment.

Some campgrounds and campsites do not allow house trailers, or do not have hook-ups for water, lights, or sanitation. Many state parks do, but very few national parks or forests provide these facilities. It is best to walk into a primitive trailer camp to ascertain if you will have room to turn your rig around or back into a vacant space. Watch out for dead-end roads where there is not enough room to turn around a car with a trailer. Turning a house trailer by hand in a confined space can be rough.

Take a knapsack along so that any member of the family that wishes can hike into a good fishing or scenic area from the road-end or from your camp. Don't forget your camera and fishing tackle.

ENJOY THE BIRDS

Did you ever watch a wren build a nest to attract a mate? What hard work and painstaking care! Did you ever watch the new bride then move in, completely tear apart and rebuild the nest the male wren had put together so carefully? Ridiculous, but true—there's a lot to learn from watching birds!

Camping and travel offer numerous chances to study many varieties of birds including some you are not likely to find around home. Try to make the most of such opportunities. It's fun! A good pair of binoculars helps. Keep notes. Use your camera when you have the chance.

If your camera has adjustable lens and shutter speeds but no telephoto lens you might try for some close-up photos anyway, through your binoculars. Make sure the binoc's are clean and focused for clarity. Set your camera to focus on infinity and use a lens opening of at least f4.5 or larger. The camera and binoculars should have a solid support; use a tripod when possible.

Position the camera close against the eyepiece of the binoculars and shoot. With Plus-X film in good light, try several shots at various shutter speeds ranging from 1/100 to 1/400 of a second. Experiment with slower shutter speeds for Kodachrome. But don't try this method through the usual coin-operated telescopes to be found at various scenic vantage points; their magnification is too great for good results.

No doubt you already know quite a few of the birds in the accompanying tabulation. It's a useful and interesting reference, however, for bird-watchers of all ages.

RESIDENT AND MIGRATORY BIRDLIFE

The first letter indicates *abundance:* Common or Rare.

The second letter indicates *season present:* Summer, Winter, Transient, or Permanent. The word "permanent" does not mean that the same individuals are present at all seasons, but means that *some members* of the species *may be seen at any season.*

Name	West	Middle	East	Name	West	Middle	East
Baldpate	CW	RW	RW	Eagle, Bald	RT	RT	RT
Bittern, American	CT	RT	RT	Egret, American	CT	CT	RT
Bittern, Least	RS	RS	RS	Egret, Snowy	RT	...	...
Blackbird, Rusty	CW	CT	RT	Finch, Purple	CW	CW	CW
Bluebird	CP	CP	CP	Flicker	CP	CP	CP
Blue-gray				Flycatcher,			
Gnatcatcher	CS	CS	CS	Acadian	CS	CS	CS
Bobolink	CT	CT	CT	Flycatcher,			
Brown Creeper	CW	CW	RP	Crested	CS	CS	CS
Bufflehead	RT	RT	RT	Gadwall	CW	RW	RW
Bunting, Indigo	CS	CS	CS	Gallinule, Florida	CT	CT	RT
Canvasback	CT	CT	CT	Gnatcatcher,			
Cardinal	CP	CP	CP	Blue-gray	CS	CS	CS
Catbird	CS	CS	CS	Goldeneye,			
Cedar Waxwing	CW	CP	CP	American	RT	RT	RT
Chat, Yellow-				Goldfinch	CP	CP	CP
breasted	CS	CS	CS	Goose, Blue	RT	...	...
Chickadee	CP	CP	CP	Goose, Canada	CW	CT	CW
Coot	CT	CT	CT	Goose, Snow	RT	...	...
Cormorant,				Grackle	CP	CP	CP
Double-crested	CT	RT	RT	Grebe, Horned	RT	RT	RT
Cowbird	CT	CT	CT	Grebe, Pied-billed	CT	CT	CT
Creeper, Brown	CW	CW	RP	Grosbeak, Rose-			
Crow	CP	CP	CP	breasted	CT	CT	RS
Cuckoo, Yellow-				Grouse, Ruffed	...	RP	CP
billed	CS	CS	CS	Gull, Bonaparte's	RT	RT	RT
Dickcissel	CS	CS	RS	Gull, Herring	CT	RT	RT
Dove, Mourning	CP	CP	CP	Gull, Ring-billed	CT	RT	RT
Duck, Black	CW	CW	CW	Hawk, Broad-			
Duck, Ring-				winged	CS	RS	RS
necked	CW	CW	CW	Hawk, Cooper's	CP	CP	CP
Duck, Ruddy	CT	RT	RT	Hawk, Duck	RT	RT	RT
Duck, Wood	CP	CP	RP	Hawk, Marsh	CT	CT	CT

Name	West	Middle	East
Hawk (Nighthawk)	CS	CS	CS
Hawk, Red-shouldered	CP	CT	CT
Hawk, Red-tailed	CP	CP	CP
Hawk, Sharp-skinned	CT	RP	RP
Hawk, Sparrow	CP	CP	CP
Heron, Black-crowned Night	RT	RT	RT
Heron, Great Blue	CP	RP	RP
Heron, Green	CS	CS	CS
Heron, Little Blue	CT	CT	CT
Heron, Yellow-crowned Night	RT	RT	RT
Hummingbird, Ruby-throated	CS	CS	CS
Ibis, Wood	CT	**RT**	...
Indigo Bunting	CS	CS	CS
Jay, Blue	CP	CP	CP
Junco (Snowbird)	CW	CW	CP
Killdeer	CP	CP	CP
Kingbird	CS	CS	CS
Kingfisher	CP	CP	CP
Kinglets	CW	CW	CW
Lark, Horned	RP	RP	RP
Loon, Common	RT	RT	RT
Mallard	CW	CW	CW
Martin, Purple	CS	CS	CS
Meadowlark	CP	CP	CP
Merganser, American	CT	RT	RT
Merganser, Hooded	CT	RT	RT
Merganser, Red-breasted	CT	RT	RT
Mockingbird	CP	CP	CP
Nuthatch, Red-breasted	RW	RW	RP
Nuthatch, White-breasted	CP	CP	CP
Oriole, Baltimore	CS	CS	CS
Oriole, Orchard	CS	CS	CS
Osprey	RT	RT	RT
Ovenbird	CT	CT	CS
Peewee, Wood	CS	CS	CS
Phoebe	RP	CP	CP
Pintail	CW	CW	RW
Plover, Semipalmated	CT	RT	RT
Quail, Bobwhite	CP	CP	CP
Rail, King	CS	RS	RT
Rail, Sora	CT	CT	CT
Rail, Virginia	CT	RT	RT
Redhead	CT	CT	CT
Redstart	CT	CS	CS
Redwing	CP	CS	CS
Robin	CP	CP	CP
Sandpiper, Least	CT	CT	RT
Sandpiper, Pectoral	CT	CT	RT
Sandpiper, Semipalmated	CT	RT	RT
Sandpiper, Solitary	CT	CT	CT
Sandpiper, Spotted	CT	CT	CT
Sapsucker, Yellow-bellied	CW	CW	RP
Scaup, Greater	RT	RT	RT
Scaup, Lesser	CW	CW	CW
Shoveller	CT	RT	RT
Shrike	CP	RP	RP
Snipe, Wilson's	CT	CT	CT
Sparrow, Chipping	CP	CP	CP
Sparrow, English	CP	CP	CP
Sparrow, Field	CP	CP	CP
Sparrow, Fox	CT	CT	CT
Sparrow, Grasshopper	CS	CS	CS
Sparrow, Lark	CT	CT	CT
Sparrow, Savannah	CW	CW	CW
Sparrow, Song	CW	CW	CP
Sparrow, Swamp	CW	CW	CW
Sparrow, Vesper	CT	CT	CP
Sparrow, White-crowned	CW	CW	RW
Sparrow, White-throated	CW	CW	CW
Starling	CP	CP	CP
Swallow, Bank	CT	CT	CT
Swallow, Barn	RS	RS	CS
Swallow, Cliff	CT	CT	CT
Swallow, Rough-winged	CS	CS	CS
Swallow, Tree	RS	CT	RT
Swift, Chimney	CS	CS	CS
Tanager, Scarlet	CT	CT	CS
Tanager, Summer	CS	CS	CS
Teal, Blue-winged	CT	CT	CT
Teal, Green-winged	CT	CT	CT
Tern, Black	CT	CT	RT
Tern, Least	CS	RT	...
Thrasher, Brown	CS	CS	CS
Thrush, Hermit	CW	CW	CW
Thrush, Olive-backed	CT	CT	CT
Thrush, Wood	CS	CS	CS
Titmouse, Tufted	CP	CP	CP
Towhee (Chewink)	CP	CP	CP
Turkey, Water	RS	...	...
Turkey, Wild	RP	RP	RP
Veery	CT	CT	CS
Vireo, Red-eyed	CS	CS	CS
Vireo, Warbling	CS	CS	CS
Vireo, White-eyed	CS	CS	CS
Vireo, Yellow-throated	CS	CS	CS
Vulture, Black	CP	CP	CP
Vulture, Turkey	CP	CP	CS
Warbler, Black and White	RS	CS	CS
Warbler, Blackburnian	CT	CT	CT
Warbler, Blackpoll	CT	CT	CT
Warbler, Black-throated	RT	RT	CS
Warbler, Black-throated Green	CT	CT	CS
Warbler, Blue-winged	CS	CS	RS
Warbler, Canada	RT	RT	CT
Warbler, Cerulean	CT	CT	CT
Warbler, Chestnut-sided	CT	CT	CS
Warbler, Golden-winged	CT	RS	RS
Warbler, Hooded	CS	CS	CS
Warbler, Kentucky	CS	CS	CS
Warbler, Magnolia	CT	CT	CT
Warbler, Myrtle	CW	CW	CW
Warbler, Nashville	CT	CT	RT
Warbler, Palm	RS	RS	RS

Name	West	Middle	East	Name	West	Middle	East
Warbler, Pine	CP	CP	CP	Woodpecker, Red-bellied	CP	CP	CP
Warbler, Prairie	CS	CS	CS	Woodpecker, Red-headed	CP	CP	CP
Warbler, Prothonotary	CS	CS	RS	Wren, Bewick's	CP	CP	CP
Warbler, Tennessee	CT	CT	RT	Wren, Carolina	CP	CP	CP
Warbler, Yellow	RS	CS	CS	Wren, House	CS	CS	CS
Warbler, Yellow-throated	CS	CS	RS	Wren, Marsh	CT	CT	CT
Waxwing, Cedar	CW	CP	CP	Wren, Winter	CW	CW	CP
Whip-poor-will	CS	CS	CS				
Woodcock	RT	RT	RT	Yellow-Legs, Greater	RT	RT	RT
Woodpecker, Downy	CP	CP	CP	Yellow-Legs, Lesser	CT	CT	RT
Woodpecker, Hairy	CP	CP	CP	Yellowthroat	CS	CS	CS
Woodpecker, Pileated	CP	CP	CP				

WATCH THE WEATHER

Weather is something we hear about, or read or talk about daily. We cannot do much about it beyond preparing in advance for either good or bad weather. Vacationing campers are especially aware of it.

When planning an outing, the new family camper must take weather into consideration. Your whole trip can become very uncomfortable if unexpected rain, wind, or snow appears after you have started on your camping adventure. If inclement weather overtakes the experienced outdoorsman, he knows how to find shelter and manages to amuse himself or keep busy until the storm is over. This is something you learn through experience. Take rain and storm gear along; it will add to your comfort if needed.

It is suggested that you plan ahead on how you will keep the children entertained and yourself occupied should you become storm bound. It can happen, you know, especially if you travel long distances.

You might follow the procedure Ranger-Pilots do before flying fire patrol or starting out on a boat patrol on large bodies of water; call your local weather bureau or Coast Guard station and ask for a short or long range forecast for the region where you are planning to camp.

The experienced person will keep a "weather eye" on cloud formations, note wind velocity and direction, and changes in temperature. The mountain climber will head for lower elevations or at least come off high peaks to avoid lightning strikes, high wind, and cold. The "salty-skipper" will head for a safe harbor, and even the animals will head for shelter when the weather becomes uncooperative.

WIND-BAROMETER INDICATIONS. Sky conditions and sky changes should be carefully watched, since this is the best guide to short-term local forecasting by the camper. The early definition of the state of the sky as clear, partly cloudy, cloudy, or overcast, is still descriptive and widely used by native woodsmen.

As a rule, winds from the east quadrants and a falling barometer indicate foul weather; winds shifting to the west quadrants indicate clearing and fair weather. The rapidity of a storm's approach and its intensity are indicated by the rate and the amount in the fall of the barometer.

The wind directions thus produced give rise to, and are responsible for, all local weather signs. The south winds bring warmth; the north winds cold; the east winds, in the middle latitudes, indicate the approach from the westward of an area of low pressure, or storm area; and the west winds show that the storm area has passed to the eastward. The indications of the barometer generally precede shifts of the wind. This has been shown by observations.

During the colder months, when the land temperatures are below the water temperatures of the ocean, precipitation will begin along the seaboards when the wind shifts and blows steadily from the water over the land without regard to the height of the barometer. In such cases, the moisture in the warm ocean winds is condensed by the cold of the continental area. During the summer months, on the contrary, the on-shore winds are not necessarily rain winds for the reason that they are cooler than the land surfaces, and their capacity for moisture is increased by warmth communicated to them by the land surface. In such cases thunder storms commonly occur when the ocean winds are intercepted by mountain ranges or peaks. If, however, the eastwardly winds of summer increase in force, with falling barometer, the approach of an area of low barometric pressure from the west is indicated, and rain will follow within a day or two.

From the Mississippi and Missouri Valleys to the Atlantic coast and on the Pacific coast, rain generally begins *on a falling barometer,* while in the Rocky Mountain and plateau districts and on the eastern Rocky Mountain slope, precipitation seldom begins until the barometer begins *to rise after a fall.* This is true as regards the eastern half of the country, however, only during the colder months and in the presence of general storms that may occur at other seasons. In the warmer months, summer showers and thunderstorms usually come about the time the barometer *turns from falling to rising.* The fact that during practically the entire year precipitation on the Great Western Plains and in the mountain regions that lie between the Plains and in the Pacific coast districts does not begin *until the center of the low-barometer area has passed to the eastward or southward and the wind has shifted to the north quadrants, with rising barometer,* is an important one for vacationists to note.

The wind and barometer indications for the United States are generally summarized in the following table:

Wind Direction	Barometer Reduced to Sea Level	Character of Weather
SW to NW	30.10 to 30.20 and steady	Fair, with slight temperature changes for 1 or 2 days.
SW to NW	30.10 to 30.20 and rising rapidly	Fair followed within 2 days by rain.
SW to NW	30.20 and above and stationary	Continued fair with no decided temperature change.
SW to NW	30.20 and above falling slowly	Slowly rising temperature and fair for 2 days.
S to SE	30.10 to 30.20 and falling slowly	Rain within 24 hours.
S to SE	30.10 to 30.20 and falling rapidly	Wind increasing in force, with rain within 12 to 24 hours.
SE to NE	30.10 to 30.20 and falling slowly	Rain in 12 to 18 hours.
SE to NE	30.10 to 30.20 and falling rapidly	Increasing wind and rain within 12 hours.
E to NE	30.10 and above and falling slowly	In summer, with light winds, rain may not fall for several days. In winter, rain in 24 hours.

SIGNS TO LOOK FOR. Here are a few weather guides that have worked fairly consistently for weatherwise outdoorsmen:

(1) If smoke from your campfire rises high in a long thin spiral, the weather will remain "good" for at least 12 hours. If it rises sluggishly for a short distance, drifts off slowly and settles, have your rain gear handy.

(2) If all the trees (particularly the maples) are showing the undersides of their leaves, and the tops of the western hemlock straighten up, rain is possible within 24 hours.

(3) Heavy dew on the grass or the forest cover presages fair weather—lack of it is likely to mean rain.

(4) Clouds, in their various formations, often give an advance hint on the weather.

(5) The big, white, puffy clouds called cumulus, mean fair weather. Go ahead and make your plans. When they bunch up they form nimbus, or rain clouds. Call the game! If they gather quickly you may expect no more than a shower. Fishing should be good! If it takes them a day or two to form in a mass, get plenty of dry wood under cover in camp. Be sure that you have made a drain trench around your tent!

(6) Small cumulus clouds indicate fair weather—go ahead and have fun! The big ones, that form like high white mountains and hide nearly all the blue, mean rain in the offing. Better not hike too far! If these clouds swell up and flatten out like an anvil, they are called "hammer-heads" and you can expect thunder and lightning. Stay away from tall trees!

(7) Cirrus clouds, or "mare's tails," those wispy affairs high up, are a bad sign. If they go scudding across the sky there is likely to be a storm within the next twenty-four hours. Better be prepared!

(8) A variation of the cirrus clouds, and somewhat denser, is known as a "mackerel sky." Look out for high wind!

(9) Clouds that move at different levels and in opposite directions are a warning of unpleasant weather ahead.

(10) If the clouds float high about sundown and are tinged with red, prepare for high wind to follow. Tighten the "guys!"

(11) Look for a change in wind and probable bad weather to follow when distant objects which have been indistinct suddenly stand out clearly. Don't get too far out on large bodies of water!

(12) When you see crows and sea gulls tumbling and pitching about in flight, batten down the hatches; tighten up the guys—there's a gale in the making!

WEATHER WARNINGS. Here are a few weather references that I learned aboard the old Sea Training Bureau ship, the *USS Iris*:

(1) Referring to the sunset: "Red sky at night, sailor's delight, red sky in the morning, sailors take warning!"

(2) A rainbow in the morning bodes no good (probably showers); a rainbow in the evening, fair weather tomorrow.

(3) When the moon "has a ring around it," look for rain in

the summer time. In the winter, look for rain at lower elevations and snow at higher ones. The same applies to a "red" moon. If the moon is clear and bright, it is safe to go ahead as you planned.

(4) In the winter, when the night is black as ink and the stars seem especially brilliant and more numerous than usual, look for rain or snow the following day. Ski mountaineers should head for shelter.

Have fun, give the above weather information a try, and see how near you come to weather bureau predictions. May the skies be clear for you in vacation land!

WATCH THAT FIRE!

For detailed instructions on building a campfire, see chapter 13.

Be fire conscious. You can prevent fires by following the few simple but important suggestions listed below.

Most people are careful with campfires. They obey state and local fire laws. They build their fires in the right places and at the right times, keep them small, and put them out before they leave. If *everyone* were careful, campfires would start few forest fires.

But an *unattended* campfire or a spark from too large a fire can cause an entire forest to burn. Wildfire damages watersheds, destroys timber, and blackens recreation areas. It kills forest animals and often leads to serious erosion damage.

The National Park Service and the National Forest Service seek to preserve our valuable forest areas from destruction by fire, in order that you and your family and your descendants and many others may enjoy them. These guardians of the public welfare deserve our utmost cooperation. We should heed the advice they offer through their signs, their literature, and the purported sayings of the very popular little creature they call "Smokey."

Your municipal, county, state, and federal parks and forest services request your cooperation in helping prevent forest fires.

NEVER LET IT BE SAID TO YOUR SHAME THAT ALL WAS BEAUTY BEFORE YOU CAME!

Learn to be a good "woodsman" and camper. Keep water supplies unpolluted. In addition to disposing properly of refuse,

(Courtesy U. S. Forest Service and the Advertising Council Inc.)

bathe and wash clothing away from springs, streams, and lakes.

Cooperate in preserving forest signs. They are posted for your information.

Never short cut a trail.

Do not disturb wildlife. Observe state fish and game laws.

Don't be a litter bug.

When in doubt, ask a Ranger.

WHAT TO DO IF LOST

(1) Stop and sit down. Keep calm. Think things out!

(2) Clear an area and build a fire. After the fire is going well, cut and place green boughs on it so there will be plenty of smoke. BE SURE THE FIRE DOES NOT GET AWAY FROM YOU!

(3) Signal by 3 blasts on a whistle, 3 shots from a gun, 3 regulated puffs of smoke, or 3 flashes from a mirror or flashlight. Repeat at regular intervals. When it is recognized by a search party, it will be answered by 2 signals. Three signals of any kind is a world wide SOS call. Use it only when in actual need of help.

(4) Stay where you are until help arrives.

CHECK LISTS FOR CAMPERS

CHECK LIST FOR THE AUTOMOBILE CAMPER (Two Persons). If you, like most other automobile campers, are limited to the trunk and possibly a car-top carrier or a small one- or two-wheeled utility trailer for storage, you'll want to think about packing the most comfort in the least space. Otherwise, you may cramp some member of the family forced to sit in the back seat with most of the baggage. Don't forget that the last things to come out of the car should be the first to go in.

The following list is made up for two people. If there are more in the party all you will need to add is additional sleeping bags, tableware and chairs.

Air mattresses (2).
Air pump (1) (or use the car pump).
Aluminum griddle (1).
Aluminum and canvas folding chairs (2).
Axe, with 2¼-pound head and 28-inch handle w/sheath (1).
Ball hitch for trailer (1) (optional).
Books and games for the family.

Broom (or small rake) (1).
Buckets (2), one canvas and one plastic.
Bug-bomb (1); insect repellent, small bottle per person.
Camera, film, filters, flash-bulbs (optional).
Camp stove, gasoline or canned gas type, two-burner (1).
Camp stove, wood, cook & heater (1) (optional).
Camp stove (1), charcoal grill type (optional).
Canteen (1), gallon type; water-bag (1).
Canvas windbreaks or tarpaulins for shade 6 x 18 feet (1).
Chain, tow-chain for car, or steel cable, hook at each end—15 feet.
Charcoal briquettes for charcoal grill (optional).
Cleaning material, detergents, sponges, soap, steel wool, etc.
Coffee pot if one in nested kit isn't large enough (optional).
Compass with sighting line and adjustable declination (1).
Cook outfit, 4-man aluminum nesting type, add kitchen and table ware, knives, forks, spoons, can opener, spatula, salt & pepper shakers, butcher and bread knives, extra plastic dishes, washpan, dishpan, etc.; broom, small child's type.
Firearms (optional, unless hunting); fishing gear and tackle.
Fire extinguisher, Du Gas or CO2 (carbon tet. not used any more).
Flares, red-glass road reflectors (3); red flags (3).
Flashlights (2) with batteries and extra bulbs.
First-aid kit, add prescriptions needed, laxative, roll of two-inch tape, wire splints (2), etc. Ask your doctor to help make a list up for your personal needs. Add snake-bite kit (suction type; if you are traveling much in the desert, antivenin syringe type); metal wound clamps (6); water purifying tablets (50); codeine; sulfa; sleeping tablets.
Funnel for filling gasoline stove and lantern (1).
Gasoline, white gas for outboard motor, gas stove, and lanterns (5 gal.).
Gasoline can, metal with strainer (5 gallon size) (1) or (2).
Ice box, insulated type (1).
Jack, bumper type (1); hydraulic type (1).
Jacket and extra clothing for each member. Rain gear for all.
Kits and kit bags, duffel bags for tent and sleeping bags, sewing kit (army type); gun-cleaning kit, etc.
Lanterns, electric (optional), gasoline or canned gas type. Extra gas mantles, generators, wrenches, canned gas for lantern and stove.
Maps, road type and Geological Survey contour, large scale of area.
Matches, large kitchen size, boxes (1).
Mattresses, or cot ticks (2) (optional).
Mirror, for shaving and toilet (1).
Night clothes, blankets, cots (optional).
Oven, camp-type (optional), reflector oven (optional).
Pick, small army type (1).
Pillows (2) (optional).
Plastic wash bowl, juicer, and jeep water can (1) each.
Portable folding toilet or "old fashion high boy," (optional).
Pressure cooker (1) (optional, but strongly recommended).
Saw, folding camp-type (1) (optional).

Scout knife with blade, leather punch, can opener and screw driver (2).
Shovel, "O" or Forester type, or Boy Scout short-handled type (1).
Sleeping bags and ground cloths (2), or jungle hammocks (2) (optional).
Tarpaulin 10 x 10-feet, (1) (optional).
Tent and fly large enough to accommodate family (1), complete with
    poles, stakes, and extra rope.
Tire and car tools and kit, patches, tire-tube, pump, rubber cement,
    tire air gauge, extra tire-tube valves, repair boot.
Watch, wrist type (2).
Water can, large mouth jeep can 5 gal. (1).
Waterproof match safe (2) (optional).

Again, be sure to pack sleeping bags, tent, air mattresses, and
other easily damaged gear into canvas duffel bags or wrap
compactly in canvas. Be sure axe and saw guards and other
sharp tools have leather or canvas sheaths or guards on them.
You will learn what you need after a few trips. You will discard
some items and add others. If you haul a canoe or boat you will
need marine safety gear and equipment. *Don't forget it!*

HOUSE TRAILER CHECK LIST (Two Persons).

Axe, single-bit.
Ball hitch for front of car (optional).
Buckets, canvas (1) plastic (1) metal (1).
Canteen, 1 gallon.
Canvas, awning for shade or windbreak (6 x 18-feet).
Chain, tow chain or cable (15-feet with hook at each end).
Chairs, folding camp type with armrests (2).
Cleaning equipment, broom, detergents, mop, sponges, dust pan, etc.
Cooking utensils, nesting camp-type 4-man, add tableware.
Dishes, plastic, non-breakable type; dishpan, plastic type.
Fire extinguisher, Du Gas or other powder type or CO_2.
First-aid kit, add laxative and personal prescriptions, snake-kit.
Flags, red road signal type (3).
Flares (3) red glass road reflectors or kerosene type (3).
Flashlight, electric, with flashing red light and white spotlight.
Flashlight with extra batteries and bulbs (1).
Funnel for filling water tank (1).
Funnel for filling gas tank (1).
Gasoline can with spout and strainer 5 gal. cap. (1).
Hose, sewer-hose, carry in 4-inch dia. hose carrier under trailer.
Hose, short piece for draining into "gopher hole" near trailer.
Hose, sink-hose, largest size that will fit standard fittings.
Hose, (2) 25-foot high pressure type for filling water tank from hydrant.
Ice-box, large enough to hold 25 pounds of ice on top of wrapped dry
    ice.
Jacks, (1) hydraulic, small to fit under trailer axle, screwtype (2).
Lantern, gasoline **or canned gas for** outside use **or for emergencies.**

Light cord, electric heavy-duty type for plugging in trailer lights, minimum of 50 feet.

Maps.

Pick, small army surplus type.

Shovel, "O" or BSA type, short-handled.

Step-up, Pullman type.

Tire pump and "spark-plug" motor operated type, (1) each.

Tires, spare car and spare trailer tire and wheel.

Tire tools, patches, rubber cement, air gauge, etc.

Tire tubes, one to fit each size tire (tire repair more rapid by putting
in tubes).

Tool kit, hammer, pliers, screwdriver, 4-way lug wrench, various types
of wrenches, nails, screws, short piece of soft wire, extra valves, butane
or gas connectors and washers for butane or propane gas tanks (don't
forget lineman's friction and rubber tape and fuses for your car and
trailer lights).

Tow rope, 1-inch manila, 40-feet.

Water can, wide-mouth army jeep type 5 gal. capacity.

Wheel chocks (2), 8 inch square material, with one end slanted to fit
against trailer wheel.

Small "bubble-levels," or a small carpenter's level will be real
handy to have along so that the trailer can rest on a level keel.
Sometimes it is necessary to park on a slight slope. A 2" x 8"
piece of planking 2 feet long will work wonders in this situation.

TRIP PLANNING SUGGESTIONS

Start early with your plans; let the children plan with you.
You can secure a *campground directory* from your automobile
club showing all the principal campsites in the United States
and parts of Canada. Campground directories list over 6,000
places to camp. They may be purchased for from $1 to $4.50.
See chapter 2 of this book on where to write for game laws and
information on travel and places of interest. All the national
parks and forests and where to write for information about
them are listed. Write for information about the states on
your route. There is no charge for this service—and the maps
are free.

WHAT ABOUT TRAVEL COST? Generally speaking, it
costs a family of four about $40 a day while touring. This in-
cludes an estimated $10 to $12 for car operation, $12 for
lodging, $12 to $15 for meals and $3 for extras. But you can
tour for less, depending on where you go, and how you go.
The most economical way to cut expenses is to camp out and

cook your own meals. With the exception of gas and oil you can live in this manner almost as economically as you could at home.

HOW TO STRETCH TRAVEL DOLLARS. Follow these driving rules for maximum gasoline mileage:

(1) *Drive steadily and at a moderate speed.* At 70 miles per hour you burn up 38% more gas than at 35 miles per hour.

(2) *Avoid "jack-rabbit" starts.* They can take up to 60% more gas than gentle acceleration.

(3) *Avoid "slam-bang" stops.* Allow your engine to slow down and you'll save fuel.

(4) *Turn off the engine when you make an extended stop.* Idling consumes about one-half gallon of gas per hour.

(5) *Check tire pressures frequently.* Tires improperly inflated waste gas and wear unevenly.*

(6) *Get a complete car check at your dealer before you start out.* Be sure to tell your car service adviser you are taking a trip so he can advise you accordingly on your car's needs. With camping gear in the car or in a trailer behind, your brakes will have a heavier load to handle. You will want to be absolutely sure they are ready to safely handle all trip requirements.

THINGS TO CHECK BEFORE YOU GO

For an extended trip, the following check lists will be helpful.

YOUR HOME.

Notify local police.
Stop milk, paper, laundry, and other deliveries.
Discontinue garbage pickups.
Arrange for safekeeping or forwarding of mail.
Lock all doors and windows—leave shades up.
Disconnect electrical appliances; turn off lights.
Turn off gas jets, including water heater.
Remove food from refrigerator; leave door open.
Turn thermostat to minimum heat requirements.
Turn off water, drain pipes in severe weather.
Arrange for care of pets and plants.

---

* For best results, tires should be inflated to recommended pressures when they are cold. A good time to do this is in the morning before you have driven even one mile.

Arrange to suspend telephone service if you expect to be gone long enough to qualify for vacation rate advantages.

Store valuables.

Leave house key with friend, along with probable itinerary, and emergency phone numbers; also color, year, license number, and make of car.

YOUR BELONGINGS.

Driver's license, expiration date.

Your car registration.

Insurance expiration and proof of responsibility.

Hunting and fishing licenses and equipment; campfire permit.

Cameras and film.

Bathing suits, beach accessories, sports equipment.

Money—preferably in traveler's checks.

Credit cards for oil companies and others.

Personal medicines and prescriptions.

Eyeglasses and prescriptions, sun glasses.

Writing materials, stamps, and address book.

Duplicate car and house keys, luggage keys.

Credentials for touring in Canada or Mexico.

Maps, trip routings, etc.

YOUR CAR.

Fill gasoline tank.

Change motor oil.

Complete lubrication; check transmission, differential, steering, and brake systems.

Check battery, oil filter, and air cleaner.

Check cooling system.

Check brakes.

Check tires for cuts and worn spots, including spare.

Test all lights, inside and outside.

Check for needed tune-up service.

Check windshield wipers and washer fluid.

Check fan belt, plugs, and ignition.

Check springs, shock absorbers, muffler, and tail pipe.

Check wheel alignment and bearings.

WHAT TO DO IN CASE OF CAR ACCIDENT

(1) STOP at once if you are involved in any way.

(2) Render first-aid if needed, but do not move injured unless they are endangered by traffic.

(3) Contact police immediately to get a doctor and ambulance, and to report the accident.

(4) Get names and addresses of witnesses and ask for identification papers of other driver.

(5) Observe car positions and surroundings.

(6) Make no liability statement prejudicial to your rights or those of your insurer.

(7) Report accident to your insurance agent as soon as possible.

(8) Do not sign any papers when emotionally upset.

DISABLED CAR DISTRESS SIGNAL

Most states have adopted this standard distress signal for use when a car becomes disabled on a superhighway or freeway: Hang a white cloth or handkerchief from the left front window and raise the hood. If it is dark, turn on the interior light and parking lights. You can help others by reporting such signals whenever you see them along the road.

TEN TIPS FOR TRAVELERS

(1) Do make breakfast and lunch a light meal while traveling. Enjoy your big meal after stopping at your overnight accommodations.

(2) Don't attempt too long a trip each day. Eight hours of driving, with occasional stops, are plenty for any one day's travel.

(3) Do make intermediate stops every 100 miles or so to relax your muscles and nerves, and to rest your eyes.

(4) Don't be a litterbug. Dispose of accumulated trash in the burners and receptacles provided in roadside parks and gas stations. Remember that some states have fines up to $500 for littering.

(5) Do start and end your trip in the middle of the week if possible. You'll avoid the heavy weekend traffic.

(6) Don't forget that your loaded car will be much heavier than normal, and stopping and starting will take longer. Be prepared to make allowances.

(7) Do try and decide on your overnight accommodations by 4:30 p.m. each day so that you can relax and explore the local area.

(8) DON'T leave small loose objects on the rear window shelf. A sudden stop can turn them into dangerous projectiles.

(9) Do travel light. If possible, wear wash-and-wear clothing that will need little or no ironing. Each person should wear one color theme so that clothes can be mixed and matched without special accessories.

(10) DON'T forget your responsibility to your fellow passengers. When you are driving, their safety and well-being are in your hands.

POISON IVY AND POISON OAK

Learn to recognize and avoid: poison ivy, poison oak, and poison sumac.

Poison ivy and poison oak, both poisonous to many people

(Drawing by Luis M. Henderson)

POISON IVY.

when touched, grow on a vine with clusters of three broad leaves. The leaf is reddish and glossy when young, matures to a fairly glossy rich green, and in autumn turns red again. It is poisonous any time of the year. The plant may climb trees and poles, or grow along fences or the ground. It also grows as a low shrub.

The poison may be carried by smoke from the burning plants, or by pets, clothing, or insects.

Poison sumac may grow as a shrub or as a small tree up to 20 feet high.

Don't risk contact, as immunity one year may be followed the next year by explosive sensitivity.

If you do come in contact, immediately wash with yellow

laundry soap. If soap is not available, rub the exposed area with sand, dry soil, or absorbent cotton. If rash or blisters develop, see your doctor.

POISONOUS SNAKES COMMON TO THE UNITED STATES

RATTLESNAKE. The various species of rattlesnakes present the greatest danger to man simply because there are more of them than any other poisonous snakes. All species have horny, interlocking joints at the end of their tails called "rattles." They attain lengths of up to eight feet and are found in almost every state.

COPPERHEAD. This snake has a copper-colored head and "hour-glass" patches on its body. It attains a length of 50 inches. It is found along the Eastern Seaboard from Massachusetts to Florida, and also in Ohio, Illinois, Nebraska, and Oklahoma.

CORAL SNAKE. Brilliant in color, with wide black and red bands separated by narrower yellow bands, the coral snake attains a length of up to 39 inches. It is found from North Carolina south into Florida and west to Texas.

COTTONMOUTH (Water Moccasin). This snake lives in wet, swampy country from Virginia to Florida. It is dark in color, with a heavy body. The inside of the mouth is white, hence the name cottonmouth.

MOUNTAIN DRIVING

If your trip should take you through the mountains, remember these things: A car has much less power in the mountains, and it takes a surprisingly longer time to pass other cars when at high altitudes, even on a level road. Get a good start when approaching steep upper grades and don't hestitate to shift to a lower gear when your speed drops down to 20 mph. Observe the posted safe speed laws for curves, and don't attempt to pass trucks on long grades. Most important of all, never coast downhill. Use your engine compression as a brake by leaving the car in gear, and always shift to a lower gear before descending steep grades.

CAVE EXPLORING

There are approximately 50,000 caves scattered through the

country, barely a fifth of them known and mapped. These caves are roughly divided into "tame" ones, and "wild" ones where cave-exploring spelunkers pursue their favorite sport. Spelunking, or cave exploring, has been called "mountaineering upside down"—and after dark, at that!

Most caves have a constant temperature between 50 and 60 degrees, and the explorer will find them more or less an air-cooled diversion on a hot summer day or night. The "tame" caves are well explored and safely marked to bring out the beautiful coloring and rock formations. There are over 150 commercially operated caverns that introduce visitors to the fun of going underground. Some have elevators, eating accommodations, and even boat trips on subterranean waterways.

The "wild" caves are for the more experienced caver. Most of the over 10,000 caves registered with the National Speleological Society are only partially explored. Amateurs should check with the nearest of the 62 local "Grottoes" or chapters of the N. S. S. before undertaking a cave jaunt.

No one should undertake a caving expedition into a "wild" cave without training or without having an experienced person or guide along. It is desirable to have at least three persons in the party. Always leave word with friends and local officials of your plans. Always carry sufficient recommended equipment along. Always carry three separate types of lights. A cave deep in the bowels of the earth, is no fit target for exploration with dead batteries in your flashlight.

GUIDE BOOKS FOR EATING AND LODGING

The following books can give you up-to-date information on where to eat and sleep:

Adventures In Good Eating, Duncan Hines Institute, 408 E. State St., Ithaca, N. Y., $1.50.

Lodging for a Night, Duncan Hines Institute, 408 E. State St., Ithaca, N. Y., $1.50.

Motel Blue Book, National Hotel Publishing Co., 179 W. Washington St., Chicago 2, Illinois.

New Horizons USA, N. Y., Simon and Schuster, $2.50.

Gourmet Guide To Good Eating, New York, Simon and Schuster, $1.50.

Hotel Red Book, American Hotel Association, 221 W. 57th St., N. Y., $6.00.

SMOKEY THE BEAR

COPYRIGHT 1952 · HILL AND RANGE SONGS, INC.   By STEVE NELSON and JACK ROLLINS

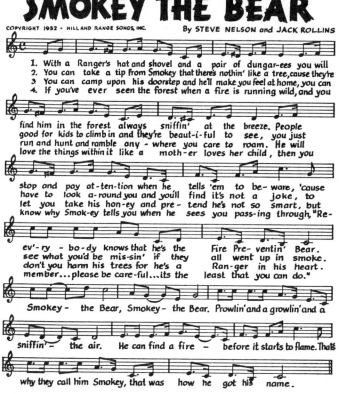

1. With a Ranger's hat and shovel and a pair of dungar-ees you will
2. You can take a tip from Smokey that there's nothin' like a tree, cause they're
3. You can camp upon his doorstep and he'll make you feel at home, you can
4. If you've ever seen the forest when a fire is running wild, and you

find him in the forest always sniffin' at the breeze. People
good for kids to climb in and they're beaut-i-ful to see, you just
run and hunt and ramble any - where you care to roam. He will
love the things within it like a moth-er loves her child, then you

stop and pay at-ten-tion when he tells 'em to be-ware, 'cause
have to look a-round you and you'll find it's not a joke, to
let you take his hon-ey and pre-tend he's not so smart, but
know why Smok-ey tells you when he sees you pass-ing through, "Re-

ev'-ry - bo-dy knows that he's the Fire Pre-ventin' Bear.
see what you'd be mis-sin' if they all went up in smoke.
don't you harm his trees for he's a Ran-ger in his heart.
member...please be care-ful...its the least that you can do."

Smokey - the Bear, Smokey- the Bear. Prowlin' and a growlin' and a

sniffin'- the air. He can find a fire - before it starts to flame. That's

why they call him Smokey, that was how he got his name.

THIS SONG HAS BEEN RECORDED, UNDER LICENSE ,BY SEVERAL COMPANIES
INCLUDING RCA–VICTOR, COLUMBIA, DECCA AND GOLDEN RECORDS.

Chapter 5

TAKING TO THE WATER

BOATS AND BOATING

Recent trends show a rapidly increasing participation in water recreation activities for over 45 million people using pleasure boats. Not all are campers too, but Americans everywhere are enjoying swimming, water skiing, skin diving, fishing, canoeing, and sailing. Hundreds of thousands are enjoying camp cruising in boats. Many watch waterfowl and study aquatic life. With increased leisure time, over 10,000,000 recreational boats were in use in a recent year. The trend is on the increase. Many of these boats were used on inland waters such as streams, lakes, rivers, or on bays near the sea.

But there is plenty of cruising water in smaller rivers, lakes, streams, and reservoirs, too, where boating is possible close to home. One can cruise and explore for hundreds of miles on over 56 large rivers in North America and along protected stretches of the Gulf of Mexico, the Great Lakes shorelines, and both the Atlantic and Pacific seaboards.

Even in water sports you don't have to go it alone. Clubs devoted to water skiing, skin diving and Scuba diving (self-contained underwater breathing apparatus) flourish everywhere. Locate one nearby, and you'll get an enthusiastic welcome from members eager to enlarge interest in their sport. If you wish, you can soon probe confidently into an amazing new world below the water, or skim across its surface in the soaring, spine-tingling excitement of water skiing or aquaplaning.

Boating can become the most satisfying sport you've ever tried, and the more you learn about it, the better you will like it. What's the boating season? You can depend on good boating weather at least six months of the year wherever you live. In many parts of the country the season lasts the year around.

Skin diving is great; beginners usually start with a face-mask, snorkel-tube, and flippers. You skim along peering into a wondrous underwater world. To explore deeper and stay down longer, you'll want a portable oxygen tank and other accessories.

Today, even in a small boat, you can wander all weekend or

138

longer, self-sustained with lightweight camping equipment, or by stopping at "boatels."

What does boating cost? The typical family taking up boating these days spends from $1,200 to $2,000, or about the price of a good used car. Here's what you get new for that amount: A 14 to 17-foot boat, a 40-horsepower motor, and a trailer, plus accessories. Used equipment costs half to two-thirds as much. Or, if you want luxury, you can get a cabin cruiser that sleeps four—with motor, trailer, and accessories—for about the same cost as a new car.

With ignition key starting, automatic choke, full gear shift, and dashboard steering wheel, today's outboard motorboat is as easy to drive as a car. With a little practice you can acquire the fundamentals of boat operation even more quickly than those of an automobile. Your dealer can see to it that you get proper beginning instructions.

You'll find that boating pleasure increases as you learn to operate your craft like a seasoned skipper. Contact one of the hundreds of outboard boating clubs across the country. Teaching newcomers the right procedures is one of their main objectives. The U.S. Coast Guard Auxiliary, the U.S. Power Squadrons, the Red Cross, and even some community high schools give instruction in safe boat handling. Any yacht club, dealer, or your nearest U.S. Coast Guard unit will gladly tell you where to take courses or get more information about them.

Coupled with the astounding growth in America's small boat industry, waterways have become more crowded; boating—increasingly subject to law and regulation. In 1958, a new and more comprehensive Federal Boating Act became effective. Most of the states had already made provision for controlling boating. There are additional policies to be observed when boating in the waters of most of our state and Federal parks and forests.

A requirement to register the small boat and receive an identifying number is now established by law, dependent on size or power of boat. Motors, too, are subject to licensing in many locales. Stiff fines are now levied for reckless or negligent boat operation.

But boating is fun! Especially if it is linked with a camping vacation near good waterways! To get the most through such enjoyable recreation activities review the tips in the accompanying Check Lists.

Before making any financial commitment, take advantage of every chance to try out as many different boats and boat-motor-trailer combinations as possible through use of those owned by your friends or through the rental of used boats. These trials should include trailering, launching, and recovery of the boats if at all possible. Trials of this kind tone down a bit of the glamour and help you analyze your boating objectives on a brass-tacks basis. As a bonus, they will also help you get acquainted with the various special laws and regulations applicable to towing a boat and trailer behind your car, and those which govern boat operation in the waters you expect to frequent the most.

Then, to help sort out your requirements and the various considerations methodically, think over each of the following Check List questions.

PLEASURE BOAT BUYER'S CHECK LIST

(1) How many people will you want your boat to accommodate normally?

(2) Do you definitely plan any living aboard—as on extended cruises—or will your boating involve mostly such casual use as fishing, water skiing, beach picnics, etc.?

(3) Do your plans for boat cruising contemplate sleeping ashore or aboard the boat each night? In case of the latter, how many persons will you want your boat to accommodate?

(4) How much interior storage space will you need for gear, normal and emergency equipment, provisions, and fuel?

(5) Will you boat mostly on sheltered waters or on exposed waters? (You will want a dry-running boat for exposed waters.)

(6) Where and how will you store your boat (and trailer) during the winter? Consider not only space but also ease in moving and handling the boat and trailer.

(7) Apart from the initial price of the boat, have you considered the following:

   a. The cost of any special fittings or equipment required by law or regulation. (This should include the cost of safety equipment.)

   b. Costs such as sales tax, if any.

   c. The expense of adequate insurance against loss or damage of the boat, motor, and trailer together with liability protection for your boat operation.

   d. Trailer hitches, hitch installations, light connections, brake connections (if needed), and possibly overload springs for your car.

   e. Fuel costs to include cost of extra fuel tank, if desired.

   f. Boat taxes (peculiar to various areas; some may relate to the size of the boat or the motor, or to both).

   g. Mooring and launch expenses (these might involve monthly or seasonal rates, the cost of any special mooring equipment you may want to own yourself, and perhaps even the cost of ferry trips to go back and forth to a desirable mooring location).

    h. Marina tie-up costs, if to be used regularly.

BOAT MOTORS—BUYER'S CHECK LIST

(1) Will it be dependable? Don't buy a motor loaded with novelty gadgets that may require constant adjustment. The simpler the motor, the better.

(2) How does it start? Manually by pulling a cord or electrically by turning a key? Either works well but, obviously, key switch starting is the more convenient system.

(3) How does it shift? Can you shift gears easily and conveniently—even from the front of the boat? Does it have a neutral?

(4) How does it steer? Is it balanced so that it turns smoothly? What about wheel steering?

(5) Is it quiet? If the mounting, the gear system, and motor cover are solid and sound, the motor should purr like an electric fan.

(6) Is it solidly built? Certainly, you want sound construction and lasting strength in an outboard motor—even if it means a little more weight.

(7) How does it run? Ask about two particular points—revolutions per minute and piston displacement. The fewer RPM's a motor runs to deliver rated horsepower, the less wear and longer life it will have. And the larger the piston displacement, the fewer RPM will be.

(8) Is it corrosion-proof? Stainless steel, plastic, special paints baked on. Such materials extend the motor's life and new appearance.

(9) Is it well designed? You want clean, trim, functional design—simplicity that stays in style—low lines that blend with your boat, and colors to complement it.

(10) What about generators? With certain motors and boats (those equipped with running lights, for example) you will want a generator with your motor, either DC or the latest alternator type. Ask if they will charge your battery while idling—and if any models have built-in generators.

(11) If you expect to tow skiers, does it have adequate horsepower?

BOAT TRAILERING CHECK LIST

(1) Make sure that your car insurance is valid. Check and see if you are covered while towing a trailer. It pays to have your boat insured respecting fire, theft, and public liability. If the policy on your car is a broad form it may cover your boat trailer, too.

(2) Check the vehicle code of your own state and those of any you may be traveling through; special permits may be needed.

(3) Be sure that your boat trailer is in good condition and that your trailer fits your boat. The craft should be supported in at least three places. If you transport your outboard motor on the boat, be sure that it has a strong enough transom support.

(4) A good strong frame hitch is preferable to a bumper hitch.

(5) Use safety chains; they are required by law.

(6) Stop and check trailer hitch and tie-downs shortly after you first get underway. Check them at all stops.

(7) When towing a trailer, know the applicable speed limit; observe it and drive at a lower speed than you would without a trailer. Always remember that it takes more room and time to pass another vehicle. In passing, be sure that you can pass the vehicle overtaken before it reaches a turn or curve.

(8) Don't forget that it takes more room to park a car and boat trailer, so look ahead for a good spot where there is room for both.

(9) Don't forget to loosen the tie-downs, if appropriate, when the outfit is parked overnight. Motors should be chained and padlocked to prevent theft.

(10) Check all tires and the rest of the outfit before leaving parking area in the morning. You might discover a slow tire leak that could otherwise cause you trouble later in the day.

LAUNCHING CHECK LIST

(1) If you plan to cruise in distant and unfamiliar waters, be sure to check ahead of time on available launching sites and facilities.

(2) It is usually difficult and sometimes impossible to launch your craft from a natural or unimproved site. If you have no other choice, look for a spot where the shore slopes gradually. The water, no doubt, will also be rather shallow at a point of this type.

(3) Be sure the site is hard enough to enable you to have proper traction.

(4) Beware of loose gravel, sand, mud and soft spots. Wet grass will cause wheels to skid and spin. Avoid steep shores when possible.

(5) Better traction can be obtained by deflating your rear tires from 20 to 25%. Be careful not to spin wheels so that the tire tube valve is pulled inside the casing or the valve is torn off in the case of tubeless tires. Be sure to re-inflate the tires as soon as you return to firm ground. Sometimes skid chains are necessary to get you free of a difficult situation; and a good tire gauge will come in handy.

(6) When backing your boat trailer into water, back in at right angles to the shoreline. If you want the rear of the trailer to go left, be sure to turn the car wheel to the right. However, this type of maneuver should be mastered long before you start out on a trailer trip. If you haven't had sufficient experience of this sort you can get into some rugged situations on a stream or lake shore where there are trees, stumps, rocks, and other obstructions to hang you up. This is the time a good "come-along" jack pays for itself many times over.

(7) Before backing your trailer into the water, be sure the boat and trailer are ready for the launch. Disconnect the electrical lines which run from the car to the rear trailer lights. Your trailer tail lights may ship water when you back the rig in. Unless you keep an eye out for this problem, a short-circuit and blown fuse could result thus leaving you with no trailer lights at dusk when you want to start for home.

(8) Protect your trailer license plate before launching. On some trailers, the only place for mounting the plate is located so low that it causes the plate to hit the ground or water during launching. The plate might get

knocked loose, possibly lost, though in most cases it merely gets bent or torn, if too low. To avoid this, some owners use the automobile dealer quick-detachable license plate bolts. With these, it is no task at all to protect the plate by removing it before launching.

BOAT OPERATOR'S CHECK LIST

(1) Know your boat and its limitations.

(2) Use the right motor for your boat; reduce speed in rough going.

(3) Know your fuel tank capacity; remember your cruising radius.

(4) Don't overload.

(5) Maintain a properly balanced boat; adjust load accordingly.

(6) Maintain a low center of gravity with both passengers and load.

(7) Know the official storm signals; boat accordingly.

(8) Angle your boat towards high waves; reduce speed.

(9) Avoid unnecessarily fast, sharp turns.

(10) Know and respect hazards associated with gasoline and fueling.

(11) Always maintain an alert lookout.

(12) Watch for swimmers; often they are hard to see.

(13) Watch your wake; pass slowly through anchorages and by other boats.

(14) Have fire-fighting and lifesaving equipment always ready to use.

(15) Obey Rules of the Road, boating laws, and local regulations.

(16) Equip children with life preservers; "all hands" wear them under hazardous conditions.

(17) Practice good housekeeping; it affects safety aboard a boat.

(18) Prevent falls; they are the greatest cause of injury afloat as well as ashore.

(19) Buoys: Know their meanings and how to pass them; never moor to one.

(20) Plan ahead on emergency routines; fire, fog, man overboard, bad leak, motor breakdown, storm, collision, loss of fuel, etc.

(21) Anchor and anchor cable: Maintain for use in length and size suitable for your waters.

(22) Maintain harness on any pets aboard; carry a boat hook—it has a thousand uses.

(23) Learn distress and other marine signals.

(24) Carry the proper charts and a magnetic compass.

(25) Maintain electrical equipment and wiring in good condition; maintain ample ventilation around batteries, fuel and engine compartments.

(26) Carry or instruct at least one other person aboard in serving as an emergency co-pilot.

(27) Review your responsibilities as a boat owner periodically. Each spring, or before resuming boating after a long layoff, go over your obligations. Consider also the following topics:

(a) *Observe Specifications.* Don't regard the number of seats in a boat as an infallible guide to the number of passengers it can safely carry. Check the manufacturer's name plate for specifications. If you follow the specifications concerning maximum power motor to be used and maximum passenger load to be carried your boat will handle well and safely. In some states, failure to follow the specifications could lead to arrest for violation of boating laws.

(b) *Loading.* Heavy objects should never be dropped or tossed into a boat. To do so could cause damage to the hull or to fastenings. Adults can usually do a better job handling the anchor than children.

(c) *Before Starting Motor:* Unless you are very familiar with the area, delay starting your motor until the boat has been paddled out to water free from the likelihood of underwater snags, rocks, or ledges. It almost goes without saying that everyone should be seated before starting the motor.

(d) *Cruising New Water:* Cruise at less than your average speed until you have become familiar with new water. By so doing you are less likely to have accidents and less likely to damage your motor if unexpected underwater obstructions are encountered.

(e) *Storms:* Head for home before the waves get too high! If storm conditions come about too suddenly to permit this, head for the nearest shore; have all occupants sit on the bottom of the boat (to lower the center of gravity). Don't gamble that you may be able to get all the way back to camp. It is always much better to risk some delay in returning to camp and be off the water than to risk capsizing; eventually the sudden storm may leave as abruptly as it arrived.

(f) *Upsets:* A capsized boat will support quite a few persons, even if it is nearly underwater. Passengers should try to stay with the boat. Resourceful boatmen have succeeded in righting a capsized boat or canoe and resumed their travel many times. If the boat can be righted, much of the water can be expelled from its interior by rocking the boat from side to side. Eventually enough water will be out so that passengers may climb back in—one at a time. In any case, guard against panic—cooperation and resourcefulness are required for survival.

(Also see Check List—Water Skiing)

WHERE TO GET INFORMATION USEFUL IN BOATING

RECREATIONAL BOATING GUIDE CG-340. This booklet should be in the hands of all boat owners. It is sold by the Superintendent of Documents, USGPO, Washington 25, D.C. for 40¢. It tells the boatman many important things including what he should know about equipment required, laws and regulations applicable to boats and boating, and other topics germane to recreational boating.

TIDE TABLES, CURRENT TABLES AND CHARTS. Write the U.S. Coast & Geodetic Survey, Washington 25, D. C. for information relative the wide variety of charts and tables available.

LIGHT LISTS. These are published by the U.S. Coast Guard and sold by the Superintendent of Documents. They describe lighted aids to navigation, radio beacons, fog signals, unlighted buoys, and day marks.

NOTICES TO MARINERS. This is a free weekly pamphlet published jointly by the U.S. Hydrographic Office and the U.S. Coast Guard. The Notices are issued so that nautical charts can be kept up to date. The Notices, incidentally, periodically give the names of agents authorized to sell various official charts, tables, and publications.

Local Notices, of interest primarily within the locale of each Coast Guard District, are issued and available from the individual U.S.C.G. District Offices.

SWIMMING—A GENERAL CHECK LIST

(1) Never swim alone. Swim with friends and use the "buddy" system.

(2) Swim in a safe locale only, away from sail and motor boat lanes.

(3) Do not swim immediately after eating.

(4) Never dive until you have established that the water is sufficiently deep and that the bottom is free of objects which might cause injuries.

(5) Don't become a victim of overconfidence; if you swim out too far, rest, tread water, or float on your back until help arrives.

(6) *Flotation devices or water toys:* Be careful using inflatable water toys; you may start out in shallow water but be carried out over your head and the float might deflate.

(7) *Currents:* Never buck a current. Swimmers move at less than 3 mph, currents, between 4 and 6 mph. When currents move directly outward from shore, a swimmer caught in the current should save his strength by drifting with the current and by swimming diagonally across it.

(8) *Undertow:* There is a difference between an undertow and a current. The undertow's pull is short and it runs deeper as it goes outwards. A swimmer caught in an undertow should turn and go with it, taking a diagonal course to the surface.

SWIMMING FROM BOAT—CHECK LIST

(1) Observe the rules outlined in the General Swimming Check List. Observe the following in addition.

(2) Select a suitable area free from other boat traffic.

(3) Anchor the boat.

(4) Make sure the motor is off.

(5) Tilt motor, if practicable, so that prop is up out of the water.

(6) Put out a line with flotation equipment within reach of swimmers.

(7) Provide a boarding line or ladder in a safe location, preferably near the stern to minimize tilting the boat.

(8) Swimmers should slide into the water from the boat instead of diving in.

(9) Swimmers should board boat near its stern.

(10) With several members in the party, one person should always be in the boat as an observer. Take turns swimming, if necessary.

(11) Stay near your boat when swimming; remember, swimmers are often difficult to see from other boats when the water is choppy or when there is surface glare.

(12) Confine after-sunset swimming to well-lighted areas.

BOAT OPERATOR'S WATER SKIING CHECK LIST*

(1) Know and conform to your State laws governing boating and skiing.

(2) Always operate in a safe area, free from shallow rocks or undesirable obstructions.

(3) Before towing a skier trim your boat with forward ballast, if necessary, to hold the bow down enough to guarantee yourself clear forward vision. As respects safety, the skier is entirely dependent upon your forward vision, not his.

(4) As a general rule you must carry another person in the cockpit of the boat to act as a ski observer while you operate the boat. Your attention should be concentrated on steering, with eyes front. The installation and use of a wide-angle, rear-view mirror allows the boat operator to check his skier occasionally without turning his head. It is a convenience and contributes to safe operation but, depending on law, may not necessarily substitute for the requirement of having a full-time observer aboard.

(5) Make sure the skier wears proper flotation equipment.

(6) Always remember you can slow down far quicker than your skier.

(7) When terminating a skier's run, slow down gradually before cutting the motor to guard against the hazard of the skier being driven against the boat by momentum.

(8) Be especially watchful for swimmers and other hazards when maneuvering the skier in for release to the beach. If the skier wants a sweeping drop to the beach, you must be both skilled and careful. First, your skier must have a clearly safe approach path. Secondly, you don't want to run your prop aground—especially on the turn. Thirdly, you need plenty of room to maneuver for your turn—free of worry about possible swimmers, low cables, floats, etc. Never practice such maneuvers near congested shore areas or without a careful preliminary safety inspection of the ski area.

(9) Avoid towing skiers in heavily traveled or restricted waters such as narrow winding channels or in areas containing docks, floats, and buoys.

(10) When your skier tumbles, approach him from the lee side.

(11) Stop your motor before taking a skier aboard; don't just shift to neutral.

(12) In bringing a skier aboard, avoid sharply unbalancing your boat. In smaller craft it is best to bring the skier aboard at the stern.

(13) Never assume a course which will find your skier running over shallow water at high speeds. A tumble, in such an instance, could be quite hazardous.

(14) Terminate the water skiing activity well before twilight hours when the hazards due to poor visibility increase.

---

* Portions through courtesy Safety Dep't., Allstate Insurance Companies, Sacramento, Calif.

(15) Inspect tow-lines and fastenings regularly; replace worn or strained equipment well before its use becomes clearly unsafe.

(16) Agree on and use a standard set of signals for communications between boat and skier. (Note accompanying signals recommended by the American Water Ski Association.)

TURN   WHIP OFF   FASTER   SLOWER

SPEED O.K.   BACK TO DOCK   CUT MOTOR   STOP

SCUBA DIVING CHECK LIST*

(1) Never dive alone.
(2) Be skilled in distance swimming.
(3) Be able to swim underwater a minimum of 75 feet.
(4) Be able to surface dive.
(5) Be able to tow a water accident victim.
(6) Be able to stay afloat with minimum of trouble.
(7) Know first-aid and artificial respiration.
(8) Remember never to surface too quickly.
(9) Never use alcohol beverages or overeat before diving.
(10) Use good equipment.
(11) Learn to use your equipment properly.
(12) Examine your equipment before each dive.
(13) Keep your equipment in good condition.
(14) Always use good air (compressed air).
(15) Never dive with a cold or sinus condition.
(16) Always descend slowly.
(17) Continue to exhale while ascending.
(18) Always have a flotation device with or near you.
(19) Avoid deep dives.
(20) Use quick release for weights.
(21) Remain calm.

* Excerpts from a report on Skin and Scuba Diving, Water Safety Service, American National Red Cross.

(22) Develop sound emergency procedures.
(23) Be in good physical and mental condition.
(24) Learn all you can about the area in which you plan to dive.
(25) Know and respect your limitations.
(26) Avoid exhaustion.
(27) Avoid filling tanks beyond rated pressure.
(28) Avoid diving in rough water.
(29) Avoid dropping air tanks.
(30) Avoid diving at night.

Most accidents to Scuba divers are caused by failure to dive with a buddy and to fully understand the operations and limitations of the equipment they are using. Most accidents can be prevented if the individual observes the generally accepted practices of safe watermanship and, in addition, learns to know and use proper equipment.*

SKIN DIVING CHECK LIST

(1) Be a better than an average swimmer.
(2) Always wear or have surface flotation gear.
(3) Treat spear guns as dangerous weapons.
(4) Avoid the combination of surf and rocks.
(5) Practice self-control.
(6) Be in good physical condition.
(7) Use good equipment.
(8) Learn how to use your equipment.
(9) Avoid overeating or use of carbonated liquids before diving.
(10) Know and respect your limitations.
(11) Know and respect the condition of the area in which you are diving.
(12) Know the location of your partner at all times.
(13) Think—don't take chances.
(14) Use a quick release belt if weights are used.
(15) Learn how to give artificial respiration.
(16) Leave the water when cut or bleeding.
(17) Stay away from piers or pilings.
(18) Stay close to boat on surface.
(19) Always carry a sheathed knife.
(20) Learn first-aid, especially artificial respiration.
(21) Be alert for moving objects under water.
(22) Give dangerous fish a wide berth unless experienced and well equipped.
(23) Avoid diving into the water while wearing a mask.
(24) Avoid a deep dive—30 feet should be deep enough.
(25) Stay away from riptides.
(26) Stay up-current from boat.
(27) Look up as you surface from a dive.
(28) Never enter a hole unless you know you can get out.

The major type of accidents in this sport results from diving alone!* Other factors, such as over-confidence, carelessness, overexertion, lack of

---

* Excerpts from a report on Skin and Scuba Diving, Water Safety Service, American National Red Cross.

good safety practices, showing off, horseplay, and panic are also high on the list of reasons why people get into trouble skin diving.

BOAT CRUISE CAMPING CHECK LIST—TWO PERSONS

Axe, single-bit (1)
Air-sea rescue orange dye (1)
Air mattress (2)
Air pillow (2)
Air pump (1)
Anchor, light & heavy (2)
Bags, sleeping (2)
Ball twine, heavy (1)
Bathing suit (2)
Barometer (1)
Bar soap and detergents (1)
Bilge-pump (1)
Binoculars (1)
Blankets, optional (4)
Boat hook (1)
Bottle and can opener (1)
Box, ice 25 lbs. cap. (1)
Box, food, watertight (1)
Boat fuel, oil and gasoline
Bucket, plastic with line (1)
Bug bomb, shore use (1)
Camera, filters, film (1)
Canteen, 1 gal. cap. (1)
Chairs, folding aluminum (2)
Canvas boat top and curtains, set (1)
Charts, navigation, area (1)
Compass, marine type (1)
Compass, w/sight line, shore (1)
Cook kit, nesting type 4-man (1)
Camp stove, LP canned gas, opt. (1)
Camp stove, two-burner, alcohol (1)
Camp grill, wire (1)
Camp lantern LP gas, shore use (1)
Dish and bath towels (2)
Dishpan (1)
Dividers, navigation type (1)
Duffel bags, canvas (2)
Emergency USCG rations (2)
Emergency hull repair kit (1)
Extra clothes, socks, etc., (2)
Flashlight, bulbs, batteries (2)

First-aid kit, personal medicines (1)
Flares, red signal (Very pistol) (6)
Food to last trip
Food locker, watertight (1)
Fire extinguisher, dry chemical (1)
Fire extinguisher, Co'2 (1)
Fishing gear and license (2)
Folding table (1)
Firearms and license, optional (2)
Matches, waterproofed, boxes (2)
Match-safe, waterproof (2)
Navigation directional finder (1)
Paddle (1)
Paper towels, rolls (1)
Paper napkins, pkgs. (1)
Portable radio (1)
Portable TV, optional (1)
Oars (2)
Rubber slicker or poncho (2)
Sea anchor, canvas type (1)
Shovel, camping (1)
Signal mirror, steel (1)
Signal flags, optional, set (1)
Rope, extra docking and spring-lines
Spare line, ¾ inch Manila (100 ft.)
Spare motor parts, shear-pins, plugs
Sponges, detergents, soaps, broom, etc.
Sun glasses and case (2)
Tableware, knives, forks and spoons (4)
Tent for shore camping (1)
Tent fly, optional (1)
Toilet tissue, rolls (1)
Tool kit, outboard motor
Water jug, 1 gal. cap. thermos (1)
Water can, 10 gal. cap. (1)
Waterproof sea chest for identification papers, personal papers and gear (1)
Very Signal Pistol (1)

BALKY OUTBOARD MOTOR CHECK LIST

Hard Starting or Misses
   (1) Out of gas; fuel line clogged or line closed.
   (2) Water or foreign substance in fuel.
   (3) Cold motor not choked sufficiently or warm motor flooded.
   (4) Gas cap air vent plugged or not opened enough.
   (5) Wrong fuel mixture. Too much oil in the mix. Smokes considerably.
   (6) Loose or broken spark plug lead.

(7) Dirty or fouled spark plugs. Outer spark plugs cracked or dirty.

(8) Breaker points need cleaning or gap reset.

Motor Idling Roughly

(1) Wrong spark plug type, probably need a hotter plug.

(2) Idle adjustment of carburetor needs attention and resetting.

(3) Wrong transom, motor may set in water too deeply, or not deep enough.

(4) Intake valve gasket may leak or has "blown."

Power Loss

(1) Wrong fuel mixture. Too little oil or too much oil.

(2) Screens clogged in fuel line.

(3) Spark plug too hot for that particular type of motor.

(4) Wrong carburetor adjustment. Mixture may be too rich or too lean.

(5) If the compression is weak, it may be due to blown gaskets, sticking piston rings or scored cylinder walls.

If Motor Knocks

(1) The spark may be advanced too far.

(2) Cylinders may be carbonized.

(3) Loose connecting rod, piston and cylinders worn, bearings bad.

(4) Pre-ignition due to motor overheating.

Vibration is Excessive

(1) Check transom bracket clamps, they may be loose.

(2) Swivel brackets may be loose.

(3) Carburetor may be adjusted too rich.

(4) Propeller may be bent or fouled.

(5) Steering gear tension too loose.

Motor Overheats

(1) Water line leaks, not enough water getting through. Pump inlet clogged.

(2) The pump itself may be clogged or defective.

(3) Exhaust gasket "blown."

(4) Motor may not be deep enough in water.

Motor Doesn't Drive Boat Or Drives It Only Slowly

(1) Motor not deep enough in water and causing cavitation.

(2) Propeller may be bent.

(3) Obstruction may be dragging; weeds, sea-weed or pulp may be causing cavitation.

The Propeller Doesn't Turn

(1) The shear-pin is broken.

(2) The propeller may be broken, or maybe even the propeller drive shaft.

Motor "Freezes"

(1) Too little oil in fuel mixture.

(2) No lubricant in gear housing.

(3) Cylinder walls are rusted.

(4) Propeller is bent or possibly the shaft.

(5) The propeller shaft could be badly fouled.

(6) Motor may have not been properly drained and low temperature caused it to freeze up.

THEFT-PREVENTION CHECK LIST—BOAT AND MOTOR

(1) On most outboard motors, holes will be found in the handles of the clamp-screws used in securing the motor to the boat. Tighten the transom clamps so that both handles point downward. A regular bicycle lock can then be passed through the holes making it impossible to remove the motor without disturbing the lock. Special locks are available for motors not having holes in their clamp handles.

(2) A boat stored outside and left unattended on a trailer, or a small camping or utility trailer is "easy picking" for a thief. All he need do is hitch the trailer to a car and drive off. If you store a trailer outside, it's a good idea to lock it in some manner. A heavy chain can be used to secure the trailer to some stationary object such as a strong post or tree. Or, you can chain one wheel of the trailer to the axle or to some other object to make it more difficult for the thief.

(3) If you keep your boat in the water, it's a good idea to keep the area lighted. Most thieves are bold under cover of darkness. Insurance won't prevent theft, but it will make your loss less serious if it should occur. It's only good sense to have your rig and other equipment insured for current value at all times.

(4) When purchasing a used outboard, make sure that the Bill of Sale (which should be kept) *includes both model and serial numbers* of the motor. To establish a record of ownership, a new motor should be registered with the manufacturer at the time of purchase. Be sure to keep a record of all serial numbers of all of your equipment so that on recovery you can identify it and prove ownership. Also mark your equipment with some extra identification marks in a secret place to further aid identification. Some thieves alter numbers and repaint their ill-gotten gains, making identification more difficult.

(5) If your equipment is stolen, report the theft to local law enforcement officers and to your insurance carrier immediately.

CANOEING

Canoe camping, or even a float trip in a life raft or small, portable boat can be a wonderful experience and an enjoyable one if you will plan and map the route out beforehand. Much more can be carried on a weekend trip in a canoe than can be carried on a back-pack trip; however, if you plan on going into a wilderness area for a week or more, you will have to cut down on weight as much as possible since the canoe and all supplies and equipment may have to be "portaged" overland to other water sources.

PHYSICAL CONDITION

As for back-packing, you must be in good physical condition for canoe camping, since you will not only be relaying over portages but will be using a new set of muscles while paddling

(Drawing by Luis M. Henderson)

the canoe. So it pays to be in tip-top shape because you will be remote from quick medical aid.

One of the country's most outstanding canoeists, Ben Ferrier, and three companions made a record canoe trip of 2700 miles from Athabaska Landing in Canada, over the Arctic Circle to Fort Yukon in the state of Alaska. These men were in excellent physical condition, as well as good swimmers, and were able to overcome the many obstacles they encountered en route.

There are many hundreds of streams and lakes that one can canoe and camp along that are not as rugged as the above mentioned trek, if one will first check and inquire about the area in which he is interested.

(Drawing by Luis M. Henderson)

Canoes on inland waters where power boats and other small craft are navigating at night should exhibit a white light. An electric lantern or flashlight of sufficient power may suffice.

EQUIPMENT

More canoemen are now using outboard motors for power these days, for one can travel faster and farther under gas power even though at times he may have the added weight of gasoline and motor to portage. The Makah and Quillayute Indians of the Olympic Peninsula have been using outboard motors on their sea-going fishing canoes for years, and many people have been startled while fishing on one of Washington's coastal streams by seeing an Indian canoe coming around the bend at a good twelve knots. In Alaska, outboard motors are used on canoes to freight supplies up rivers that other types of craft cannot negotiate.

Like any other type of camping, one should know what type of equipment and supplies to take along. Of course, for a short trip one may have a wider range of food to select from; however, for the extended trip, the dry or concentrated, dehydrated type is best since it is light, less bulky, and very nutritious. Be sure to have a good compass and the best map of the region that can be secured, an extra paddle, the know-how to propel a canoe and to load it and carry it, and, of course, how to repair it if damaged on the trip.

If the canoe doesn't have duckboards in the bottom to keep the load clear of the bilge water, you can use small branches to help raise the load off the bottom where water has collected from paddle drip or rough seas.

The canoe load should be packed in waterproof duffel bags and not heavier than a man can pack comfortably on a packboard. Put heavy loads on the bottom for ballast and balance. The load should be securely lashed down with the tent on top and a canvas tarpaulin over all to keep it dry. Be sure everything is secured and lashed in case the canoe should capsize in rough water. This way you would be able to salvage the canoe and its contents on some sand bar or shore downstream; otherwise, you might find yourself in a survival situation miles from supplies and help.

When it is not windy, cargo should be stowed so that the bow will ride slightly high. Cargo can be stowed to balance

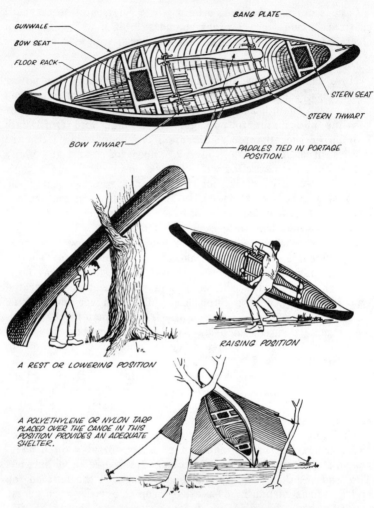

GUNWALE

BOW SEAT

FLOOR RACK

BANG PLATE

STERN SEAT

STERN THWART

BOW THWART

PADDLES TIED IN PORTAGE POSITION.

A REST OR LOWERING POSITION

RAISING POSITION

A POLYETHYLENE OR NYLON TARP PLACED OVER THE CANOE IN THIS POSITION PROVIDES AN ADEQUATE SHELTER.

CANOE TIPS showing how to raise or lower a canoe, how to improvise canoe shelter, and canoe nomenclature.

the craft and even out differences in the weights of occupants. If there is only one occupant, the canoe should be trimmed to remain slightly bow-high regardless of the position the canoeist may choose to paddle from. But when it is windy, trim the load so the bow is low and less exposed to the wind. Otherwise it would be difficult to keep the canoe on course. A low bow is also desirable when running with surf or in white water (rapids).

Be sure to take a packboard for each person, and only two or three persons to a canoe. There are several types of canoes, such as aluminum, plastic, glass, and canvas. Canoes are quite sensitive to wind. It follows that canoes with high sides and ends are more affected by wind than those having low sides and low ends. This is a good thing to keep in mind when choosing one for your particular uses. A 16 or 17-foot aluminum canoe is more easily portaged than heavier types. For larger bodies of water, a heavier canoe is needed. An 18-foot canoe weighing about 80 pounds is about the minimum size for rough going. All types should have open gunwales so they may be drained easily. One can travel faster and more safely, with less fatigue, by kneeling on floor pads rather than by sitting up to paddle. The paddle should be a minimum of six inches wide and should come to about the tip of your nose while standing. A lightweight spruce paddle is right for smooth water, but one made from hard wood is best for rough water.

PADDLING

If there are two of you in the canoe, the bowman sets the pace which should have a smooth stroke of about 30 to 34 strokes per minute. With only one person in the canoe, the bow sometimes has to be weighted so that it is slightly lower than the stern when running into a stiff breeze, to keep it from yawing from side to side.

Paddling on the local mill pond or at a summer camp does not qualify you to take a wilderness canoe cruise on your own or with an equally inexperienced companion. First, go with a competent canoeist or a professional guide. Observe what he does and follow his advice. In time you will have enough experience to take charge yourself.

Even if you have had a lot of experience in paddling a canoe in local waters, when you take a wilderness trip by canoe, you can copy with profit the Indian's method of paddling. His stroke looks awkward, but the canoe moves with remarkable speed.

BOW STROKE

J-STROKE

SWEEP

PUSH-OVER

DRAW

BACKWATER

CANOE STROKES.

Note on the next page the picture of paddling Indian fashion. Instead of the normal stroke when paddling on the right-hand side from the stern, in which the left arm pushes and the right arm pulls the paddle without the paddle touching the canoe, the Indian rests his paddle shaft against the gunwale. He holds his left arm stiff and uses the weight of his body to drive the paddle blade back through the water. His right hand holds the shaft in position. As he pushes the blade backward, the Indian turns the paddle butt in his left hand in a counterclockwise direction, making the blade turn outward as it is driven back. This keeps the canoe on its course instead of heading to the left. The paddle is held so that the butt is always in front of the paddler, where he can bear his weight against it, the gunwale acting as a fulcrum for the paddle.

(Drawing by Luis M. Henderson)

INDIAN METHOD OF PADDLING.

At the completion of the paddle stroke the Indian's body is leaning well forward and he then swings erect without effort. At the same time as he raises the paddle he twists the paddle butt with his left hand so that the blade is ready for the next stroke. This method of paddling cannot be called graceful but it takes less effort and is much faster than the long push-and-pull stroke of the average canoeist. The Indian method tends to wear down both the gunwale and the paddle shaft but it does make for speed.

CANOES—HIGHLY MOBILE

CANOE CARRYING. A heavy-duty ski rack or the standard car-top carrying bars are suitable as the supporting framework for carrying your craft on a car. The canoe should be anchored at both ends. Extend a line from the bow end to the radiator grill or front bumper. This line is important and should be checked for tightness just before you drive away because it prevents air pressure and wind from causing the canoe to slide backwards when the car is moving. But also tie a line from the stern to the rear bumper. This helps prevent the canoe from rocking when your car goes over sharp bumps or when you are forced to make a sudden stop. At least one tension-strap should extend down from each side of the canoe to the rain gutters of the car as "tie-downs." If you do not own car-top carrying equipment, two old tire carcasses may be used on the car roof with the canoe tied securely as described above.

(Drawing by Luis M. Henderson)

HOW TO CARRY A CANOE.

In portaging, a single-man carry is easier than a two-man carry. This leaves the other member of the party free to pack the duffel. One person can pack a moderately light 18-foot canoe by means of a center thwart carry. If carrying yoke pads are installed on the thwart, the carrying will be reasonably comfortable and the bearer will have better control in negotiating steep ground or when carrying during windy weather.

LANDING AND EMBARKING. Improper boarding or disembarking from a canoe can inflict severe damage to it if the proper technique isn't used. The canoe should be carried to the water by two persons holding the gunwales and facing each other amidships on either side of the craft. It is launched by sliding the stern into the water using the hand-over-hand motion along the gunwales, and the bow then is lowered gently to the water's edge. The bow man keeps the canoe in an upright position between his knees; the stern man (after he has washed the sand and gravel from his feet), steps into the stern, sliding his hands along the gunwales for balance, and assumes his paddling position. The bow man then steps in amidship until the craft floats and can be moved off shore, he then shifts to his paddling position forward towards the bow.

Debarking may be accomplished by coming along side a dock, rock, or broadside to the shore or landing place. If the water is too shallow, the landing can be made at right angles to the shore. When the bow man steps out, he should hold the craft until the stern man is out. Never try to pull the canoe up on shore, first, as is often done; to do so could ruin the bottom.

PORTAGING. Portaging can be fun or, again, hard work; it will depend on the kind of an outfit you have made up for the trip, type of pack and canoe, and the amount of equipment you plan on taking along. Portages vary from a few yards around some obstruction to several miles in length. In the far north, portages are marked by the number of days it takes for the average traveler to negotiate them. A "portage day" is usually an average of ten miles per day. If a portage is marked—say two days—that would mean that you would have to pack everything, including the canoe, for two days overland to the next water. This is not for the tenderfoot, but for the hardy, explorers, trappers and Indians.

Locating portages on large lakes calls for a good compass and an excellent map of the region. Many canoeists use the skyline method by looking and searching for a notch in the hills or through the timber if the terrain is more-or-less flat. The portages are usually at the lower or upper ends of the lake and can be spotted as a notch in the hills. With the exception of very remote northern woods, portages are marked by signs or blazes. If you have to leave part of your dunnage and make two or more trips, be sure to cache it high so that bears and other animal prowlers will not damage or destroy it.

CANOE SAFETY CHECK LIST

(1) Don't be ashamed to don a life jacket in rough weather—it can be your life that you are saving. Buoyant cushions, in contrast, are hard to hang on to and could slip away when most needed in an emergency situation.

(2) Be sure that all members can swim, and that they understand mouth-to-mouth resuscitation (see chapter 24) since more oxygen can be forced into a drowning person's lungs by this method.

(3) Don't forget the canoe repair kit—a small roll of balloon silk and a can of marine glue for canvas canoes—aluminum solder for aluminum canoes.

(4) Be sure to notify several people or officials where you are going and when you expect to return.

(5) Stick to the route you planned. If you take a different route and run into trouble or have an accident, the search party would be looking for you in the wrong area.

(6) Make up several bundles of waterproofed matches and scatter them among your packs.

(7) Be sure to wear footgear that will not injure the canoe bottom. Hobnailed and other types of rough soles can be injurious to all boat decks and canoe bottoms.

(8) Wrap or pack all cutting tools or sharp articles so they cannot puncture or damage your craft or other equipment.

(9) Boil or use Halazone tablets if you are unsure of your water supply. A few drops of iodine per gallon will also purify water.

(10) Beach your craft well above high water or flood line each night.

(11) Secure paddles or other articles containing traces of salt from perspiration so that they will not be damaged by porcupines or rodents.

(12) In primitive back country never be caught without a good map and compass. You can get turned around where countless islands look like thousands of others and portage trails just seem to disappear if you don't keep a sharp lookout for them. Most portages are marked by signs in the States—in Canada they are sometimes marked by blazes.

(13) Never run a stretch of rapids or white water without knowing exactly what lies ahead. Get out and walk along the fast stretch, check conditions and study out the route before you decide to attempt to run the river. If there is the least doubt that you can't make it safely, line the canoe through, or portage.

(14) It is dangerous to be caught in wind-lashed waters. Make it a rule to get off the water at the first warning of a gale or storm.

(15) Never stand up in a canoe; it is safer to change places by going ashore to do so.

(16) Carry a properly stocked first-aid kit aboard; know how to use it.

(17) Plan your course according to estimated predictable winds; be especially alert when rounding a point.

(18) Be sure your canoe is in proper balance and "set" in the water when it is loaded; don't overload, try to have at least six inches of free-board amidship.

(19) If you get caught in a squall, sit in the bottom of the canoe; if conditions warrant it, lie flat on the bottom in such a position that you can bail. Always keep a bailing can aboard and a large size sponge to remove paddle drip or wave spray.

(20) If the canoe capsizes, hold on to the canoe and kick-swim it to the shore. Canoes are buoyant and will float; it is safer to stay with the craft than to attempt to swim ashore. Learn the proper method of righting an upset canoe; also learn how to reenter a swamped canoe.

FOLBOTING

Some campers like a light boat that can be easily carried on top of the car for trips where boating and fishing opportunities are possible. Apart from canoes, there is a wide variety of small boats suitable for such use; these range from rubber and plastic boats through the smaller prams and up to the larger more de luxe craft. Some are fabric covered and can be folded into two or more packages and carried in the car as luggage.

One of these is the Folbot, an increasingly popular hand-paddled craft. As versatile as a canoe (perhaps even more so), the Folbot in both appearance and handling most closely resembles the kayak of Eskimo usage. But much improved over its more primitive cousins, the Folbot has a staunch reputation for carrying its users safely over amazingly rough waters and through very heavy rapids when managed expertly. Adequate overnight or trip camping gear for two people can be carried under the unusual decking arrangement of the longer Folbot models. Float trips involving overnight camping stays by groups often employ Folbots instead of canoes. One or two persons is the normal Folbot load.

Occupants of a Folbot sit practically on the very bottom of the craft, on low seats with backs which swivel for comfort. This seating arrangement results in a very low center of gravity and greater stability—much more than characteristic of the average boat and most canoes. The occupants of a Folbot ride low in a small, elongated open well, shielded if they like by fabric decking drawn about their waists much in the manner of Eskimos in kayaks.

In such a riding position, the Folbot occupant stretches his legs forward, and can move them enough for comfort unless the cruise is prolonged. Then, even though leg movement is only slightly restricted, the wise Folbot user will periodically step ashore to stretch his legs as opportunity offers. A board can be placed across the cockpit as a seat and as a means of occasional relief for leg muscles; this is fine when anchored as in fishing some quiet cove. But changes do effect the craft's center of gravity, and are best made only in coordination with movements of the other occupants.

The long, low, fully enclosed and pointed bow together

with the almost matching, tapered stern give the light 17½-
foot Folbot characteristics of speed and feathery maneuver-
ability. The craft's silhouette somewhat suggests that of a
stretched out pumpkin seed. In quiet waters, the craft responds to the double-end paddle like a dart. In breakers or
ocean swells, the Folbot is a remarkable performer because
of the special advantages of its design and general con-
figuration.

With average loads, Folbots are usually of shallow draft.
Like many canoes, they can be used in very shallow waters.
They have been safely used in ocean swells. In contrast to
the average canoe, however, the special fabric which forms
the outer shell of the Folbot is much more resilient and rock-
resistant. The Folbot tends to bump off rocks—even sharp
ones—noiselessly, and with no damage. In rough rapids, the
Folbot can be adroitly maneuvered through waters too exciting for most canoeists.

Extensively used in Europe for many years in place of the
canoe, Folbots have enjoyed a growing place in the American
outdoor scene and seem to increase constantly in popularity.
Many summer youth camps employ them almost exclusively
due to their relative safety. They are also very popular with
hunters, fishermen, explorers, and today's highly mobile
campers. When air-inflated bags or Styrafoam blocks are
mounted under the covered deckings, the Folbot cannot sink,
even if capsized. Unlike most canoes, a person in a Folbot
can sit on a center side rail with his feet in the water and
the craft will still not tip over.

Campers not exclusively wedded to the outboard motor and
its numerous accessories and impedimenta have already found

Folbots ideal for many a back-waterway excursion. From the standpoints of portability and storage, Folbot's are unexcelled. A complete craft can be disassembled and stored away in two packages to fit into the average closet or car trunk. The packages are not awkward to handle. The weights are easy to manage and within 20 minutes, or thereabouts, the Folbot can be assembled at the water's edge, ready to go.

Some Folbots are expressly designed for use with motors or sail. Both small motors and sail can be used with the kayak-type Folbot; other Folbots have a more conventional boat shape with the square stern for larger motors and afford more interior room.

WHERE TO GET INFORMATION. Folbot has become a common name for this class of kayak-type boats but it is actually only one of several boats made or imported in this design. Neither does the name imply that all such craft can be folded away. Some are of rigid, rather than folding construction; some are available in kit form as well as in stock models finished at the factory. The cost of a Folbot, paddle, etc., is less than the average boat and motor rig. More information can be readily obtained from the firms listed below.

FOLBOT
Folbot Corporation
Stark Industrial Park
Charleston, South Carolina

KLEPPER FOLDAWAYS
Hans Klepper
820 Greenwich St.
New York, 14, New York

FOLDBOAT
The Banton Corporation
15 California St.
San Francisco, 11, California

**Every time a forest fire strikes
You Get Burned**

Chapter 6

CB RADIO GOES CAMPING

IT IS DIFFICULT, indeed, to keep up with the amazing technological revolution which brings us so many new and useful items of camping equipment each year. But we should not overlook the dramatic advances in electronics which today make two-way radio communication as feasible in camping as in many other forms of work and play.

Until a few years ago, the main users of our airwaves were amateurs or professionals. Many of the former were known as "ham operators," or simply "hams." A lot of these amateurs were licensed and sufficiently interested in radio to not only learn the dot-dash code, but to study and progressively pass more difficult examinations so they eventually became holders of relatively advanced radio operating licenses. Many of them were so technically proficient that they designed and built much of their own equipment—often from old or second-hand parts. Of course this is also true of many amateurs today.

But breakthroughs in costs and equipment design have brought radio voice communication to thousands who do not now share the amateur's interest in the finer points of radio. With justifiable pride in their traditionally respected amateur standing, some of the present amateurs tend to look down their noses at today's relatively new breed of radio operator— the Citizen Bander—whose only presently needed passkey to the airwaves is the price of a low-powered transceiver. And no wonder the old-line amateurs tend to feel a bit critical of the casual ignorance and lack of radio courtesy discernible in some of the younger and more impatient newcomers to CB radio!

Small transistor radio receivers have been popular in camping since their advent several years ago. Their lightness, small packing or storage space occupied, and the miracle of their quality operation from such tiny batteries won them acceptance everywhere. With them campers can receive useful weather and highway reports, news, and entertainment.

Even campers who have radios in their cars often bring along one or more of the small transistor receiving sets for use away from the car, especially if there are young people in the party.

Now campers with two or more miniaturized two-way radio transceivers can talk to each other over practical ranges, and without special license. A far cry from the jumbo-sized but short-range "walkie-talkies" of World War II, today's transceiver houses its speaker, receiver, antenna, and transmitter in a single small plastic case roughly the combined size of two packs of king-sized cigarettes laid end to end. Such a transceiver weighs only about a pound; a few penlight batteries or a tiny 9-volt battery will operate the set for about 50 hours—often longer.

A TYPICAL 'WALKIE-TALKIE'

In some models a 12-volt battery is used for power; often such a battery can be easily recharged by simply plugging it into any 110 to 117-volt AC wall receptacle. The 12-volt cigarette lighter receptacle of the automobile has also been tabbed as a power source for some transceivers or for recharging transceiver batteries.

The term "transceiver," incidentally, is not reserved exclusively for these small "walkie-talkies." The term merely refers to a radio unit that will both send and receive. Hence transceivers are also to be found in other than CB radio.

But CB radio has many uses. Some fuel oil dealers, for example, control the dispatching of their supply and servicing trucks with two-way radio, using CB or assigned commercial frequencies and equipment. There are other applications, usually involving a licensed station and a master transceiver.

Most of the small CB transceivers now being marketed permit the user to plug in a tiny earphone, if he wishes, when receiving calls. This is of advantage should one wish to avoid annoying bystanders while receiving. On occasion, such as in a high wind, the earphone also helps make it easier to understand incoming calls. Deer hunters, as a rule, prefer the earphone to minimize noise in hunting areas. Hunters have, in fact, found it possible to communicate via earphones and whispered transmissions.

More and more CB transceivers are appearing on the market. Many are made in Japan; their prices are competitive and their quality good. A leather carrying case and shoulder strap enclose most of the sets; by and large, the sets are easily operated without removing them from the carrying cases.

No one, of course, can accurately predict design trends for "walkie-talkie" equipment. Several models are made with built-in regular broadcast receivers. The ordinary receiver portion of such sets is powered by the same battery employed in "walkie-talkie" use. The two-way frequency controlling crystals may be easily interchanged (plug them in) to enable operation on another channel.

REGULATION. The Federal Communications Commission controls all radio communications including Citizens Radio Service, or CB (Citizens Band) as it is popularly called.

In general, there are two forms of Citizens Radio operation. One is licensed, the other is not. This is sometimes mystifying to the newcomer to Citizens Band radio whose first questions usually seek to determine whether he will or will not have to obtain an FCC license. The answer to this depends upon what kind of equipment he is buying, and how he plans to use it. If the equipment has a limited power input (less than 100 milliwatts), no license is needed to operate it *unless* it will be used to communicate with licensed stations. Use of the remainder of Citizens Band equipment (with power input up to as high as 5 watts) does require a license. Five watts of power, the maximum permitted in CB use, is not impressive to most radio amateurs. However, Pioneer V was equipped with only a

5-watt signal. It was heard 8,000,000 miles away, with special equipment, of course.

If you are interested in using the more powerful Citizens Band equipment, the matter of getting a license presents no formidable obstacle. You need to: (a) Send $1.25 to the Superintendent of Documents, The Government Printing Office, Washington 25, D.C. and obtain a copy of Volume VI, FCC Rules and Regulations; (b) obtain an application form (FCC Form 505) from the Federal Communications Commission (from any of their Engineering Field Offices or from Washington, D.C.), and fill out and mail the application to FCC, Gettysburg, Pennsylvania; (c) allow time for processing the application. Details are supplied by the FCC with the application instructions. Presently, there is no undue expense or special fee in filing an application. Any citizen of the United States who is 18 or more years of age (or 12 years of age for a Class C station—for remote control, models, etc.) may obtain a license if his application meets requirements.

Most outdoorsmen and campers are primarily interested in the use of the low-powered equipment, the kind that entails no license for use.

Under FCC rules, no license is required to operate a two-way CB radio which meets the following requirements:

a. The power input to the r-f final stage is less than 100 milliwatts.

b. The r-f carrier (wave) is between 26.97 and 27.27 mc.

c. Total length of the antenna to be used is less than 60 inches.

d. Undesirable, spurious radiations from the antenna are at least 20 decibels below the carrier wave.

Limitations on the power input to the r-f final stage, together with controls on the length of the antenna affect the power and range of transceivers; the other limitations promote clarity of voice communication and confine use of the equipment to stipulated channels.

But you don't need to worry about the technicalities involved so long as you buy a set which is certified by the manufacturer as meeting the FCC specifications for *unlicensed* use. The cost of two separate transceivers (one for you and one for the person you want to communicate with) ranges from about $55 (kits) to over $200. Beware; some of the small "walkie-talkie" sets are rated higher than 100 milliwatts and do require licensing for use. Read the specifications for the set carefully.

Regarding operating technicalities, don't be misled. So long as you use such equipment exactly as it was designed and intended to be used, you should have no problem. But whenever a Citizens Bander starts to improve his equipment, trouble looms. For example, the movement you try to boost the power of your tiny transceiver by clipping its antenna connection to a longer more powerful one, you invoke an FCC regulation which requires that such a set-up be a licensed station. Operation of the small transceivers may also be boosted through other technical subtleties—but they are definitely frowned upon by the FCC.

To avoid difficulties, the responsible CB user must be familiar with FCC regulations and the instructions which come with his set. FCC has the job of keeping order within our crowded airwaves; its regulations must be strictly followed. Penalties for infractions of rules are severe.

CRYSTALS AND RANGE. The typical small transceiver for

unlicensed use boasts two crystals; one is a receiving crystal, the other a transmitting crystal. They are not exactly identical. Replacement price of either crystal is from $2.50 to $3. The crystals in your matched sets are designed for use on only one (and the same) channel frequency. As a rule, you cannot hear or talk to persons using a set having crystals made for a different channel. But there are exceptions.

Sometimes you can hear and understand other transmissions one or two channels adjacent to yours, or hear their overtones. This depends upon the locale, your proximity to the other transmitter, atmospheric conditions, etc. Of the 23 channels among those available and set aside by the FCC for CB use, unlicensed CB transceiver operators have access to all except channel 1. The manufacturers usually pick the original channel you will use through installation of the crystals. But in many transceivers you may interchange crystals rather easily to use a different channel.

The task of changing crystals usually involves plugging in the new ones in place of the old, but before using the new channel you must be absolutely sure your set is properly tuned for FCC tolerances. A qualified serviceman can easily check this for you with a frequency meter. With the more expensive equipment used in licensed service, channel changing is easier to accomplish. Merely turn a switch or dial to your choice of four or more of the other channels. The more elaborate equipment, by the way, may or may not use crystals for frequency control; range may extend from 1 to 30 miles depending upon terrain and conditions.

If you are enjoying minimum interference while using your equipment on the channel it was originally set for, there should be some very special reason to justify a change. The new channel, after all, may carry a lot more traffic and therefore be less desirable to use.

Though you might change crystals from time to time, you still cannot call a U.S. Park or Forest Ranger with the transceivers now authorized for unlicensed operation. Nor can you call Police, Sheriffs, Forest Fire control points, Highway Patrols or many of the other public service categories you might wish you could reach fast in some emergency. The low-powered transceivers simply do not send nor receive on the radio frequencies used by such service classes.

Referring to Citizens Radio Service, FCC says in its SS Bulletin 1001: "Frequencies available to stations in this service are shared among licensees. During periods of normal operation no protection can be afforded to the communications of any station in this service, even when involving the safety of life or property, from interference which may be caused by the proper operation of other authorized Citizens Radio stations, or from stations in other radio services properly operating on frequencies shared with the Citizens Radio Service."

This, of course, applies equally to the unlicensed CB transceiver user.

But factors entirely apart from crystals affect range: the terrain, length of the antenna, the number of transistors, and the set's rated power output. Even within the models carrying approval for unlicensed use there are power variances in design. Some of them have shorter antennas than others; many of them also have fewer transistors than others—for example, 4 to 6 versus 8 or 9. Thus, as a general rule, their range will be shorter than the larger sets. The manufacturer's literature should be carefully reviewed in determining the expected range of any particular model. Your mobile communications equipment dealer can tell you quite specifically what ranges to expect of his sets, but such dealers do not always carry CB equipment. Many radiotelephones are operated on special frequencies other than those assigned to Class D use.

A range of about one mile is reasonable to expect of most of the small CB transceivers in unlicensed use. Radio waves peculiar to this form of communication bend slightly, but mostly they follow a straight line instead of the expanding sphere patterns suggested with the use of radio equipment in other broadcasting.

Occasionally, unusual atmospheric conditions will bring about a phenomena known as "skip." When this happens, the Citizen Bander may be startled to find himself listening (or talking to) someone on his channel but located several states away. When this happens, the natural inclination is to ask for the exchange of courtesy postcards confirming the contacts. But FCC never intended that small transceivers would be used over long ranges; postcard collecting activities are likely to net you as many enemies as friends, and may invoke FCC intervention.

As with other radios, there are freak conditions which may temporarily extend range beyond your expectations. In general, however, the range will be found to expand in high elevations, across open country, and across large bodies of open water. Our larger rivers form excellent conductors. The tall buildings in a city, on the other hand, have a restrictive effect upon range. Two CB users separated by a mountain peak may encounter trouble communicating because of the terrain massed between them.

INTERFERENCE. Quality of reception and transmission is affected by ignition and other interference. This may be experienced in trying to communicate from a running boat or car without benefit of a permanent installation. FCC has said that Citizen Radio users must expect and tolerate interference not only from other legally operating Citizens Radio stations, but sometimes from stations legally operating in other radio services (military, etc.). And, as you know if you own such equipment, a transceiver user has no exclusive monopoly on his particular channel; he must often wait until others are through using the channel before he can call someone himself. The old rule: "First come, first served," is followed.

Both policy and courtesy also require that the user not "tie up" a particular channel with prolonged and useless talk—or, as the FCC puts it, "frivolous communications." Your radio conversations, incidentally, are hardly a private affair. Anyone having the properly attuned radio receiving set can listen.

CONVERTER. If you have an ordinary car radio, you can easily have a mobile converter unit installed which will enable you, through the flick of a switch, to tune in most any CB channel on which you wish to listen in. And if one of the members of your party carrying a low-powered transceiver should stray out beyond normal range you may be able to receive a message from him in this way, even though you can't talk back. The American Electronics Co., 178 Herricks Road, Mineola, New York is but one of several companies making such a converter. Prices for the unit run between $20 and $25.

In wilderness or remote country there is a lesser amount of competitive radio traffic; in such an ideal locale the average transceiver user should have few problems.

CHANNELS. Some of the CB channels seem to get special usage; this pattern will vary in different parts of the country. Most Citizen Banders develop their own traffic charts—the accompanying one is an example only, but you might check it against your local traffic. Then enlarge it through your own additions.

Channel	Notes
2, 4	Popular with various commercial firms such as the dry cleaners, etc.
9	Frequently used by commercial boats.
11	Usually a high-traffic channel; often used as a calling channel by operators with flexible equipment. They listen but switch to another channel for business upon receiving a call.
13	Pleasure boats often stand by on this channel for calls.
15	This channel is often used as a standby channel by operators of motor clubs, motels, service stations, and commercial organizations serving tourists through affiliation with the National Travel Service.
18	Popular in marine use.

EQUIPMENT USES. Consistent with FCC regulations and technical limitations, campers are finding two-way radio a handy thing—even with the lowest-powered equipment. Advantages start whenever members of the party separate.

Interestingly enough, only one state—Minnesota—has a law (passed in 1961) which specifically concerns the use of 2-way radios in hunting. This singular law prohibits the use of radio and walkie-talkie equipment ". . . for the purpose of assisting in or facilitating the taking of any wild animals . . ." The Minnesota law applies as follows:

(1) It does not prohibit hunters from possessing 2-way radios during open hunting seasons.

(2) As intended, it does prohibit the use of such equipment in assisting or facilitating the taking of *protected* wild animals. To Minnesota hunters this ordinarily means deer, rabbits, squirrel, and raccoon.

(3) Special radio-user permits may be obtained on application by hunters of *unprotected* animals. Such special permits

automatically become invalid, however, during regular open deer-hunting seasons.

(4) The special permits are subject to cancellation by the Commissioner of Conservation upon justified complaint of the misconduct of any of the holders during hunting activities.

But elsewhere sportsmen are using radio on a wide scale. In many areas fishermen exchange word on where the fish are biting. Groups of hunters are using radio to coordinate their movements afield or in the woods. Exploring parties, too, use walkie-talkies to keep in touch with their main camp. And camping parents can now stay in touch with Suzy or Bill who may be out fishing, down the beach some distance, or exploring elsewhere. The beach lifeguard may use a transceiver to talk with other lifeguards rowing along swimming lines some distance away. Depending on the amount and kind of traffic on the channel open to you, you might find the transceiver a help should your car, trailer, or boat require servicing assistance in some out of the way spot. Persons in camp can relay unexpected weather warnings to members of their party out on the lake fishing. Similarly, the fisherman who runs out of gasoline with his outboard, or who finds the fishing too good to leave and is therefore delayed in returning on schedule may notify the rest of his party in camp.

Because of the flexibility of operation permitted with a licensed station, the advantages are apparent. Camp operators and professional packers, too, have already discovered uses for two-way CB radio. And for many ordinary campers, some party member might be dropped off with a small transceiver in some crowded but potentially desirable campsite area while the rest of the party continues the search for a site. When a site is determined upon, all can quickly get together to set up camp.

Some of the senior citizens who enjoy the outdoors will also find the small transceivers useful. Comfortably wrapped against the evening's coolness and sitting on the porch of their cottage overlooking a northern lake, a wife recovering from illness recently had only to press the "mike" button of her transceiver to visit with her husband fishing a mile away.

And the Citizen Bander cruising along the turnpike may, as many do, turn his set on to hear interesting samples of the radio traffic zones he passes through. Conceivably he may even discover some fellow Citizen Bander who runs a motel and make an advance room reservation for the night by radio—it has been done.

CB RADIO IN CANADA AND MEXICO. In Canada, the equivalent of the U.S. Citizens Radio Service is called General Radio Service. Canada, unfortunately, has no provision for permitting the operation of the transceivers brought in by tourists, hunters, or campers. The practice is for Canadian Custom officials to seal such equipment when the visitor enters Canada. With the passage of time and the growth of CB radio the conventions which govern reciprocal radio services between the United States and Canada may change.

Mexico does not object to the operation of CB equipment by visitors.

WHERE TO GET INFORMATION. To obtain information on the various models of Citizens Band radio equipment browse through any of the radio or electronic magazines, then write in for free details. Many stores now stock and display CB equipment; auto supply stores and the mail order stores, for example, usually carry transceivers. Your local radio store and CB equipment dealer will be glad to fill you in on the details and recommend equipment best suited to your communication objectives.

Part 15, FCC Rules governs the small units for unlicensed use. This is a leaflet available at no cost from your nearest FCC office or from the FCC, Washington 25, D.C. Part 19, FCC Rules is available at a cost of 10¢ from the Superintendent of Documents, Washington 25, D.C.; this section of the Rules deals with equipment requiring license.

CITIZEN-BANDERS CHECK LIST

(1) Be sure to learn and follow strictly the FCC rules applicable to your equipment.

(2) If your equipment is powerful enough to require licensing, *don't use it until you get your license.*

(3) Don't try to communicate with license stations unless you, too, are licensed (see FCC rules).

(4) Don't begin a transmission when someone else is already using the channel—wait your turn. First come, first served.

(5) Speak slowly and clearly when transmitting. Avoid poor transmissions through carelessness in holding the transceiver too far from your mouth.

(6) Remember that while you are transmitting, you cannot hear an incoming call or message.

(7) Limit your message exchanges to the shortest necessary time. Present rules of "on 5 minutes, off 2," may soon have to be changed to "on 3 minutes, off 2" because of traffic increase.

(8) Don't tie up the channel trying to stretch your communication range records.

(9) Do not use the airwaves for unnecessary testing; instead, patronize a qualified repairman.

(10) If you are licensed, give your call letters as required (at the start, the end, and every 10 minutes while communicating).

(11) Expect and tolerate some interference; some will be from other CB users—some from other sources.

(12) Always pratice courtesy; respect the needs and right of others.

(13) Before changing crystals so you can use a different channel, be sure the new crystals will enable transmission within FCC tolerances on the new frequency. Have your equipment tested before going on the new channel if you are not sure. The help of a qualified repairman in advance may spare you an FCC citation for off-frequency operation on the new channel; always consult and follow FCC rules before changing frequencies.

(14) Also keep in mind that extremes in temperature such as encountered in severe below-zero weather may alter crystal characteristics; such temperatures are also notoriously adverse to standard battery life.

(15) Follow the manufacturer's recommendations regarding the use and care of your equipment; carry extra batteries against unexpected power needs.

(16) Don't let anyone use your CB equipment unless the borrower is under your direct supervision, or unless you are sure he knows the rules, is licensed—if necessary—and is responsible. Don't allow anyone to use or treat your equipment as kids treat toys.

(17) Always remember that CB radio is *not* just another amateur band and that it is *NOT for unnecessary or frivolous communications*.

(18) Always remember: The FCC may be monitoring *you!*

Chapter 7

DESERT CAMPING—ALL SEASONS

SOME PEOPLE are amazed when one mentions camping in the desert, yet people are traveling the desert routes in increasing numbers. No doubt this trend is due to an increase in leisure time, improvements in accommodations, and better road conditions than were encountered a few years ago.

WHERE TO GO

Desert state parks and national monuments in the great southwest desert country are increasing and improving their campgrounds, such as, for instance, Anza-Borrego State Park, Death Valley, and Joshua Tree National Monument in California.

There are many other fine county and state parks throughout the southwest desert belt of Arizona, Nevada, New Mexico, and parts of Colorado and Texas. There is a considerable range in desert animal and plant life, ranging from below sea level in Death Valley and the Salton Sea up to the 500-foot dry-tropical zone along the Colorado River in the extreme southwest part of Arizona. This is the land of the Organ Pipe and Senita Cactus, of magnificent distances and small lizards—and some say not much else. From the lower Sonoran zone at 500 feet to an elevation of 4,500 feet in the Sonoran, Chihuahuan, and Mojave Deserts, grow the Ocotillo cactus, Creosote, and Salt bush. Coyotes, jack rabbits, desert fox, and several species of rattlesnakes roam this area. The foothills and mesa lands extend from 3,500 feet to nearly 7,000 feet in elevation where one may find deer, cougar, and sometimes roaming wild burros, horses, and Mexican wild pigs or peccary.

Thousands of people are taking trips into the desert in the spring to see the wild flowers and to enjoy the resorts at Palm Springs and Death Valley in the winter months. Rock hounds and prospectors are heading out into remote sections of the desert at all times of the year hunting for uranium, gold, and semi-precious stones. Some people go to study the flora and fauna, some go for rest or health reasons, others to take

177

COYOTE.

(Drawing by Luis M. Henderson)

movies or still pictures of whatever may strike their fancy. Hunters find excellent bird, deer, and wild pig shooting in season. Excellent fishing may be had along the Colorado River in Arizona and Nevada.

PLANNING YOUR DESERT TRIP

Organize and plan your trip well in advance. This gives you time to make any changes in route or plans. Study your map well if you are going off the beaten path! Maps may be obtained from federal and state agencies, railroads, bus depots and gas stations. A large-scale topographical map of the area should be purchased if you go into the interior.

If you plan on passing through a desert en route to some other destination, it is best to travel at night or very early in the morning during the summer months to avoid the heat. During the heavy vacation travel season, try to make overnight reservations in advance, or stop early if you plan on camping to insure a good campsite.

IN THE DESERT

Be sure to obey safety and warning signs. They do mean what they say! If you are pulling a trailer, find out what steep grades may lie ahead. Never let your gas tank get below half full.

If you plan on using side or back roads, it is best to use a pickup with four speeds ahead. Four-wheel drive jeeps or power wagons are better off-the-pavement vehicles, and it is much easier for them to negotiate high-centered dirt roads. If you are driving a conventional car or station wagon, be sure to inquire at each opportunity regarding your route and road conditions ahead. If you go into remote sections of the desert, be sure to leave word with your family and friends where you plan on turning off the regular traveled roads; or better still, also notify and check out with the local sheriff's sub-station or ranger station where you plan on going and when you expect to return. Again check in with these officials when you return. *This is important!*

Camping in a house trailer along the regular routes, and staying in a state or national monument campground is deluxe desert camping, but camping in primitive interior country can be dangerous unless you have the right equipment and some desert knowledge or lore. The following is a check list for a rambling trip off the main road for three days (summer exploring trip—two people).

EQUIPMENT FOR JEEP OR POWER-WAGON.

(1) Axe, single-bit.
(2) Canteens (2), 1 gallon capacity.
(3) Flares, red signal, minimum of 3.
(4) Ice-box, large enough to hold 25 lbs. of wet ice and several pounds of paper-wrapped dry ice. Dry ice placed in bottom, so when wet ice melts the dry ice will continue to freeze the melting ice for minimum of 3 days.
(5) Jacks (2).
(6) Spare gas tank mounted in back holding from 20 to 30 gallons, plus full car tank.
(7) Shovels (2).

(8) Thermos jug (1), 2-gallon type, for cracked ice.
(9) Tire tubes (2).
(10) Spare tire and tire repair kit.
(11) Spark-plug type air pump for inflating tires.
(12) Tool kit, with spare spark plugs, fan belt, tire tools, and tire pump.
(13) Water cans (2), 5-gallon jeep cans.
(14) Vehicle in good mechanical condition with 6-ply tires and spare.

PERSONAL ITEMS.

(1) Air mattresses (2).
(2) Ammunition (optional).
(3) Blankets or sleeping bags (2).
(4) Bug repellent.
(5) Canteens (2), one-quart belt type.
(6) Compass, declinator adjustable with sighting line.
(7) Canvas cots (2), or jungle-type sleeping hammocks (2).
(8) Canvas, a couple of extra canvas tarpaulins for windbreaks.
(9) Cooking kit, nesting type.
(10) Dishes, plastic.
(11) Emergency firemakers (flint & steel, small magnifying glass).
(12) Firearms (optional).
(13) Flashlights (2), with extra bulbs and batteries.
(14) First-aid kit, snake-bite kit, suction type, also antivenin with syringe.
(15) Gasoline, 2 gallons white gas in leak-proof can with spout.
(16) Hat, cap, or sun helmet.
(17) Handkerchiefs (2), bandanna, large size.
(18) Knife, BSA type with screwdriver, leather punch, blade and can opener.
(19) Map of area (topographic type).
(20) Matches.
(21) Mirror, steel.
(22) Stove (1), two burner, Coleman gasoline, or stove using propane canned gas.
(23) Sun glasses.
(24) Stick of white lipstick for sun or wind-burned lips.
(25) Sunburn lotion.
(26) Thermos jug.
(27) Toilet kits for each.
(28) Towels, one each; one dish towel, one dish or wash rag, one roll paper towels.
(29) Toilet tissue, one roll.

Take food for four days. Canned goods and smoked and dehydrated foods can be carried since weight isn't a problem. A menu should be made out in advance. A few emergency rations, "C" or "K" type, may come in handy.

WARNING. Do not depend on regular waterholes. They may have dried up. Carry all water you will need for the trip.

Don't camp in dry washes; they can become death traps during a flash flood from a rain storm miles from your camp. Camp in the shade of desert brush if possible, high on the bank beyond the reach of any flash flood. A sudden cloudburst can cause floods that crest at better than 20 to 40 feet at times. Watch out for rattlesnakes. It is safer to sleep off the desert floor on a cot or in a jungle hammock. Shake out your shoes, socks, and other clothing. There may be a scorpion or centipede in them.

Remember animals and snakes will attempt to avoid you. It is only when they are molested that they strike back in self-defense. You are safer in the back country than you would be crossing a street in town.

Don't put a hair rope or lariat around the spot you plan to sleep on to keep rattlesnakes out—it won't work! They can, and will, crawl over it.

Respect the desert, but never fear it. Next time, try snow camping!

Chapter 8

SNOW CAMPING—WINTER OR SUMMER

MORE PEOPLE are enjoying camping in snow country than ever before! Most of these hardy folks, both men and women, belong to a mountaineering or ski club where they have learned the technique of camping in the snow while ski-touring cross country, or while hiking over snow-covered ranges at high elevations during the summer. The technique is basic whether one pitches his tent on summer snow or camps in any region during the winter months.

PHYSICAL CONDITION AND STAMINA

Snow camping varies from the usual back-pack trip in the summer in many ways. In winter camping, one must wear skis or don snowshoes to enable him to travel on top of the snow. With the added weight of skis or snowshoes on his feet and having to use both arms to maneuver ski poles, he will bring in to play an entirely different set of muscles and will burn up considerably more energy than the summer hiker on a dry trail.

Therefore, the ski camper must be in excellent physical health and condition, and have the stamina to cope with cold, wind, snow, ice, and avalanches. In addition, he must be able to take care of any member of his party who may become ill or injured on the trek and get himself and his party safely home again.

WINTER EQUIPMENT

The greatest difference in winter camping is the importance of maintaining body warmth. Weight must be kept at a minimum and all equipment must be of the very lightest, warmest, and strongest type obtainable.

Warm clothing, shelter, dehydrated food, an eider-down sleeping bag, some type of gas or spirit stove, good boots, skis, and, of course, snowshoes if the job calls for them, are needed. A good rucksack is necessary to carry the supplies and equipment. The lighter the pack weighs the more pleasant the trip. and the better control one has of his skis.

182

CHOOSING YOUR PARTY

Be very careful in choosing companions on a journey of this type, since it calls for a quite rugged individual with lots of character. The party should all be about equal in strength and skiing ability. At least one member should be an experienced ski mountaineer and have some knowledge of the region to be traveled. Never go solo in the winter. A minimum of three is safe, preferably four, especially if there is any rock or ice climbing to do. In this manner, if a member of the party becomes injured, someone can stay with him and make some kind of shelter while the other man can go for assistance. It takes a good-sized party of experienced mountaineers to remove an injured person from the back country under winter conditions, sometimes entailing the use of "snow-cats," helicopters, toboggans, and a lot of grueling work.

Before the last war it was very difficult to secure sufficient experienced skiers and mountaineers for the rope and ice-climbing type of rescue. During World War II the Army picked these experienced men for instructing our ski troopers and mountaineer divisions. After the war, some of these men organized ski clubs or mountain rescue teams so that it is now easier to obtain sufficient competent help when an accident occurs in the snow country. These men are the unsung heroes of the mountains. They leave their jobs in the cities, or whatever they may be doing at the time, and are gone for hours or days in recovering an accident victim's body, or bringing an injured person to medical aid. This is done at a considerable personal sacrifice in time and money.

Winter camping is as safe as any other type of camping, if one isn't reckless. This way one can really get away from the crowds and relax and enjoy the crisp mountain air. It's quite a thrill to ski over unmarked snow, knowing you are on your own, far from the job and from city cares. One returns with more zest and memories of the "mountain" and fine companions, and takes pleasure in showing the pictures taken on the trip to friends who were unable to go.

CLOTHING TO TAKE

Clothing for winter camping should be chosen very carefully. Underwear, loose-weave wool, heavier than that used in summer camping; two pairs, one to wear in daytime and one to sleep in while the other pair is drying in the sleeping bag; should be of the two-piece long-john type—better still, try the new loosely knit type used by the military forces.

Shirt, lightweight wool; two, if trip is longer than a week.

Ski pants, windproof, water repellent, long enough to stay in boots, loose-kneed, smooth finish.

Socks (two pairs); inner, lightweight wool, outer, heavy wool half-size larger.

Cap, visored, with ear muffs (Balaklava helmet, optional).

Ski boots, box toe, large enough to insert felt inner sole and two pairs of wool socks; rubber-cleated Bramani-type sole, or ski boot with sponge rubber heel center, heel plate and Tricouni nail pattern.

Parka, windproof, water repellent, hooded, hip length, zipper front, with thong.

WINTER APPAREL—CHECK LIST

(1) Keep clothing as clean and dry as possible to maintain maximum insulation properties. As an alternate to regular dry-cleaning, woolen shirts and trousers should be washed periodically. Wash them at least every three months, but exercise special care to prevent shrinkage.

(2) Snow should be brushed from boots and clothing before entering any shelter.

(3) Carry extra dry socks, dry gloves, and glove-liners if work entails exertion and possible sweating. To dry socks, gloves, or mittens, put them inside the parka.

(4) Keep clothing items loose and free from binding, particularly on the feet. Get your clothing, particularly woolens, big enough to allow for considerable shrinkage with moisture or washing. When more than one pair of socks are worn from inner to outer layers, the socks must increase progressively in width as well as length to prevent constriction or pressure on the feet. Any sock-boot combination must allow free movement of the toes. Constant toe and foot exercising when the feet begin to numb will prevent a freezing injury in the back country.

(5) Don't sweat; keep comfortably cool at all times. Underdress, rather than overdress. You may spend much time changing clothing layers but the effort pays off.

(6) If you get hot, take the following steps until comfortably cool:
  (a) Take your gloves or mittens off.
  (b) Loosen or remove belt or parka waist-tie.
  (c) Open shirt or parka throat.
  (d) Remove hat or throw parka hood back.
  (e) Shed middle pants if wearing them.
  (f) Shed sweater, shirt, middle coat, or parka.
  (g) When through exercising, put on spare clothing *before* you chill.

(h) Don't touch bare metal with bare hand at temperatures below freezing.

(i) Pull thumbs into palms; move arms out of sleeves and inside parka if extremely cold.

(j) Keep big mittens tied together and to you. If one or both are lost, a hand may be frozen. If some garments are removed to keep cool be sure they are safely stowed and will be dry when you wish to put them on again.

(k) In cold regions always control your comfort through changing intermediate layers of clothing rather than by dispensing with the outside layer (windproof parka and trousers).

SHELTERS

The lean-to is simple and easy to construct. You can make the frame from dead poles with or without using an axe. The success of a lean-to depends on building an adequate fire to spread warmth evenly throughout the shelter. This means that it must be placed properly in relation to the prevailing wind. This applies for all types of shelters.

Tents of course are the best type of wilderness shelter. They keep the rain off, the cold out, and the heat in. Those with the canvas floors and mosquito bars keep the snakes and insects out.

A lightweight tent is the most satisfactory shelter for high elevation winter camping or traveling through snow country. The tent should be made of some lightweight, strong, windproof material, such as Neoprene-treated cloth, sail-cloth, or balloon fabric. Nylon tents are satisfactory, and also the more economical Army arctic tent secured from surplus stores. The tapered three-man tent is a favorite of mountaineers and will hold four persons by crowding. All types should have a floor cover of heavier material with a sod cloth that can be turned back for cooking space, or at least a zipper vent in the floor, so spilled liquids or melted snow may be drained. The entrance should be of the sleeve or tunnel type that can be closed tightly to keep snow and wind out. Waterproof tents must have a ventilator to avoid condensation and the danger of monoxide poisoning, since most of the cooking is done inside. Care must be observed that the tent is not snagged or punctured by sharp objects.

It has been found through experience that the Arctic, Meade, Logan, and tapered three-man style tents have proven best for winter use. Various types of tents, shelters, snow caves and

PEAK

CEDAR "ROPE"
MAIN POLE

BASE LOG

POLE AND CEDAR BARK LEAN-TO.
(Note cedar bark siding bent to proper shape, lower right.)

This lean-to is an efficient means of shelter in an emergency. Bark from a recently fallen cedar tree is stripped off in lengths of 3 to 6 feet. The lighter inner portion of the bark is separated from the outer portion. This material is used in lieu of twine or rope for lashing the pole framework together. Though the cedar strips are satisfactory for most of the framework, rope should be used to lash the main poles to the support trees. The need for rope at this point can be eliminated by using a large log to elevate the main poles instead of trees.

After the framework is up the siding comes next. Pieces of bark are bent S-shaped. The upper end is then hooked over the main pole. When all the siding has been hung the base log is placed to hold the lower ends in place.

The roofing comes next. Bark strips are placed on the low end first; 2 or 3 layers are best. The next course generously overlaps the first and so on to the peak.

It may be necessary to add a log on each side of the roof to help hold the ends of the siding in place.

lean-to's are shown in chapter 4; also in the accompanying illustrations.

BIVOUAC SHEET. Every good mountaineer should carry a bivouac sheet, or poncho, in his pack for it may save his life if he is caught away from camp in a sudden snow storm. The sheet can also be used as a drop cloth, roof, or floor in a snow shelter.

EMERGENCY SHELTERS. Snow caves and snow shelters involve the use of both skis and poles and a poncho or bivouac sheet for the roof. For making an igloo, the snow must be of the right consistency to do a good job. A snow knife, machete, or an aluminum shovel is needed to cut snow blocks. It can be done with a ski but is very slow and difficult to do this way.

SLEEPING BAGS. Many winter travelers use the Army double arctic bag since it costs less than most feather bags. The three and a half pound inner bag can be used for summer trips. Eider-down bags weighing from four to six pounds are sufficient; however, a wool inner liner should be used for added warmth. Pound for pound, down-lined sleeping bags are still the warmest and usually cost the most but bags lined with dacron, as distinguished from other synthetic materials, follow closely on the heels of down, or combinations of down and feathers, in terms of providing efficient insulation and light weight at reasonable cost. The type bag one invests in can mean the difference between sleeping in warmth and comfort or spending a miserable, cold night. The mummy type bag has proven best since it is more compact when used in a small tent.

Sleeping habits have a good deal to do with the choice of a bag. Some people like a snug fit. This is most efficient. Some people feel restricted and want a loose fitting bag. The size of sleeping bag cannot be based on body size alone. In getting ready to buy a bag it may be best to pin a sheet into the size stated for the bag you have in mind and actually try it on for fit. Sleeping habits also determine the type of bag. For example, the Mountain Sleeper (Gerry) is one of the most efficient combinations possible, giving greater warmth than any other bag of equal weight; however, it has a narrow mattress, and the sleeper must stay on the mattress with the top draped loosely over him for best results.

Sleeping in any position except on the back requires some technique to keep the head covered without breathing moisture into the bag. If you cannot develop these techniques, then an all-down bag in an Alpine shell will give you the same protection, more easily, and with only a pound additional weight. Choose the sleeping bag to suit your own needs and sleeping habits.

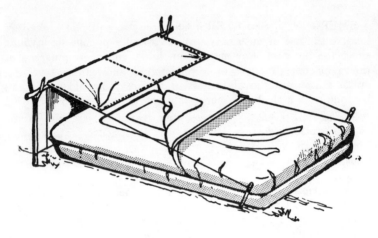

The Army sleeping bag which opens down the middle of the top may be satisfactory if you sleep flat on your back all night without moving. In case one moves during sleep, and most people do, a bag which opens across the top and down the side is more satisfactory, unless one wishes to sleep in his jacket, parka, or balaclava when camping in cold weather. A woolen watch cap or stocking cap pulled over the head and down around the neck will keep the head warm. A bare head and neck may allow 25 percent heat loss in a sleeping bag. Bags should be large enough so the user can make adjustments for comfort without rolling off the pallet or air mattress. A good Arctic, Alpine, or Mountaineer model cold weather bag should assure at least 6 hours comfortable sleep at night.

Many persons wish to use the same sleeping bags all year around. But bags designed for zero or below would be too uncomfortable in the milder seasons. Use two medium or lightweight nested-bags in this case for the winter months rather than individual heavier bags. Blankets and blanket liners may be inserted inside such a set, or inside any sleeping bag, for that matter, to increase considerably the warmth of the bag as needed.

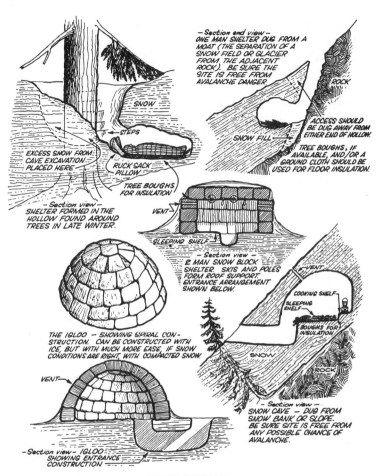

SNOW SHELTERS.

THE DOUBLE-BED. If you wish to make a double-bed out of two single sleeping bags (they must have separating, full-length L-shaped zippers), open each bag and unzip completely. Each bag should open flat (same as a quilt). Place one bag on top of the other so that the bottom of each zipper will meet; connect zippers where they meet. Zip together.

Paired double bags which permit two or three persons to sleep together, will be warmer than the same bags used individually.

AIR MATTRESS. An air mattress is a *must* since it provides insulation between the cold tent floor and the sleeping bag and, if properly inflated, adds greatly to sleeping comfort. Plastic air mattresses cost less initially than the rubberized material type. Plastic mattresses are also much lighter but difficult to fold when very cold.

Some type of air mattress pump should be provided since it takes lots of breath to blow up a mattress in the high, rare atmosphere and burns up a great amount of needed energy. Inflating a bag by mouth at a high elevation can sometimes cause severe nose bleed. Nevertheless there is a way of inflating your air mattress without a pump and without incurring a nose bleed. It will take longer than most any other method, but it works. First, be sure the valve is open and that the stem is sufficiently warm to put between your lips safely. Lie down beside your mattress, make yourself comfortable, and place the opened valve stem in your mouth. Breathe normally, but be sure to exhale through your mouth and the valve. Eventually your mattress will be ready for use—and you will be ready to use it! The pump, however, is preferable to most.

When camped in timber, or at timber line, prospectors sometimes used fir boughs laid shingle-wise instead of an air mattress; however, the National Park Service forbids this practice and the Forest Service frowns on anyone lining his bed with green boughs. It would not be long before timber line would be denuded in camping areas if this practice was permitted.

AIR MATTRESS SIZES. The 30-inch mattress width will usually fit into the corresponding size of sleeping bag pocket but some may require considerable effort to install. With an oversized sleeping bag, choose a 30 or 32-inch air mattress width. If you prefer to place your mattress under the sleeping bag, then this width mattress will provide ample room and sleeping comfort.

Station wagon sleepers should use a 46 or 50-inch air mattress width. Double-up sleepers will need 46 to 50-inch mattress widths. Two 25-inch singles, or one extra-wide mattress will, of course, serve the same purpose.

SNOW SNOOZER'S CHECK LIST

(1)   Breathe outside the sleeping bag to keep moisture and frost out.

(2)   Sleep bare or in long underwear; better—sleep in a "sweat suit."

(3)   Do not sleep in a bag having a completely waterproof cover, or moisture will gather and you will become cold. In extreme cold weather, frost can add about one pound per day to bag weight.

(4)   Sleeping bags should be insulated from the ground or snow. Use an air mattress, Li-Lo, or cot pad for insulation between bag and ground.

(5)   Air mattresses should be inflated by pump rather than breath to prevent internal moisture or icing.

(6)   A ½-inch "Raidoprene" or "Ensolite" blanket next to the sleeping bag absorbs moisture and prevents the bag from freezing to the air mattress or ground insulator.

(7)   Sleeping bags should be turned wrong-side out and exposed to the sun and air whenever possible.

(8)   For cold weather, hunters and explorers have found that placing a pocket warmer or two, a canteen full of hot water, or a hot-water bottle at the foot of the bag makes entry to the bag most luxurious. Using a hot-water bag or canteen will also insure drinking and cooking water in the morning, save on fuel used for melting ice or snow, and save time.

(9)   Sleeping bag liners will help keep bags clean, and will prolong the life of the bag.

(10)   Zippers should be handled carefully and slowly to prevent bag material from catching. Lubricate zippers, if necessary, with soap, Vaseline, or light lubricating oil; apply full length.

(11)   If you prefer to sleep in long johns or in your underwear, keep a set just for sleeping in, for they must be dry. If you sleep in clothing worn during the day you are apt to sleep cold due to the moisture absorbed from your body. Adding one pair of wool socks to your kit just for use in sleeping also will aid your comfort. The socks must be clean and dry; not the ones you hunted in all day.

TIPS FOR THE SNOW CAMPER

WATER. While traveling on skis or snowshoes one can become very thirsty, since open water is not always available due to freezing of streams and lakes. One may quench his thirst safely by eating snow if he will hold it in his mouth and let it melt slowly so as not to chill the stomach. Sucking on a piece of hard candy will improve the flavor of the snow considerably, and the sugar in the candy will add energy to the system. In securing water from pools or open stretches of streams, be very careful not to break off the snow-lip, else you might accidentally slip into the water. By tying a can or cup to a ski pole one may safely dip water from a stream or pool.

Should you accidentally fall into a stream or get wet fording a creek, you should immediately build a fire and dry your clothing. Change socks and wet clothing even though the weather is warm and sunny. Otherwise, if a cold spell sets in or you do not reach camp as early as planned, you might be caught out after dark when freezing temperature occurs. This can lead to trouble.

A spot close to the tent should be set aside for gathering clean snow to be melted into water and should be kept from contamination. Wet snow will melt more rapidly than powder snow. If compelled to use dry snow, it will be necessary to compress it as compactly as possible and the kettle must be watched carefully so that the bottom doesn't burn out. If any water is available, adding it to powder snow will quicken the melting process.

A thermos bottle for each member is worth its weight and some ski mountaineers even carry a hot water bag in their pack. The thermos bottle can be used for a hot drink on the trail, in camp, or for holding water overnight to keep it from freezing. The hot water bag will add warmth to the sleeping bag, will provide water for toilet purposes, or can be used for dish washing.

The boiling point of water decreases with the altitude but food requires increased cooking time—about fifty percent for each 5,000 feet rise in elevation.

FOOD. Weight and bulk must be cut to the very minimum for snow camping. Food taken should be of the lightest dehydrated type with the least bulk, easily digested, and with the highest nutriment value. Some pre-cooked food may be added. Don't forget to take some hard candy, nuts, and chocolate bars for quick energy on the trail. High altitude foods should be chosen somewhat differently than those used in a normal diet, since at high elevation the oxygen intake is reduced and it is more difficult to digest certain foods. Therefore, one should depend more on carbohydrates for body fuels. However, high protein foods are necessary and fats also have their place in the diet. Some skiers take booster vitamins along and have found they help to maintain one's vitality. Food chosen must be easy to prepare with a minimum of simple cooking equipment. Most cross-country skiers and rangers on patrol use the one-pot method—cooking everything for the meal in one kettle. This saves time and extra dish washing.

COOKING KITS. Cooking equipment must be cut to bare essentials. A pot to melt snow, a pot for the one-pot meals, a cup, a small 2½-inch sportsman type knife with spoon and fork attached, should enable one to manage very well for a short period. Some ski mountaineers take only one pot and a roll of aluminum foil for cooking. Of course, a nice, nested cook outfit is much handier if the extra weight is distributed among the group. (Don't forget the dish towel and rag.)

STOVES. Some type of knapsack model stove is needed to melt snow for water and, of course, for cooking. Even though the stove may be small, it will help warm up a cold tent or snow cave. The following stoves have been found to be most practical for winter mountain use since they are compact, lightweight, and use very little fuel. The G.I. type uses the top and bottom covers for kettles; however, the Primus, Meta, and Knapsack models weigh less. Heat-Tab stoves are not much larger than a pack of cards and weigh only a few ounces including the fuel tablets. The Heat-Tabs are wonderful in assisting in getting wet fuel started. They are too small and too slow for general cooking, but are useful for heating a hot drink.

FUEL. Liquid fuel needs will run approximately a pint per day per stove; however, the amount of fuel consumed will depend on how much snow or ice melting is necessary to obtain water. A pint will burn for about two hours, so it pays to have everything ready and the meal prepared and cooked as rapidly as possible to save on fuel if one is to be above timber line very long.

Liquid fuel must be carried in a moisture and gas-proof bag, and the can must have a spout and be leak proof. Use only white gasoline and, for safety, be sure to fill and light the stove outside your tent, for any spilled gas on the tent floor can be serious if it should become ignited. Some tents are treated with highly flammable waterproofing and will flash-burn in a second. A small two-man tent can be very difficult to get out of in a hurry.

RUCKSACK. There are many types of rucksacks being used today. The Kelty Pack seems to be increasingly popular and is seen on trails and in camps all over the country. The sleeping bag can either ride on the top or the bottom of this outfit.

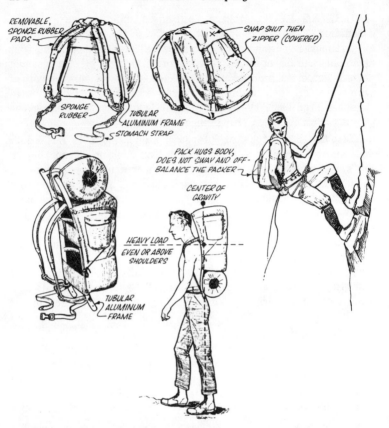

Top: **THE DAVIS SUMMIT PACK.** This is an extremely well built, comfortable, lightweight rucksack. It is completely adjustable. Strapping set-up makes rucksack hug the body in almost any position. This is representative of the finer high-altitude rucksack.

The metal frame rucksack is for loads up to approximately 20 pounds and is designed to ride low on the back so as not to hinder stability in precarious spots.

Bottom: **THE KELTY MOUNTAIN PACK.** The above position shows the packing arrangement for hiking where greater stability is needed.

The position at right shows the comfortable, energy conserving posture that can be maintained for long distance, heavy packing when the pack sack is high on the frame and close to the packer's center of gravity.

The metal frame Kelty Mountaineer can be arranged to carry heavy loads high on the shoulders and close to the body. This allows an almost vertical stance for the packer. Or, when more stability is mandatory, the load can be lowered closer to the hips. (See detail pack illus.)

The rucksack should have a rigid frame, fit close to the body, and have a low center of gravity. A belly strap is necessary to keep the pack from riding overhead if one falls, and the strap will keep side sway to a minimum while skiing. The Ski-Pack is only good for a one-day stand for carrying lunch, camera, and extra ski wax. It is entirely too small to carry a sleeping bag and camping equipment. The Bergans-Meis and the Army Frame-Pack are excellent choices and the many pockets they

(Drawing by Luis M. Henderson)

THE BERGANS-MEIS PACK.

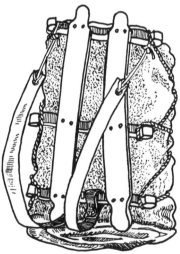

PACK FRAME with load.   (Drawing by Luis M. Henderson)

contain are handy since one doesn't have to dig all through the pack to find small articles. Various types of knapsacks, sleeping bags, and other equipment are shown in the accompanying illustrations.

GLASSES. Dark glasses should provide protection from snow and side glare. Pilots and ski mountaineers prefer yellow lenses because they provide better depth perception. The Ray-Ban "Kalichrome" type is best. Polaroid glasses remove only a small amount of glare. Calobar glasses are fair. Whatever type of sun glasses are used, they should be ventilated to retard fogging. There are several types of anti-fog sticks on the market that will prevent moisture from collecting on the lenses for several hours after each application. One stick will last for weeks.

FIRST-AID KIT. A small first-aid kit, about 2x4x6 inches in size, should be adequate for most minor accidents, such as burns and cuts. To this kit should be added a dozen codeine-aspirin tablets, a few sulfadiazene tablets, six sleeping capsules, and, of course, a 2-inch roll of adhesive tape. The sudden change from regular diet to concentrated dehydrated food sometimes causes constipation, so some kind of mild laxative should be taken along.

SKIS. Skis for cross-country travel should be of good quality, flexible, and of laminated construction. A shorter ski can be maneuvered to better advantage in climbing in the higher elevations than the longer cross-country type. A quarter-inch hole should be drilled near the tip of each ski so they may be trailed when walking on top of snow crust. One can tie a rope on the tips for a pulling harness if the skis are used for a ski ambulance. Each ski should be equipped with an ankle strap so the skis will not be lost if one should fall.

Ski poles should be long enough to reach from boot bottom to armpit. Ski poles of metal are stronger than the hardwood type and are worth the slight extra cost.

EMERGENCY REPAIR KIT. An emergency repair kit for mending a broken ski or other equipment is good insurance. The kit should contain the following: aluminum snow shovel; combination wrench-pliers-screwdriver tool; Philips screwdriver and screws to repair metal ski edge; four slender 1½-inch non-rust bolts with nuts and washers; two slender

1½-inch aluminum screws and two heavy ¾-inch screws; 6 ft. braided iron picture wire; 6 ft. ¼-inch rawhide thongs; ski tip and contraction band with key or nail; ski pole mender and small piece of sheetmetal; 30 ft. of ³⁄₁₆-inch nylon rope, orange color; and a toe strap.

SKI CLIMBERS. Some sort of canvas ski or sealskin climbers are necessary at times to enable one to mount steep slopes. Climbers can also be made from ¼-inch rope by using a diamond weaving hitch from either front or back of ski where it should be tied to the toe harness. However, climbers made from rope will not glide down hill as well as sealskins.

SKI WAXES. Several types of ski wax for various snow conditions should be carried, or, at least, a climbing wax and one for fast snow.

SNOWSHOES. Snowshoes have their place in the winter travel scene; however, most skiers will not concede this.

Some woodsmen say, "Why carry a pack on your back when you can haul it on a toboggan sled?" A sled is fine for rolling or level terrain but is slower and next to impossible to use in really steep, rough country.

If you can ski well enough along level or slightly sloping ground, the chances are you will not find it hard to get used to snowshoes. For cross-country travel in fairly open snow country many prefer skis, but the long and rather narrow snowshoe having a slightly upturned nose is also useful. In heavy woods with lots of underbrush, however, the long trailing ends of such shoes tend to become entangled with the brush too easily, thus restricting the user's movements. Hence, many prefer a different design such as the "bear's paw." But, keep in mind that the differing shapes of various makes and models of snowshoes indicate only an effort to provide the right compromise shape for the individual's use. Some experimentation may be necessary to help you arrive at the right shoe shape for your expected use.

AVALANCHES. Avalanches are always present dangers in some areas. The steeper the slope, the greater the chance of an avalanche. Most avalanches fall in gullies or couloirs. If conditions are right, they can occur on a slope of only 20 degrees. Dangerous slopes should be crossed as near the top of the ridge as possible. Members of the party should spread out a hundred yards or more apart. It is much safer to go straight up or straight down the slope when on terrain where avalanches may occur. Of course, there are always a few skiers who dare not move straight down for fear of losing ski control. It is safer to cross snow fields on foot if possible. Under certain conditions when crossing a slide area it takes very little to start an avalanche—the cut of a ski in the snow, the vibration of voices, or a shot. The National Park and Forest Service have snow rangers whose job it is to clear the winter sports areas of avalanches by the use of explosives or artillery fire with a mountain howitzer or field gun. However, the ski tourist or winter camper is on his own when in the remote back country. A person should study the terrain very carefully before going into slide areas; however, sometimes there is no route around a slide area and the decision must be made on the spot whether to risk it or give up the trip.

USING DOGS

Dog teams are still used in some of the northern states of this country and in Canada for recreational camping, racing, ski pulling sport, and winter rescue operations. They are also used for backpacking. In the latter case, the family dog carrying a homemade pack is often involved. The size and weight of the load depends on the health, capability, and general disposition of the individual dog.

The American Kennel Club recognizes four breeds of sled-dogs which are more or less wolf-like in appearance. The most famous dogs used for recreational sledding or for carrying camp loads, the fastest and smartest, the boldest and bravest, the greatest pranksters, and the most deadly killers have been crossbreeds of Huskies or Malemutes with wolves, Collies, St. Bernards, Labradors, and other big dogs. The most useless dogs, also, are usually crossbreeds. In the wilderness areas, it is said by experts that the dog carrying his tail in a sickle-shaped plume over his back makes a good sled-dog. The least desirable sled-dog has a wolf's tail slinking below his hind quarters.

Teams for dog-sledding usually consist of 5 to 15 dogs. They may be driven single-file (tandem hitches popular in freighting), or in a double-file called the "Alaska hitch." The latter arrangement requires a good lead-dog but has the advantage of involving less trail breaking for the remainder of the team in loose or deep snow. It is also possible in this arrangement for fights to badly tangle the harness and to find shirkers not pulling their share. Another hitching arrangement resembles a "fan." In this system, dogs are driven in a fan formation by means of individual traces of equal length. But there are variations in hitching arrangements; these depend upon the region, the customs, and the kind of terrain.

How much a dog can be expected to pull is a question closely linked with the team's speed of travel. Here are some approximate load capabilities which are reasonable to expect:

Speed of Dog	*Load Potential*
2 to 4 mph	One and one-half times the dog's weight
6 to 8 mph	About equal to the dog's weight
20 mph (gallop on good snow)	Half of the dog's weight

The load, of course, must be suited to the number of dogs, their physical condition, the type of terrain to be traveled, and the elevation. As elevation increases, pulling capacities fall off sharply. Dogs can rarely be used for sledding at altitudes above 8,000 feet. When weather and snow conditions are good, some dogs will pull from 75 to 100 pounds of load; this drops quickly, however, on inclining terrain with 10 to 15 percent grades. Such grades are about the steepest that dogs can negotiate under load; even then a load-pulling loss of 40 to 50 pounds per animal is not unusual.

A common type of sled used is called the Yukon model. It is five to nine-feet long and also varies in width from sixteen to about thirty inches. Clearance over the snow will be about four inches. There is some overhang along the sides; the overhang effects the width of the sled by about four inches.

In starting a sled load and in breaking sled runners free from deep snow or ice, dog teams may require assistance. The problem is compounded if too much of the load is packed in the front of the sled. Never pack anything in front of the first forward upright since this makes for hard pulling. Load the heaviest gear on the bottom and the lighter supplies on top. Cover the load with a waterproofed canvas or tarp and lash down securely by bringing the "bull-rope" straight back along the center of the load and fastening it to the handlebar. Side lashings are then fastened and tightened across the sled.

Control of a dog team is accomplished by voice. "Gee" is used for right, "Haw," for left. To start, you may have your own variation but "All Right," or "Let's Go" are common. The lead dog does not exercise any physical control over the rest of the team; rather, he is selected on the basis of being most responsive to command.

Harnesses vary, but each dog wears a collar—somewhat on the order of a small horse collar. The traces may be hitched to this directly; a back or belly-band is used to hold the traces in place. Spacing between dogs, and the specific harness to be used as well as method of hook-up to sled vary depending on whether the load is for racing, freighting, skiing, etc. The reader interested in using dog teams in winter sports will find pertinent information available from time to time in *Alaska Sportsman* magazine (Box 1271, Juneau, Alaska) as well as other outdoor periodicals. (Also see chapter 22, Care of Saddle and Pack Animals.)

SKIING CHECK LIST

(1) A winter ski sportsman dresses warmly and comfortably.

(2) Takes lessons, in beginning.

(3) Is sure that his ski boots fit properly.

(4) Travels with a companion on long treks.

(5) Never skis alone.

(6) Never takes a dare.

(7) Learns to fall correctly.

(8) Never skis out of control (tumbles instead).

(9) Fills in his sitzmarks; skis across ruts—not in them.

(10) Avoids overexertion, never takes chances.

(11) Gives way on call of "T-R-A-C-K!"

(12) Uses a recommended cable-release binding.

(13) Never wears hair loosely, nor wears loose clothing while using the rope ski-tow.

(14) Is always courteous to fellow skiers.

(15) Never attempts to ski on slopes too steep for his ability.

(16) Always cooperates with the Snow-Ranger or Ski-Patrolman.

CHECK LIST OF EQUIPMENT FOR WINTER CAMPING:

Aneroid barometer (optional)—an aid to identifying elevation and keeping records.

Anti-fog stick to keep eye glasses from fogging.

Balaklava wool helmet (optional).

Bandannas (2), large size.

Belt or suspenders.

Camera and accessories (one each), share film expenses (optional).

Can opener, turn-twist type, leaves edges of can smooth, safer.
Compass, declination adjustable with sighting line.
Firearms and ammunition (optional, unless hunting).
First-aid kit, small size, plus 12 codein-aspirin tablets, 12 sulfadiazene
    tablets, a mild laxative, and 2-inch roll of adhesive tape (sufficient for
    party of four).
Flashlight and batteries, fountain-pen type, one each member.
Flashlight, head-lamp type, one per party.
Foil, aluminum, one roll.
Glasses, dark, extra pair, with case.
Handkerchief, white, one or two.
Hat with brim or billed cap with ear muffs.
Hot-water bag for sleeping bag comfort and storing water overnight.
Knapsack, Kelty Mountaineer Model or Bergan type.
Knife, BSA or utility type, with can opener, screwdriver, etc.
Map, topographic, large-scale, of area to be traveled.
Matches, waterproofed, in waterproof container.
Mittens, (2 pair) wool liners, ski cloth outers.
Moccasins or snowpacs to wear inside shelter.
Muffler or wool scarf (headband optional).
Notebook and pencil.
Parka, close weave, water repellent, windproof, knee length, zipper front.
Poncho or ground cloth, can be used as roof in snow cave.
Sewing kit, small Army type (optional).
Shirts, (2) lightweight wool.
Ski boots, good grade.
Ski pants, windproof, water repellent, loose-kneed, smooth, tight weave
    with zippered pockets.
Ski wax, climbing and gliding waxes.
Skis with bindings and poles.
Snow pacs, if snow shoes are worn (insulated type).
Snowshoes, Bear-paw type for climbing, Yukon type for cross-country
    (optional).
Soap, small hotel bar size.
Socks (2 pair), lightweight wool inner; 2 pair heavyweight outer socks
    half-size larger.
Sunburn lotion, zinc oxide or cream type.
Sweater, lightweight wool.
Tent, 2-man Army arctic 6 lbs. 6 oz. or Mountaineer Model 3 lbs. 4 oz.
Thermos bottle for hot drinks and storing water (optional).
Toilet paper.
Towel and toilet articles (razor, optional).
Underwear (2 suits), wool, long-handled two-piece type, loose weave. Sleep
    in one pair while pair worn during day dries in sleeping bag. (New
    knitted or insulated type best.)
Watch, water and shock-proof, wrist type.
Whisk broom for sweeping snow off clothes and out of tent.

Try something different next vacation; try knapsack camping without need for skis or snowshoes!

Chapter 9

KNAPSACK CAMPING—ANYWHERE

THE KNAPSACKER is a different breed of outdoor camper. Usually he is, or will soon become, a good woodsman and mountaineer. He may belong to a hiking club or he may be a free lance, on his own. In any event, he is eager to get away from the crowd and the beaten paths, and to roam at will through the wilderness back country of our national parks and forests. The area he covers is only limited by the supplies he can carry comfortably on his back or secure along his route.

A HARDY CHARACTER

Several times while rangers were making an inspection tour of the high mountain trails in remote areas of Olympic and Yosemite, they encountered one of these hardy characters who had been traveling for weeks with nothing more than a small bag of ground parched corn or pemmican, a blanket, fishing pole, and sometimes a small belt-axe and a hunting knife, plus the clothes on his back. All appeared to be in good health and spirits; however, it was noticed that they could really store the grub away when asked to share a camp meal. Must have been the rangers' cooking!

Ranger John Bingaman and his trail crew apprehended a man holed up in a trail crew cabin near Rancheria where he was hiding out while trying to dodge the draft during World War II. He had lost his pack several months earlier while attempting to ford the Tuolumne River and had been living off the land, mainly on plants, berries, and raw rattlesnakes.

There is no need or reason for one to be hungry or unclean on a back-pack trip if he has the knowledge and makes proper plans and preparations. With the modern dehydrated, highly concentrated foods now available, anyone can have maximum nourishment and energy for minimum bulk and weight and a wide range and variety of menus.

ADVANTAGES IN HIKING

The hiker-camper will have better hunting and fishing than

202

the non-hiker. He also will see more beautiful scenery and animal life than any other type of camper, since he can travel over territory that pack and saddle stock cannot negotiate. Of

(Drawing by Luis M. Henderson)

course, folks using pack stock can ride and let the mule carry the load; however, it is obvious which method is the most economical way to travel.

TAKE A FRIEND

It is more fun and much safer to back-pack with a friend or two, for no matter how good a woodsman or how experienced a mountaineer you may be, sometimes you can get into difficulties. This can become serious for a lone hiker. Be careful in your choice of a companion—he may be the salt of the earth at home but a stinker in the back country when difficulties occur. A camping trip can bring out the good or bad qualities and reveal a companion's character very quickly.

HIKING TRAILS—EAST OR WEST

The largest system and longest stretch of trails in the United States or, in fact—the world, are the Pacific Crest and Appalachian Trail systems.

The PACIFIC CREST TRAIL traverses the United States from Canada in the northwest, to the Mexican Border in the southwest, for over 2,156 miles. Most all this trail passes through state parks, national parks or national forests and wild, primitive areas. The route climbs over the backbone of the Cascades through Washington and Oregon, and up over some of the roughest and highest ridges of the famous Sierra Nevada range (John Muir Trail section) where it drops down over the Tehachapis before it reaches down the last 406 miles into the foothills of the Mojave and Sonora deserts and ends at the Mexican border.

There are hundreds of miles of lateral trails leading east and west from the main trail that will bring the hiker to places where he can terminate the trip or replenish his supplies. You can pack over the Pacific Crest Trail system with saddle and pack-stock. However, there are stretches where grazing is poor.

It is best to check these stretches from section to section well in advance with the forest and park service officials to insure forage and water for your pack animals.

THE CASCADE CREST TRAIL. The first section of the Pacific Crest Trail of over 445 miles passes through Washington's Cascade Range. This route passes through five national forests and is one of the most primitive and rugged in the northwest, with the possible exception of the Olympic mountains in Olympic National Park. The trail starts near Mount Baker, and passes through Mount Rainier National Park, Glacier Peak Wilderness Area, Mount Adams, and Goat Rocks Wild Areas. This section is called the Cascade Crest Trail. It provides access to some of the finest hunting and fishing in the Pacific Northwest. Fishing is allowed, but hunting is prohibited in the national park stretches. The required travel time for this section is approximately 40 days. This will allow for resting and cleanup periods.

THE OREGON SKYLINE TRAIL. Next comes the Oregon Skyline Trail where the land is a bit more gentle and the route follows an unbroken divide covered with heavy stands of Douglas fir and abounding with beautiful lakes and wildlife. This section goes through six national forests. It passes through the woods of Mount Hood Wild Area, Mount Jefferson Primitive Area, the Three Sisters Wilderness Area, and Crater

Lake National Park. This stretch is 412 miles long and requires about 30 days travel time.

THE LAVA CREST TRAIL. The California portion of the Pacific Crest Trail is divided up into sections. The Lava Crest Trail begins at the Oregon border and runs through the mountains of northern California for 339 miles to Yuba Gap. The beautiful Tahoe-Yosemite Trail from Yuba Gap traces the famous High Sierra Nevada Range and enters Yosemite National Park at Bonds Pass. It ends at scenic Tuolumne Meadows after traversing 239 miles.

THE JOHN MUIR TRAIL. The John Muir Trail from Tuolumne Meadows to Mount Whitney is 175 miles long. It requires about 21 days to travel comfortably. This stretch is the most rugged to be found in the United States. On it there is an 11-mile gap where no grazing is available for stock. It is best to load some firewood on top the pack loads for camp wood is also unobtainable in this high, rough desert of granite rocks and bluffs. Knapsack hikers should carry a lightweight Knapsack stove on this trail. While traveling through Sequoia-Kings Canyon National Parks you will cross Forester Pass, elevation 13,200-feet, on the way to Tehachapi Pass.

The route from Tuolumne Meadows to just beyond Mount Whitney is one of the most beautiful and spectacular in the world. Within this area lies the Mammoth-Sierra Recreation Area and the famous High Sierra Primitive Area. There are some peaks that exceed 14,000 feet, and many over 13,000 feet. This section contains famous Mt. Whitney, 14,496 feet tall, the seventh highest mountain in the United States. Forty air-miles east of Mt. Whitney is Death Valley where the elevation at Bad Water is 272 feet below sea level.

THE SIERRA CREST TRAIL. The Sierra Crest Trail from Mount Whitney is 137 miles long and extends over the Tehachapi Range to Tehachapi Pass.

THE DESERT CREST TRAIL. The Desert Crest Trail passes through the Mojave Desert and up over the Sierra Madre and San Bernardino ranges, then enters the Sonoran Desert where the temperatures range well over 120 degrees during the summer months. This section should be traveled during the cool of night. Campsites may be found approximately 15 miles apart. Water is uncertain during prolonged dry spells in the lower section. The distance from Tehachapi Pass to where the trail ends in old Mexico at Campo is 406 miles.

The total trailway route through California stretches for over 1300 miles from Yuba Gap to Mexico and requires approximately four to five months of steady travel over very rough terrain. This, of course, includes time out to rest pack-stock one day a week, and to reshoe animals, as required. Man also needs rest from the arduous riding and hiking found in a trek of this magnitude. Time should be allowed to explore some of the scenic east and west side trails.

Snow, sleet, hail, wind, and lightning storms occur frequently in this region at the higher elevations. Travelers should have some mountaineering experience before attempting to negotiate this formidable terrain and desert land.

THE APPALACHIAN TRAIL SYSTEM. This trail extends for 2,056 miles from Mount Katahdin in Maine and meanders through the state's wilderness lakes and streams for over 266 miles before going on into New Hampshire. There, it travels over the famed White Mountains, climbs over the interesting Presidential Range, crosses Pinkham and Franconia passes, then wanders through Vermont for 100 miles. The section then follows the crest of the storied Green Mountains and heads over part of Vermont's Long Trail. It continues through the Berkshire Hills of Massachusetts, climbs over beautiful Mount Greylock and the lower ranges into Connecticut's renowned state forest reserves; it travels through part of New York's state forest and park system, crosses Bear Mountain Bridge, and goes over Bear Mountain to the New Jersey section.

Up to this point, the trail has crossed mountain ranges. Now it follows natural topography along ridgetops and down through Delaware Water Gap. Then it meanders into the wilderness area of the Kittatinny Range where it is a joy to camp. In Pennsylvania, the trail follows the rim of the east range of the Alleghenies and the northern Blue Ridge Mountains, a hiker's delight. Next, it cuts across the Cumberland Valley.

In Maryland, 38 miles of trail follow a narrow ridge crest, a part of the abandoned Chesapeake and Ohio Canal, and then bridges the Potomac River near historic Harper's Ferry.

Approximately one-fourth of the Appalachian Trail lies

within Virginia. It crosses a considerable amount of wilderness mixed with old ridge roads. Here one travels a 100-mile route through the famous and beautiful Shenandoah National Park. In the Tennessee-North Carolina section, the trail follows the state boundary rather closely, passing through spectacular and scenic national park and forest land and up over the most primitive and highest ridges and peaks east of the Rocky Mountains. In Georgia, the trail continues for 100 miles through the Chattahoochee National Forest, a very rugged and high wilderness region. Roads and highways cross at intervals of about a day's hike. Mount Oglethorpe is the southern terminus.

TRAIL TIPS. While traveling either trail system be sure to secure fire permits, where they are to be used, well in advance of your trip. Also hunting and fishing licenses, if you plan on this sport, and maps of the sections you plan to travel. Be sure to check state firearms laws. Firearms are prohibited in national parks and in game refuges. In some areas, dogs and other pets are not allowed on trails. You must have reservations to secure accommodations in the lean-to shelters, cabins, and lodges that are along the route. Many sections along the trail pass through country broken by roads and towns where one can freshen up and renew supplies. It is necessary in certain sections of the trail system to carry full camping gear.

WHERE TO GET TRAIL INFORMATION. It is suggested that you write the Appalachian Trail Conference, 1916 Sunderland Place, N.W., Washington, D.C., and request the pamphlet "The Appalachian Trail." The price is 15 cents. The pamphlet describes the trails and lists many guide books, maps, and other pertinent references. It describes the trail system, section by section, and covers names of lakes, streams, side trails, peaks, and climatic conditions.

For details on the Pacific Crest Trail system, write for Joseph Hazard's "Pacific Crest Trails," from the Superior Publishing Company, Box 2190, Seattle 11, Washington.

To secure other maps, write to the Regional Forester, Forest Service, Northwest Region, Portland, Oregon, for the Cascade Crest and Oregon Skyline Trail recreational maps. The maps are marked from the Canadian border to the California state line. For maps from the Oregon-California line to the Mexican border you may write to the Regional Forester, U.S. Forest

Service, California Region 5, 630 Sansome Street, San Francisco 11, California. For maps of the sections of trail running through national parks, write the Superintendent, Mount Ranier National Park, Longmire, Washington; Crater Lake National Park, Crater Lake, Oregon; Lava Beds National Monument, Tule Lake, California; Lassen Volcanic National Park, Mineral, California; Yosemite National Park, Yosemite, California; Kings Canyon-Sequoia National Parks, Three Rivers, California.

PLAN YOUR TRIP

Back-packing is a sport requiring careful planning and efficient execution as it is the one form of travel in which you are entirely dependent on your own resources to get you into the scenic area once you have left the road head behind you.

Make your acquaintance with the back country gradually. Take a few overnight camping excursions into the woods to test your equipment and get the feel and the hang of your pack. If you are new at the game, it is a good idea to join some hiking club where you can go on organized hiking and camping expeditions. In an organization of this kind you will be under the guidance of experts and will be able to learn from them the fundamentals of safe hiking and camping.

(For trips which combine hiking with the use of a pack animal or burro, see chapter 11, Saddle and Pack-Outfit Camping.)

HOW TO HIKE

Remember that a wilderness trip into isolated, primitive back country is not an endurance test. You can take all the pleasure and fun out of an experience of this kind if you push too rapidly. Take it easy the first few days until you gradually break into the routine and become acclimated to your pack and the elevation.

FOOT CARE. Anyone planning on entering a primitive area should be in good physical condition. His feet should be toughened up ahead of the trip and his boots well broken in. If his feet or boots, or both, are not in shape, blisters are bound to appear. The quickest way known to break in a new pair of boots is to wade in water over the boot tops and wear them all day. This will shape them to your feet. Then let them dry at room temperature. When dry, dress them down with neats-foot oil. This will preserve them and keep them soft and pliable. At night, place your hiking boots alongside and under the edge of your sleeping bag so they will be warm and much easier to put on in the morning; otherwise, they may become cold and stiff. A boot placed on each side of the bag will keep you from rolling off the ground cloth and thus assist in keeping the sleeping bag clean.

Since good old "shank's mare" must get you there and back, you must take good care of your feet. It is a good idea to soak your feet in a cold mountain stream or lake each night. This should be done after your feet have cooled off—otherwise it can induce blisters right after a hard hike. Soaking your feet will toughen them and refresh you considerably. Be sure to dry your feet carefully and put on clean, dry socks and a pair of tennis shoes or moccasins. This will give your hiking boots a rest and a chance for any perspiration to dry out during the night. Should your boots become damaged beyond camp repair for any reason, you can always fall back on the moccasins or tennis shoes in an emergency.

For foot comfort on the trail, one should wear a light pair of wool socks with a heavier pair over them a half-size larger than the inner socks. Of course, have a change. On a hiking trip lasting several days, wash your socks each day and let them hang dry from your pack straps. At noon stops, lay them out in the sun, rehang them on the pack and by evening they should be dry.

At the first sign of a tender spot on your feet be sure to stop immediately and tape the spot before it turns into a blister. Blisters and sore feet can spoil an otherwise delightful trip.

TRAVELING ON FOOT. Most of us have lost the art of walking. In hiking, use a gait that is comfortable so you can breath normally. Point your toes straight ahead, coming down lightly on your heel, reach forward with your toes and push up off your toes. In this manner you will acquire what mountaineers call a swinging gait that will eat up the miles. Set a pace that you know from past experience you can keep up all day with a minimum of rest stops. The point is that you want to arrive at your destination early and with enough strength and energy to make and enjoy a comfortable camp.

You will soon be able to adjust your pace to the weight and distance you must tote your pack. Two miles an hour is fast enough when back-packing. A good rule of thumb when climbing steep terrain is to climb about a thousand feet an hour and at a pace that you can reach the ridge without being out of breath. This is important if you are hunting because if you are panting hard you will be unable to hold a steady aim when game is sighted. This is standard procedure with the Army mountaineers.

CLOTHING, EQUIPMENT, FOOD

CLOTHING. Clothing for summer mountain travel should provide necessary protection with least bulk; therefore, it must be of strong, lightweight material. Lightweight, long-handled, two-piece underwear is best. Avoid 100% wool underwear. About a 40% to 60% content is best. A lightweight wool sweater can make you very comfortable in camp at night. Cotton underwear and shirts may be more comfortable in hot weather, but they become cold and clammy when wet with perspiration. Some hikers have been seen in the wilderness wearing shorts, with their legs badly sunburned or mosquito bitten, or both.

Blue jeans and poplin trousers are used more than any other type of pants. Soft, lightweight, canvas-weave pants are good if you don't waterproof them; however, any hard material is noisy when contacting brush and while hunting will frighten game.

A comfortable brimmed hat or cap will keep the sun out of your eyes and rain off your head. Don't forget the old "poncho" for it can be used as a lean-to, ground cloth, or cover for you and your pack if it should rain.

TENT. For shelter a 3½-pound tent is best if you can afford one. Otherwise, a tent ranging from 4 pounds up to 8 pounds will do if you can handle the extra weight. It should be made of lightweight plastic, nylon, or balloon silk. Canvas is too heavy for back-packing. You can get by with a plastic tarpaulin 6x9 feet by hanging it over a nylon rope strung between two trees. Some hikers use only a poncho for shelter.

SLEEPING BAGS. How well you sleep will depend on the type of sleeping bag you have purchased. Sleeping bags are filled with eiderdown, duck and goose feathers, chicken feathers, wool, kapok, dacron, polyester, or celacloud acetate. Prices range from about $8.00 to over $100.00 A mummy-type bag takes up less room than the rectangular robe or bag. Anyone having a double arctic Army bag in summer may use only the 3½-pound inner bag. This type may be purchased at most Army surplus stores and is the best of the economically-priced feather bags

AIR MATTRESS. A lightweight plastic air mattress will add to sleeping comfort. It does not cost very much—about $2.98 for the full-length type. This type will snag or puncture more readily than the rubberized mattresses. Do not over-inflate any air mattress or it will be as hard as sleeping on the ground. Fill it with air and then lie on the mattress and expel air until your hips nearly touch the ground. Close the valve at this point for comfortable sleeping.

KNAPSACKS. One of the most important pieces of equipment is your knapsack. Most experienced hikers and campers use the new Kelty, Himalayan Pak, Davis Summit, or the Bergan Meis type. Next best is the Army frame rucksack. It has nearly the same lines as the Bergan Meis. Some hikers prefer pack-boards such as the Trapper Nelson or Alaskan type frame.

BACK PACKING. Back-packers have found from experience that the amount of weight that can be packed comfortably depends on physical condition, age, and general health. A basic load rule for the average person is about 35 pounds for a man and 25 pounds for a woman. This is for average hiking on trips of two or more days over mountain country.

For heavy loads, an Alaska pack frame is an excellent choice. So is the Everest Assault Pak, and that old stand-by—the Trapper Nelson. The Duluth and Cruiser or Canoe pack sacks are used mostly in the East and in northwood areas. They do not have frames, but are used for short hauls where bulky or heavy loads are to be carried over portage trails between lakes. This kind of pack is rather hot and uncomfortable, but it will hold larger amounts of equipment than other models.

Some interesting philosophy on packs has been furnished through the courtesy of Gerry, Inc., Boulder, Colo. A pack is supposed to apply the equipment load to the body in the most comfortable way possible. In order for a man to stand in equilibrium with a pack on, the combined center of gravity of his body and the pack must be directly over his feet. But the body must lean forward to compensate for the load. A simple force diagram will show that the more the body leans, the lower is the mechanical advantage. Were it practicable, a load balanced on the head would offer optimum mechanical advantage.

A heavy rucksack bulging far out behind may represent a 50 percent loss in mechanical advantage. Translated to the user, however, this means twice the normal energy must be expended to carry the given load by pack rather than on the head. A person carrying a pack must spend extra energy in maintaining his balance.

The comfort of a pack depends on two factors; first, the placement of the center of gravity. A high load over the shoulders requires less forward lean than a lower load protruding behind. Another comfort factor involves the way in which the load is attached to the body. Most rucksack packs are designed to fall away from the back thus tending to pull backwards on the shoulders affording a very low mechanical advantage. Ideally, the shoulder straps should serve only to hold the pack on the back; the lower back should bear the load—not the shoulders.

If your pack feels as though it might fall off backwards, the plague is a low mechanical advantage. But if it stays in place against your back, you enjoy high mechanical advantage and will be better off in hiking. While a comfortable frame is desirable for the heavier pack, it is of lesser importance in the smaller ones. For maximum comfort, choose a pack with a capacity slightly larger than you expect to need.

When using a packboard, your outfit must be kept tightly covered to keep contents dry. Employ a ground cloth or some special cover. Using your poncho or tent for a cover is not recommended unless you have absolutely nothing else. But you may need the poncho to keep yourself dry, and there is always some danger of snagging or ripping a hole in exposed tent fabric, if used as a pack cover.

Make your pack as thin, flat and compact as possible. Rucksacks have the advantage, here, since small articles can be stowed in the several outside pockets they offer.

HOW TO PACK YOUR KNAPSACK. A good system is to put your toilet article kit in one small bag, mess kit in another bag, food in still another, etc. In this way, you make the most effective use of the pack's compact space. Small bags of nylon, plastic, or muslin are handy. Heavy objects go to the bottom of the pack; lighter ones higher, together with any you might need in a hurry. Incidentally, a waistbelt from which a lot of heavy gear depends can become very tiring and burdensome. Stow your belt-axe inside the pack or lash it on the side or back of the pack instead of carrying it from a waistbelt to avoid strain.

COOKING KIT. For a lone hiker, a one-man nested cook kit such as that used by the Boy Scouts will do. For larger groups, the nested units come in 2, 4, and 6-man units. They can be purchased for 10, 25, and 50-man units through government warehouses for large organizations. A small canteen and a BSA knife containing a screw driver, can opener, leather punch, and blade will be handy.

FOOD. In the line of food, the back-packer has a wider choice of food than the ski-tourist. He won't have the weight of skis and poles, nor the heavier-weight clothing; therefore, he can carry more weight in food and have a more varied menu. Being weight conscious, he will stick to the dehydrated or pre-cooked, highly concentrated, nutritious food he can purchase. See chapter 13 for menus and dehydrated food lists.

KNAPSACK STOVE. There are long stretches near Muir Pass on the John Muir trail in the Sierra Nevada of California that are barren of fuel wood; consequently, in such areas, it might be wise to carry a small, compact Knapsack model stove weighing 1¼ pounds. It will hold one pint of gas, naphtha, or benzine and will boil a pint of water in four minutes at high elevation. Otherwise, it is suggested that the hiker cross this high rocky area before making camp.

Don't forget your Fire Permit, a good map of the area, and, of course, a good compass with a sighting line—you may need it badly before the trip is over, especially if you decide to cut across country. It is fun to study maps and to find one's way over the land.

TRAIL GUIDES. One of the best trail guides to the Sierra Nevada range is Walter Starr, Jr.'s *Guide To The John Muir Trail, And The High Sierra Region*. This manual is a gem in trail mileage and lore of the mighty Sierra Nevada. For the person who wants to become a real dyed-in-the-wool backpacker, ski-tourer, rock-climbing mountaineer or woodsman, you are guided to the following handbooks or manuals for complete details: *On Your Own In The Wilderness*, by Col. Townsend Whelen and Bradford Angier, The Stackpole Co., Harrisburg, Pa.; *The Handbook Of Wilderness Travel*, by George & Iris Wells, Harper & Brothers, Publishers, New York, N. Y.; *Handbook Of American Mountaineering*, by Henderson; *Manual Of Ski-Mountaineering*, by the National Ski Association of America, University of California; *The Cascades And Olympics*, by Beckey; Martin & Pargeter's *Map Of The Olympics*. Top it off with a Boy Scout Field Manual, and you will have combined more knowledge of the outdoors than the pioneers and explorers had in the past.

INDIVIDUAL CHECK LIST FOR KNAPSACK CAMPING:

Air mattress, ¾ size, plastic or nylon for lightest type.
Axe, small belt type. (optional).
Bag, sleeping, 3½-pound eiderdown.
Bandannas, large (2).
Belt and/or suspenders.
Boots, 8-inch tops, hobnailed or Tricouni nailed soles.
Camera and accessories (optional).
Can opener, twist type for cutting smooth can edge.
Chapstick, white, for lip protection.
Compass, declinator, adjustable with sighting line.
Cook kit (one-man nesting type).
Fire permit.
Firearms and ammunition if hunting.
First-aid kit, small size, plus mild laxative, roll of two-inch adhesive.
Flashlight, small fountain-pen type, extra batteries and bulbs.
Glasses, dark sun type or prescription ground, with case.
Handkerchief, white, pocket (1).
Hat with wide brim or billed cap.
Head net for mosquito country.
Hunting and fishing licenses, if required.
Insect repellent.
Jacket, wool windbreaker.
Knapsack, rucksack or pack-board.
Knife, with screw driver, can opener, leather punch, and blade.
Map, topographical, large scale of area.
Match safe, waterproof.
Matches, waterproofed.
Moccasins or tennis shoes to wear at camp or for emergency shoes.
Notebook and pencil.

Pants, blue jeans or poplin.
Poncho, ground cloth or tarpaulin (lightweight).
Sewing kit (optional).
Shaving kit (optional).
Shirt, lightweight wool, two if gone over a week.
Snake-bite kit.
Socks, two pair lightweight wool, two pair heavy wool, ½ size larger.
Sunburn lotion.
Tent, lightweight (3½- or 4-pound), one or two-man mountain style (optional).
Toilet articles, toothbrush and paste, comb, soap, steel mirror.
Toilet paper.
Towels, one dish towel, one hand towel.
Underwear, two-piece long-handled type, lightweight wool.
Watch, wrist or pocket waterproof type.

For types of shelters, and woodcraft in general, note the illustrations.

EQUIPMENT CHECK LIST FOR MAN AND WIFE—KNAPSACK TRIP:

Woman	Lbs.	Oz.	Man	Lbs.	Oz.
1 Rucksack	3	8	1 Rucksack	5	
1 Sleeping bag	4		1 Sleeping bag	4	
1 Air mattress	2		1 Air mattress	2	
1 Poncho	2		1 Poncho	2	
1 Change of underwear		10	1 Change of underwear		10
2 Pr. extra wool socks		6	1 pr. Extra wool socks		6
2 Bandanna handkerchiefs		2	2 Bandanna handkerchiefs		2
2 White handkerchiefs		2	2 White handkerchiefs		2
1 Hand towel		8	1 Hand towel		8
1 pr. Boot laces		1	1 pr. Boot laces		1
1 pr. Camp moccasins		14	1 pr. Camp moccasins		14
1 BSA knife		6	1 BSA knife		6
1 Enameled cup		6	1 Enameled cup		6
1 Flashlight, pen type		6	1 Flashlight, pen type		6
1 Toilet article kit	2		1 Toilet article kit	2	
1 Snake kit (suction)		4	1 Snake kit (anti-venin)		8
1 Compass		2	1 Compass (Sportsman type)		4
1 Waterproof match safe		2	1 Waterproof match safe		2
1 Insect repellent		3	1 Insect repellent		3
1 Lightweight sweater		12	1 Lightweight sweater		12
1 Army type sewing kit		8	1 Map, topographic, area		4
2 Small boxes matches		2	1 2-man nested cook kit	3	
1 Magnifying glass, small		1	1 First-aid kit	1	8
2 Large face cloths		6	1 Camera	2	
1 Roll toilet tissue		6	1 Fishing gear & Poles	3	
TOTAL 20 lbs. 3 oz.			TOTAL 30 lbs. 6 oz.		

DEHYDRATED FOOD. If all food taken is dehydrated, about 15 pounds will be added to the equipment packs for two people for one week. Adding five pounds of food to the woman's pack would bring her total weight to 25 lbs., 3 oz. Adding the remaining ten pounds of food to the man's pack would make his load weigh 40 lbs., 6 oz. As food is consumed, the packs should weigh 2 lbs. lighter each day.

The equipment kit could be trimmed slightly, and in this manner several more pounds of dehydrated food could be added, extending the trip for a few more days. This could be done without boosting the weight beyond comfort. Concentrated, dehydrated foods bulk fast when water is added.

One 7-lb. Bernard Kamp-Pack makes 20 lbs. of finished food when water is added, and contains 21,000 calories, or 3,000 per person a day for seven days; two, if two persons make a week-long hiking trip. Figure on a pound of dehydrated food per person per day and you won't be far wrong. Wet packs can add weight very rapidly. TAKE IT EASY—GO LIGHT—KEEP A CLEAN CAMP—PREVENT FOREST FIRES! For a change, why not try the saddle and pack-outfit next time?

Chapter 10

MOUNTAIN TRAVEL AND CLIMBING TECHNIQUE

FOR THOSE with a taste for scenic grandeur, there is nothing more thrilling than mountain climbing. Each peak along the route offers a view of never ending beauty. Thousands of acres of untouched forest country sweep towards the horizon. As far as you want to go, you will find the scent of pines and firs, and the sound of water. Every river bend hides another breathtaking sight.

THE FEEL OF THE MOUNTAINS

You must have a basic knowledge of what is required before entering this great domain of rock and snow that reaches to the heavens. After you have acquired this "know how," *and not before*, you ought to try for the "feel of the mountains."

Most of those who have hiked or ridden in the high country, "back of beyond," are convinced that the "feel of the mountains" is reserved for those who love to tread the timberline or above. This is not true for you may also join the ranks of these pioneer mountaineers by affiliating with one of America's climbing-mountaineering clubs, and thereby learn the secrets of the "high places."

A famous mountaineer once wrote: "There is much comfort in high peaks, and a great easing of the heart." How true this is—try it and see!

HEALTH

First, before you ever attempt hiking or climbing in mountainous country, be sure you are in excellent health. Next, unless you are an experienced camper and outdoorsman, join some mountaineering club and learn the ropes; go on a few camping trips, then a few short easy climbs with other beginners, and have an experienced club member along to teach you the proper technique in this exciting sport.

MOUNTAIN WALKING

Mountain walking is similar to walking in any rough and rugged terrain. The long swinging stride used by the hiker on the trail can seldom be used for the feet must be lifted to clear rocks and other obstructions when traveling off the trail.

Mountain walking, depending on the general terrain to be crossed, involves four different techniques. However, two fundamentals apply to all four techniques, and you must master both in order to conserve energy and time.

You must keep the weight of your body *directly* over your feet. The sole of the foot should be placed *flat* on the ground, even on *sloping* ground. This is to distribute your weight as widely as possible and to obtain a better purchase. Boots and soles that will not slide nor slip on rock are a *must*. For most climbs, nailed or Bramani boots, or boots with heavy-lugged soles are necessary. When climbing, keep the lift of each step low; swing *around* obstacles rather than over them. High steps are usually unnecessary and become very fatiguing. In descending, a lean will bring the body nearer perpendicular to the slope, increase acceleration, and relieve the shock to the knees and spine that so many otherwise experience on long descents. Taking small steps and moving at a slow steady pace aids in accomplishing the fundamentals —body in proper balance and the feet flat.

HARD GROUND. Hard ground is generally hard-packed dirt that will not give way under the weight of a man's step.

Ascending. Apply the two fundamentals already described, and the following in addition:

You must lock your knees briefly at the end of each step in order to rest the leg muscles.

You must traverse steep slopes and, if necessary, climb in a zigzag; *not* straight up.

You must turn at the end of each traverse by stepping off in the new direction with the uphill foot. This prevents having to cross your feet and possibly losing your balance.

Traveling. When traveling, you can place the full sole of your shoe down flat most easily by rolling your ankle away from the hill with each step.

Narrows. For narrow stretches, you must use special steps such as the herringbone. Ascend straight up a slope with your toes pointed out and use all the other principles already outlined. You can also use the sidestep in ascending. Similar methods are used when climbing slopes on skis.

Descending. Descending is easiest if you can find a safe way down without traversing.

Keep your back straight and the knees so bent that they take up the shock of each step; this helps prevent slipping. Remember to keep your weight directly over your feet and place the full sole on the ground with each step.

Walking with a slight forward lean—your feet slightly toed out (pigeon-toe fashion)—makes descent easier.

GRASSY SLOPES. In mountainous terrain, grassy slopes usually are made up of small hummocks of growth rather than a continuous field of grass.

Ascending. While all the techniques previously mentioned apply, it is better to step on the *upper side of each hummock* where the ground is more level than on the lower side. Be very cautious in crossing wet grassy cover, for it sometimes is very slippery.

Descending. Traverse with a slow, rhythmic walking motion. *Never run* because hard running on uneven terrain can result in a sprained or broken limb.

SCREE SLOPES. These consist of small loose rocks and particles which have collected under cliffs or bluffs. Scree varies in size from sand particles to pieces the size of a baseball.

Ascending Scree. This is extremely difficult. Avoid it when possible. All principles of ascending hard ground apply but you must pack each step carefully so your foot does not slip down when weight is applied. You can do this best by kicking in with the toe of the upper foot and the heel of the lower foot. (The same applies to climbing in snow).

Traversing Scree. When a scree slope must be traversed and no gain nor loss of altitude is desired, use the hop-skip method. This is a hopping motion in which the lower foot takes all the weight; the upper foot is used only for balance.

Descending Scree. Come down in a straight line. It is important to push your feet out in a slightly pigeon-toed position, as well as to keep your back straight and knees bent. Since there is a tendency to run down scree, take care not to go too fast and lose control. Leaning forward helps.

TALUS SLOPES. Talus slopes are similar to scree slopes, except the rock pieces are larger. To walk on talus, step on top and onto the uphill side of rocks to keep them from tilting and rolling downhill. All previously mentioned fundamentals apply.

Loose Rocks. It is of utmost importance that you *do not kick* loose rocks so they roll downhill. Falling or rolling rocks are extremely dangerous to anyone below. Carelessness by anyone in this respect can cause serious injury or death by rocks no larger than baseballs. The noise of rolling rock can also "spook" game, spoiling an hour or more of careful stalking.

Obstacles. Step *over* rather than on top of obstacles such as rocks and fallen logs to lessen fatigue. (Watch for snakes.)

Talus Vs. Scree. Talus is usually easy to ascend and traverse, while scree is a better avenue of descent.

CLIMB SAFELY

Keep a margin of safety by never attempting to climb to the full limit of your ability. Carefully assess your own climbing ability and that of all other members of the party. The ability and condition of the party are very important. Responsibility is assumed by every member of the party, and it is the leader's responsibility to get the entire party up and back safely.

If some member is unable to complete the climb or becomes ill, he should not be left behind or the party divided unless the disabled can be left with another person competent to assume responsibility for him. The first section or group should return with any person who is unable to continue. *Never leave a person with the possibility of his climbing alone.* Solo climbing is universally condemned.

Before attempting the climb, study the terrain to be covered. Make every effort to plan climbs so that the least able climber in a group is *never pushed* to the fullest extent of his ability.

STEEP SLOPES

BALANCE CLIMBING. Balance climbing is the type of movement used to travel on steep slopes. It combines the balanced movements of a tightrope walker and the unbalanced climbing of a man ascending a ladder.

Body Position. Climb with the body in balance; that is, with your weight poised over your feet or just ahead of them, as you move. Your feet, not your hands, carry the weight except on the steepest slopes or cliffs. Your hands are for balance. Your feet will not hold well when you lean in towards the bluff or rock face.

Movement. With your body in balance, move with a slow rhythmic motion. The pace is extremely important. Climbing should be smooth. One position should flow smoothly into the next. Try to adjust your speed to the climb and distance to be traveled so no rest stops are necessary or at least held to a minimum. Travel slowly but with an even pace so that your gain in elevation will be approximately 1,000 feet an hour. Thus you will be able to "top out" without being completely out of breath.

Support. Use three points of support, such as two feet and one hand, whenever possible. Handholds that are waist to shoulder high are preferable. It is better to use small intermediate holds rather than stretching and changing to widely separated big holds. Avoid the spread-eagle position in which you stretch so far that you cannot let go.

Descending. In descending, face out when the going is easy, sideways when it is hard, and face in when it is extremely difficult. Use the lowest possible handholds. You must keep relaxed because tense muscles tire quickly. When resting, keep your arms low so that circulation is not impaired.

MAIN HOLDS. *Pull Holds.* These are the kind you pull down on. They are easiest to use but also the most likely to break out.

Push Holds. These are the kind you push down on. They allow you to keep your arms desirably low. They rarely break out, but are more difficult to hold in case of a slip. A push hold is often used to advantage in combination with a pull hold.

Friction Holds. These depend solely on the friction of your hands or feet against a smooth surface. They are difficult to use because they give you a feeling of insecurity. Most climbers try to correct improperly for this feeling by leaning close to the rock, thereby increasing their insecurity. Friction holds often serve well as intermediate holds, some of which give needed support while you move over them. But they would not support you were you to stop on them.

Jam Holds. These involve jamming some bearing part of your body or an extremity into a crack in the rock surface. Put one hand into a crack and clench it into a fist, or put one arm into a crack and twist the elbow against one side of the crack and a hand against the other side.

COMBINATION HOLDS. You can combine or vary the main holds described. The number of variations depends only upon the limit of your imagination. A few combination holds are as follows:

Pinch Hold. Pinch a protruding piece of rock between your fingers.

Lie-Back. Lean to one side of an offset crack with your hands pulling and feet pushing against the offset side.

Inverted Pull or Push Hold. This hold is also sometimes called an *under hold.* It permits cross pressure between your hands and feet.

Chimney Climbing. Exert cross pressure between your back and feet, hands or knees. In this manner you can inch up or down if the chimney is not too wide or too narrow.

Foot Hold. A good climbing boot with a rubber-lugged sole is a *must,* and will hold on rock slabs that slope as much as 45 degrees. On steep slopes, keep your body vertical and use small irregularities in the slope to aid foot friction.

USE OF HOLDS. A hold need not be large to be good, nor must it be solid as long as the pressure you apply keeps it in place. Experienced mountain climbers use holds so small that they are hardly visible.

Movements. You must roll your feet and hands over your hold—*not* try to skip or jump, one to another. When traversing, however, it is often desirable to use the hop-step in which you change feet or a small hold so that you may move sideways more easily. This useful step involves a slight upward hop followed by precise footwork.

Testing Holds. Carefully test each and every hold before applying full pressure to it.

ROPE CLIMBING

BELAYING. In group climbing, two or three persons are tied together with a 120-foot rope. Belaying provides the necessary safety factor that enables each person to climb. When any one person is climbing, he is belayed from above or below by another person to whom he is tied with a belay-rope. Without belaying skill, using a rope is a hazard and not a help in group climbing.

What a Belayer Must Do.

(1) Run the rope through his guiding hand (the hand on the rope running to the climber) and around his body to his braking hand, making certain that the rope will slide easily.

(2) Be sure the remainder of the rope is so laid out that it will run freely through the braking hand.

(3) Be certain that the rope does not run over the sharp edge of a rock.

(4) Constantly use the guiding hand to avoid letting too much slack develop in the rope as the climber moves.

(5) Gently tug the line running to the climber to sense his movements.

(6) Avoid taking up slack too suddenly since this may throw the climber off balance and cause him to lose control.

(7) Brace well for the expected direction of a fall so the force of a fall, whenever possible, will pull the belay man more firmly into position.

(8) Neither trust nor assume a belay position that has not been tested.

Falls. In case of a fall, the belayer must be able to perform the following movements automatically:

(1) Relax the guiding hand.

(2) Let the rope slide enough so the braking action is applied gradually by bringing the braking hand slowly across the chest.

(3) Hold the belaying position even if this means letting the rope slide several feet.

The Sitting Belay. The belayer sits or leans against the rocks and attempts to get triangular bracing between his two legs and buttocks. Whenever possible, his legs should be straight. The rope should run around his hips in such a manner that a fall will maintain the belayer more firmly in position. This is facilitated by making certain that the rope always runs along the belayer's *best braced* leg to the climber.

Signals. After a belayer has found a good belay position and has settled himself there, he calls, "ON BELAY," which is answered by the climber with, "UP ROPE," in order to have the belayer take up the slack.

When the slack has been taken up, the belayer calls, "TEST." The climber then calls, "TESTING" and puts his weight gradually on the rope. The climber must use care not to jerk the rope suddenly as this might affect the belayer's position.

If the position is satisfactory, the belayer calls "CLIMB," and the climber calls, "CLIMBING."

If the belayer finds his position unsatisfactory, he must call "OFF BELAY." The climber must then release all tension at once. The belayer *must then find another position and repeat the test procedure.*

ROPE CLIMBING—TWO-MAN PARTY.

(1) One man is chosen as leader because of his ability and experience; he always climbs first.

(2) Both men tie in with a bowline knot or a bowline on a coil.

(3) The second man takes a belay and starts the *test procedure.*

(4) After finding that his position is satisfactory, he gives the order, "CLIMB."

(5) The leader then climbs to a suitable belay position. He should not take long leads, particularly where climbing is difficult. If there is no suitable belay position and he must take a long lead, or if climbing is precarious, the leader should lay the rope whenever possible over rock nubbins. In such a case the belay man adapts his position to an upward pull of the rope.

(6) The belayer should watch the slack and inform the climber, "TWENTY FEET," "FIFTEEN FEET," "TEN FEET," "FIVE FEET," or whatever it may be, by estimating the length of the rope left at the belayer's position.

(7) When the climber has reached a belay point, he establishes a firm belay position and follows test procedures. The Number 2 man climbs to his position; then Number 1 man climbs again. Only if it is determined that both climbers are of equal ability, is leapfrogging permissible.

(8) The procedure is repeated until the objective is reached.

ROPE CLIMBING—THREE-MAN PARTY. In a three-man party each person has a number. The leader is Number 1, the middle man 2, the end man 3.

The signals are the same as for a two-man party except that the number of the man involved must be used with signals. For example, the middle man may give the order, "NUMBER 1, CLIMB," or "NUMBER 3, CLIMB."

The leader climbs from the starting point to the first belay position. He provides what security he can while Number 2 brings up Number 3. Number 2 then follows Number 1 who climbs to the third belay position. If not climbing, Number 3 acts as an anchor man in support of Number 2 when he is belaying.

No man climbs *until ordered* to do so. *Only one man* climbs at a time.

GENERAL ROPE SIGNALS. Certain other standard signals in addition to the belay signals are useful.

(1) "UP ROPE," is used when a climber discovers excess slack in his delay rope.

(2) "SLACK," is used when the belay rope is too tight to permit maneuvering.

(3) "TENSION," means the climber is in trouble and wants a tight rope.

(4) "FALLING," is used to warn the belay man if the climber believes he is about to fall.

(5) When silence is necessary or when high wind distorts voice signals, you can convey information by a prearranged system of jerks or gentle tugs on the rope.

SIMULTANEOUS MOVEMENT. When a slope becomes gentler for a stretch, the entire group can move expeditiously by having all persons in the party move at once. The Number 2 and 3 men carry the slack rope in neat coils which can be paid out or rolled up as the distance between the men varies. The rope must be kept off the ground, but not taut.

RAPPELING. A climber with a rope can descend quickly by means of a rappel—sliding down the rope which has been doubled around such rappel (or holding point) as a tree or projecting rock.

Establishing A Rappel. In selecting a route, be sure that the rope reaches the bottom or an intermediate point from which additional rappels will reach the bottom. Otherwise you are in for trouble!

Test the rappel point carefully. Inspect to see that the rope will run freely around it when one end of the rope is pulled from below to retrieve it after the rappel has been completed.

The Body Rappel Position. Face the anchor rope and straddle it. Then pull the rope from behind and run it around either hip, diagonally across the chest, then back over the opposite shoulder. From there the rope runs to the braking hand, which is the hand on the same side as the hip which the rope crossed; for example, the right hip to the left shoulder to the right or braking hand.

The climber should lead *with the braking hand down* and turn so he faces slightly sideways. He should keep *the other hand on the rope above him* just as a guide, and not as a brake.

He must lean out at a sharp angle to the rock. He should keep his legs well spread and relatively straight for lateral stability, and his back straight to reduce unnecessary friction.

Turning up a shirt or jacket collar helps prevent rope burns on the neck. Wear gloves and select other articles of clothing as padding for the shoulders and buttocks. Leather sewed to clothing where the rope touches body points at shoulder, buttocks, and legs will help prevent rope burns or sores.

Chapter 11

SADDLE AND PACK-OUTFIT CAMPING

THERE IS almost nothing finer to recall than a successful pack trip into the mountains, whether it was planned in order to "get away from it all" or just a grand old hunting or fishing trip. The trip will bring back many fine memories over the years of outdoor scenes shot with camera or gun, of fish eaten, and of tall tales about "the big one that got away." You will recall the fragrance of the pine and the fir, the aroma of coffee and bacon, and the "bull fests" around the campfire with fine companions. The experience will have enriched your life and will bind friendships ever closer. The memory of magnificent views and even the far-off tinkle of grazing bells will remain with you through life!

GETTING READY FOR THE TRIP

The pleasure begins in anticipating a pack trip and planning ahead with the companions who will join you on the trip and share the expenses.

If you have hired a packer and have chosen the right type of equipment and supplies, you are 'way ahead of the game. However, if you plan on doing it all by yourself, you certainly must have some knowledge and experience in the care and handling of saddle and pack stock. You, or at least one of your party, should be experienced. Fail to heed this advice and you may be assured that you will run into trouble with sore-backed, sick, or crippled stock. You will probably be left on foot, to hike back to the pack station where your stock has probably drifted back hours or days ahead of you.

USING A PACK-OUTFIT

WHEN YOU OWN THE OUTFIT. If you own your stock, of course, you can pack in to the national parks and forests without a packer or guide; otherwise, government regulations require that you hire a licensed packer who holds a valid "Special Use Permit" to operate in that section. This is for

(Drawing by Luis M. Henderson)

your protection as well as the park or forest operator, who has a considerable investment in his pack station and is required to operate under government regulations and supervision.

WHEN YOU HIRE. Some families have a packer bring them in to their favorite camping or fishing spot, as also do some hunting parties, and then have the packer return at a later predetermined date to pack them out. This, of course, is the more economical way. Others like to keep the saddle and pack stock with them, moving every few days from one scenic spot to another.

STATUS OF YOUR PACKER. Your guide and packer is a professional man in his line; consequently, he should be given every courtesy due him. Some "guides" and "dudes" become lifelong friends. Your packer will take care of your saddle mount and feed and take care of you. He will show you where the best fishing is to be had and will put you in game country. That is what you pay him for—but don't treat him like a servant or push him just because game has "spooked out" of the area or moved on to another feeding range. It is beyond his power to control such things. You can't blame him if you miss a fair shot at game or fail to catch as many fish as you thought you would for fish move about, too. Again, you may not be as hot a hunter or fisherman as you thought you were!

There are many fine saddle and pack-outfits throughout the United States and Canada, especially in the West, such as the high Sierra Nevada region of California.

One of the outstanding guide and pack-outfits is operated by Joe Barnes who owns the "Lazy Me Ranch" near Oakdale, California. Joe Barnes maintains a deer hunting camp on the Clark Fork of the Tuolumne River in Tuolumne County, during deer season, and a pack station at Mather, California.

COSTS

The cost of a pack train trip will vary, depending entirely upon the extent of the service rendered. On an expedition where the outfitter supplies everything, such as cooks, guide, wrangler, food and camping equipment, it will average about $25.00 per person a day.

Saddle mounts and pack animals average about $6.00 per animal a day if you supply your own equipment. In most cases, you are required to have a packer along. This will cost approximately another $15.00 per day, plus the packer's food and equipment. With four or more in the party, the cost is somewhat cheaper.

THE HIKING-PACK TRIP

A less expensive way to enter a wilderness region and not have to pack your supplies and equipment on your back is the hiking-pack trip. This is a compromise between the hiking trek and the pack trip, or, in other words, a pack animal car-

rying the load, ambling along on a lead rope behind the unbur-
dened hiker.

Burros are coming into the camping scene more and more as
vacationists head for the tall timber in the summer. The average
pay load for a burro is from 50 to 75 pounds, depending on its
size, age, and general health. A large, strong, young burro will
pack 100 pounds if he is grain-fed and not pushed too far. The
average burro-day trek will be 8 to 12 miles, depending upon
roughness of the terrain.

A pack horse, mule, or burro may be used. A single mule or
horse will cost about $6.00 a day. Burros rent for about $3.00
each a day. You should figure one burro per person; however,
if each person carries a small pack, you could get by with one
burro for two persons. By using this method you can carry a
few extra items that you might have had to leave at home if
you had to do all back-packing. Anyone unwilling to back pack
or unable to afford a pack trip can still gain access to the back
country by using burros. Riding burros may also be obtained
for children who are unable to hike. In this way, whole families
are able to vacation in remote country, enjoying the secenery,
fishing and taking pictures. A most helpful discussion of burro
travel is contained in the Sierra Club's *"Going Light With Back-
Pack and Burro,"* recommended for anyone considering a burro
camping trip. It may be purchased for $2.00 from The Sierra
Club, Mills Tower, San Francisco, California.

Arrangements for camping trips can be surprisingly flexible
as far as many of the commercial packers are concerned. For
example, you can make a "spot pack" trip. Your packer will take
your party to a desirable campsite, then return for you at some
specified time. The average cost for "spot pack" trips begins at
about $25 to $30; costs depend upon size of party, destination,
etc.

Or, you can arrange to make a "hiker's spot pack" trip; this
means your dunnage will be packed in to a specified camp location while you hike in to reach it by prearrangement. Since this
is essentially a freighting rather than a guided pack trip, costs
are nominal. Costs of $5 to $7.50 per mule load, plus $15 to $18
per day for the packer and food costs for the packer constitute
most of the trip expense.

See chapter 21, Saddling and Packing, and chapter 22, Care
of Saddle and Pack Animals.

PACK OUTFIT EQUIPMENT CHECK LIST

PERSONAL GEAR
Toilet kit
Hunting and fishing license
Compass and maps
Wash cloths and towels
CLOTHING—Inner
Lightweight wool shirt
Heavyweight wool shirt
Medium weight wool pants
Wool underwear (2)
Socks, 6 pr., wool
Bandanna handkerchiefs
CLOTHING—Outer
Saddle slicker
Hunting cap with ear flaps
Red hunting hat with brim
Down jacket
Wool cruiser coat
Mountain climbing boots
Barker (or Sno-Paks) boots
Rain parka and pants
Leather work gloves
Wool mittens
Suspenders
Camp moccasins
MISCELLANEOUS
Sun glasses (yellow lens)
Binoculars
Spotting scope, small tripod
Extra inner-soles
Extra bulbs and batteries
Flashlight
Pocket knife (BSA model)
Sheath knife (3½-inch blade)
Battery-powered shaver
Hot-water bag or bottle
Thermos bottle (qt. size)
Sharpening stone
Boot waterproofing
First-aid kit
Personal medicines
Smoking gear and tobacco
Pocket warmer
Flannel pajamas
Hooded sweatshirt and pants
Air mattress
Down sleeping bag
Bed roll
Air pump
Camera, extra film, and gear
Duffel bags
Saddle bags
Snake bite kit
Waterproof match **safe**

Waterproofed matches
FIREARMS GEAR
Rifle, scope-sighted
Rifle, iron sights or
  Shotgun (if bird hunting)
Hooded leather scabbard
Cleaning kit, firearms
Ammunition
Scope hoods
CAMP GEAR
Light canvas fly, 12 x 12 ft.
Tarpaulin, canvas, 10 x 10 ft.
Coleman lantern
Axe, single-bit 3 lbs. head
Camp saw, folding
White gas, square 5 gal. can
Strainer
Extra generators and mantles for
  lantern
Shovel, forester type 3 lbs.
50 ft. ½-inch rope
Ball twine
Toilet tissue
Pliers, lineman type
Aluminum grill
Wire grill
Reflector oven
Pressure cooker (optional)
Cooking pans
Kettles
Kitchen gear, knives, forks,
  spoons, pancake turner, etc.
Tableware
Bottle and can-opener
Aluminum foil
Lunch gear, wax paper, sacks
Salt and pepper shakers
Soap and dish towels, detergents
Kitchen Maid, S. O. S. pads
Pot holders
Paper towels
Large cooking fork
Dutch oven
Large iron fry pan
Nesting cook kit
Coffee pot
Dish pan
Wash pan
Oil cloth
Plates
Cups
Butcher knife
Paring knife
Insect repellent

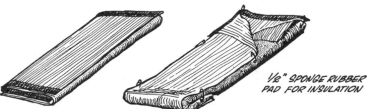

½" SPONGE RUBBER
PAD FOR INSULATION

INTERLOCK TWO
WOOL BLANKETS

TURN UNDER, PIN AS SHOWN

MAKE YOUR OWN SLEEPING BAG FROM BLANKETS.

Chapter 12

NATIONAL PARKS AND NATIONAL FORESTS

MEET YOUR HOSTS, THE RANGERS

SHOULD YOU choose to visit a national park or national forest, you will want to know more about your hosts, the rangers. The rangers are your friends and are there to help you enjoy your visit. Much of the general camping public believe that all rangers are Forest Rangers. This is erroneous since each belongs to a different branch of government service. They perform entirely different duties, with possibly the following exceptions: both make water and snow surveys, work on insect control measures, fight fires, and do rescue work when necessary.

YOUR FOREST RANGER. Your forest ranger is a career professional man and has to qualify as a forester, research forester, range conservationist, or other specialist work in forest land management, and have a college degree in forestry or a related subject. This is a prerequisite necessary to taking the Civil Service examination for entrance into the professional ranks.

DUTIES OF A UNITED STATES FOREST RANGER. The duties of a forest ranger are many and varied. He is the business manager of a large ranger district consisting of several hundred thousand acres for which he is responsible. He is the field representative of the Forest Supervisor. Under government timber management and regulations, he sells timber, he leases grazing land to cattle, horse, and sheep men, and leases summer cabin sites in recreation areas, makes land and boundary surveys, and assists in land exchanges with other agencies.

RANGER NATURALIST. Ranger naturalists are seasonal employees. Incumbents of these positions are selected from the registers for that grade which are maintained in the regional offices of the Civil Service Commission.

DUTIES OF A UNITED STATES PARK RANGER. A park ranger's job encompasses a multitude of duties. The primary objectives of his work are to protect the park visitor, protect the park from fire, theft, vandalism, poachers, timber trespass, direct traffic, enforce park rules and regulations, and state and federal laws. Added to this work are such duties as sanitation; supervising fire, road, and trail crews; building maintenance; inspection of concessionaires and their operation; stocking streams and lakes with fish; making water and snow surveys; recording statistics and office detail; care of live stock; supervision of employees in the district; study of wildlife and wildlife ranges; tree disease and insect control measures; and campground inspection, sanitation, and management. He must be able to drive a patrol car at high speeds when necessary, operate patrol boats, motorcycles, and go as an observer in a plane, and handle pack and saddle stock in remote areas. He must have a knowledge of crime prevention and be able to carry on successfully cases brought before the U. S. Park Commissioner by him, and investigate violations in the park and carry on any special assignments given him. He must be able to carry out rescue operations and search for lost persons; plus numerous other duties peculiar to his district.

WHAT ARE NATIONAL PARKS AND NATIONAL FORESTS?

It is apparent that many people are not clear regarding the difference between a national park and a national *forest*. Even newspaper accounts often misinform the public by reporting that an incident took place in a national forest when it actually occurred in a national park and vice versa. This is an erroneous picture and the following statement by The National Park Service, United States Department of The Interior, and by The Forest Service, United States Department of Agriculture should clarify the issue.

Millions of people annually visit both national parks and national forests, or receive benefits of one kind or another from them, without realizing that there is a definite distinction between these two kinds of federal reservations. Perhaps you, too, would like to know what that distinction is.

Both the national forests and the many kinds of areas that comprise the National Park System exemplify conservation— the wise use of our resources; and both play an important part in the lives of the people of our Nation.

THE NATIONAL PARK SYSTEM

National parks, of which there are now 31, all established
by acts of Congress, and a number of national monuments,
have been set aside to preserve superlative examples of natural
beauty permanently for public enjoyment. Geological features
and all plant and animal life are carefully protected in them.
The law requires that they be administered to provide for
public enjoyment "in such manner and by such means as will
leave them unimpaired for the enjoyment of future generations." They are thus, in a sense, great outdoor museums. Only
such developments are permitted as are needed for the protection and administration of the areas or required for the
comfort and convenience of those who visit them for the
recreation and inspiration they offer. Research into and inter-
pretation of the natural phenomena of these areas are an
important part of the Service's work.

All animal species are given equal protection, subject to
sensible controls; virgin forests remain unlogged to go through
their natural cycles; grazing is limited and is being steadily
decreased, with the ultimate objective of eliminating it completely; lands, with a few exceptions specifically authorized
by Congress, are not subject to mineral entry; impoundment or
"artificialization" of lakes or streams for irrigation, hydro-
electric power, or other purposes is opposed in accordance
with the principle recognized when the parks and monuments
were exempted from the provisions of the 1920 Federal Power
Commission Act. The basic policy is to preserve nature as
created while providing for visitor appreciation and intelligent
use.

The National Park System also includes other national
monuments of historic or prehistoric significance and many
areas of special historic interest in other categories. As of
January 1, 1962, there were 30 national parks, 8 national historical parks, 83 national monuments, 12 national memorials,
11 national military parks, 10 national historic sites, 10 na-
tional cemeteries, 5 national battlefield sites, 3 national park-
ways, 3 national battlefield parks, 1 national memorial park,
1 national seashore recreational area, and the national capital
parks—a total of 190 areas covering over 25,700,000 acres.
In addition, the Service administers 3 national recreation

areas on reservoir sites; 2 under agreements with the Bureau of Reclamation and 1 with that Bureau and the Office of Indian Affairs.

THE NATIONAL FORESTS

National forests are established by proclamation of the President, or, in some states, only by act of Congress. The earliest national forests were established by reservation of lands in the public domain. Under authorization of the Congress, lands may also be acquired for national forest purposes by purchase, donation, or exchange.

National forests are administered for the protection, development, and use of timber, water, range, and other resources in the public interest. A basic purpose is the management and protection of watersheds, to safeguard water supplies, prevent erosion, and reduce floods. Timber resources are managed to contribute toward a permanent supply of timber and other forest products and to serve as demonstration areas of forest management for the benefit of private timber owners and operators. National forest ranges are managed to provide a sustained supply of forage for the grazing of livestock. The forests are managed also to preserve their beauty and attractiveness for the recreational enjoyment of the people; to maintain a favorable habitat for wildlife; and in other ways to make their resources contribute to the economic stability and welfare of the nation.

All these uses of the national forests are provided for under a management principle known as "multiple use." Multiple use means that most of the national forest areas yield not one but several different products or services. Thus, timber harvesting, livestock grazing, various uses of water, mining, hunting, fishing, berry picking, and similar activities may take place at the same time—each is so adjusted that it does not seriously interfere with the others. At some places, of course, one use may be so important as to give it the right-of-way over the others; multiple-use management provides for this. The controlling objective is to maintain for the national forest as a whole a coordinated pattern or use that will produce the largest net total of public benefits.

There are 154 national forests and 18 national grass lands containing almost 186,000,000 acres. The Forest Service also maintains nine regional forest and range experiment stations and a Forest Products Laboratory for research into the basic facts necessary for proper management and utilization of all forest resources and conducts programs to encourage and support better management and protection on forest lands in state and private ownership.

VISITING AREAS OF THE NATIONAL PARK SYSTEM

In carrying out the mandate which established the National Park Service, roads, trails, and campsites have been constructed by the Service where necessary. Other facilities, including hotels, lodges, cabins, and bus transportation, are provided in the larger areas by private concessionaires. The Federal Government, itself, does not operate public accommodations or transportation. Park rangers protect the parks from fire and acts of vandalism, and perform many services for visitors. Park naturalists or historians give talks and conduct tours, and this service is supplemented by many museums.

Moderate fees are charged in some areas for guides, admissions, or motor permits. These fees have been established in the belief that part of the expense of administration should be borne directly by those who use the areas.

Rules and regulations, which must be observed, are those of good manners and are for the protection of the natural features, as well as for your safety, comfort, and convenience.

VISITING THE NATIONAL FORESTS

National forest lands are open for recreation use; restrictions are imposed only when necessary for your health and safety and for protection of the forests. National forests provide opportunities for camping, picnicking, swimming, skiing, hiking, hunting, and fishing. Numerous nearby resorts are operated privately under special permits.

In times of extreme fire hazard certain areas may be closed to all use. Such closed areas are conspicuously posted.

Campers and picnickers are urged to use regular camp and picnic areas where fire grates, tables, sanitary facilities, and safe drinking water are available. Campfire permits are required in some forests, even at regular camp and picnic areas. At a few of the larger camp and picnic grounds a small fee is collected by the concessionaire.

National forests are a home for about one-third of our country's big-game animals. Also, they furnish part of the forage for eight million domestic animals.

Wilderness and wild areas, 82 in all, have been set aside in national forests to be permanently maintained in their primitive status.

WILDERNESS—WILD—PRIMITIVE AREAS

The Forest Service has established 83 areas in which primitive conditions of environment are preserved for the use and enjoyment of those to whom the wilderness means many things and yields experiences which are unattainable elsewhere. All of these areas are generally referred to as Wilderness Areas because they are all managed for the same purpose.

Actually, there are four classifications or kinds—Primitive Areas, Wild Areas, Wilderness Areas, and the Boundary Waters Canoe Area. Wilderness Areas must be over 100,000 acres in size, and are subject to classification by the Secretary of Agriculture; Wild Areas are smaller, and are classified by the Chief of the U.S. Forest Service. A Wild Area is comprised of between 5,000 and 99,999 acres.

The Boundary Waters Canoe Area, in Minnesota, is a compromise between important wilderness and commercial values. Its management plan provides for the protection of wilderness values while permitting certain utilization of its resources.

Some of our Primitive Areas may ultimately be classified as Wild or Wilderness Areas; as a matter of policy, the Forest Service is now managing all Primitive Areas just as though they were so classified.

The Forest Service does not, however, have complete control over all developments in Wilderness Areas; some private lands are included in them, and the western Wilderness Areas, are of course, subject to the provisions of U.S. mining laws.

HOW TO OBTAIN A FOREST SERVICE SUMMER HOME

Summer homes are permitted in most of the national forests under certain restrictions governing site, construction, maintenance, and use.

At present there are approximately 18,230 summer-home permits in effect. The minimum fee is $25.00 but on choice sites the fee may run as high as $100.00 or more per year.

Since a summer home is an exclusive private use of national forest land, such use must not be allowed to interfere with public or semi-public uses such as reservoirs, flood-control projects, highways, public campgrounds, and other distinctly public uses. Summer homes may only be permitted on areas which because of topography or location are unsuitable for public use, or on areas which as far as can be foreseen will not be needed for present or future public use. The presence of summer homes must not interfere with public needs on other areas. In several national forests the pressures of gen-

eral public needs have become so great that summer-home sites are no longer available; but this is not so everywhere.

In order to prevent unnecessary intrusion into the forest scene and interference with general public uses, summer homes are not allowed within sight of highways or lakes, along fishing streams, near public use areas, nor near scenic attractions. Nevertheless the objective is to locate them in suitable places and in attractive country with good forest cover. Occasionally they are within convenient distance of fine recreation areas.

Areas suitable for summer homes are selected by experienced forest officers in accordance with the above principles. Such areas are subdivided into lots or units of about one-third acre in size. It is, however, both impracticable and undesirable to permit individual summer homes in isolated, scattered locations.

Persons desiring summer homes should get in touch with the forest supervisor of the particular national forest in which they are interested. If summer home sites are available, the forest supervisor will arrange for an inspection of the sites and the prospective summer-home owner may take his choice of unoccupied lots. The location and surveying of summer-home areas is just one of many things which men of the Forest Service do, hence it is not possible to have many sites ready at all times.

If no summer-home lots are available in a particular forest, the supervisor will, if practicable, direct the prospective summer-home owner to another forest where lots are available. An application for a specific lot must be made on application forms available from the forest supervisors. The application should be filed with either the district ranger or the forest supervisor of the national forest concerned. A special use permit will be issued upon approval of the application.

Buildings on summer-home lots must be appropriate to the forest environment. The location of all buildings is approved by the forest officer in charge. Construction plans must also be submitted to the forest supervisor for approval before starting to build.

Builders of summer homes at the higher elevations in the mountains must expect winters when the snow will be ten feet or more in depth, and this should be taken into consideration in preparing building plans, and figuring building costs. All buildings must be finished in a color harmonizing with the forest background.

Only one residence building may be constructed on a lot. Construction must be completed by the end of the second season after the permit is issued, and no improvement of a temporary nature will be allowed after that date.

Toilets and garbage disposal must meet state and county sanitation laws and national forest regulations.

Summer homes are for personal—not commercial use. Subleasing is allowed only for short periods, if first approved by the forest supervisor; it will not be approved as a general practice. Summer homes may be sold or transferred, but only after the written approval of the forest supervisor has been obtained. The premises and improvements must be maintained in an orderly condition and in good state of repair; they will be inspected from time to time by a qualified forest officer. All national forest regulations and state laws as to fire protection, fish and game, etc., must, of course, be observed.

Permits for summer homes authorize their use as a recreation residence—not as a permanent residence. The keeping of livestock, saddle horses, or poultry is prohibited in summer-home areas.

Each holder of a summer-home permit pays an equitable fee for the privilege of using the land. The fee for each lot is determined on the basis of its value for summer-home use.

MISSION 66 AND OPERATIONS MULTIPLE USE

The National Park Service is catching up in all phases of its "Mission 66" program, a ten-year expansion plan that is already moving into high gear. More and better facilities have been observed throughout the system.

The National Park Service will be concluding "Mission 66" in the near future, and will again move forward with a newer program to improve camping and other facilities for the increasing millions of park visitors.

The National Forest Service has concluded "Operations Outdoors," and started in on "Operations Multiple Use." This development program includes all renewable resources of the National Forest System—water, timber, recreation, forage, and wildlife habitat. It includes both specific proposals for the next ten years and long-term proposals to the year 2000.

These programs will mean more and better recreational facilities for millions of outdoor-minded people who every season roam through 382,000 square miles administered by these two services. Over 180,000,000 visits are expected by 1966, when "Mission 66" will have been completed.

CABIN OWNER'S SAFETY CHECK LIST

(1) We know that the forest ranger or fire warden checks our summer cabin for our own protection and that we are liable for damages when our negligence causes a forest fire.

(2) The forest ranger or fire warden has inspected our cabin and found that it meets all state, county, and National Forest fire regulations.

(3) All leaves, pine needles, grass, and debris have been cleared from our yard.

(4) We have removed and destroyed all rubbish, oily rags, and flammable material from our cabin.

(5) Paint, cleaning fluid, and gasoline are kept in a safe cool place.

(6) Our roof is cleared regularly of leaves and pine needles.

(7) Our chimney and fireplace flues are clean and fire-proofed.

(8) We have checked to make sure our power lines are clear of branches.

(9) Our telephone, radio, and TV antennas are equipped with grounded lightning arresters.

(10) We know and follow the state, county, and National Forest burning regulations.

(11) We practice safety when handling fire of any kind.

(12) Fire extinguishers and fire fighting tools are kept handy and in good working condition.

(13) We know where to report a fire. The telephone number is ......

(14) When in doubt—we ask a Forest Ranger.

Chapter 13
THE CAMPFIRE

FIRE HAS BEEN a comfort and friend of man for centuries—it will keep him warm, cook his food, dry his clothes, and even add a flickering light of friendship to dispel night's shadows. Yet, at times when he has lost control of it, fire has destroyed him and his possessions.

CONTROLLING THE CAMPFIRE

Fire, recognized as necessary and useful, is a dangerous instrument when used carelessly. Every year hundreds of forest fires are started by careless campers and others who use the out-of-doors. The true woodsman reveals his character

(Drawing by Luis M. Henderson)

and experience in the woods by the way he builds and takes care of his campfire. The type of fire you build will depend on the use you plan to make of it, whether for warmth, drying clothes, cooking, or for heating water.

Soft woods like ponderosa pine, sugar pine, cedar, lodgepole pine and spruce burn much more rapidly than do the hard woods of ash, birch, hickory, or oak. However, the hard woods make better coals for cooking and hold the heat considerably longer.

CAMPFIRE PERMIT

Be sure before leaving on the trip that you have secured a campfire permit if it is required in the area in which you plan to camp. The permit may be obtained free of charge at most sporting goods stores or from the local headquarters of the

National Park or Forest Service. Permits may also be secured from the park or forest ranger in the area before you leave the end of the road for your camping spot. However, don't expect the ranger to feel too friendly towards you if you awaken him in the middle of the night or at four o'clock in the morning requesting a fire permit or asking where the best fishing may be had, just because you neglected to get a permit and information in town during office hours. This happens many times during the summer months when thoughtless city folks sometimes fail to realize that the ranger loses plenty of sleep as it is, on fires and rescues, without having to issue fire permits or give information in the middle of the night. Be certain before you build a fire that you are not in a closed or restricted area.

STARTING YOUR CAMPFIRE

For wet country, matches should be waterproofed by dipping the head of the match into melted wax or fingernail polish. There are several good fire starters on the market—some woodsmen use candles to assist in getting the campfire going. In the rain forest of the Olympics where the annual rainfall averages 144 inches, woodsmen use Army issue Heat-Tabs in getting damp wood lighted. Some sportsmen carry a fully filled cigarette lighter, with several extra flints. The lighter should be tightly taped with waterproof adhesive and used only in emergencies. This will provide between 600 and 800 lights, depending on how long one keeps the flame lighted each time it is used.

Dry tinder will get your fire going quickly since tinder is the intermediate between match and heavier fuels. Small, dry, dead branches found under pine and fir make excellent tinder. A fuse or fire stick as illustrated will assist in igniting damp fuel. Hard, pitchy sections of wood can be found in some half-rotted logs. This is a quick fire starter. Heavy fir bark makes fine cooking coals.

A good way to start a fire, especially if you have only one match, is the fuzz stick. This woodsman's standby is made by "shaving" a dry piece of wood with a knife or an ax, allowing one end of each shaving to remain attached to the wood. Prepare two of these sticks and prop them against each

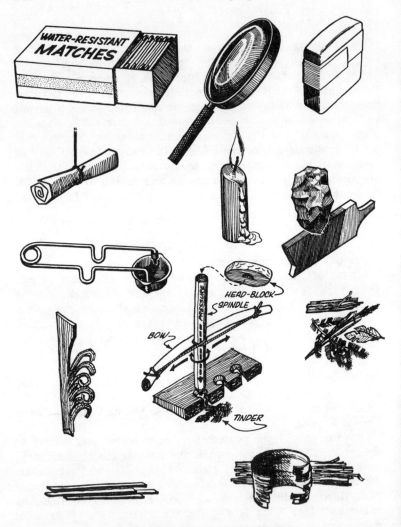

FIRE MAKES AND PRIMARY FUELS.

Included are the magnifying glass, candle, lighter—filled and taped shut, newspaper dipped in wax or cut up milk cartons, flint and steel, welder's torchlighter (flint and steel), fuzz stick cut from dry stick, the friction method, tinder (any fine, dry, combustible material), cedar kindling, and two ideal prime fuels—dry cedar and birch bark.

other with some loose shavings leaning on them. Hold the

lighted match under the fuzz sticks—and you have a fire!

A small magnifying glass and a piece of flint and steel for emergency use can come in awfully handy if one should lose all his matches or if they should accidently become too wet to light.

TYPES OF FIRE LAYS

The pyramid or tepee fire lay is the quicket and simplest. It is good for boiling, making a bed of coals, or for warmth.

The log cabin or criss-cross allows for plenty of draft, and a bed of hot coals can be made more quickly by this method for baking pan-bread, broiling or frying steaks or other meat. If a grill is placed on top of the coals you can make excellent pancakes.

For baking, the half-tepee reflector lay is a good choice. This fire is made by tipping a large thin slab of rock on its side or using the base of a large rock wall. Stack the tinder with kindling and other fuel sticks on top and up against the rock wall in a half-tepee. The rock will reflect the heat back onto whatever you are baking. A sheet of aluminum foil placed across the face of this wall will increase heat reflection. If you expect to depend upon a log type reflector to warm your open tent, place a sheet of foil across the log and it will throw more heat.

One of the most popular types of fire lays is the "keyhole." With this you can cook on one end and have your evening campfire at the other. It is used more in fixed or permanent camps since it takes more time and rocks to construct. The lay is formed by making a rock border in the shape of a large keyhole. It is very likely that you will find one already made at your campsite in the back country.

The hunter type of lay is used more than any other by hunters in a hurry to "get out and at them." It can be constructed by laying two rows of rocks parallel and about 6 to 8 inches apart, and building a fire between. It can also be made by cutting two green logs 8 to 10 inches in diameter and 2 to 4 feet in length. The length of either will depend on how many people there are in the party, and how many pots and kettles you want on the fire at one time. In either case, the walls should be placed just far enough apart so that the cooking utensils do not fall in between; build the parallel rocks or logs with the wind direction so that the fire will have proper draft. Draft then can be regulated by placing different sized rocks in front of the windward side.

The "pit" or "prairie" lay should be used on windy days. This keeps the fire or a spark in the hole where it belongs, and it cannot be blown into the forest litter where it is very apt to start a brush or forest fire. Sod should be placed on the windy side, and the dirt removed from the pit on the windward side. The sod will prevent dirt from being blown into the cooking pot.

The "trench" fire lay is made by digging a narrow trench about 8 inches deep and 6 to 8 inches wide; just wide enough so that the pot will not drop in between when the dirt walls dry out. The mouth or entrance should be wider so that fuel sticks can be shoved in to feed the fire. Build to face the wind so that breezes can enter for draft.

For a single pot lay, use three rocks placed triangle-shape so that a pot will sit on top.

The "star type" fire lay is used for sitting around. Mainly, this is a camp or warming fire. The lay is fashioned star-shape and, as the center fuel burns up, the ends are shoved to the center. Long lengths of wood can be used in this method and do not have to be cut up.

WILDERNESS CAMPFIRE LORE

1. Start your fire with dry, dead, soft wood. It should be secured from a standing dead tree if possible. Standing wood is normally dry wood in most areas.

2. Gather sufficient wood to cook your entire meal and for your warming camp fire before you light your fire. Be sure to have enough dry kindling for the breakfast fire put away in a safe, dry place.

3. For quick burning, all wood should be split. Round wood will last longer for a warming fire.

4. Fires are controlled by draft. Lay your fire so you can control it properly. Arrange it so it will receive more air and you will receive more heat. Remember, the less air, the less heat.

5. For boiling, frying, searing, and reflector oven baking, use soft woods.

6. Use hard woods for heating, broiling, stewing, slow frying and baking in a fry pan.

7. Never use rocks from lakes or stream beds or shale for they may explode when heated.

8. Never leave a camp fire, even for short periods of time. A sudden gust of wind may blow sparks where they may cause a grass, brush or forest fire.

9. Unburned fire logs which haven't been fully consumed should be dipped in a stream or lake if one is nearby; if not, they should be well soaked with a pail of water. Small embers should be wet down and damp earth stirred up with them. Wet and stir until the last spark is out. Feel through the ashes before you leave the camp to make sure you didn't leave a spark that might cause a forest fire.

10. A good woodsman will leave the site better than he

CLEARING AREA FOR CAMPFIRE: This is mandatory, to be done FIRST. Dig down to solid mineral soil. Area must be at least six feet in diameter.

found it. Burn all garbage. Burn, flatten, and bury all tin cans. Erase all signs of human use. That is the mark of an experienced sportsman.

Careful people use the *fireplaces* provided at some places in national forests, national parks, state forests, and even on some private forests.

However, where there are no fireplaces, the careful hunter, camper, fisherman, or hiker makes a safe place for his fire. He then follows these eleven commonsense rules:

(1) He builds his fire away from overhanging trees. Embers and sparks drift upward with heat and can start a fire in the tree branches.

(2) He makes sure the ground area is free from exposed roots. Fire can burn downward and travel through roots, coming to the surface days or weeks later.

(3) Before he starts his fire, he scrapes away all litter, leaf mold, and humus, and other material that will burn, so that the soil is bare on an area from six to ten feet in diameter. This will keep small campfires from spreading.

(4) He builds his campfire where it is protected from wind and sudden breezes. If no natural wind protection is available,

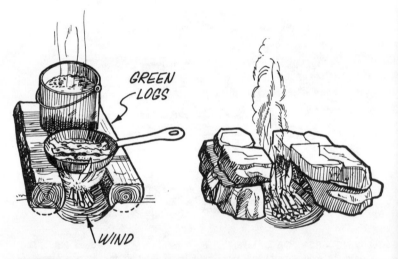

FIREPITS: Left, dual green log pit. Right, dual stone pit (note upper stones are slightly cantilevered).

he stretches canvas or a raincoat between two poles or trees several feet to the windward of the fire.

(5) He sometimes builds his fire in a hole. This helps save wood and protects the fire from the wind. It also makes it easier to put the fire *dead out* before leaving it.

STONE FIREPITS, showing cooking support, wind direction, fuel, and sleep area.

(6) He starts his fire with twigs and small sticks, and adds larger sticks as the fire builds up. This prevents a sudden flareup with its shower of sparks.

VERY SIMPLE CAMPFIRE ARRANGEMENT.

(7) He keeps his fire small. A small fire or good bed of coals gives plenty of heat for cooking and reduces both fire hazard and smoke.

(8) He puts his campfire *dead out* before leaving it. He puts water on it and stirs it until he can *safely* put his hand in it. When both smoke and steam are gone, he feels each stick to

make sure there are no hot coals. If there is no water handy, he stirs moist dirt or sand into the coals until they are all dead out.

(9) He extinguishes, if possible, any uncontrolled fire he finds burning and immediately reports it to the nearest park or forest ranger or state fire warden. If he cannot put out the fire he goes to the nearest phone and calls the ranger. Anyone who answers will help him get the message to the ranger station. The ranger would like to know the location of the fire and its size and whether it is smoldering or moving fast; also if anyone else knows of the fire and is fighting it.

(10) He leaves a clean camp. He burns as much of the garbage

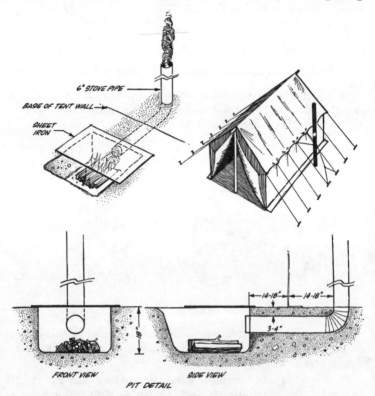

6" STOVE PIPE

BASE OF TENT WALL

SHEET IRON

14-18" 14-18"

3-4"

18"

FRONT VIEW   SIDE VIEW

PIT DETAIL

FIRE PIT IN FLOOR OF EMERGENCY SHELTER TENT.
Rocks may be placed around the fire in pit to help retain heat.

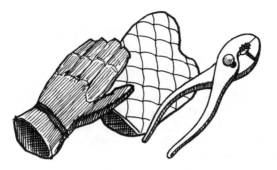

THREE GOOD POT LIFTERS.

as possible, especially fish heads and other fish waste. He puts the rest of the garbage in the cans or pits provided. If there are none, he buries all garbage and refuse. He is careful not to leave straw or pine boughs scattered around.

(11) He does not smoke while traveling—whether by auto, horseback, or foot—except while on a surfaced highway or in an improved campground. He breaks matches in two before throwing them away to be certain they are out. He crushes out all cigarettes, cigars, or pipe heels on rock or in mineral soil.

The accompanying illustrations show various types of campfire arrangements and aids.

CAMP HELPERS. Forked stick, coat hanger wire, and old oven grate.

SMOKEY BEAR SAYS—ONLY YOU CAN PREVENT
FOREST FIRES!

Chapter 14
CAMP COOKING

A CAMPER can now solve his cooking and dishwashing chores by using versatile aluminum foil to broil, fry, and bake his food. Cooking food in aluminum foil is a simple process. You need nothing to hold the foil-wrapped package together, since the foil will mold to the shape of any food wrapped in it.

Your food, no matter if it is a roast, vegetable, fruit or what have you, will have that sealed-in flavor that is the mark and seal of the expert camp cook. You will also find that foil cooking can be used to advantage in patio cooking, on beach parties, and even in the home. Most men enjoy cooking on an outdoor fire.

WRAPPING THE FOOD PACKAGE

Some outdoorsmen wrap and mark food packages in aluminum foil before leaving on a pack horse or canoe trip. By preparing foil-wrapped parcels in advance, much camp cooking time is saved, and there are no dishes, pots, or pans to wash. This gives one more leisure time to fish, hunt, or just loaf around the campfire visiting with camp companions.

Each food package should be wrapped in one regular weight foil. It has been found that by rewrapping this with an outside heavy-duty quilted foil, the food inside can be protected if one layer should become punctured. This will also prevent ashes or dirt from entering and possibly spoiling the contents. It is best to purchase regular foil in 12-inch width rolls and the heavy-duty type in 18-inch width.

COOKING WITH FOIL

Of course, it will take a few trial runs to become expert at foil cooking. One needs to have plenty of coals. Hard woods, of course, are best for making a good bed of coals; however, in the West unless you are in the lower oak regions, you will have to depend on fir, pine, or one of the soft woods. With care you can build up a good bed of coals with these woods, although fir bark is the best fuel for coals.

WRAPPING. If you haven't packaged your food in advance, proceed as follows: after you have prepared a good bed of hot coals, place your food on a single sheet of regular foil large enough to allow a fold over and a three-fold crimp of each of the three open sides. Now fold over and crimp in the open ends and top, folding each over at least three times to insure a tight seal. Next, take the heavy-duty quilted foil, which should be at least two inches larger in size, and wrap the food package again. Fold over the open edges the same as you did the first time but reverse top and bottom so that the crimp is on the opposite side.

COOK IN HOT COALS AND SERVE. Dig a hole in the hot coals and bury the package. Rake the coals back over the foil-covered food so that it will receive heat from all sides. When it is ready, take it out and place it where the foil will cool for several minutes. The seams can now be opened and folded back and the food can be eaten while still in its foil wrapping. Some kind of gloves are advisable for lifting the package out of the coals. Use cheap cotton work gloves when working around a campfire to save yourself from burns. They are well worth it.

COOKING MEATS AND VEGETABLES. You can cook practically anything in foil and camp menus are many and varied. You should add cooking oil, shortening, butter, bacon or oleomargarine when cooking meats. A tablespoon of water should be added when cooking vegetables. This will prevent food from sticking or burning.

You can cook vegetables and meat together to save time. Hamburgers, steaks, and chops will cook in 15 to 20 minutes but pork and lamb chops require longer cooking. When cooking vegetables, be sure to shoestring, slice, or dice them since they require longer cooking time than meat. It will take over an hour to cook a roast or large game birds. Fish will be well done in about 15 minutes.

OUTDOOR RECIPES. Remember, the higher the elevation, the greater the change in atmospheric pressure and the effect on cooking. Cooking takes more time, and more water must be added to the ingredients to make up for rapid evaporation.

Here are a few tested trail recipes.

CAMP COFFEE
2 cups of water per person and add one extra. 1 tablespoon of instant coffee per cup. Add boiling water. Add Pream, canned milk, or drink black. Sweeten.

COWBOY COFFEE

2 cups of water per person and add one extra. 2 tablespoons of regular grind coffee per cup. Add egg shells from breakfast. Bring to boil, strain and lace with whiskey.

NORTHWOODS TEA

1 pinch of bulk black tea per cup. Bring to boil and serve with lemon.

SIERRA TEA

1 pinch of powdered instant tea or 1 tea bag per cup. Fill cup with boiling water. Serve with powdered lemon or Pream.

TRAIL PANCAKES

1. Heat must be just right. Test by dropping a few drops of water on the skillet. If the water skitters around the skillet, the heat is right. (Batter should be thin).
2. Grease pan or griddle slightly. Pour batter-mix to desired size.
3. Turn cakes when puffed and full of bubbles, but never before they break.
4. Serve as soon as each batch is completed.
5. Or, use prepared flour. (Ingredients that are already mixed and sifted.) 10 cakes; 1 cup flour, ¾ cup milk, 1 egg, or use powdered eggs, 1 teaspoon butter or oleo, shortening or cooking oil. Mix until smooth. Bake on hot griddle or in fry pan. In an emergency they can be cooked on a camp shovel blade or on a large hot rock. Cook cakes all at one time if hot rock is used.

CAMP BREAD

In making camp or foil bread, it is quicker to use one of the prepared biscuit flours. The tendency is to use too much water. Use just enough to make an easy working dough. Dust the loaf; grease the inside of the foil with butter, cooking oil, or shortening; and wrap loosely so the foil package will not burst when the dough rises. Place the bread package at the edge of the coals, and turn sides often so each side will receive equal cooking time. For the last three minutes, place the bread in the center of the coals. This will put a good crust all around it. Don't let a crust on your meat fool you, either—it just seals in the good meat flavor.

FRY PAN BREAD

Mix prepared flour or Bisquick with water and enough milk to make thick dough. Grease pan and bake on hot coals.

(For Two)

HIGH SIERRA BISCUITS

2 cups of flour
2 teaspoons baking powder
1 cup instant dry milk
½ teaspoon salt
4 tablespoons shortening

CANADIAN CAMP BISCUITS

2 cups prepared flour
⅜ cup canned milk
Mix until stiff and sticky, grease pan, and place on hot coals or put in reflector oven.

For these biscuits, mix dry ingredients thoroughly, cut the shortening in, then add sufficient water or milk to make a thick dough soft enough to be handled easily. If batter becomes sticky, dust with more flour. The batter can be flattened out by hand or rolled out until dough is one inch thick. From the sheet of batter, cut out the biscuits with the baking powder can top, or use a cup. Dust each biscuit with flour and place in lightly greased pan. Place in a reflector oven or close to the campfire coals. Bake until golden brown. Keep turning so all sides are done. Test with a toothpick or a pine needle. When done, the dough should not adhere to needle. Biscuits will raise 2-inches high. The above recipe may be cut in half if used for one person. Multiply the ingredients by the number of people in camp to secure sufficient servings.

MINER'S SOURDOUGH BREAD

For a small party (4) in a fixed camp.

4 cups of flour; mix warm water into flour until a thick creamy batter is obtained. Add 3 tablespoons of sugar, 2 tablespoons of salt. Mix well and place in warm spot for several days, or until it turns sour. A speedier method is to add a cake of yeast to hasten fermentation. The container should be large enough so that the sourdough doesn't "boil over." Keep the mix covered to keep out dirt and insects. When the mix is "ripe" or ready to use, mix ½ to ¾ of batter with 1 cup of flour, 1 teaspoon full of baking soda. Mix well and add 1 tablespoon of cooking oil or shortening. Next, add whatever additional flour needed to work into a smooth kneading dough. Do not knead more than necessary. Shape and place in greased baking pans. Place in sun or a warm spot until raised to about twice its original size. Baking time, about 1 hour. Test with fork or toothpick. If fork comes out clean, bread is done.

CAMP CORNBREAD

½ cup corn meal
½ cup cold milk

1½ cups boiling water
¾ teaspoon salt

Mix ingredients. Beat 1 egg slightly, add milk and shortening. Combine with dry ingredients, stir only until moist. Pour into well-greased pan and bake in reflector oven until done. Serves three.

WOODSMEN'S CREAMED POTATO SOUP

2 cups of potato flakes
½ cup chopped onion
1¼ cups of boiling water
3¼ cups of milk

1 tablespoon butter
2 slices of chopped well-done bacon
Salt and pepper to taste

Boil onions gently until tender; add milk, butter, salt, pepper, and chopped fried bacon. Bring contents to slow boil. Add potato flakes. Cook for several minutes. Stir constantly to keep from scorching.

FISHERMEN'S CLAM CHOWDER

Prepare 2 servings of Pillsbury's cooked diced potatoes. Drain well. Melt 1 tablespoon butter in large saucepan. Blend in ⅛ cup of flour, ¼ teaspoon salt, and pinch or 1/16 teaspoon pepper. Gradually stir in 1 pint of milk and drain liquid from one 7-oz. can of minced clams. Add minced clams and 1½ tablespoon chopped onion. Cook over medium fire, stirring constantly until chowder thickens. Makes 2 to 3 servings.

MULE SKINNER'S MUSH

Cut leftover cornmeal mush into ½-inch slices. Pan fry in small amount of hot shortening until golden brown. Serve hot with syrup or honey.

FISHERMEN'S FRY

Salt fish, dip in cornmeal or in seasoned mixture of egg and milk, then in cornmeal, and fry slowly over hot coals.

ALPINE CLAM PADDIES

One 7-oz. can of minced clams.
Place in bowl and crumble up dry soda crackers. Mix 1 egg with ingredients. Grease pan and fry. Salt and pepper to taste. Serve with lemon.

SALMON RIVER PADDIES

Prepare the same as clam paddies. Season and serve with lemon.

PIGS-IN-A-BLANKET

"Pigs-in-a-blanket" take about 15 minutes and are delicious. Mix some Bisquick or other type of prepared flour with water and roll it out as thin as you can. Use a round glass jar or a tin can to roll the dough out flat. Dust your hands with flour to keep the dough from sticking to them. Cut the dough large enough to completely cover the frankfurter except at the ends. Wrap in foil and cover with coals and in about 15 minutes you will enjoy a delicious meal.

HIKER'S FRANKS

Put 4 frankfurters, small cabbage wedge, small carrots, and fresh or frozen peas on double thickness of foil. Salt, and put in teaspoonful of butter or margarine. Close package, sealing tightly. Grill 15 to 20 minutes. Serves four.

SQUAWMAN'S BEAN STEW

Allow 1 cup of precooked Lima, Navy or other beans for each member. Cook until done. Add one small can of meat cut in small cubes, 1 can of tomatoes, 2 medium onions (diced), celery salt, and parsley flakes; season to taste with salt and pepper. Simmer until ingredients are well done. Ham, frankfurters, or any other leftover meat will add to the flavor of this stew.

MOUNTAINEER'S HASH BROWN'S

Cook a half-package dried diced potatoes in 3 cups of water, add 1 teaspoon salt and bring to boil. Simmer 15 to 20 minutes until potatoes are tender. Drain well. Melt ¼ cup of butter, shortening or cooking oil in medium size skillet, add potatoes, ½ teaspoon salt, ⅛ teaspoon pepper. Press down and fry until brown crust forms on bottom. Turn potatoes, a portion at a time, and continue to fry until a golden brown.

CAMPER'S DELIGHT POTATOES

Prepare 4 servings of Pillsbury's hash brown potatoes. Combine with 2 tablespoons butter, 2 tablespoons parsley flakes, and ½ tablespoon salt; sprinkle with paprika. Serves four.

256   *All About Camping*

RANGER'S HASH

Here is an old favorite of the trail. Empty 1 package of dehydrated potatoes in a kettle; cover with water. Soak until potatoes are fully swelled. Cover with water again, and boil for 10 or 12 minutes with lid on. Add teaspoonful of dried onions, bell peppers, and diced carrots. Throw in 1 pound of ground beef or contents of a 12 oz. can of corned beef.

Mash or mix with fork, and add salt and pepper to taste. Grease pan and cook until brown on bottom, turn and brown other side. Serves 4.

PACKER'S MEAT PIE

A complete one dish meal. Start ingredients like stew. Sear or brown 1-pound of beef in fry pan, cover with water and boil. Add diced potatoes, one large diced onion and a carrot, and salt. Mix enough Bisquick dough to cover top of pan; cover and bake in skillet.

DESSERT RAT (BREAD DESSERT)

½ cup cornmeal
2 cups milk or powdered milk
2 eggs, or powdered eggs
½ tablespoon sugar
½ teaspoon baking powder

1 teaspoon salt
1 tablespoon melted butter
 (margarine or cooking oil)
¼ cup of raisins or chopped prunes

Scald milk. Do not boil. Stir in cornmeal. Cook for 2 or 3 minutes. Keep stirring to avoid sticking. Egg yolks should be beaten until stiff. Fold in all ingredients. Pour into a well greased baking pan and bake for 30 or 40 minutes or place in a reflector oven until done. The bread dessert should have a golden crust on top when done. Cover with syrup, honey, or jam.

HUNTER'S CORN BEEF CASSEROLE

Prepare 2 servings Pillsbury's cooked diced potatoes. Drain well. Combine ½ can condensed cream of celery soup and 1/6 cup of milk in 1 quart-size pan. Add half of a 12 oz. can of whole onions. Mix ingredients and bake until sauce bubbles. Makes from 2 to 3 servings.

COWBOY'S MULLIGAN

Brown 1 pound of cubed beef in cooking oil. Add water to cover and let simmer slowly until tender. Add carrots, onions, green pepper, celery and potatoes. Cook until all vegetables are tender, season with salt and pepper. Serves four.

LAST CAMP STEW

Last camp stew is made from any scraps of leftover meat, gravy, soup stock, and vegetables. If leftover scraps have been cooked all you have to do is warm and serve. If meat scraps are raw, cook and add to pot. It's as simple as that!

CANOEIST MASHED POTATOES

Bring ¾ cup of water to a boil in a medium-size sauce pan, add ½ teaspoon salt, 1 tablespoon butter, and half an onion chopped fine. Simmer, then remove from heat and add ¼ cup cold milk. Slowly add ¼ of a 3.2 oz. package of powdered potatoes and stir gently for a minute or two. Whip lightly and serve hot. Serves three. (Powdered potatoes are excellent for thickening soups, gravies, and stews. A whole package will serve six. Leftover potatoes may be used for potato patties for breakfast. Any leftover corn adds to flavor.)

RANGER'S DELIGHT

Brown half package of Rice-A-Roni mixture in 1½ tablespoons butter or margarine in fry pan. Make a broth with contents of envelope in 1⅛ measuring cups of boiling water. Add broth to browned Rice-A-Roni, ½ cup corn, and ½ half-cup pitted olives, then cover pan. Simmer without further stirring until all liquid is absorbed. Serves two. Use full package for four persons.

SHEEPHERDER'S HASH

Chop up any kind of camp meat, corn beef, or leftovers with an equal amount of boiled potatoes. Add leftover corn or other vegetables, and chopped onions. Season with celery salt and dry parsley flakes. Moisten with soup stock or a small can of mushroom soup. Spread mixture on a greased pan and bake.

HUNTER'S TAMALE PIE

½ cup cornmeal
½ cup cold water
1½ cups boiling water
1¼ teaspoons salt
¼ lb. ground beef

⅛ cup chopped onions
½ can chili-con-carne
¼ cup minced ripe olives
¼ cup grated cheese

Mix cornmeal with cold water, add boiling water and ¾ teaspoon salt, and cook over low heat for 20 minutes, stirring occasionally to prevent sticking.

Brown ground beef and onions in fry pan; add ½ teaspoon salt and chili-con-carne. Mix olives with cooked cornmeal; use 2/3 of mixture to line greased pan. Pour meat mixture and cover with remaining cornmeal. Sprinkle grated cheese over top. Bake in dutch over (or in reflector oven) for about 20 minutes until heated through. Serves three people. This is the type of food that will stay with you!

SHEPHERD'S RICE PUDDING

2 cups of cooked rice or leftover rice, enough powdered milk to make 3 cups of milk, 1 teaspoon powdered eggs, 1/3 cup sugar (brown sugar preferably), ½ teaspoon salt, ½ cup raisins or dried chopped prunes. Season with nutmeg or cinnamon to taste. Add a few chopped nuts if you wish. Grease a deep pan and combine ingredients. Bake in camp stove or reflector oven until a light brown crust appears on top. Serve with milk.

PIONEER TOAST

Toast sliced bread on sticks over a bed of coals. If you have an old fashioned square-wire toaster, you are in business. They are back on the market again for $1.00.

MOUNTAINEER'S TOAST

Dip bread or toast in leftover flapjack or pancake mix and fry like French toast. Serve with honey, syrup, jelly or jam.

FRUIT

Dried and fresh fruit, such as bananas, can be cooked in foil. Baked apples are delicious. Core the apples, put in a tablespoon full of dark brown sugar, wrap in foil and bake. Prunes and apricots should be soaked in enough water to cover them in a kettle overnight. When ready to cook, add brown sugar and more water if necessary and let them stew until soft.

HIKER'S STICKOBOB

Cut a green stick about 2-feet long and about as thick as a lead pencil. Sharpen one end. Cut ¼ lb. lamb or mutton into 1½-inch cubes. String the following on the stick: meat, then a strip of bacon that has been folded together 3 times lengthwise, a small peeled onion, meat, green pepper, small tomato; then start again with a cube of meat and so on until sufficient food is on the stick to feed two persons. Force stick into ground over hot coals until meat and vegetables are thoroughly cooked.

COMMANDO PINOLE

The sustaining power of pinole, jerky, and pemmican has it all over any other type of dry or dehydrated food manufactured so far. With it pioneers and explorers have traveled over the world's wilderness.

A simple way to make pinole is to get a dozen or more ripened ears of corn; either "Indian" or regular field corn. When the corn is in seed condition, remove the seed from the cobs and place in flat pans in a moderately hot oven. Stir occasionally so that all kernels are parched evenly on all sides. When kernels have turned a golden brown, remove from oven. The next step is to secure an old fashioned small-size coffee grinder, or have the corn ground at your grocery store until the corn has been reduced to the "regular" (coffee) grind size. Dry for a short period in the oven to be sure that the pinole is as moisture-free as possible. Remove and place in plastic or moisture-proof bags until you are ready to use on a back-country trip. It keeps indefinitely.

ALASKA PEMMICAN

Some explorers swear by pinole, others by pemmican; some carry a little of each in their emergency kits. An old Ranger recipe requires the following ingredients:

5 pounds of lean beef   1 pound dried fruits
5 pounds of beef suet   1 pound brown sugar

The meat must be "jerked." Jerky is simply sun-dried raw beef which may be eaten uncooked. The meat is cut into ½-inch strips, ½-inch thick, and sun-cured or dried until the meat turns hard and black. Salt and pepper are hand rubbed into the meat before the drying process.

The long strips of jerky are tied to a line in a sunny spot to cure. The meat should be hung under a framework enclosing the meat with cheesecloth to keep flies and insects off. When the "jerky" is completely cured it should be ground up like pinole. Next melt the suet down. Mix the dry ingredients—then pour the suet over the concoction. Be sure to mix the fat well into the other ingredients.

ALPINE ERBSWURST

Erbswurst is the European outdoorsman's version of pinole. European armies have used it for emergency rations for years. Erbswurst requires a little more patience to prepare than other types of dried food. It is made as follows:

2½ pounds pea meal ½ pound bacon or ham
2½ pounds bean meal ½ pound onions
Salt and pepper (to taste)

To prepare, boil ingredients to pasty consistency. Boil off remaining water; be careful not to burn ingredients. Pour into pan and place in moderate oven until mixture is completely dry. Pulverize in mixing bowl until ground to coarse powder. Store in waterproof bags until needed. Be very careful that no moisture reaches contents or mold-spoilage will result. Eat dry or use as a soup.

OTHER RECIPES AND TIPS. Without a doubt one of the best friends a camper can have in the cooking department is the book *Wilderness Cookery* by Bradford Angier (The Stackpole Co., Harrisburg, Pa.).

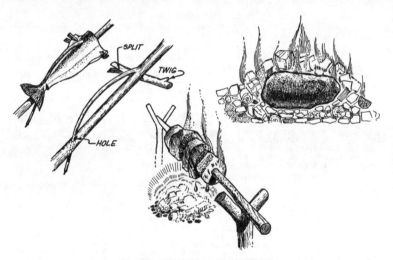

COOKING WITHOUT UTENSILS.

Upper left: Fish on green willow. Upper right: Potato surrounded by coals. Center: Kabob made with cubed foods threaded on a skewer.

COOKING WITHOUT UTENSILS

If for any reason you are going light or something has happened to your cooking utensils, you still can get along by cooking your food the primitive way. You can broil steaks on top of a good bed of coals. Blow off any white ash and sear the steaks quickly on both sides. This retains the juices. Then finish broiling to your liking.

You can cook by the stick method. Lace vegetables and meat after they have been cut into 2-inch cubes, on a green stick and broil over hot coals. You can fry eggs on a hot rock. After broiling bacon on a stick, you can trail bacon grease from the bacon onto the hot rock and then fry the eggs. In an emergency, you can use your shovel blade for a fry pan. Another method is to wrap food in green leaves and cover with mud, then bake the food in the coals.

DISPOSING OF USED FOIL

When you finish with the foil cooking wrappers or kettles, be sure to burn off all food that may be stuck to them, roll them up in a ball and bury them. If you leave a particle of food adhering to the foil, bears and other animals will smell it through the soil and dig it up, making an unsightly camp spot.

Aluminum foil will not burn. Many camps have had to be cleaned up because the campers threw their used foil in the fire or just on the ground. All camp refuse should be burned and then buried.

Never let it be said that all was beautiful *before* you came! Even though you may have to camp at someone else's dirty camp, be sure to take time to clean up the whole mess, yours and the other fellow's, so it can't be blamed on you or be said that you, Mr. John Doe Outdoorsman, left it that way!

HELP PREVENT FOREST FIRES!

Chapter 15

CAMP GRUB LISTS AND EMERGENCY RATIONS

FOR DIETARY reasons, most people like to make up their own food lists. Each individual has his likes and dislikes in the way of food. Making up "grub" lists and camp menus can be as much fun for the "first timer" as it is for the "old timer," for we all enjoy eating.

BREAKFAST

Breakfast should be a hearty meal to fortify and sustain the active outdoorsman. Camp breakfasts are formed around combinations of three or four items, such as: fruit—fresh, stewed, canned, or juice; bacon, sausage, steak, or ham and eggs; pancakes, cereal, biscuits, or toast; and drinks—coffee, tea, milk, or chocolate.

LUNCH

Lunch is usually a cold one because most of the time you will be out hiking or fishing and will not care to take the time to cook a noon meal. The lunch menu will normally be some kind of sandwich, probably combined with the following: sweets —fruit of some kind, nuts, candy, etc.; snacks—cheese, vegetable strips of carrots or celery; and a drink—water, tea, coffee, milk or a fruit drink.

SUPPER

Dinner or supper will likely be a main dish centered around meat, vegetables, and starchy foods. The amount of fresh items such as meat, vegetables, and dairy products depends upon their availability at your camp. If you are camped in the back country you will not have these items after the second day or so and you will have to depend on food that will keep, such as dried, smoked, canned, dehydrated, or pre-cooked kinds which do not spoil.

Try something new in the food line next time!

FOOD LIST—TWO PERSONS—TEN DAYS

STAPLES

1 lb. shortening	8 oz. Tang (Orange)	2 dish towels
1¼ lb. Bisquick	8 oz. chocolate mix	2 dish cloths
1 lb. corn meal	16 tea bags	1 roll toilet paper
5 loaves bread	1 lb. dry milk	3 candles
1 pkg. Rye Crisp	½ lb. salt	1 box matches
2 lb. butter	1 can pepper	1 bug bomb
5 lb. sugar	1 lb. raisins	1 "Chore Girl"
1 bottle Mapleine	1 bottle catsup	
8 oz. instant coffee	2 bars Ivory soap	

BREAKFASTS

5 lb. bacon	3 lb. dried fruit	1½ doz. eggs
3 lb. pancake flour	1 lb. oatmeal	

LUNCHES

½ lb. dried beef	3 cans pork & beans	1 lb. hard candy
1 lb. cheese	3 cans sardines	½ lb. nuts
1 jar jam (large)	1 lb. sausage	1 lb. lunch ham
1 jar peanut butter	6 pkg. Kool-aid	12 lunch bags
1 lb. cookies	20 candy bars	

SUPPERS

2 8½-oz. Rice-a-Roni	2 Kraft dinners	4 cans tomatoes
1 lb. weiners	1 can chili	9 oz. hash brown potatoes (8 servings)
1 can beef steak	1 can carrots	
1 can corned beef	1 can peas	2 pkg. powdered potatoes
1 can Spam	2 cans corn	
1 can chicken fricassee	1 can beets	3 pkg. dried soups
1 can beef stew	1 can mixed vegetables	½ pound onions
1 can meat balls	1 can string beans	6 pkg. powdered desserts

MENUS—TWO PERSONS—TEN DAYS—FIRST WEEK

SUNDAY

Breakfast:	Lunch:	Supper:
Oatmeal, toast	Baked beans	Chicken soup
Eggs & bacon	Peanut butter sandwich	Weiners
Beverage	Cookies	Mixed vegetables
	Beverage	Mashed potatoes
		Beverage

MONDAY

Stewed fruit	Sausage sandwich	Steak
Pancakes, bacon	Cookies	Hash brown potatoes
Beverage	Beverage	Corn pudding
		Beverage

TUESDAY

Oatmeal, toast	Cheese sandwich	Pea soup
Scrambled eggs	Canned fruit	Roast beef hash
Bacon	Beverage	Pudding (mix)
Beverage		Beverage

WEDNESDAY

Stewed fruit	Baked beans	Chicken fricassee
Pancakes, bacon	Jelly sandwich	String beans
Beverage	Beverage	Mashed potatoes
		Beverage

THURSDAY

Oatmeal	Sausage sandwich	Beef stew
French toast	Fruit, candy	Hash brown potatoes
Bacon	Beverage	Pudding
Beverage		Beverage

FRIDAY

Fruit	Cheese & Spam sandwich	Soup
Pancakes, eggs	Cookies	Kraft dinner
Bacon or Spam	Beverage	Carrots
Beverage		Beverage

SATURDAY

Oatmeal, toast	Peanut butter-jelly sand-	Sardines or fish
Fried eggs	wich	Rice-A-Roni
Ham	Beverage	Hash brown potatoes
Beverage		Tomatoes, stewed
		Beverage

Note: Don't make the mistake most tenderfeet do of eating all the favorite and tasty food during the first part of the trip. Save the best toward the last. It makes the trip more pleasant. A person craves sweets in the wilderness.

FOOD STORAGE SUGGESTIONS FOR CAMPERS

As a rule, campers who keep a clean camp, and use a minimum of odorous foods, are less bothered by bears than those campers who do not keep a clean camp and allow garbage to collect. Any food or food container that emits an odor is a natural target for bears. Food left on tables or in open boxes is a definite invitation to bear damage. Here are some good rules:

(1) Food should not be stored on a table or in your tent.

(2) Seal surplus food in clean wrapping material or in airtight containers.

(3) Keep your food as cool as possible.

(4) Metal chests with good locks make fair storage receptacles, although experience has shown that not all metal chests are bear-proof.

(5) Campground and back-country campers often suspend their supplies high between two trees out of a bear's reach.

(6) Burn all garbage and food containers, including cans, in back-country camps.

SUGGESTED GRUB LIST FOR TEMPORARY STUB CAMPS

For food lists and supplies, use the unit measure and multiply for the number of days stub camp is to be used.

10 men, one day: Unit #1.
20 men, one day: Unit #2.
30 men, one day: Unit #3.
40 men, one day: Unit #4.
50 men, one day: Unit #5.

Article	Unit	1 Unit	2 Units	3 Units	4 Units	5 Units
Fresh meat	lb.	10	20	30	40	50
Ham, cured	lb.	4	8	12	16	20
Bacon	lb.	2	4	6	8	10
Ham, boiled	lb.	2	4	6	8	10
Bread, large	loaf	9	18	27	36	45
Soda crackers	lb.	1	2	3	4	5
Jam, assorted	qt. can	2	4	6	8	10
Cheese	lb.	2	4	6	8	10
Peanut butter	lb.	2	4	6	8	10
Ham, minced	lb.	2	4	6	8	10
Eggs	doz.	3	6	9	12	15
Sugar	lb.	4	8	12	16	20
Coffee, ground	lb.	2	4	6	8	10
Tea	lb.	1/4	1/4	1/2	1/2	1
Milk, canned	tall	4	8	12	16	20
Butter	lb.	1 1/2	3	4 1/2	6	8
Prunes, dried	lb.	1	2	3	4	5
Peaches	qt. can	2	4	6	8	10
Apricots	qt. can	1	2	3	4	5
Pears	qt. can	1	2	3	4	5
Pineapple	qt. can	1	2	3	4	5
Tomato juice	15 oz.	5	10	15	20	25
Grapefruit juice	15 oz.	5	10	15	20	25
Tang (orange)	jar	1	2	3	4	5
Shortening	can	1	2	3	4	5
Beans, dried	lb.	3	6	9	12	15
Macaroni	lb.	1	2	3	4	5
Tomatoes	qt. can	3	6	9	12	15
Potatoes	lb.	10	20	30	40	50
Rice	lb.	2	4	6	8	10
Onions	lb.	1	2	3	4	5
Flour	lb.	5	10	15	20	25
Salt	lb.	1	1	1	2	2
Pepper	oz.	2	2	4	4	4
Mustard	jar	1	1	2	2	3
Catsup	bottle	1	1	2	3	4
Pickles	qt. can	1	2	3	4	5
Peas	qt. can	3	6	9	12	15
Corn	qt. can	3	6	9	12	15
Beans	qt. can	3	6	9	12	15
Pancake flour	lb.	2	2	4	6	8
Syrup	bottle	1	2	4	6	8
Baking soda	pkg.	1	1	1	2	2
Baking powder	can	1	1	1	2	2

Also, consider additions from the following list if you expect to try some of the recipes given in the preceding chapter.

Apples	Cornmeal'
Bananas	Frankfurters
Beef, ground or corned	Honey
Bell peppers	Jelly
Bisquick	Lamb or mutton
Brown sugar	Mushroom soup
Cabbage	Nutmeg
Carrots	Olives (variety)
Celery	Paprika
Celery salt	Parsley flakes
Chile-con-carne	Raisins
Cinnamon	Rice-A-Roni
Clams	Yeast

STUB CAMP SUPPLIES

Article	Unit	1 Unit	2 Units	3 Units	4 Units	5 Units
Towels, dish*	no.	3	3	5	8	10
Towels, hand*	no.	5	10	15	20	25
Soap, Ivory	bar	2	3	4	6	8
Detergent	pkg.	1	1	1	1	1
Paper bags	size #8	12	24	36	48	60
Paper towels	roll	1	2	3	4	5
Matches, large	box	1	2	3	4	5

Article	Unit	1 Unit	2 Units	3 Units	4 Units	5 Units
Toilet tissue	roll	1	2	3	4	5
Cook outfits†	10-man	1	2	3	4	5
Pot cleaner, mesh	no.	1	2	2	3	3
Coleman lanterns†	no.	2	3	3	4	4
Gasoline	gal.	1	2	4	5	5
First-aid kit†	no.	1	2	3	4	5
Radio†	no.	1	1	1	1	1
Axes†	no.	1	1	2	3	3
Shovels†	no.	1	1	1	1	2
Saws, bucking†	no.	0	0	0	1	1
Tents, cook†	no.	1	1	1	2	2
Hammers†	no.	1	1	2	2	2
Nails	lb.	¼	¼	¼	¼	½
Chloride lime	no.	1	2	3	4	5

* Total requirement may be decreased by adding laundry soap where camp laundering facilities can be used.

† Quantities shown are not related to duration of stay.

Chapter 16
DEHYDRATED FOOD

IN THE OLD DAYS the pioneer hunter and explorer traveled far and fast with lightweight food. In those days the traveler had little choice as to what food he could carry. It consisted chiefly of parched ground corn called "pinole," and of "jerky" made from venison. On occasion some old timers made pemmican, a powdered mixture of dried beef, suet, raisins, and sugar. These three types of lightweight food are still used for emergency travel rations by many people in Mexico, Canada, and in some areas in the United States. Pemmican is still used by our Armed Services along with various types of dehydrated and wet-pack rations.

ADVANTAGES OF THE NEW DEHYDRATED FOODS

The outdoorsman today is more fortunate. He may choose from a wide variety of deliciously seasoned, concentrated, moisture-proof, non-perishable, lightweight foods that need no refrigeration and will keep for years. This food is packaged for all types of camping, and is also used aboard planes and boats where space and weight are at a premium. It is not only used by all experienced back-pack campers, canoeists, explorers, hunters, fishermen, rangers, and other woodsmen who travel to the out-of-the-way places in the back country, but by the military as well.

As world tension grows, people are storing dehydrated food for their Civil Defense home needs. Many carry a survival kit in their car trunks in case they are caught away from their home supply in sudden emergency. The U. S. Coast Guard has approved survival rations with a storage life of twenty-five years. These kits contain six sealed cans of water, and enough rations for one person for six days.

Tremendous advances have been made in the past five years in the development of precooked and dehydrated foods. In the past year newly developed freeze-dry foods that combine the taste, texture, and eye appeal of fresh meats and vegetables with extremely light weight and long storage life are now being marketed. Distribution of the new freeze-dry dehydrated foods is being handled through sporting goods stores, outdoor divisions of large department stores, and direct mail outlets.

Freeze-dry foods appeal to any person because they are fresh tasting and may be stored anywhere, including the kitchen cupboard or the trunk of a car.

Why carry the weight and bulk of wet-packed canned food when it is easier to carry dehydrated food and add the water at camp? The compactness and lightness of the new dehydrated foods is truly remarkable. A few ounces of carried weight yields pounds of prepared food whenever you want it. About one pound per person per day of dehydrated food will provide full and varied menus for average activities. For strenuous mountain climbing or ski-mountaineering and other arduous outdoor activities, an average of two and one quarter pounds per day is necessary. Under survival conditions a person could get along very well for weeks on half a pound per day. By using this type of food, the saved room and weight can be used by the camper to carry many other conveniences that usually must be left behind.

Wherever weight is a problem or transportation difficult, the use of dehydrated food is indicated. It may also be used where temperatures are extreme as in the desert waste lands, the freezing cold of the Arctic and Antarctic, or the steaming tropical jungles of the world.

Use dehydrated food products put out by a reputable manufacturing company. Most of the food manufacturers packaging dehydrated food use only the choice cuts of meat and the better portions of vegetables. This eliminates subsequent consumer waste.

DIRECTIONS FOR PREPARING DEHYDRATED FOOD*

Always read and follow the simple instructions on each food envelope for best results. When directions say to soak the contents, pour the contents in water before cooking, measure the water accurately, and stir in the contents of the package as soon as you reach camp. Stir the food occasionally as you proceed with making camp. If you can set it in a warm place to soak, do so; just be sure that it warms slowly during soak-

---

* Courtesy of Bernard's Food Industries (KAMP-PACK), San Jose, California.

ing time. When your directions say to make a paste of the contents, pour the dry contents into a pan or bowl and add water from the directed amount slowly, stirring steadily until the material makes a thick paste. Be sure to mash out all lumps, then add more water slowly until the material will mix readily into the rest of the water. When food needs simmering or boiling, let it come to the bubbling point fairly slowly and then continue to cook slowly—just enough to keep the bubbles coming up. Hard boiling is not necessary or good for these foods. It will help to keep a lid on your cooking container; but remember to watch for things that boil over, and stir things often enough so that they won't stick on the bottom of the kettle.

Remember to burn and bury, or to pack out, the empty package. This cannot be emphasized too strongly.

HIGH ALTITUDE COOKING

Replace the water as it boils away. Water evaporates very rapidly in high altitudes, so in order to keep the water content sufficient for the absorption of the dry contents plus evaporation loss, extra water must be added.

Increase the soaking time, and soak in warm water when possible.

Increase simmering time, but cook slowly. Flavor and texture improve in any case with long, slow cooking.

Keep the cooking container covered. This helps to retain both moisture and heat. Watch things that tend to boil over, and stir things that tend to stick.

SPECIALLY PACKAGED DEHYDRATED FOODS

Ann Benedict of Dri-Lite Foods has many tasty menus for breakfasts, no-fire trailside lunch snacks, and a variety of dinner suggestions. Dri-Lite comes packaged in 2, 4, and 8-unit servings.

Bernard's Kamp-Pack is packaged for 4-man and 8-man units. Kamp-Pack menus are packaged for four persons for one day, and contain material for breakfast, lunch, and dinner. The 4-man unit contains 12 full meals with approximately 12,000 calories or 3,000 calories daily per person. The 8-man unit contains twice as much of everything. By adding water the smaller pack will make up to 20 pounds of finished food and drink including dessert. The larger pack will double this amount.

BERNARD'S KAMP-PACK AND MENUS. The Alaskan Air Command is now using four-man units of Kamp-Pack for survival purposes in the far north. From the Kamp-Pack list you can make up your own survival food kit for your Civil Defense shelter or car by adding canned or bottled water to the kit. Add containers for cooking.

Bernard's Kamp-Pack includes a variety of well-seasoned, concentrated, non-perishable foods, packaged especially for campers. There is nothing to add but water. Quick and easy to prepare—great for camping, hunting, and fishing trips—ideal for back-pack, foldboat, pack train, car, or plane portage. Packed in waterproofed kraft-covered foil envelopes, lined with polyethylene plastic, Kamp-Pack foods are completely protected against the rough conditions of camp life. Kamp-Pack is airtight, waterproof, lightweight, and compact, and needs no refrigeration.

INDIVIDUAL KAMP-PACK ENVELOPE LIST

STANDARD ITEMS:	4-Man Size (Use Double for 8-Man Size)
	Net Wt. Ozs.
Apple sauce mix	4
Mixed fruit sauce mix	6
Hot biscuit mix	10
Instant Farina cereal with milk & sugar	6
Instant Ralston cereal with milk & sugar	6
Sweet cream buttermilk pancake mix	12
Ginger sweet cream buttermilk pancake mix	12
Orange sweet cream buttermilk pancake mix	12
All purpose french toast batter mix	6
Boysenberry flavored pancake & waffle syrup mix	8
Maple flavored pancake & waffle syrup mix	8
Egg omelette de luxe	4
Scrambled eggs de luxe	4
Chicken gumbo soup	2½
Chicken noodle soup	2
Chicken rice soup	2
Minestrone soup	5½
Potato soup supreme	8
Tomato noodle soup	5½
Vegetable noodle soup—beef flavored	3½
Barbecued beans, hickory smoke flavored	11
Boston baked beans	11

	4-Man Size (Use Double for 8-Man Size)
	Net Wt. Ozs.
Camper's vegetable stew	7
Casserole with rice and cheese	9

Chicken stew	8
Chili & beans (meatless)	11
Chow mein dinner (meatless)	5½
Macaroni and cheese	14
Macaroni in cream sauce	14
Pizza pie (instant—complete)	5½
Minestrone dinner (meatless)	11
Mulligan stew	7
Pot pie—beef flavored (with biscuit bread)	17
Pot pie—chicken flavored (with biscuit bread)	18
Spaghetti tomato dinner	11
Spanish rice dinner	9½
Vegetable noodle stew—beef flavored	7
Mashed potatoes with chicken gravy	4
Hashed brown potatoes	6
Hashed brown potatoes with onions	6
Cabbage flakes	1¾
Carrot dice	2
Spinach flakes	2
Creamed mixed vegetables	5
Potato pancake mix	8
Potato salad mix	4½
Chocolate drop cakes with icing	9
Chocolate fudge mix	12
Creamy rice pudding	11
Banana instant Stir'N'Serv pudding	8
Butterscotch instant Stir'N'Serv pudding	8
Chocolate instant Stir'N'Serv pudding	8
Vanilla instant Stir'N'Serv pudding	8
Whole milk powder	4½
Hot or cold chocolate	8
Chocolate flavored milk shake	7
Strawberry flavored milk shake	7
Vanilla flavored milk shake	7
Fruit punch	8
Pink lemonade	8
Lemonade	8
Limeade	8
Orangeade	8
Orange juice crystals	4
Beef flavored gravy mix	3
Chicken flavored gravy mix	3
All purpose detergent with miracle sponge (Makes 6 gal.)	3

SPECIAL LOW-MOISTURE DRY MEAT ITEMS:

Beef vegetable stew	8
Beef pot pie—(with biscuit bread)	18
Beef camper's stew	8
Beef rice dinner	10
Beef macaroni dinner	10¾
Beef mulligan stew	8
Beef minestrone dinner	12
Beef chili with beans	11
Spaghetti with meat sauce	14
Beef hash	10

SAMPLE KAMP-PACK MENUS

Breakfast
Ginger sweet cream buttermilk pancakes
Maple flavored syrup
Hot chocolate

Lunch
Spanish rice dinner
Hot biscuits
Fruit punch

Dinner
Chicken rice soup
Camper's vegetable stew
Banana instant Stir'N'Serv pudding
Chocolate milk shake

SAMPLE LOW MOISTURE MEAT ITEM MENU

Breakfast
Scrambled eggs de luxe
Hot biscuits
Hot chocolate

Lunch
Minestrone dinner
Hot biscuits
Limeade

Dinner
Potato soup supreme
Beef mulligan stew
Butterscotch instant Stir'N'Serv pudding
Vanilla milk shake

Supplementaries: Both menus contain miracle sponge and detergent, pure vegetable shortening, salt, hard candies, and toilet tissue.

SOURCES OF EMERGENCY RATIONS AND DEHYDRATED FOODS

EMERGENCY RATIONS:

Emergency food rations may be purchased from the following:

FIREFLY SURVIVAL RATIONS
(Coast Guard type)
Safety Research & Mfg. Co.
Seattle 4, Washington

BERNARD FOOD INDUSTRIES
217 N. Jefferson Street
Chicago 6, Illinois

ALL TYPES OF DEHYDRATED FOODS:

ANN'S KITCHEN
1500 Wisconsin Avenue
Washington, D.C.

ANN BENEDICT'S
Dri-Lite Foods
8716 Santa Fe Avenue
South Gate, California

BERNARD'S FOOD INDUSTRIES
Plant #1
559 West Fulton Street
Chicago, Illinois

BERNARD'S KAMP-PACK
152 West 3rd Street
North Vancouver, B.C., Canada

BERNARD'S KAMP-PACK
Plant #2
1208 E. San Antonio Street
P. O. Box 487
San Jose 27, California

CHUCK WAGON
Bolton Farms Pkg. Co., Inc.
P. O. Box 66
Newton 64, Massachusetts

CRAMORE FRUIT PRODUCTS
90 West Broadway
New York, N.Y.

DRI-LITE FOODS
8716 Santa Fe
South Gate, California

E-Z FOOD PRODUCTS
  COMPANY
1420 So. Western Avenue
Gardena, California

MEGDEN INDUSTRIES
6808 Marshall Road
Upper Darby, Pennsylvania

AD SEIDEL
1245 W. Dickens Avenue
Chicago 14, Illinois

SEIDEL TRAIL PACKETS
David Abercrombie Company
97 Chambers Street
New York 7, New York

TRAIL MEALS
J. B. KILSKY
1829 N. E. Alberta Street
Portland 11, Oregon

TRAILWISE-SKI HUT
1615 University Avenue
Berkeley 3, California

TRIP-LITES
S. GUMPERT
812 Jersey Avenue
Jersey City 2, New Jersey

TRIPPEROOS
HILKER & BLETSCH
614 Hubbard Street
Chicago, Illinois

YAKIMA CHIEF
709 N. First Street
Yakima, Washington

You can also contact your local Park and Forest Service warehousemen and the U.S. Coast Guard for manufacturers of "K" and "C" rations and names of other companies that distribute dehydrated foods.

Chapter 17

WILDERNESS CRAFTSMANSHIP

WILDERNESS craftsmanship is not a lost art, as we are sometimes led to believe, for there are many millions of outdoor people practicing it today. Full credit must be given to the pioneers of another day, especially to Lord Baden-Powell, Chief Scout of the world, who gave us scouting and campcraft.

VALUE OF CRAFTSMANSHIP

Some day, your very life may depend on your knowledge of woodcraft and skill in woods lore. You will need to know how to start a fire without matches, how to build a fire in the rain, and the types of fires needed for warmth and cooking. You will need to know how to cook without utensils or containers, and the proper and safe location to pitch a tent or build a primitive shelter in the woods. You will need to know how to sharpen a knife or axe, and how to use them safely. It is advisable to know how to make and set traps, deadfalls, and snares, to be able to purify or filter unsafe water, whether alkali, muddy, or polluted, and how to find and stalk game and prepare it for storage.

Wilderness craft also means skill in reading map and compass correctly, how to travel safely over rough mountainous terrain, how to build rafts, and how to build caches to store food away from rodents, wolverines, and bears.

Your knowledge of camp and woods lore, and how to improvise, may be the deciding factor of your staying alive under survival conditions, if you ever become lost in a wild primitive region; or if you are ever forced to live off the land in case of a nuclear attack.

WHEN YOU'RE ON YOUR OWN

The supreme test of wilderness craftsmanship comes when all equipment has been destroyed or lost by some disaster—a canoe swept away, a forest fire, or some other accident. A person without a gun will depend on trapping fish, and upon such small game as he can capture with snares or deadfalls.

272

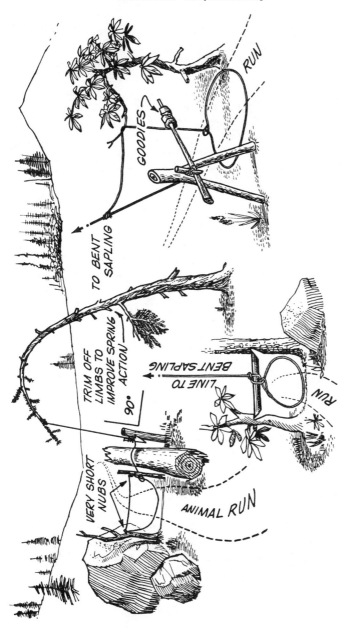

HANGING SNARES. All snares should be adjusted to hair trigger performance. Fine steel wire makes a good noose because the catch can't chew his way to freedom.

In a survival emergency, there is but one law; that of self-preservation. Sportsmanship and game laws may have to go out during the ordeal. A victim will kill and eat anything he can get that will give him strength, no matter how unpleasant the food may taste.

The larva of pinebark beetles have a nutty pine needle flavor; roast grasshoppers and lizards are not too bad. Snake is somewhat oily, but nourishing. Raccoon is not bad if properly prepared by removing the scent glands before roasting. Muskrat, ground squirrel, woodchucks, and skunk are good if parboiled and then roasted. Porcupine, skunk, and opossum are very rich and greasy. Pack rats are very good. Of the smaller animals, rabbits are the easiest to snare and most palatable.

SNARES

There is no use in setting a snare in a runway unless there are fresh tracks or animal droppings indicating that it is being used. The snare must be set in a narrow part of the runway or dry sticks must be driven in a semicircle around the edges of the runway to force the animal to pass into the snare. Rocks may also be used to narrow the runway.

Rabbit snares may be baited with wild fruit or succulent roots. For other small animals bait with whatever you can catch—beetles, grubs, grasshoppers, frogs, snakes, etc.

Several types of snares are shown.

AXEMANSHIP

Without the axe, our pioneer forefathers could not have cleared land for cultivation, built cabins for shelter, nor cut wood for fences and for their fires.

It is rather surprising how few outdoorsmen understand the axe and how to use it properly and safely. Men who make their living in the woods soon become experts, but the once-a-season camper usually has to learn the hard way, unless he seeks assistance from an expert. An axe can become a dangerous and lethal tool in the hands of the inexperienced.

The so-called belt or hand axe that so many vacation people carry is fine for splitting kindling, but a larger and heavier axe is needed and used by the experienced outdoorsman for cutting wood.

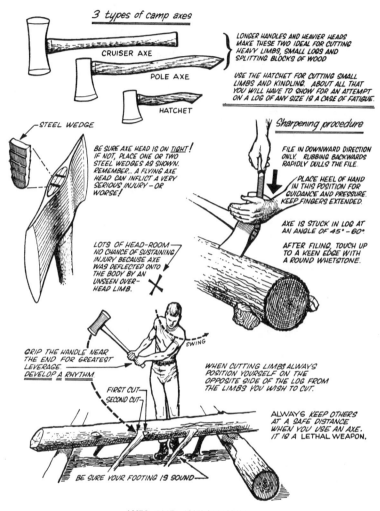

3 types of camp axes

CRUISER AXE

POLE AXE

HATCHET

LONGER HANDLES AND HEAVIER HEADS MAKE THESE TWO IDEAL FOR CUTTING HEAVY LIMBS, SMALL LOGS AND SPLITTING BLOCKS OF WOOD

USE THE HATCHET FOR CUTTING SMALL LIMBS AND KINDLING. ABOUT ALL THAT YOU WILL HAVE TO SHOW FOR AN ATTEMPT ON A LOG OF ANY SIZE IS A CASE OF FATIGUE.

STEEL WEDGE

BE SURE AXE HEAD IS ON TIGHT! IF NOT, PLACE ONE OR TWO STEEL WEDGES AS SHOWN. REMEMBER... A FLYING AXE HEAD CAN INFLICT A VERY SERIOUS INJURY – OR WORSE!

LOTS OF HEAD-ROOM NO CHANCE OF SUSTAINING INJURY BECAUSE AXE WAS DEFLECTED ONTO THE BODY BY AN UNSEEN OVER-HEAD LIMB.

Sharpening procedure

FILE IN DOWNWARD DIRECTION ONLY. RUBBING BACKWARDS RAPIDLY DULLS THE FILE.

PLACE HEEL OF HAND IN THIS POSITION FOR GUIDANCE AND PRESSURE. KEEP FINGERS EXTENDED.

AXE IS STUCK IN LOG AT AN ANGLE OF 45° – 60°.

AFTER FILING, TOUCH UP TO A KEEN EDGE WITH A ROUND WHETSTONE.

GRIP THE HANDLE NEAR THE END FOR GREATEST LEVERAGE. DEVELOP A RHYTHM.

SWING

FIRST CUT SECOND CUT

WHEN CUTTING LIMBS ALWAYS POSITION YOURSELF ON THE OPPOSITE SIDE OF THE LOG FROM THE LIMBS YOU WISH TO CUT.

ALWAYS KEEP OTHERS AT A SAFE DISTANCE WHEN YOU USE AN AXE. IT IS A LETHAL WEAPON.

BE SURE YOUR FOOTING IS SOUND

AXES AND AXEMANSHIP.

There are many types of axes; however, the types used most in the woods are the lightweight double-bitted Cruiser axe with a twenty-six or twenty-eight-inch handle, and a two and one-half pound head; its big brother, the double-bit axe with a thirty-six-inch handle, with either a three and one-half or

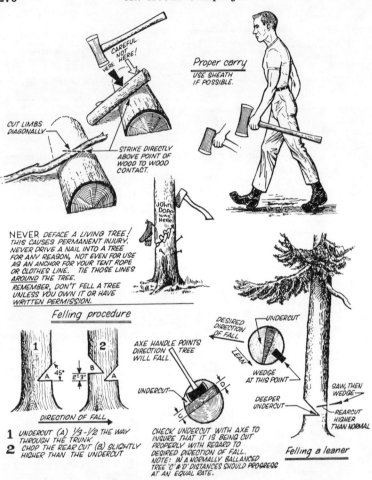

CARRYING AND USING THE AXE.

five-pound head; the lightweight single-bit pole axe with a twenty-six-inch handle and two and one-half pound head; and its big brother, the full-sized pole axe with a thirty-six-inch handle and carrying a three and one-half pound head, which is used by pulpwood men.

For recreational use, the lightweight, single-bit pole axe with a twenty-six-inch handle and a two and one-half pound head is correct for all types of camp use. You can cut through a downed log in the trail, drive tent stakes, or cut camp wood with it. The Hudson Bay model with a two pound head is also an excellent choice.

AXE SAFETY CHECK LIST

(1) When through with a pole axe, stick it in a stump or log; never leave it leaning against anything or lying on the ground.

(2) Never leave a double-bit axe sticking in a stump or log. Place it face down under a log's edge.

(3) Indoors, place all axes in a corner; the pole axe with the blade pointing toward the wall and the double-bit with both edges touching the walls in a corner.

(4) When carrying a double-bit axe, grip the handle close to the head and carry at the side, blade up and down. Grip a pole axe the same way, but with the blade pointing outward on the downhill side. If you happen to stumble, throw the axe away from you.

(5) Avoid cutting into knots in wood. They can cause a blade to glance and cause an accident. Cut around them. They can chip an axe blade, especially if the blade is cold.

(6) In cold weather, warm the axe slightly before using it. Steel is very brittle when cold.

(7) If the axe has a sheath, use it when the axe is out of service. Don't leave an axe sheath where it may become lost.

(8) When chopping a log in two, stand on top of it, if it is too large and heavy to be rolled over. A log is chopped in two by cutting a "V" in one side of it, then cutting another "V" in the opposite side so that the two meet.

(9) The width of the "V" depends on the size or diameter of the log. The width of the "V" should always be cut as wide as the log is in diameter.

(10) For safety reasons, always lop off limbs by having the log between you and the limb. Clear limbs from one side of the log, then move to the other side to finish.

The illustrations show examples of correct axemanship.

CAMP SAWS. A camp saw will cut several times more wood in a given period of time than can be cut with an axe, and with much less expenditure of energy. There are several excellent folding camp saws on the market. A small collapsible saw with a 24-inch rake-tooth blade is very useful in the "high back country." When not in use, be sure to protect the blade with a piece of old lawn hose, or with heavy canvas.

CAMP AND OUTDOORS KNIVES. Among Rangers and experienced woodsmen, a man is often judged by the size and type of knife he packs on his belt when he enters the woods.

A tenderfoot can be spotted along the trail carrying anything from a "Bowie" fighting knife, bayonet, or bolo. These types of knives may have their place in jungle fighting, but not in the recreation field. If a large knife is needed for brushing, a machete is needed to do the job; but there is no need today for anyone to have to hew out a campsite with one. If you must, use an axe!

For general camp use, the author uses a Marble or Sheffield skinning knife with a 4½-inch blade. The heft of the Sheffield is better because the handle is somewhat thicker and it is not quite so tiring to use when dressing out an animal as large as deer, elk, or moose. It handles better for general whittling, too. The Boy Scout sheath knife is also a good buy in a blade of 4 to 5 inches. Most expert guides use this length, or shorter.

A good grade of carborundum whetstone is a *must* to keep both axe and sheath and pocketknives sharp. It is necessary to sharpen a skinning knife every few minutes when dressing out large game. Hide and hair will dull an edge very quickly. Working in confined space is where the jack or pocketknife with two blades about 2½ inches long comes in mighty handy. Use due caution when working in tight places for it is easily possible to cut your fingers in some of them. If you ever do cut yourself while cleaning game, be sure to wash and treat the cut as quickly as possible to prevent any possible animal infection.

Whatever type of knife you have or purchase, it should be of the best steel possible. Of course, good things do not come cheap. When backpacking, the author carries either a Marine or Boy Scout pocketknife that has a leather punch, can-opener, screwdriver, and blade. The blade and leather punch take care of leather repair, the screwdriver is handy to tighten up ski-binders or the metal edges on the skis (incidentally you will need to file the screwdriver a little thinner to fit the screwheads), and the blade for whittling prayer or fuzz-sticks for the fire and other camp chores. Such a knife sells for $1.95 and should be in everyone's stampede kit. The U.S. Marine pocketknife may be preferable to some users because the handle is metal and cannot be broken; sometimes they can be purchased at surplus stores. A good pocketknife, a good sheath knife, a good grade axe, and a camp saw should be in every camping outfit.

Treat your wood cutting tools with the respect due them, and they will last you a lifetime. The longer you have them and have used them on the high trails, the more you will cherish them and recall the many fine hunting, fishing, or vacation trips in which you have packed them.

PATHFINDING

For instructions in pathfinding by means of a compass, see chapter 18. For instruction in reading and using maps, see chapter 19.

Chapter 18
PATHFINDING BY COMPASS

TOO LITTLE is said in manuals and outdoor books on that small but important gadget, the compass. With it, man has traveled and covered the earth by air, land, and sea!

EARLY HISTORY

Discovery that a lodestone or magnetized piece of iron seeks to place itself in a north and south position has been attributed by various historians to the Chinese, Arabs, Greeks, Etruscans, Finns, and Italians. Earliest historical records on the use of this physical phenomenon in navigation date back about 700 years. Since that time, various types of magnetic compasses have been used for navigation and land surveying.

DIFFERENT KINDS

The least expensive types of compass merely contain a pointer needle, magnetized at one end and mounted on a pivot bearing over a paper marked with the various directions, and cheaply encased. You have undoubtedly seen these and perhaps noticed how the needle fluctuated wildly whenever the compass was suddenly moved, carried past or placed in the vicinity of a piece of metal mostly made of iron. These cannot be recommended to the outdoor man because they break easily and the markings on the dial are inadequate for practical use with maps except in dire emergency. In the latter case, any compass is better than none.

Next higher, in terms of price and quality, are compasses better marked and additionally using an ingenious magnetic induction method for stabilizing the needle or dial. Needles will not swing wildly about in these compasses, and many of them have luminescent markings which permit their use even in the dark. Although the dial markings are not as sufficiently detailed as the more professional instruments, they are adequate for many camping uses and quite sturdily constructed. A camper once left such a compass (it happened to be a wrist

THE SILVA PIONEER. Needle stabilizes without fluid.

compass) in the bottom of a fishing tackle box where it became completely immersed in water during a prolonged rainy spell. It remained under water for several days. After discovery, removal, and a drying out period of several days, it seemed as good as ever, the rust gradually receded, and it yet remains in active use.

Better grade compasses employ liquids suggestive of glycerine in which the needle or even the entire compass face appear to float on its pivot bearing. You may notice a small bubble in the face of one of these when you first pick it up. This, of course, does not interfere with its use. You will also notice that if you turn suddenly while watching the dial, it or the needle alone, depending on construction, will very quickly stop swinging to afford a reading of the changed direction. Many of these compasses come with an outer snap-shut cover much like that of pocket watches having the old-fashioned hunter case. If you do not now own a compass, this grade will most satisfactorily serve your hunting and camping purposes, especially if you should develop a serious interest in using

maps and exploring more remote back country areas. The
Army Lensatic, the Leupold Sportsman, and several of the
Silva compasses are of this general type and quality.

USE OF THE COMPASS

Many people own compasses of one type or another, but
haven't the slightest idea how to operate one beyond the fact
that the needle points to magnetic north. This precision instrument is not of much help as a pathfinder if one doesn't
know how to use one correctly. Every year a few hunters,
fishermen, and hikers become lost. It is up to you, Mr. Sportsman, as a woodsman to own a good compass and to know how
to use it if you plan on going into primitive or wilderness areas.

CHECK YOUR BACK TRAIL. Hindsight is foresight when
traveling through unfamiliar country. Stop and look back over
the route you have traveled. Note some of the prominent peaks
and landmarks and the direction the streams are flowing. Then
if you have to backtrack you can find your way back to camp.
It can be quite a shock, when you must backtrack and have
failed to check your back trail to discover suddenly that the
country looks quite unfamiliar. Camp can become lost very
easily by this negligence, especially after dark in new country.

TYPES OF COMPASSES

With early compasses and simple pocket compasses, directions are "reckoned" by estimating the angle from the north-
south line of the magnetic needle to the line of direction. To
obtain more accurate readings for land surveys, the sighting
compass was developed.

The sighting compass is equipped with a sighting line or
wire which is "aimed" in the direction to be determined. The
angle of this direction from north is then read at the point
on the face of the compass indicated by the north-seeking end
of the magnetic compass needle.

A Leupold sighting compass is shown in the accompanying
illustration, and is designed after the surveyor's transit. East-
west dial readings are reversed on the face of the compass so a
direct reading of the sighting line direction can be made from
the north end of the magnetic needle.

This type of compass is one of the most accurate and versatile pocket-size compasses available. It is the simplest of all

compasses to use for charting and following map courses, determining bearings, plotting rough maps, and making preliminary land surveys. Army pocket lensatic compasses obtainable from surplus sales stores, are used in a similar way but dial readings are not reversed as with the Leupold.

There are several other good compasses on the market today, such as the Marble, Taylor, and Silva, all relatively inexpensive. The simple box-type compass has the azimuth graduations reading clockwise from zero to 360 degrees.

The Surveyor's or Cruiser's compass reflects a reverse order with the azimuth reading counterclockwise, since this reduces the chances of error in reading, and the north end of the needle may still be read for convenience and simplicity. Many rangers and woodsmen like the Sportsman model compass manufactured by the Leupold & Stevens Instruments, Incorporated, 4445 N.E. Glisan Street, Portland, Oregon. This

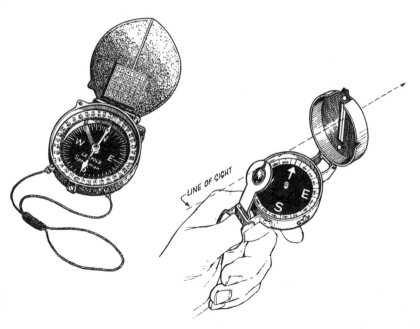

Left: THE LEUPOLD SPORTSMAN'S COMPASS. Right: U. S. ARMY LENSATIC COMPASS (illustrating "Line of Sight").

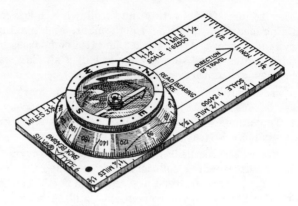

THE SILVA RAMBLER COMPASS.

is one of the best medium-priced lightweight compasses.

MERIDIANS AND MAGNETIC DECLINATIONS

A true meridian may be defined as a north and south line on the surface of the earth passing through the north geographic pole. A magnetic meridian is a line defined by the compass needle and passes through the north magnetic pole. In pointing to the north magnetic pole, the needle will only rarely coincide with a true meridian. This is due to the fact that the north geographic pole and the north magnetic pole do not coincide. The angle between the magnetic meridian or line defined by the compass needle and a true meridian is called the magnetic declination. This declination, or angle, is shown on all U.S. Topographic maps because it varies enough from place to place to affect accurate orientation of the maps in relation to specific terrain.

Magnetic north is approximately 1300 miles south of the geographical north pole on the Boothia Peninsula. At about the location of Cincinnati, Ohio, magnetic and true north will be in line. West of Cincinnati the compass needle will point east of true north. If proper declination has been set off on your compass no converting is necessary; however, if using magnetic bearings and you wish to read them as true directions, always *subtract easterly magnetic variation** or *add western magnetic*

---

* Declination; also—"compass error."

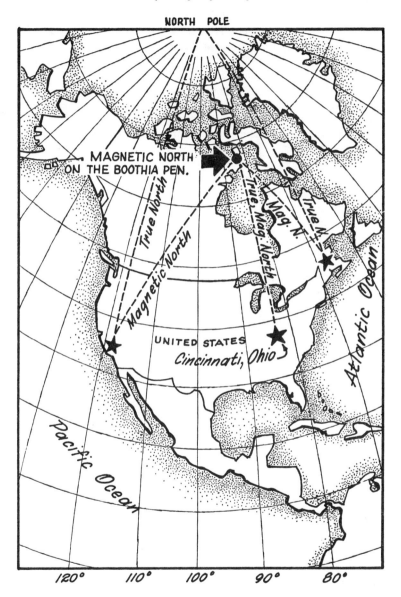

NORTH POLE

MAGNETIC NORTH
ON THE BOOTHIA PEN.

True North

Magnetic North

True Mag. North

Mag. N.

True N.

UNITED STATES
Cincinnati, Ohio

Atlantic Ocean

Pacific Ocean

120° 110° 100° 90° 80°

MAP SHOWING "MAGNETIC DECLINATION."

variation as indicated by your map. A rhyme used to help remember how to apply magnetic variation to convert a magnetic compass bearing to a true bearing is, "Magnetic *east* is *least*."

The reader is reminded that variations exist in features of the different makes of compasses available to campers and sportsmen. The explanatory material here will generally apply to use of a compass such as the Sportsman model. You may already have a satisfactory compass or prefer some other which does not have the same reversed East-West dial layout, sighting features, or pattern of adjusting or marking degrees. In any case, the explanations and examples which follow should easily enable you to develop a satisfactory system for most efficient use of your own or another style of compass.

For some compass work it is sufficient to read angles directly and ignore the magnetic declination. In rough work, especially in a locality where the variation between true meridian and the magnetic is not great, the declination may be disregarded and readings made will be sufficiently accurate for practical purposes. In such a case, N on the dial is left at the index point directly in a line with the notched cover latch and sighting line, and readings are made from the face of the dial as though this line coincided with the true meridian.

However, if it is desirable to take account of the magnetic declination, it can be set off by shifting the compass dial so that the sighting line will reflect an exactly true geographic meridian when the needle reads north. Be sure to read the directions that come with your compass, and the declination shown on your map so that you may make the adjustment correctly.

DETERMINING DIRECTION. In determining direction, the sighting line is pointed in the direction you desire to identify, and the compass held until the needle comes to rest. It may be brought to rest by gently lifting it from the pivot and lowering it again by operating the needle lifter with the finger, if your compass is so equipped. The direction in which the line of sight points is then read in terms of degrees from the north end, or zero point, of the needle. (See Reading Angles below.)

This procedure is applied in a practical way in surveying, timber cruising, exploring, hiking, and, in fact, at any time direction is desired.

SIGHTING. In sighting towards an object or in a given direction, either hold the compass level in the hand, even with the eye, and sight through the notched cover latch along sighting line, or press the rear edge of compass firmly to body midriff and point the sighting line in the desired direction. The compass may also be placed on a tree stump or other convenient support to provide a steadier rest and thus allow a closer reading of the needle.

READING ANGLES

Angles are usually read in terms of number of degrees from the north end of the needle. As has been pointed out before, in the surveying compass the needle automatically points the true direction in which the sighting line is pointing. For example, this sighting direction may be N 40 degrees W on the quadrant scale. The same direction would read 320 degrees on the azimuth scale (360°—40°.)

We can now further illustrate why E and W are transposed on the dial. For example, hold the compass so that the N end of the needle points to N on the dial—the sighting line will then indicate magnetic north. Now turn the compass to the right, in an easterly direction, until the N end of the needle rests on 30 degrees. Your sighting line will have also turned but its correct reading will now be N 30 degrees E with the quadrant graduation or 30 degrees with the azimuth instead of north as it was before you turned the compass. This, of course, is correct, whereas if the E and W on the dial were not reversed you would read N 30 degrees W which would be entirely incorrect.

"ORIENTING" THE MAP. Frequently hunters, fishermen, and woodsmen wish to travel across some piece of wilderness where there are no trails or guideposts. If a map is to be used it should first be oriented with the direction of the earth's surface. This may be done by placing the compass on the map with the sighting line pointing to the north on the map. The map is then turned until the needle reads north. The directions on the map now coincide with the directions on the surface of the earth and the map is said to be oriented. (See chapter 19.)

TAKING A COMPASS BEARING FROM A MAP. Now if you draw a line on the map connecting the point where you are located and the destination to which you wish to go, the direction of the line may be found by placing the compass on the oriented map with the sighting line of the compass parallel to the line on the map, and noting the compass reading of this line.

This direction is read directly from the compass. As an example, in the accompanying illustration, a line has been drawn

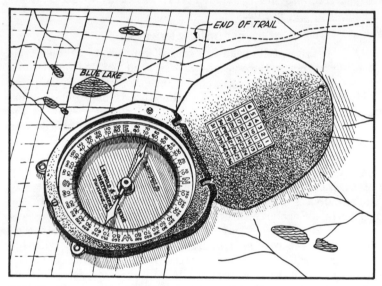

EXAMPLE OF USE OF MAP AND COMPASS TO LAY A COMPASS COURSE ACROSS COUNTRY.

Draw a line between Blue Lake and the end of the trail. Orient the map so that the top of the map points due north. Now lay the compass parallel with the line you drew on the map. Let the compass needle come to rest. Now read the north end of the compass needle: on the quadrant scale it reads North 64° East; on the azimuth scale it reads 64°. Now sight along the sighting line of the compass and pick out a prominent object as a landmark. Move toward the landmark and you will be on your desired course of direction.

connecting Blue Lake with the end of a trail. The direction of the trail from the lake is N 64 degrees E.

APPLYING THE COMPASS BEARING TO THE GROUND. After thus determining the correct course of travel, the compass is held in the hand and turned until the needle reads N 64 degrees E. The line of sight now points the proper direction of travel. A sight is then taken along the sighting line and some object picked out, such as a tree, top of a hill, gap in the hills, or other conspicuous landmark, toward which to proceed. After reaching the first object, the procedure may be repeated and a second object along the same direction may be selected toward which to travel. In this way the destination can be reached by the shortest distance.

THE OPPOSITE DIRECTION ("BACK AZIMUTH"). Having known the direction in which you came, the compass will guide you back again. On the return trip, of course, the opposite direction would be followed with compass observations in the same manner as on the trip in. However, you will return on the back azimuth course. For example, your foresight was N 64 degrees E, or 64 degrees on the azimuth dial. In returning, your back reading would be S 64 degrees W. To obtain a back azimuth you would add 180 degrees and your back course would be 244 degrees on the azimuth dial.

RULE FOR OBTAINING A BACK AZIMUTH READING. (a) When the azimuth is 180 degrees or *less,* add 180 degrees to obtain back azimuth. EXAMPLE: If the primary course is 30 degrees, add 180 degrees to secure back azimuth reading. The back azimuth will then be 210 degrees, or 30 degrees plus 180 degrees.

(b) When the azimuth is *more* than 180 degrees, to obtain back azimuth, *subtract* 180 degrees. EXAMPLE: The primary course has an azimuth of 210 degrees, so you *subtract* 180 degrees. The back azimuth will then be 30 degrees, or 210 degrees minus 180 degrees.

NOTE CHANGES IN DIRECTION OF MOVEMENT. In case of unexpected detours, changes of direction and distance should be noted and recorded on the map, if possible.

In hunting, where the hunter covers a territory with frequent changes of direction during the day, the general direction of travel is usually observed. Each time a change in direction is made it will be helpful to note the general direction of camp with reference to the new direction being followed, so one can return directly to camp without retracing the full day's travel.

USING A PROMINENT LANDMARK. Some times it is possible to keep oriented with reference to some landmark which is known to be in a certain direction from camp.

COMPASS—CHECK LIST

(1) If it is necessary to take into account the magnetic declination, be sure that the proper declination for the locality is set off on the compass.

(2) To find direction to an object, point the sighting line at the object and read the N end of the needle. Always follow the line of sight and not the direction of the needle.

(3) To find or follow a given course, turn the compass until the N end of the needle is on the given bearing and note the course indicated by the sighting line. Always trust your compass directions rather than rely on your own judgment as to the direction.

(4) Hold the compass level so that the needle floats freely. Always read the N end of the needle. When sighting up hill or down hill, you must lower or raise the sighting eye in relation to the compass.

(5) Don't change the alignment of the compass between the time of sighting and the time of reading.

(6) In reading the compass, always observe the direction in which the numerals are progressing and also the quadrant in which they are located if using the quadrant scale.

(7) Don't use the compass in close proximity to steel rails, wire fences, guns, axes, etc., since iron or steel will deflect its needle and cause errors.

(8) Take note of one or more objects, such as a tree or rock, along the line of sight. When in doubt, take another compass reading.

(9) Walk to the most distant object you have noted along the line of sight and then at that point take another sight ahead with the compass.

(10) Take a back sight occasionally, to be sure that you are on the line of sight you have chosen, since you might have had to make offsets to reach your line-of-sight object.

(11) Keep the compass cover closed when not in use to prevent the needle from riding the pivot unnecessarily. A worn pivot will make the action of the needle sluggish and cause errors.

(12) If water gets into compass, remove the glass and dry out thoroughly. Otherwise, the steel pivot may rust and destroy the sensitivity of the needle.

TRAVELING BY COMPASS

A woodsman will use his compass to guide his direction under certain conditions, such as the following:

(1) In fair weather, to record changes in direction from one landmark to another in order to retrace his steps over the route he came.

(2) To travel a direct line of march in storm or darkness when visibility is zero from directions taken from the map.

An outdoorsman must learn when compass bearings are necessary and when they are not. If he plans on climbing a ridge or peak, naturally the ridge or peak is the best guide

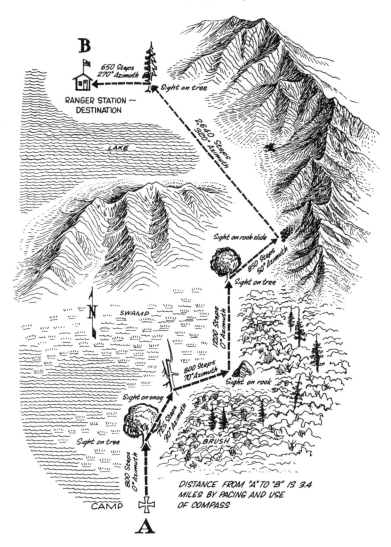

B

650 Steps
270° Azimuth

Sight on tree

RANGER STATION —
DESTINATION

2640 Steps
320° Azimuth

LAKE

Sight on rock slide

850 Steps
50° Azimuth

Sight on tree

1200 Steps
0° Azimuth

N

SWAMP

800 Steps
70° Azimuth

Sight on rock

Sight on snag

725 Steps
90° Azimuth

Sight on tree

BRUSH

800 Steps
0° Azimuth

DISTANCE FROM "A" TO "B" IS 3.4
MILES BY PACING AND USE
OF COMPASS

CAMP

A

COMPASS COURSE USING SUCCESSIVE LANDMARKS.

Assume you are in camp at "A" where an accident has occurred to a member of your party. You want to move the injured person by stretcher across some rough country to the ranger station "B." None of your party has been to the ranger station but you have a sketch of the best route, prepared by to direction. However, if he encounters obstructions, such as large brush or snow fields, he must take frequent bearings. Always take bearings on the return route when there is any doubt about a change in direction. Always trust your compass unless it has become badly damaged.

Of course, rock features provide better landmarks than do ice, snow, or brush fields; however, fog, snow, or darkness can markedly change the appearance of the terrain so that it may become unrecognizable. The smart woodsman will take bearings forward and backward along his route at each change of direction. *Be sure these bearings are recorded at the time taken.*

Compass courses should always be taken so that travel may be accomplished in a given direction with as little deviation as possible. In most cases it will be impossible to travel a straight course for canyons, swamps, brush, snow fields, and many other obstacles will intervene and force one to detour around them. However, by allowing for deviation from the observed compass course, one may reach his objective.

Example: A hunter wishes to travel from point A on the accompanying illustration (see below) to his camp at point B. His magnetic bearing is observed to be 80 degrees. Following this course a large brush field (x-x) is encountered at (1). He decides to turn a 90-degree angle to the right. By changing the compass course 90 degrees, the new course becomes 170 degrees (80 degrees plus 90 degrees). The obstacle is cleared in 100 paces at point (2) where another 90-degree angle is turned to the left. This brings him back to the original course of 80 degrees, but 100 paces below. The original course of 80 degrees is assumed until the brush field is cleared at point (3). Here he makes another 90-degree turn to the left. The new course will be 350 degrees or the reverse of 170 de-

a friend who was at your camp some weeks earlier. You have a sighting compass; with friends carrying the injured person, you start out. Your sketch says your first landmark, a tree, is due north (Azimuth 0°). You sight your compass at 0° and locate the tree and move to it, a distance of 800 steps. The next landmark is a bare tree trunk at an azimuth of 30°, which you find with your compass, and move to it. In the same way you proceed successively to each landmark shown on the sketch (next a large rock, then another tree, then a rock slide, another tree, and finally the ranger station) using the compass to determine the direction in which to go by sighting it at the indicated azimuth reading, and going the indicated distance.

grees. Following this course for 100 paces puts the hunter back on his original line of sight at (4). At this point he should take a foresight (80 degrees) and a backsight (260 degrees) to ascertain if he is exactly back on the A-B line course of 80 degrees.

Further on, a swamp is encountered at y-y at point (5) running obliquely to the line of travel. Here he may turn a 90-degree angle and go around, or take a bearing parallel to it. He decides to take the parallel bearing, angle to the right. The parallel bearing he finds to be 120 degrees. This bearing will differ from bearing A-B by a certain amount which will be called the deviation angle (da). Its sign will be plus if the

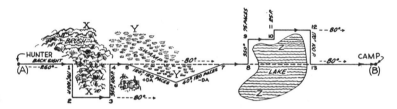

EXAMPLE OF PATHFINDING WITH A COMPASS.

deviation is to the right of the primary course and minus if to the left, thus: (+da or —da). He finds that the swamp was cleared at 120 paces at point (6) and here the angle was turned to the left leg or minus angle of 40 degrees. The primary course is 80 degrees from the plus (+da) which gives our new course of 40 degrees to point (7) after traveling 120 paces. Again, the hunter should take a foresight and backsight along with the primary course to verify that he is on line A-B. On continuing along line A-B a small lake is encountered at point (8) at z-z, and he decides to turn a 90-degree left angle at (8); thus, he continues to pace and turn 90-degree angles at point (9), (10), (11), (12), and (13), and on into camp.

WHEN HUNTING

The serious hunter, fisherman, camper, and explorer will want a high grade compass and up to date maps. He will become proficient in their use. On the other hand, there are many individuals whose only requirement for a compass is related to

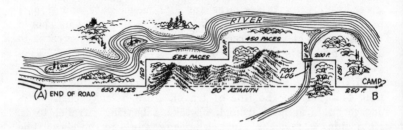

ANOTHER EXAMPLE OF PATHFINDING WITH A MAP AND COMPASS.

A fisherman is looking for a camp site. His map shows the location of the camp ("B"), also the end of the road where he has parked his car ("A"). By orienting the map with the ground, and by use of his compass (see page 164) he lays a compass course on the map from the road end to the camp. His compass tells him the direction is azimuth 80°. He starts out but soon finds a straight line is impracticable because of rough terrain. He records in his notebook the azimuth of each change of direction and the number of paces he moves on each leg of his course. (In this example, for the sake of simplicity, all turns are shown as 90°.) He finds he goes a total distance of 2575 paces, offsetting to the left twice and then, to get back on course offsets an equal distance to the right.

To retrace his course back to the end of the road would be a simple matter, even in fog or rain, as he knows the direction and distance of each leg of the course. The BACK azimuth, the direction of the return course from camp is, of course, 260° (80° plus 180°).

their occasional hunting trips. For the latter, a very simple and unique compass has been on the market for several years. This refers to the small compass which is available in many sporting goods stores and deliberately designed for installation behind the comb of a rifle or shotgun stock—down towards the heel. It requires drilling a small hole approximately ½ inch deep and about ⅝ inch in diameter. A small but well built compass is then inlayed in this hole so that when the firearm is held parallel to the ground, trigger guard down, the face of the compass is easy to read.

The compass is simplicity itself. An outer knurled ring which the hunter may turn aligns a small luminescent white dot with the short, white magnetic pointer needle (half needle) on the face of the compass. If aligned so that the gun barrel also points in the same direction as the dot and pointer, the gun will be pointing north. You can readily see applications of this simple arrangement.

Before starting to hunt, face the main direction you expect

to go, then take a few moments to familiarize yourself with landmarks to your right and left to identify the area (—they represent the base line) from which you are about to depart and to which you will later return. Next, point the gun in the direction you will generally be following during your hunt. While pointing, align the white dot in its ring so it is exactly opposite and as far away as possible from the white tipped end of the pointer needle. Later on, wherever you are, to find your way back from hunting, simply hold your gun horizontally and turn yourself around until the little compass needle points to the white dot. Your gun will then point to the area (base line) from which you started.

Users report that although this system won't bring them out exactly to their car or camp, it will invariably bring them back to the area (somewhere along the base line) from which they started. By the time this is reached, landmarks observed near the point where the hunt originated begin to look familiar and the starting point is then usually easy to find. While it is hard to beat carrying a more elaborately graduated compass and map, I must say I have never had to go out and look for a lost hunter who had one of these little instruments imbedded in the stock of his gun.

Another excellent compass is the Silva Huntsman. It is liquid filled, has a pin-on fastener, sun watch, and luminous points.

Chapter 19

PATHFINDING WITH MAPS

READING A MAP

A MAP is a representation on a flat surface and at a convenient scale of a part of the surface of the earth. Reading a map intelligently requires considerable thought and study. Everyone is familiar with a road map but not everyone can quickly relate the map to the area it represents. A map is a picture of the land; if you can understand the picture, you can understand the map. It is a bird's-eye view of the terrain. Maps show the roads, trails, streams, lakes, bridges, peaks and elevations, and by standard symbols all the features that assist one to recognize the land and terrain when you travel over it. Therefore it is essential that you understand the symbols on the margin of the map, and also how to use the mileage scale. Every car or truck driver uses a road map. Experienced foresters, rangers, and other outdoor people also use the topographic maps made by the United States Geological Survey Service. To secure a map of this type, first write to the Director, United States Geological Survey Service, Washington 25, D. C., and ask for an index to topographic maps of your state or the area that you are particularly interested in; this will enable you to order the correct maps from the index.

MAP NORTH. The top of most maps are usually true north. Most Geological Survey maps have a compass rose or arrow pointing to true north, with a half-arrow pointing to magnetic north. The correct declination for the area is shown on these maps. All marine and air maps carry compass roses printed thereon.

MAP SCALE. Map scale may be shown in several ways:

(1) By a statement of how many miles are represented by an inch on the map—two inches to the mile, one-fourth or one-half inch to the mile, etc.

(2) The scale may be represented by a fraction, such as 1:24,000. This means that every unit of measurement on the map is represented by 24,000 similar units on the earth's sur-

face. The representative fraction is used on all topographic maps of the United States. A conversion table of the most frequent ones in use is as follows:

1:24,000 —1 inch equals about ⅜ mile or 2,000 feet.
1:31,250 —1 inch equals about ½ mile or 2,640 feet.
1:48,000 —1 inch equals about ¾ mile or 4,000 feet.
1:62,500 —1 inch equals about 1 mile or 5,280 feet.
1:125,000—1 inch equals about 2 miles or 10,560 feet.
1:250,000—1 inch equals about 4 miles or 21,120 feet.
1:500,000—1 inch equals about 8 miles or 42,240 feet.

(3) By a line divided into intervals and marked to indicate what these intervals represent on the ground. This is called a visual or graphic scale.

GEOLOGICAL SURVEY TOPOGRAPHIC MAPS

Most anyone can read an automobile club map. These and the small trail maps issued by the Forest and National Park Service are the simplest to read. They show the roads, trails, and towns, and a considerable amount of other pertinent information; however, for the woodsman or mountaineer going into remote sections of the back country, the best available map is a must! These are the Geological Survey topographic maps sold at most Forest and National Park Service headquarters, or at most up-to-date stationery stores for around $1.00. They may also be purchased through the Superintendent of Documents, Washington, D.C.

Smaller quadrangle maps of the area you intend to travel through may be secured for $.40 to $.50 each. Most of these maps do not have the section lines printed thereon as the larger maps do; however, they are of a larger scale. A good map should have at least a half-inch scale, as a quarter-inch scale is too difficult to read. A county map shows the section lines, townships, etc., and is a good buy.

VARIOUS LINES ON MAPS

CONTOUR LINES. The arrangement of contour lines on a map indicate the form of the land. The contour lines around a ridge point down hill, and those in a river valley point up stream. The spacing of the contour lines indicate the steepness of the slope. Those that are very close together indicate a steep slope, and the widely spaced lines a gentle slope. It should be remembered that slopes measured from a map are average slopes.

Contour lines are a series of lines which connect points of equal altitude. Such lines are broken at intervals by figures that indicate the height in feet above mean sea level of the points connected by contour lines.

Some lines carry no identifying figures, but when one knows the contour interval, one can determine the height of any unnumbered line from its relationship to numbered lines. Often the contour lines are at fifty, one hundred, or two hundred foot intervals.

PRINCIPAL MERIDIANS. Most good maps will show one or more principal meridians. These are north and south lines established as a control by which the east or west boundary lines of townships may be determined.

BASE LINES. Base lines are started at given points and run east and west, and assist in making a starting point for surveys. They further assist in proper land description and location.

STANDARD PARALLEL LINES. These lines run east and west, and parallel base lines at intervals of twenty-four miles. These lines also serve as correction lines for range boundaries.

GUIDE MERIDIANS. Guide meridians run north from the standard parallel meridians every twenty-four miles and lay off the land in theoretical rectangles twenty-four miles square.

TOWNSHIP LINES. These lines are more or less six miles apart and are east and west lines that mark the north and south boundaries of townships. The six-mile strip of land that lies between them is known as the "range" and is numbered east or west from the principal meridian from which that survey was made. These lines divide the country into six-mile squares and are called townships.

SECTION LINES. Townships are next divided into sections of 640 acres and are as nearly one mile square as possible. The subdivision lines are made east and west and north and south at intervals of one mile. There are thirty-six sections to the township. Convergence of lines sometimes prevents establishing thirty-six regular square miles, so the extra large or small sections are put in the north and west sides of the township. In some instances, one might note wide and narrow sections on his map caused by crowding, since surveys were started in various parts of the country, and when connected did not merge exactly on line with each other.

SECTION NUMBERS. Sections are numbered from one to thirty-six and can be further divided and subdivided into smaller units such as half and quarter sections, and quarter-quarter sections. This can be broken up further into smaller blocks or lots.

CORNERS. Section and quarter-section corners were set in the first surveys made by the U. S. Land Office. These "corners" may be found to be iron pipes driven into the ground, wooden stakes, concrete posts, etc. If trees were nearby they were marked by carving the description of the section, township, and range thereon. These trees were called "bearing" or "witness" trees and were blazed on the side facing the "corner." If a woodsman became turned around, he could find his way back to camp if he found one of these section corners. Once he located himself on his map, he could follow the survey blazes out to the nearest road, trail, or land that he was familiar with.

SURVEY TAGS. Nowadays, one will find metal location survey tags or section posters at quarter-section or section corners with the section, township, and range inscribed thereon. Where section lines cross roads, trails, and sometimes private property lines, one will usually find these metal survey tags. Where section lines cross a road or trail, the tag is marked as to how many chains it is to the section line, and any woodsman worth his salt should be able to "pace" and know how many paces he takes per chain (a chain being 66 feet) and thereby find the section line quite easily.

It is fun to be able to read maps properly, and of course it is a "must" for all rangers, woodsmen, and others who work or live in the outdoors.

HOW TO STAKE A MINING CLAIM

Right to certain mineral lands owned by the United States and the various states is yours for the asking if you are an adult U. S. citizen or have applied for citizenship. That "asking" includes—first, discovering mineral on the land; second, locating the claim; third, recording the location at the county recorder's office in compliance with state laws; and fourth, continuing development of the claim by doing annual assessment work worth a minimum of $100.

A good quality compass such as the Leupold is an invaluable aid to the prospector who seeks a fortune in gold, uranium, or other mineral. Such a compass will enable him to travel confidently through the unmarked terrain of wilderness areas. And, after minerals are located, the prospector can use his compass to stake the boundaries of his claim and plot a rough map showing its location.

Federal mining law requires that a location be established by staking the corners of the claim, posting notice of location thereon, and complying with state law regarding the recording of the location at the county recorder's office. Whether your claim is made on Federal or state land, you must comply with mining laws of the individual states. Information on how to make a proper location can be obtained at the county recorder's office where you expect to file location notice.

Mineral lands available for the "asking" include most vacant Federal and state-owned public domain lands, national forests in the public-land states (forest regulations must be observed), lands entered or patented under the stock-raising Homestead law (title to *minerals only* can be acquired), lands entered under other agriculture laws but not perfected and where prospecting can be done peacefully, and lands within railroad grants for which patents have not been issued.

Lode locations for minerals discovered in lode or vein formation may not exceed in length 1,500 feet along the vein, and in width 300 feet on each side of the middle of the vein; the end lines of the location to be parallel to each other. Placer locations, which include all minerals not occurring in vein or lode formation, may be for areas of not more than 20 acres for each locator.

THE GOOD PATHFINDER IS OBSERVANT

Next to map reading, an outdoorsman must be a good observer and be able to read "signs" and be especially observant as he travels. He should note special landmarks, the direction in which streams are flowing, how many streams he has crossed, sun direction, trails, peaks, animal and man tracks, and other objects that will assist him in finding his way through the woods safely.

ORIENTING A MAP

In order that a map may be used and understood properly as a means of identifying places in any area, it first must be oriented with the terrain. This can be done quickly if you have a compass with you. (See chapter 18). If you do not have your compass with you, it will then be necessary to use some other method, such as follows:

(1) Orient a map by rotating the map until the direction of a line drawn from any point to any other point on the map will be the true direction between the two points on the ground.

(2) Another method requires that the observer's position on the map be known as closely as possible, and that one point shown on the map can be identified on the land.

Imagine a line to be drawn between the observer's position on the map and the position of the identified point. Turn the map around until this line, if extended, passes through the point on land. The map is then oriented and lines drawn from the position occupied to any other point on the map will pass through the actual points on the terrain.

PATHFINDING WITHOUT A COMPASS BUT WITH A MAP

TO ORIENT THE MAP AND LOCATE A POSITION. Assume the hunter has the map shown on the next page. If the hunter knows his approximate location on both the ground and the map and can recognize some of the prominent landmarks, he proceeds as follows:

1. To orient his map approximately, he lays it out flat with the top toward the north.

2. He looks around the country and identifies Piute Peak. Off to the northeast he spots the Storm King Lookout.

3. He now locates Piute Peak and Bear Pass on his map.

4. He shifts the direction of the map slightly so that, when sighting over the map, the line joining Bear Pass and Piute Peak on the map coincides with the line between these two objects on the ground. The map is now oriented.

5. The hunter can now locate other landmarks, such as Mono Peak and Butte, both on the map and on the ground and

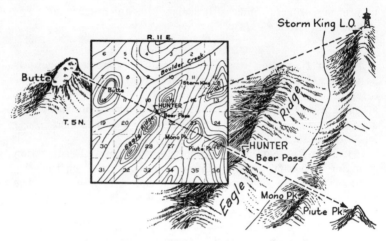

PATHFINDING WITHOUT A COMPASS (See text).

determine their direction and distance from where he is by measuring on his map.

If the hunter does NOT know his location on the ground or on the map, he still may locate his position from recognized landmarks. Assume he has the same map (shown above) but does not know just where he is.

1. First he searches for landmarks. He notes that Piute Peak rises slightly higher than Mono Peak and that they are in line.

2. He lays his map out flat and rotates it until a line through Piute Peak and Mono Peak on the map coincides with a line through these two points on the ground. This orients the map.

3. Now he locates his own position by looking around for other landmarks he can identify on the ground and on the map. He sees the Storm King lookout station about 2½ miles northeast of where he is. He locates this landmark on the map and finds that 2½ miles southwest of the lookout station is Bear Pass in a saddle in Eagle Ridge. He compares the ground forms where he is with those shown on the map and they agree. He now knows he is on Eagle Ridge at Bear Pass.

FINDING DIRECTION WITHOUT COMPASS OR MAP

SHADOW METHOD. Place a vertical pole firmly in the

ground with the top four feet above the ground, in **direct sunlight**, as shown below. Fasten one end of a string or length of vine to the top of the pole, and attach a stick at the other end. Now in the morning draw a circle on the ground with the stick with the pole as the center, and the length of the pole's shadow as a radius. Now mark on the circle with a stake or rock the point where the tip of the morning shadow touches the circle. Then in the afternoon similarly mark the circle where the shadow tip again touches the circle and the shadow is the same length as that marked in the morning. Halfway between the two marked points is north. (Not always reliable.)

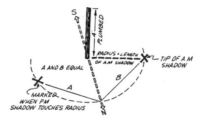

FINDING DIRECTION BY SHADOW METHOD.

WATCH AND SUN METHOD. Using standard time, point the hour hand toward the sun, as shown below. In the **northern** hemisphere, halfway between the hour hand and 12 o'clock is south. (Not always reliable.)

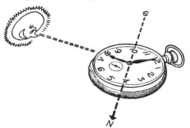

FINDING DIRECTION WITH WATCH AND SUN.

OWENDOFF "SHADOW-TIP" METHOD. The fastest, most accurate method of finding direction without compass **or map** but using the sun, was developed by Robert Owendoff, a versatile young scholar-athlete, of Falls Church, Virginia. Select a smooth spot where the sun is shining. Drive a straight stick three or four feet long firmly into the ground. Be sure it is vertical. Now mark on the ground with a match, stick, nail, or similar object, the exact tip of the stick's shadow. After a quarter of an hour or more, again mark the exact tip of the shadow which meantime will have moved a few inches. Now connect these two marked points with a straight line, extending it in each direction. This line runs in an east-west direction. Draw another straight line across the east-west line and at right angles to it, and passing through the base of the stick. This new line points *north*. *Note.*—In the southern hemisphere (and at certain times of the year in the tropics) the line will point *south*. If you are ever uncertain as to which direction is east and which is west, observe this simple rule: The sun rises in the east and sets in the west. The shadow, of course, moves just the opposite. Therefore, the first shadow-tip mark is always

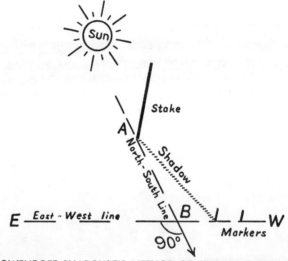

OWENDOFF SHADOW-TIP METHOD OF FINDING DIRECTION

Drive a stake in the ground. Mark with a peg or nail the tip of the stake's shadow. The shadow will move. About 15 minutes later mark the new location of the shadow tip. Connect the two marks with a straight line, extending it both ways. This line runs EAST and WEST. Draw a line at right angles to the east-west line (at B) passing through base of stake (A). This line runs NORTH-SOUTH, with south toward the stake.

in the west direction and the second mark is always in the east direction, everywhere on earth.

TELLING TIME WITH THE OWENDOFF METHOD. The "Shadow-tip" method will not only help you find direction; it may also be used to tell the time of day. To tell the time of day, consider the vertical stick casting a shadow as an improvised sun dial. The *north* line will extend from the shadow stick northward, and in the northern hemisphere will point toward 12 o'clock on your improvised sun dial. To lay out a 6 o'clock line, draw another east-west line parallel to the first one and passing through the base of your shadow stick.

Having determined the correct direction by the shadow-tip method, move the stick to the intersection of the east-west line and the indicated north-south line (i.e., from A to B on the diagram) and set the stick vertically in the ground. The east-west line now becomes the 6 o'clock line on your improvised sun dial. The west half of the line indicates 6 A.M. and the east half 6 P.M. The north line has become the noon line.

To complete the face of your sun dial, draw a half-circle of a convenient radius with the base of the stick as its center. Using the noon line and the 6 o'clock lines as your guides, divide and mark the half-circle into 12 equal angular parts to

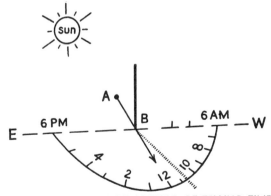

OWENDOFF SHADOW-TIP METHOD OF TELLING TIME

Shift the stake used in finding direction from A to B and mark out a clock face on ground as an improvised sun dial. Mark 12 equal angular parts to show the hours. The west end of the east-west line is 6 A.M., the east end 6 P.M. The shadow mark of the stake as it moves across the clock face will indicate local "sun" time, just like a sun dial.

represent the hours. The shadow of the stick becomes the hour hand and you can read the time as the shadow passes along the face of your clock. This will be standard "sun time" for your area. (Add one hour for daylight saving time.)

Note. In the southern hemisphere the south line becomes the noon line. When south of the Equator or in the tropics, observe the direction of rotation of the shadow around the stick to establish the correct way to read the shadow clock.

NORTH STAR. At night, in the northern hemisphere, the star Polaris can be seen in the direction of true north. Polaris can be found quickly by locating the Big Dipper (Ursa Major). The "pointers," the two stars in the dipper farthest from the handle, point to Polaris.

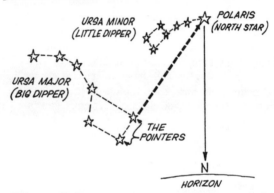

FINDING DIRECTION BY LOCATING THE NORTH STAR.

Chapter 20

OUTDOOR MEASUREMENT

THERE ARE times when an outdoorsman needs to know how far it is across a lake, the width of a stream or canyon, how tall a certain tree is, or how high a cliff is from where he is standing. He may need this information should he have to swim across a body of water; or he might want to know how many logs of a certain length he can secure from a tree; and again, he might wish to scale a cliff. Normally a woodsman doesn't carry an engineer's chain, yardstick, or tape measure with him; however, nature has provided him with a ruler—his own measurements!

A RULER YOU ALWAYS HAVE WITH YOU

Take a tape measure and note and remember the following measurements:

(1) Your height in feet and inches.

(2) Your vertical reach; the distance from the ground to the tip of your fingers when standing with your arm held vertically.

(3) Your horizontal reach; the distance from the finger tips of one hand to the finger tips of the other when both arms are held horizontally.

(4) The distance from the ground to the level of your eyes.

(5) The length of your foot.

(6) The length of your step.

(7) The length of your pace (Note: a "Roman pace" is two natural steps).

(8) The span of your hand, from tip of little finger to tip of thumb.

(9) Now find a unit on your body that is exactly one inch, such as a finger joint; then a unit of exactly one foot, which could be the length of your shoe, or from your elbow to a point on your wrist; next a yard measure, possibly the distance from the tip of fingers to the tip of your nose when your arm is held outstretched horizontally.

A belt can be used for a tape measure by simply marking off the inside of the belt into inches and feet.

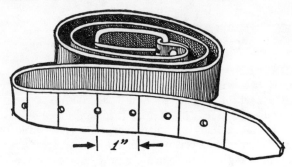

A CONVENIENT MEASURE—YOUR BELT.

Several examples on how to measure a stream width or tree height are shown in the accompanying illustrations.

PACING—A "MUST" FOR THE WOODSMAN

With practice, any person can obtain sufficient accuracy for most field measurements by knowing the length of his pace and how many paces he takes per chain. A chain is the land surveyor's unit of linear measure. One chain is sixty-six feet long and is the basic unit for measuring distance on the land. There are eighty chains in one mile.

A convenient unit is the "Roman pace," which is the distance on level ground between the heel of one foot and the heel of the same foot where it next touches the ground while walking at your natural gait—in other words, it is two natural steps.

Because each person's pace varies with the individual, it is necessary for each person to learn the length of his normal pace. This can be determined by measuring off a number of chains with a steel tape and driving a stake at each end. Next, walk normally from one stake to the other, count your paces and divide by the number of chains in the course to obtain your average paces per chain. Do this a number of times so that you are certain of your average pace, and remember it for future use.

Pacing is used in conjunction with compass work when making detours or off-sets in cutting across country, or in land measurement, and for locating section corners.

HOW TO MEASURE THE WIDTH OF A STREAM, RIVER, OR CANYON

Example (1) (see illustration below). To measure the width of a stream or canyon one must select two points A and B which are close to the shore or canyon edge, and squarely opposite each other. At point A lay off the right angle CAD. From point

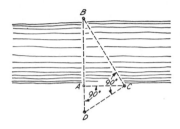

MEASURING WIDTH.

A along the line AC measure off an estimated one-third of the width of the stream or canyon, or in fact any convenient distance, to point C. At point C lay off the right angle BCD. Now find point D on this last line CD, where CD intersects BA extended. Then measure, by pacing or other means, the distances AD and AC. Now you can compute AB, the width of the stream, by means of the formula: $AB:AC::AC:AD$.

Let us say that when you stepped off the distance AC you found it to be 40 steps. Your step is 30 inches, or 2½ feet. AC, then, is 100 feet. You now step off AD and find it to be 26 steps, or 65 feet. Applying the formula $AB:AC::AC:AD$, you find that—

$AB:100::100:65$

Hence $65AB = 10,000$

And $AB = 154$ feet.

Example (2) (see illustration). If you happen to be in open country, or there is room for making longer measurements, the method illustrated below is more convenient, since CD is the same as the width desired, AB.

Lay off the right angle BAC.

Select point C on the line AC a convenient distance from A (approximately the distance AB). At C lay off the right angle ACD, and extend line CD away from from the stream until point D is exactly in line with both point B and point E. (Point

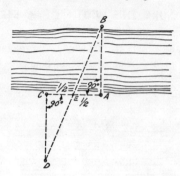

MEASURING WIDTH. (This is a more convenient method if space is available.)

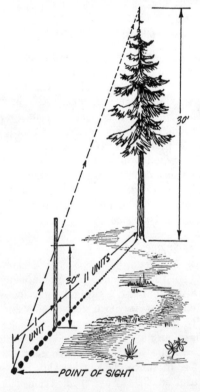

MEASURING HEIGHT.

E is marked half way between A and C so as to be easily sighted on from D toward B).

Now measure CD; this equals AB, the width of the stream.

TO MEASURE THE HEIGHT OF A TREE OR OTHER OBJECT

The "One Inch To One Foot" method, shown on the next page is convenient. Move on level ground in a straight line from the base of the object to be measured exactly 11 units of whatever measuring scale you wish to use—11 steps, 11 stick lengths, or any other unit. At this point drive a straight stick or staff far enough into the ground to be steady. Measure one more unit beyond this point. Mark on the ground where this 12th unit ends and at this point lie down with your eye as near the point as possible and sight across the vertical staff at the top of the tree or other object. Note where your line of sight crosses the staff, and measure on the staff the height of this line from the ground in inches. One inch on the staff equals one foot on the object. If the measurement on the staff is 30 inches, the tree is 30 feet high.

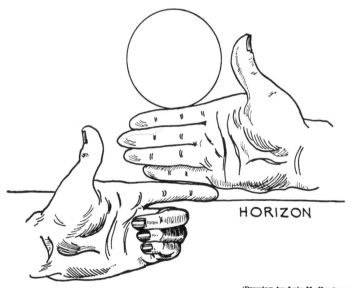

(Drawing by Luis M. Henderson)

HOW LONG UNTIL SUNSET?

HOW TO TELL HOW SOON THE SUN WILL SET

You may find yourself without a watch and you want to make camp or row across the lake before the sun is down. Or perhaps you have your watch but you don't know what time the sun sets. You want to know how much time you have before sundown. Here is a way to get a quick approximation. Face the setting sun. Extend your arms at full length toward the sun, your wrists bent inward, your fingers just below the sun. Disregard the thumbs. Count how many finger widths separate the sun from the horizon. Allow fifteen minutes per finger. If four fingers fill the space between the horizon and the sun with your arms fully extended, sunset is an hour away; six fingers would mean an hour and a half.

Chapter 21

SADDLING AND PACKING

SADDLING A HORSE

Most sore backs are caused by improper adjustment of saddle blankets. Be certain that the animal's back has been brushed clean, and that the blanket is as clean as possible; that there are no wrinkles, burs, pine needles, or other objects or dirt on or under the blanket that might abrade or gall the back.

Poorly constructed saddles and improper saddle and cinch adjustments are another source of trouble and may cause saddle sores. A curry comb and brush are a "must" to keep an animal clean and well-groomed. Be gentle with comb and brush, especially at tender points.

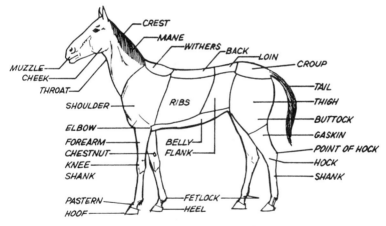

NOMENCLATURE OF A HORSE.

FOLDING THE BLANKET. The so-called Army fold should be used. Take a full-sized blanket and fold lengthwise once, then crosswise in even thirds, making six thicknesses of blanket. The blanket should be placed so that it will fit squarely under the saddle, so that the pressure will be distributed evenly from the backbone down each side to the edge of the saddle skirts. Place the blanket well forward, then slide it back so that it is seated properly, with about two inches of blanket ahead of the front saddle skirts. This will comb the hair back so that it will lie smoothly. The front margin should come to the center of the withers.

PLACING THE SADDLE. Never throw a saddle on an animal so that it lands harshly, otherwise the stirrups will slap down hard, causing a sharp blow to the animal's side. This is painful, and will cause any horse or mule to shy after this sort of rough treatment.

The simplest method is to place the right stirrup and cinch or breeching over the seat of the saddle. Now grip the horn with the left hand, and the back center of the saddle skirts with the right hand. Raise the saddle high enough so that it can be gently swung into position, and settle the saddle down to correct position on the blanket. Now slide the cinch and the right stirrup over the right side gently, and they will fall into their proper place.

TIGHTENING THE CINCH. Most riding and pack saddles in the West, where steep mountain trails prevail, are of the double-rigged type. Reach carefully under the animal and secure the cinch and bring it up to the near side; then thread the latigo through the cinch ring from the inner side. The latigo is next passed upward and through the ring fastened to the saddle rig from the outer side, downward again, and through the cinch ring from the inner side, then upward again and tied into the rig ring.

Some latigoes are made to buckle. These are less complicated, and may be adjusted quickly. Be sure all slack is taken up between the cinch and the rig, or the buckle tongue may work loose on this type and lead to an accident. After the front cinch is secured, the rear cinch is treated in the same manner. The front cinch should not be so tight that one cannot get at least two fingers under the cinch. The rear cinch is left looser so the animal can breathe properly. Too tight a cinch can cause a bad cinch welt or sore. Having the cinch too close to the arm or front leg can cause a hard-to-heal sore.

Use a breeching and breast strap harness when going into mountainous country, especially on a horse that has very little belly. This will prevent the pack or saddle from slipping forward or backward while negotiating steep trails.

PROPER STIRRUP LENGTH

It makes one shudder to think of how many inexperienced riders have suffered over the years because they used too short a stirrup. A few still can be seen in the back country—dismounting stiff-legged and sore of knee from improperly adjusted stirrups. The old rule of thumb—by measuring the stirrup from armpit to saddle rig with arm extended full length—is not a cure-all. Some people happen to be long or short-armed, and their legs can also vary in length. In any event, the stirrups should be long enough so that there is about a two-inch clearance between your seat and the saddle when standing upright in the stirrups.

MOUNTING AND DISMOUNTING

MOUNTING. Always mount from the near (left) side of any riding animal. Nothing will show up an inexperienced horseman more quickly than his trying to mount from the offside. Cheeking is the safest manner in which to mount a strange animal, or one that moves out the moment you hold the reins and grab a stirrup. Secure a firm grip of the bridle cheek with the left hand, then turn the near stirrup forward with the right hand until you can insert your left foot into it. When the left foot is firmly in the stirrup, release the stirrup and cheek and with the reins in the left hand, grasp the horse's mane or the saddle-horn and mount up. If the animal should lunge forward or start moving ahead as some horses do, the forward momentum forces the rider up into the saddle if he has his foot seated well into the stirrup, and all he has to do is throw his right leg over and he is seated. Having a tight left rein will force the animal into a tight left turn if he insists on moving ahead and you happen to miss or fumble mounting on the first attempt. This action will slow him down and keep him close to you so that you can reach the stirrup and remount. Be sure to inquire of the packer or person who rents stock to you regarding any bad traits that the animal may have so that you may be on the alert.

The horse cavalryman mounted by taking the reins in the left hand with the little finger between them and the bight of the reins falling on the right side, and adjusting the reins so they give a gentle, even bearing on the horse's mouth, and placed the left hand on the horse's crest near the withers, taking a lock of mane between the thumb and forefinger. He then placed the left foot in the stirrup, assisted by the right hand, brought the left knee against the saddle, with the right hand on the cantle. He then mounted by rising by an effort of the right leg assisted by the right arm, releasing his hold on the cantle as he carried the right leg over the cantle and down on the right side, inserting the foot into the right stirrup.

DISMOUNTING. Dismounting sounds simple, but there is a right way and a wrong way. The safest method is to grip the saddle horn with the right hand, holding the reins with the left hand. The right foot is then withdrawn from the stirrup, the left foot is moved backward until the tip of the toes rest in the stirrup, the right leg is carried over the cantle and downward to the rear of the left leg, and the left foot is finally released from the stirrup by tipping the heel downward. This enables the rider to land on both feet and at the same time leaves him facing forward or the same direction the horse has been traveling.

The cavalryman, to dismount with the reins in the left hand, placed that hand on the horse's crest near the withers and put his right hand on the pommel. He then removed the right foot from the stirrup and carried the right leg over the croup without touching it. He then changed the right hand to the cantle of the saddle and lowered his right foot to the ground, followed by the left foot.

YOUR HORSE CAN FIND THE WAY BACK

If caught out in a snow storm or after dark and lost, with visibility nil, you can normally give your horse or mule his head and he will bring you into camp.

SADDLING AND LOADING A PACK ANIMAL

A tenderfoot packer and an inexperienced pack animal make a poor combination. If you are a tyro and not an old hand at packing, insist on a gentle animal.

Make sure that the pack saddle fits the pack animal. A long, narrow-treed saddle will injure the back of a fat, short-coupled horse and a wide, flat saddle should not be put on a narrow-backed animal. Use plenty of pads or blankets under the pack saddle. Be sure that they are wrinkle-free and also that no pine needles or other abrasives are under them.

Saddle the pack animal and allow him to stand with moderately tightened cinches for several minutes before putting the load on him. This "warming up" period will often prevent a horse from humping up his back, loosening cinches, and possible "blow-up" from a cold packed animal.

Saddling pack stock is accomplished in the same manner and by the same method as used with the riding saddle, except that most pack saddles have breast collars or straps and breeching attached. There are many ways to pack a horse or mule, and the method usually varies with the area and the individual packer. The Forest Service uses the Decker saddle for cargo packing supplies and equipment into remote areas. It also uses the sawbuck or cross-tree pack saddle—so does the National

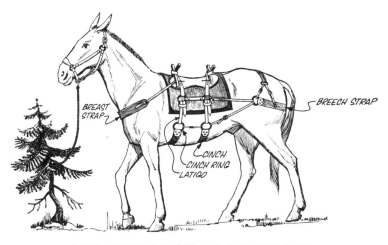

BREAST STRAP

BREECH STRAP

CINCH
CINCH RING
LATIGO

PACK ANIMAL SADDLED AND READY TO PACK.

Park Service. The Army prefers the Phillips pack saddle, an elaborate leather and metal outfit. In any case, the breast strap and breeching should be snug, but not tight. Once fitted to an animal, it should be consistently used on that particular animal if at all possible; otherwise, it will have to be readjusted for each individual animal on which it is placed.

The breast strap keeps the pack saddle and load from slipping backward, and the breeching straps keep the load from **riding forward,** an important matter when negotiating steep **trails.** Be careful in placing breeching over an animal's **rear,** and while clearing an animal's tail from the breeching. Some horses or mules are skittish in that area and will sometimes kick viciously either backward or sidewise.

Be sure to balance carefully the weight of the panniers, kyacks, or side loads if you are using "slings" before loading and have top packs, manta covers and lash ropes laid out conveniently so packing, once started, can proceed without interruption. Make final tightening of the cinches only when ready to start loading the pack. Work from the front of the

BALANCE EVENLY THE PACK BOXES OR KYACK BAGS.

animal, left side first, and in crossing to the right side, always cross in front where he can see you. If you approach with equipment from the rear where the animal cannot see you, he may "spook" and kick the outfit all over creation. Avoid sudden motion, stumbling, flapping of canvas, or undue noise.

Always avoid entangling of lash or sling rope. Speak quietly to the animal.

A person working on each side of the animal is best. While the packer on the left side laces the load, the person on the right side can adjust its hang and balance. When the person on the left or near side "throws" the hitch and takes up the slack, his opposite partner can pull the slack across and around his side of the pack.

LEADING PACK STOCK

With several pack animals in a "string," lead the first and tie each of the following animals to the tail of the preceding animal or to a rope loop fastened for that purpose around the rear fork of the pack saddle. A lead horse tied to the lash rope on top of the pack may pull back and unbalance the load.

In leading one or more head of pack stock, be sure to keep a minimum of six feet between animals. The horse in back may crowd the one in front, and the front one may in turn kick the rear horse or mule and cripple the animal, or he might take a nip at the horse immediately in front.

In most national forests and parks, stock must be led; otherwise, pack stock left loose will lag back to graze, or lie down, or run ahead and take the wrong trail, and sometimes head for the home corral. Leading the pack animals is a safety measure, and also regulates the speed of the pack train.

ON THE TRAIL. Most western horses and mules know where to step, so give them their heads. If your saddle horse stumbles for some reason, don't yank up hard on the reins; he needs to swing his head to assist in regaining his balance. When you come to a difficult or dangerous spot or crossing, size up the situation before you cross, or go around. It's safer and good horse sense to get off and lead an animal over or around any bad spot. Get off and walk up or down very steep slopes or trails. This will be appreciated by your steed, for he, too, is flesh and blood, and it might save both of you from a bad fall. Get off your mount and lead him across all bridges as a safety measure.

If your saddle or pack animal should ever bog down in a swampy or boggy spot, there is only one thing to do—unpack him, and repack on firm ground.

Get moving as soon as possible after packing all stock. Delay can cause stock to become restless and cause rubbed backs, kicking animals and general confusion.

Keep moving. Do not stop to allow the animals to mill and rub each other or to graze. Only short rest periods are necessary on zig-zag switchbacks. On arriving at the camp or evening stop, remove the packs immediately, clean the sweaty backs, and allow the animals to roll, drink, and feed. Be sure to bell the leaders and hobble the animals that are apt to stray or head back to the home pasture or corral. The care and welfare of the stock is the first consideration of anyone handling a pack string.

See also chapter 11, "Saddle and Pack-Outfit Camping."

PACK LOADS FOR HORSES, BURROS, AND MULES

Too many pack animals are overloaded, especially so by inexperienced persons who own their stock.

WEIGHT OF LOAD. For burros, the average load is seventy-five pounds for an extended trip; however, if you are lucky to have a large, young burro, a maximum of one hundred pounds can be carried. Burros have hauled 175 and 200-pound persons up mountain trails, but that, of course, is live weight. Inert dead weight is a "horse (or burro) of a different color!"

Average pay loads for horses and mules are the same, and range from an average of 150 to 185 pounds in rough country for grass-fed animals. Some stock may be packed heavier for longer trips if the animal is carrying food supplies and the load is somewhat lighter each day, but where the load remains constant, such as on an animal who carries only equipment, it is advisable to keep to the 150-185 pound limit if the stock is worked nearly every day.

LENGTH OF DAY'S TRAVEL. Average mileage for burros is from eight to twelve miles per day. Average mileage per day for horses and mules is fifteen miles; however, it will fluctuate from twelve to eighteen miles. It depends upon where sufficient grazing range, water, fuel, and a safe camping place can be located.

PLANNING THE TRIP. It takes some planning and organization to prepare for a pack trip into the mountains or a wilderness area, before the outfit ever leaves the pack station corral. If you have to rent pack and saddle stock, reservations must be made well in advance of the trip with the outfitter. He will want to know how many will be in the party, how much weight (if possible), how many days the stock will be used, and where you want him to pack you; also, if you will require a cook if the party is large enough to warrant one.

Some packers will pack you and your equipment into hunting or fishing country and leave you, and then pick you and your outfit up at a prearranged date and place, and pack you out again. This is the most economical way, and is called "spot packing."

Always prepare a menu in advance with a few extras. Also, it is a good idea to prepare a detailed itinerary; however, allow an extra day in case a storm blows up, or some other delaying action develops.

The following is a check list of equipment necessary for each saddle and pack animal.

PACK AND SADDLE EQUIPMENT

(1) Tie rope for each animal, 10 feet of ½-inch cotton rope.

(2) Halter for each animal, preferably leather.

(3) Blankets, two each, a good wool or hair sweat blanket next to back, and a good wool pad or blanket on top of the sweat pad.

(4) Pack saddle, saw-buck type, double-rigged with breast and breeching straps.

(5) Stock saddle for each horse to be ridden.

(6) Bridle for each saddle horse.

(7) Kyacks, panniers, or slings—two of either type per pack animal.

(8) Boxes, two per animal, the type that two five-gallon kerosene cans come in. These empty boxes are slipped into kyack bags to keep articles from becoming broken.

(9) Pack rope, 40 feet of ½-inch manila with cinch attached.

(10) Morralies (feed bags), one for each horse.

(11) Manta, or canvas pack cover for each pack animal, 5 x 7 feet.

(12) Grazing bell, size No. 5—one bell for every fourth animal.

(13) Hobbles, one set each for those animals that are strayers.

(14) Shoeing outfit (minimum tools to do the job).

(15) Horse and mule shoes (one front and one hind shoe for each animal).

(16) Horseshoe nails.

(17) Curry brush for grooming.

(18) Small can of healing powder.

(19) Small jar of carbolic vasoline.

PACK HITCHES AND KNOTS

When camping in the wilderness, there will be times when knowing how to tie the proper knot, lashing, or throwing the correct pack hitch will add to one's comfort, solve various camp and trail problems, and may even be the means of saving a life.

The camper or boatman should select the few that are of real use and learn to tie them, and exclude the ones that have little practical use for the average outdoorsman.

There are three basic qualities to a good knot, lashing, or hitch: that it is easily tied, that it is easily untied, and that it will hold until untied or the rope breaks.

Outdoorsmen have analyzed the knot situation, and have arrived at the conclusion that the camper and boatman can get along with ten knots, three lashings, and ten hitches. Three of these hitches are used on pack horses or mules.

(1) The Slip Knot is for tying up packages or making a noose.

(2) The Reef, or Square Knot is used for joining ropes of equal thickness, and in tying and fastening bandages in first aid.

(3) The Bowline or Bowline on a Bight is an emergency knot. It will not slip under strain, and is used for tying a rope around an animal's neck, and for many other purposes. Note that it forms a fixed loop.

(4) The Prussik Knot is used in climbing a rope.

(5) The Carrick Bend is for joining heavy lines and ropes.

(6) The Figure 8 Knot is for packages.

(7) The Lariat Knot makes a loop for a riata or lasso.

(8) The Stevedore Knot keeps the end of a rope from running through a pulley.

(9) The Fisherman's Knot is for joining nylon or gut leaders

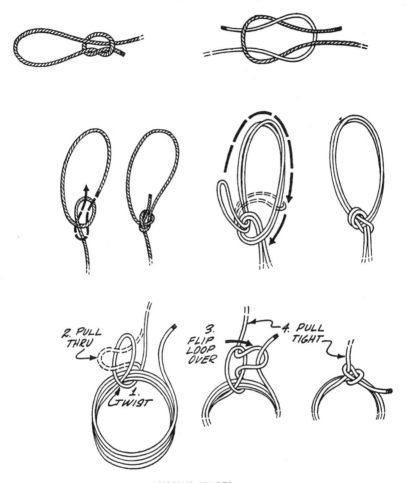

USEFUL KNOTS.
Top to bottom, left to right: Slip Knot, Reef or Square Knot, Bowline, Bowline
on a Bight, Bowline on a Coil.

to line; it is also useful for making one longer line out of a number of short pieces.

(10) The Sheet Bend is for joining ropes of two different thicknesses.

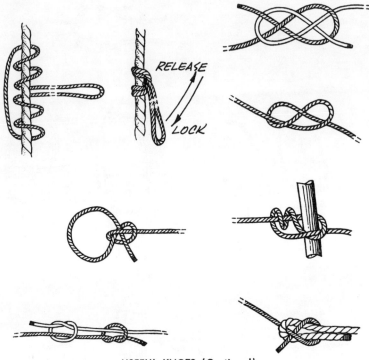

USEFUL KNOTS (Continued).
Top to bottom, left to right: Prussik Knot (for rope climbing), Carrick Bend, Figure 8 Knot, Lariat Knot, Stevedore Knot, Fisherman's Knot. Sheet Bend.

HITCHES.

(1) The Timber Hitch is used to pull timber. It is also used in lashing.

(2) The Two Half Hitches; an easy way to tie a rope to a ring.

(3) The Barrel Hitch is used to hoist barrels or round objects.

(4) The Clove Hitch—most lashings start and finish with it.

(5) The Tautline Hitch forms a loop that will not slip when the rope is tight. It is used to tighten or loosen tent guy lines. hitch.

(6) The Standard Government Diamond Hitch—a pack-horse hitch.

(7) The Lone Ranger Hitch.

(8) The Box Hitch is used in packing boxes or flat objects.

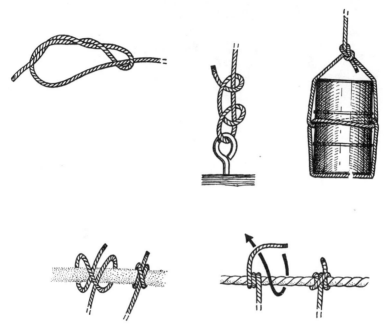

HITCHES. Timber Hitch, Two Half Hitches, The Barrel Hitch, Clove Hitch, Tautline Hitch.

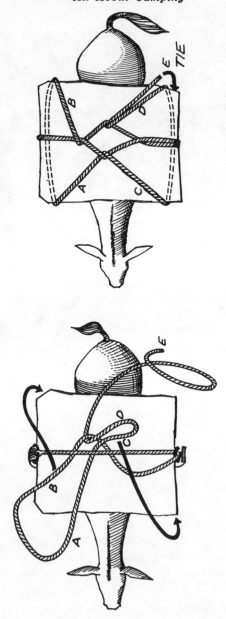

ONE MAN OR GOVERNMENT DIAMOND HITCH.

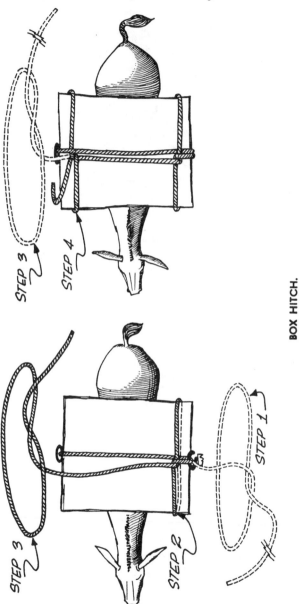

BOX HITCH.

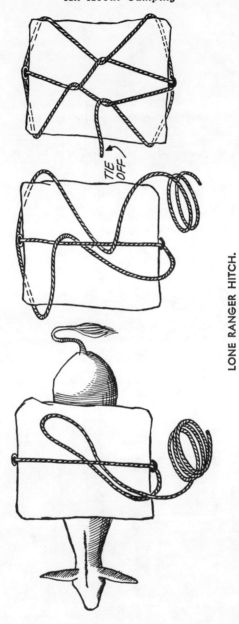

TIE
OFF

LONE RANGER HITCH.

LASHINGS.

(1) The Square Lashing is used for tying two poles together at right angles.

(2) The Diagonal Lashing is used to "spring" two spars together.

(3) The Shear Lashing is used when constructing shear logs or a tripod for a tepee.

The Bibliography will guide you to more detailed works on the subject. A few of the more important knots are shown in the illustrations.

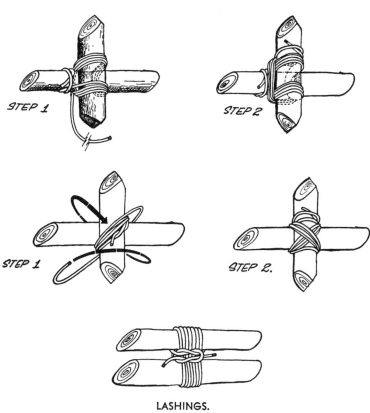

LASHINGS.

Square Lashing
Diagonal Lashing
Shear Lashing

Chapter 22

CARE OF SADDLE AND PACK ANIMALS AND SLED DOGS

CERTAIN characteristics, good or bad, may develop as a result of improper training or treatment of an animal. Find out about the traits and habits, and pass on the information to anyone who may use the animal, to aid in avoiding accidents.

GET TO KNOW THE ANIMALS

Some animals turn out to be kickers or biters; others will leave you afoot in the back country if not properly hobbled when turned out to graze. Some are very difficult to catch in the morning and have to be roped. Horses and mules spook easily, especially if a bear or mountain lion is close by. Expect spirited or partly-broken stock to be afraid of strangers, and to require special handling after not having been packed or ridden for a prolonged period. All strange stock should be handled as though they are dangerous until you learn their peculiarities. Keep cool, move quietly, speak quietly, and treat them kindly, and the animals will serve you well.

Be gentle but firm with all stock, for a horse or mule will quickly lose confidence in you if you become frightened or are inexperienced and get the animal into trouble. Never trust a horse or mule, no matter how much of a pet he may become, for sooner or later he will leave you afoot for various reasons of his own, and it may be a long hike back to civilization.

When approaching an animal, give him a chance to see and smell you. If the animal must be approached from the rear, talk to him softly, thereby avoiding frightening him or taking him by surprise. Avoid sudden motions, for these may frighten the animal.

FOOD AND WATER

WATER. A horse, like a person, can get by on short rations without too much harm for a short period; however, also like a human, he needs a reasonable amount of water. He should not be allowed free access to it while he is extremely hot or fatigued. He should never be given water immediately after being fed, since it will wash the grain or forage directly into the intestines before the stomach has digested the food properly. This often results in a case of colic. It is best to water stock that is hot and tired after it has been allowed to rest about a half hour, and before it is fed.

FEED. Various methods and kinds of feed prevail in different sections of the country, and the stock should be fed that which it is used to, and the local custom followed.

BARLEY AND OATS. Rolled barley and oats are the chief grain feeds used in the West, and it is customarily put up in sacks weighing seventy pounds. A sack of grain will ordinarily provide approximately fourteen to sixteen feeds for a horse or mule weighing between 850 to 1200 pounds. A normal feed is one gallon of grain in the morning and one gallon at night, if the animals are idle or in pasture. If the saddle and pack stock are working, then an average ration per day will be around ten pounds of oats or barley, and fourteen pounds of timothy or prairie hay. Crushed or rolled oats are more easily digested, but must be kept from molding. Rolled barley is a good substitute for oats. Clover is good if it is properly cured. Feeding straight alfalfa hay causes an excessive laxative condition, and therefore it should be fed in conjunction with other kinds of hay. It will run from twenty-five to thirty bales per ton. If on dry feed, be sure to water stock before feeding.

ROUGHAGE. This consists of green range grasses, hay, and fodders. Bran may be given every two weeks in the morning and evening feedings, as needed for a laxative if stock is worked each day. The bran should be well mixed with water so that the stock will not choke on the dry meal.

SALT. Stock obtain so little salt in their daily diet that it is necessary for them to have free access to it at all times. Rock salt is best for pack and saddle stock, and block salt is best for cattle.

SHOEING

SHOEING KIT. Every pack outfit, of course, has a full shoeing outfit at the home ranch or at the pack station, consisting of a shoeing hammer, rasp, nippers, paring or toe knife, and a buffer. When working saddle and pack stock on the trail, each outfit carries a minimum shoeing outfit with a few horseshoe nails, and a proper size malleable or cowboy shoe, one front and one rear for each horse and mule in the string. A curry brush for grooming and keeping the animal's back clean is a "must," and it's a good idea to throw in a can of healing powder to boot.

Rangers have come across some pretty sorry-looking outfits while on patrol, and have not only had to re-shoe or tighten shoes on some private stock, but have had to lay over a day or so to heal up saddle galls and sores, before stock could be returned to the pack station. It would be interesting to hear what the packer had to say to the returning would-be horseman!

The importance of proper care of an animal's feet or legs, and proper shoeing, cannot be over-stressed. A horse or mule is no better than his legs or feet, and a poor job of shoeing has ruined many a good animal. Knowledge of the natural formation of the feet and hoofs is essential for a good horseshoer; otherwise, he will be unable to understand the correct principles of shoeing and balancing an animal on its feet.

Horse and mule feet are similar in anatomy, but differ in conformation, condition, and size, depending somewhat on the breed. A good farrier will inspect and examine each animal carefully to determine the natural position of its feet, and correct any hoof irregularity, if possible.

FITTING THE SHOE. Malleable shoes are usually used in the back country, since they are made of softer metal, and therefore can be shaped more readily, and are less apt to slip on rock than steel shoes. This type of cowboy or malleable shoe may be fitted cold. The shoe should be wide enough at the heel to prevent it from resting against the frog, and the outer edges should be flush with the edges of the hoof. In attaching the shoe, drive one of the rear nails first. Inspection of a horseshoe nail will indicate that the point is beveled to one side. In driving the nail this bevel is placed toward the center of the hoof, which forces the nail out, rather than into the hoof wall. After the nail has been driven up close, the nail point projecting out is then twisted off with the claw part of the farrier's hammer. The opposite nail at the rear is then driven in similarly, and the remaining nails are driven in.

FINISHING THE SHOEING. When all the nails have been driven in they are "set" securely by holding the buffer against the clinched nails, and tapping the nail heads sharply with the hammer. When the clinches have been set, they are clipped back to not more than one-eighth inch in length, and then are flattened against the hoof wall after the ragged edges of the nails have been rasped away.

SHOEING MULES. Mules are shod in the same manner as horses, except that they have a longer and narrower hoof which requires a broader heel base for proper support. Burros are usually worked barefooted.

SAFETY WHEN SHOEING. Some horses and mules are vicious, and have to be thrown and their feet secured before they can be shod. A shoeing rig is sometimes necessary.

DISEASES OF HORSES AND MULES

Horses, burros, and mules are susceptible to many diseases and ailments, but it is beyond the scope of this manual to deal with more than just a few common illnesses, since it would require too large a volume. Also, it is wiser to leave the serious horse trouble to the trained and experienced veterinarian; however, there are a few things you can do in an emergency, if caught with a sick or injured animal in the back country away from the pack station.

Wind colic, spasmodic colic, and foundering are three of the most common ailments of horses. Mules are not so susceptible to these ailments, and are a little more careful in their eating habits than horses. Colic is usually caused in the majority of cases by over-feeding, watering while the animal is hot and tired, use of too much green feed, or feed that an animal has not become accustomed to, and indigestion from poorly masticated food. This affection is caused by the accumulation of large masses of undigested material entering the intestines, preventing the escape of natural gases caused by fermentation, and thereby causing terrific pressure against abdominal organs. This, of course, causes extreme distress and pain. Horses, mules, and burros cannot belch up gas, and therefore it has to pass on through their intestines. Wind colic is not as pronounced as spasmodic colic and the animal does not try to roll as much. However, in both types the animal will sweat profusely due to pain and gas pressure.

COLIC TREATMENT. Lead the animal around slowly and prevent it from rolling on the ground. To relieve gas pressure caused by colic, some packers carry a can of "Turcapsol" in their pack outfit. Turcapsol is manufactured by the Pitman Moore Company and can only be secured by a prescription from a veterinarian. If you do not have Turcapsol, use a solution made up of two ounces of aromatic spirits of ammonia (from your camp first-aid kit) to one pint of water as a drench. Sometimes just a plain drench of four ounces of table salt (from the camp kitchen) in a quart of water will turn the trick. At times a purgative is indicated and used at the ranch or pack station since you probably would not have the ingredients to make one in the back country. In this case use one quart of raw linseed oil and one pound of Epsom salts. Mix with two quarts of mineral oil, shake well, and administer to the sick animal.

Another camp remedy that is very effective, but hard to administer in the field is a gallon of warm soapy water used as a rectal enema.

FOUNDER. This can be caused in some cases, by over-feeding or over-watering an animal when it is too hot and tired, or by it being pushed too rapidly over steep trails or made to run over very rough terrain without proper rest periods. In some cases founder will attack the fore feet, the hoofs of which will eventually grow out long and irregular and turn up at the toe. If the soles are affected, they will extend downward. This prevents the edges of the hoof from resting properly on the ground.

Colic symptoms sometimes appear with founder. When founder appears, the fore feet are extended in a forward position with much of the body weight supported by the heels while the hind feet are well under the animal to relieve pressure on the front feet. The victim's nostrils will be dilated, and the breathing rapid and heavy with a sob-like sound at times. The pulse will be rapid, hoofs will be hot and painful, and the victim will lie down for long periods.

Hot and cold applications should be given the hoofs for several hours by placing each front foot in a bucket. The animal should be given plenty of rest until it is fully recovered from all symptoms.

CLOGGED INTESTINES. Clogged intestines may appear at times with colic. Ordinarily one does not have the proper medicine on hand in a wilderness camp, nor the knowledge for proper treatment. However, there are a couple of ways to relieve the situation. Normally the intestines are clogged at a point where the obstruction can be reached by hand, and most of the material removed.

Treatment for this condition is as follows: For safety reasons, first throw a rope loop around the animal's neck and catch a hind foot with the running end and tie this foot up so the animal can't kick you. Next grease your hand and arm with whatever lubricant is available in camp, such as butter, margarine, lard, or cooking oil, so that the delicate membrane of the lower bowel will not be injured. Then with your hand remove as much of the material as possible. Large injections of warm soapy water nearly always turn the trick, but equipment for this operation is not usually found in the back country.

GALLS AND SADDLE SORES. If open, gall and saddle sores may be relieved by the application of healing powders. The hard lumps or sores can be softened and healed by using bacon grease, lard, butter or cooking oil if carbolated vaseline isn't available.

SNAKE BITE. Poisonous snake-bites should be treated the same as a person would be treated. (Check chapter 24 on first-aid.)

LAMENESS. Lameness is a common ailment of horses, mules, and burros. Lameness can be caused by a sharp blow, a bruise, losing a shoe, or traveling over rocky terrain with bare foot stock. It also can be caused by the animal stepping on a stone in the trail and twisting or spraining one or more joints of the foot or leg. Treat lameness the same as you would for a person. (See chapter 24 on first-aid.)

DEAD STOCK. Animals dying from suspected contagious diseases must be burned and buried. Stock injured beyond recovery on trails and near streams or water-supply sources must be destroyed. Park and forest regulations state that dead animals must be hauled away from water sources and buried. If it is necessary to cremate an animal during the fire season, you will have to notify the district ranger and get permission to burn the carcass, otherwise you will have to pack in quick lime to cover the victim. Some horse and mule diseases can be contracted by humans, so due caution must be exercised when handling sick stock.

INJURIES AND AILMENTS. The injuries and ailments most common to livestock are external or internal poisoning, cuts, burns, puncture wounds, abscesses, bruises, lameness, and broken bones. In serious cases a veterinarian should be called or consulted.

Wounds on stock should be treated in the most sterile manner possible, since warm-blooded animals can become infected if not properly cared for.

While pleasure horse activities continue all year throughout the United States, Canada, and Mexico, they reach a peak during the summer months. In summer, families pack into the high mountain country, trail rider clubs cut across country, a sheriff's posse may hit the trail, and rodeo and riding clubs put their mounts through their paces. During the summer months there is an increase in horse deaths, due to the larger number of stock used, and to inexperienced riders pushing their mounts beyond their endurance. This can be corrected by the riders reading up on the subject and by talking to packers and experienced horse handlers.

CHECK LIST FOR CARE OF STOCK

(1) If on dry feed, water before feeding grain or hay. Hay should be fed ahead or before animal is grained.

(2) Pastured or corralled stock should have access to pure, clean water at all times.

(3) Wait an hour or so before watering after grain has been fed.

(4) During the day, horses and mules should be allowed to drink whenever dry, and should be allowed plenty of time to drink their fill.

(5) Let stock drink before they cross a stream or river when fording.

(6) Let animals cool off before watering at the end of a day or trip.

(7) Never hurry or run an animal that has just been watered.

(8) Be sure to curry and brush an animal's back before saddling. This also gives one a chance to inspect the animal's back for sores or injuries.

(9) When grooming or saddling an animal, be gentle, and be careful not to harm sore or tender spots.

(10) To toughen up an animal's back at the start of the season, make a solution of one tablespoon of salt and one of vinegar in one quart of water. Bathe animal's back at the end of trips for a week or so.

(11) Always walk an animal slowly the first few minutes after saddling up so he can warm up properly.

(12) Stock should be rested frequently for short periods when climbing steep trails.

(13) On long trips, the pace should be changed occasionally—trot a little on level terrain, then get off and walk a little. This rests both the horse and the rider.

(14) Get off and walk up steep or dangerous places. In this way, the pack and saddle stock can control their motion more safely. Walk down the very steep places.

(15) Sudden stops, or riding down steep slopes or trails gives one a very jarring ride. Get off and walk for a distance. Riding under these conditions causes stock to have stiff shoulders.

(16) Whenever a stop is made for any length of time, loosen up the cinch on your saddle horse. Cut stopping periods short, since it is uncomfortable for pack stock to have dead weight riding their backs.

(17) Never leave stock exposed to hot sun with sweaty backs or it may cause back scalding and the animal will either lose hair in spots or the hair will turn white in places.

(18) Never take unshod stock over rocky terrain or trails for long distances. Doing so will cause them to break their protective hoof edges.

(19) Always examine an animal's back at the end of a trip for galls from the cinch or other injuries. If sore, treat at once.

(20) Always tie animals in a shady, level spot, if possible.

(21) Tie to a strong, limber tree, when possible.

(22) Tie the rope approximately four feet above ground.

(23) Allow the halter to reach the ground with about six inches of slack. This will allow the animal to lie down and also prevent him from getting a foot or leg over the tie rope.

(24) Always feed animals from morralies or feed bags, never on the ground. Use a canvas or blanket if you haven't nose bags.

(25) Hobble and bell animals that are prone to stray.

(26) Always check stock and keep them above camp, so that you are between them and the home corral before retiring for the night.

BUYING A SADDLE HORSE

The outdoorsman should look for the following characteristics if he is purchasing a saddle horse for his personal use, and wants the best.

The animal should be between five and eight years old, since he will reach his growth between four and five years; he should be alert, gentle, and well-broken. He should neck-rein readily, and stand when the tie-rope or reins are grounded. He should be between fourteen and sixteen hands high (one hand equals four inches) and weigh between 1000 and 1200 pounds. His head should be medium size, broad between the eyes, and the line from poll to muzzle straight, with nostrils widely expanded. Eyes should be clear, bright, and full. Ears should be pointed, active, and well apart.

The neck should be strong and swell smoothly to shoulder with crest arched. The windpipe should stand out large. The chest should be deep and the floor low between his legs. The horse's body should be close coupled to hips, full, and deep. His back should be well-muscled, smooth, short, and only slightly curved. His withers should be well-formed, and not too thick. Hips should be wide and level, well-muscled, and smooth. His croup length and width should be well-proportioned. Thighs should be long, muscular, and well-spread. Hocks, of course, should be straight, broad in front, and sharp behind. Front legs should be flat and well-corded or muscular. They should be long from elbow to knee, and short from knee to ground, with straight lines side and front. The knee should be broad and deep; the cannon short, flat, and clean appearing. The pastern should be properly proportioned and slope 45 to 50 degrees, and should be strong and elastic.

Judge the animal's actions as he is being ridden about, and then mount him yourself and put him through his paces. Notice if he rides smoothly and appears to be well-balanced; that his legs unfold gradually, and steadily, that knee action is easy, and hock movement smooth and springy; that his step is light, measured, very deliberate and sure. His feet should be lifted clear of the ground, and placed down evenly with an elastic movement. His legs should be carried well under his body. The hind legs should be thrown well forward in stride. His head should be carried well up and not with a jerky motion. An animal in good health will have a gloss to his hair, with smooth skin.

SLED DOGS

Sled dogs have personalities as varying as those of people. Study of individuals and their habits should always be a constant interest of the driver if he is to get the most out of his team. Some dogs just don't get on together and must be used in different teams. Fights must be broken up if all attack one dog, and fights must never be allowed on the march. In camp, some bullying by leaders is normal. Fight wounds usually heal normally without care.

TRAIL DOG FOOD. On the trail, dogs are fed once daily at the end of the run with one pound of dog pemmican (for the average-sized dog). In parts of Alaska and Canada, dry fish may be substituted for pemmican. A good dog pemmican formula is:

Meat Meal	42%	Wheat Germ	5%
Tallow	40%	Molasses	2%
Whole Wheat Meal	10%	Cod Liver Oil	1%

Many drivers and owners of dog teams tie up only the trouble-makers in camps where there also may be cattle or game, for untied, the dogs invariably kill ranch animals or seek wild game. On the trail, time will be saved and fights between teams will be limited by using chain leashes tethered to chain picket lines. If rope tethers are used the dogs will chew through them.

CHECK LIST—HANDLING SLED DOGS

(1) Don't lie down near an untied team; they may mistake you for game and tear you to pieces.

(2) If you fear a dog, he can smell it; gentle overtures to gain his friendship may cost you a hand.

(3) Even if you love *all* dogs (and they like you), don't spoil the other fellow's team by over-attention to his dogs; don't spoil a strain he may be trying to perfect by letting your own dogs run wild and mix with his.

(4) In handing out a pat or a roughing to your own team, treat all dogs alike; dogs resent favoritism.

(5) Doubled whips or whip-handles—not axe handles—break up dog fights quickly, safely, and with little damage to the dogs.

(6) Don't leave rags soaked in animal fats about camp. Dogs will eat the rags and the rags will block a dog's intestines; the dog may die.

(7) Don't expect to use dogs at elevations over 8,000 to 10,000 feet.

(8) Don't use dogs to break trail for motorized winter equipment (Sno-Cats, tractors, etc.) for dogs easily cross bridges that heavy equipment will fall through.

(9) Attend to your personal toilet downwind and out of sight of your dog team.

Chapter 23

SAFETY IN THE OUTDOORS

BE CAREFUL!

THE A-B-C of outdoor safety is—*Always be careful!* This applies to the experienced outdoorsman as much as it does to the tyro or novice. No matter how much experience one may have in the back country, he still can slip, trip, and fall. He can cut himself with a knife, axe, or even on the sharp edge of a can that he has opened with the old-fashioned type of can opener. He can be struck by a rattlesnake, stung by a scorpion, bitten by insects, or become lost, just to name a few of the perils. Obviously, he must always be on his guard. It follows that one must be constantly alert for his own safety as well as for the safety of his party if he happens to be the leader. The further one penetrates into the wilderness and leaves civilization behind with its fast means of communication, transportation, supplies, and medical aid, the more sharply alert one must be.

A minor injury in a remote area, especially in the winter, can sometimes become a serious matter. A sprained ankle while traveling on skis or snow shoes at high elevation is a good example of this. Cuts and puncture wounds can become infected or one can contact pneumonia or become ill from food poisoning. Every year a flood of such emergencies reach national park and forest rangers, especially during the summer months when they are extremely busy fighting forest fires, hunting lost persons, assisting at traffic accidents, and taking care of millions of visitors who use our national parks and forests.

DON'T TAKE CHANCES. It is not uncommon to have three or four search or rescue missions going on at once in the Sierra Nevada range in California alone. Consider all the recreational areas all over the United States, and this amounts to a staggering figure in manpower and vehicle expense to the taxpayer. It costs approximately $150 per hour to operate a rescue helicopter, plus overtime for ground searchers, and the added expense of operating pack trains to supply and maintain search operations in the field.

In one national park in one season there were over 36 rescue missions, two of which cost an estimated $10,000. In Yosemite National Park during one July 4th week, a large part of the ranger force was out searching for a lost woman from July 1st to July 6th, leaving the remainder of the rangers to handle and give protection to one of the largest crowds ever to visit Yosemite; yet, more and more inexperienced campers enter our recreational primitive areas in poor physical condition and overexert by hiking too far, too fast, and too high. In addition, some are poorly equipped or do not have adequate equipment; therefore, they come to grief—usually far out and on a busy holiday!

BE PREPARED. In spite of the increasing millions going into the back country each year, it is surprising how infrequently accidents and illness befall people who go prepared and use "good sense." Every person who plans on an outing to our seashores, deserts, and mountains should take the Red Cross standard first-aid course. The advanced first-aid course should be taken by all ski-mountaineers, rock climbers and cross country hikers.

It is essential that one stop and think things out and be certain that he knows what he is doing before he makes a decision on the action to be taken when a serious accident occurs in the back country. The same principle applies before going on a camping trip with the family to a less primitive locale. The seasoned camper may require few safety reminders but families of infrequent camping experience, as well as novices, should devote some thought in advance of their trip to safety topics and plans for a trouble-free camp. Here are a few items for review.

(1) Campsite Selection: If the area is wooded, avoid a site in which tree limbs might come down in a strong wind or storm. Before setting up camp, be sure to check the site for broken glass, nails, cans or can covers which might lead to cut feet—especially if small children are along.

(2) Children: The new surroundings in camping are of almost immediate interest to the little tots. Their curiosity often leads them directly away from the camp site. Try to

form a scheme for controlling them and avoiding the even temporary problem of a lost child. A set of signals, simple rules, or some other method should be worked out to give you peace of mind on this score.

Outdoor cooking and use of a campfire pose some burn hazards to children unaccustomed to camping utensils. Emphasize the use of heavy gloves in handling hot pans and dishes. Remind them of the hazard of scorching their clothing when they warm themselves by the campfire.

An empty pop bottle lying on the ground can roll and cause a nasty fall to the unobservant. If broken, it can cause a nasty cut. Designate a place and method for disposing of the empties.

Swimming and wading should be confined to properly designated and supervised areas.

(3) Flashlights At Night: A flashlight is indispensable to anyone who may have occasion to move about at night amidst unfamiliar tent stakes, guy lines, poles, and perhaps even trees. Each person should have his own and place it within easy reach before retiring.

(4) Disposal Of Hazardous Items: if you use disposable propane gas cylinders in your stove or lantern be sure the empties are properly disposed of—never throw them into a campfire or leave them around where children may pick them up in play. Plan to keep the family medicine kit in a secure place where contents will be out of reach of the little ones.

(5) Overexertion: Considerable physical work can be involved in getting a tent camp set up, the boat in the water, the motor on the boat, and so on. In some tents the canvas alone weighs more than 45 pounds, even when not wet. Some grub boxes, outboard motors, and other containers used in camping can weigh as much or more. Camping was meant to be fun—not to cause overexertion. Take your time!

ACCIDENTS AND ILLNESSES

MOUNTAIN SICKNESS. People living at or near sea level sometimes contract what the layman calls "mountain sickness." It can be caused by several things, such as hiking or climbing too rapidly, becoming overheated or too cold, improper diet, sudden change from home cooking to eating highly concentrated dehydrated foods, and, of course, not being acclimated to high elevations.

The symptoms are generally headache, nausea, dizziness, vomiting, diarrhea, and a general weakness. In mild cases, only part of the above-mentioned symptom will appear. In more severe cases, all of the symptoms may occur. Acclimatizing usually occurs within a few days. If not, you should return to your home and consult your family physician. (It could be something more serious.)

BLISTERS. It is easier to *prevent* blisters than to cure them. To treat a blister, sterilize a needle and the surrounding skin. Prick the blister at its edge to release the fluid, drain, and let dry. Apply adhesive tape and leave on until healed. If the skin or flap covering the blister is torn, be sure to cover with a band-aid or gauze covered by adhesive tape. Prevent blisters by stopping the moment you feel a tender spot and apply adhesive tape. Blisters should not occur if you have the proper boot and sock combination! A good grade of boot that fits properly and has been well broken in before the trip should do the trick. Be sure the socks fit and have no wrinkles in them.

SUN AND WIND BURNS. The sun's ultraviolet rays are stronger and much more intense at higher elevations. If one hasn't acquired a protective coat of tan, he must assist nature by providing clothing or medicants. There are some excellent sunburn lotions on the market. Treat snow burn the same as sunburn or wind burn. Snow burn is caused by reflected sun rays.

Over exposure to sun can interfere with sleep and rest and sometimes the effects can completely ruin what might otherwise have been a perfect vacation. *Prevent* sunburn is the best advice—quick cures are hard to find. The wearing of long-sleeved shirts and full-length slacks will minimize sunburn problems, especially if the family plans on a good deal of boating.

SNOW BLINDNESS. Snow blindness can be very painful since the eyes are one of the most sensitive parts of our bodies. They are especially sensitive to bright sunlight on snow. However, one can also become blinded by long periods of exposure on snow fields when the sky is overcast. Since it is impossible to skirt all snow fields, it is imperative to protect one's precious eyesight by using the proper type of sun glasses or goggles. The type with side shields gives added protection from the sides.

BURNS. Painful burns can be prevented around the campfire by using pot-holding pads, or better still, "cooking gloves" which can simply be cheap cotton gloves. They are handy in picking up hot pans, dishes, and kettles. They are also useful in gathering campfire wood by keeping pitch off and splinters out of the hands.

SOAPY DISHES. Be careful to rinse all soap suds off dishes and kettles. This can cause diarrhea if you don't. By properly rinsing the dishes in scalding water, they are not only sterilized but completely cleansed of soap.

WATER. A supply of pure water is necessary for health reasons. If you are uncertain about the water, boil it for 15 minutes or use purification tablets. Never drink too much water when hot and tired, as this can cause cramps and vomiting.

HOW TO PURIFY WATER.

(1) Boil water for at least 15 minutes. Boil for a longer period if the water is muddy or looks questionable.

(2) If the water is roiled or full of debris, filter through sand or cloth and boil it for half an hour.

(3) To remove the flat taste from boiled or melted snow water, aerate it by pouring it back and forth from one container to another. A small pinch of salt will improve the flavor.

(4) Bad tasting water may be made more palatable by dropping in several pieces of charcoal from the campfire and letting the water simmer for 20 minutes or so. Next skim away the foreign material or let it settle to the bottom, then strain through a clean cloth.

(5) Another method—put two Halazone tablets in each quart of water, and let it stand for half an hour. Be sure to purify the cork or cap and outside mouth of the canteen before capping.

(6) In tropical regions, iodine water purification tablets containing active tetraglycine hydroperiodide should be used. One tablet will purify one quart of water. If the water is discolored or full of decaying vegetation, use 2 tablets.

(7) You can also use 3 drops of 2% iodine from your first-aid kit, per quart of water.

(8) Water may be purified for long storage by adding 10 drops of sodium hypoclorite per gallon. (Clorox, Purex, Sani-Clor, or any other comparable solution.)

(9) Usually pure water can be obtained from a spring issuing from live rock or clean soil, if it is away from contaminating influence.

(10) Better yet, use the commercially made Sure Pure Water Filter. This filter is small, light, and easy to pack. The filter part is composed of molecularly charged particles which are treated with bactericidal agents; it takes only 8 squeezes on its small bulb pump to deliver a glass of pure water. The manufacturer's leaflet advises that their filters are used by the U.S. Government for the President's personal airplane as well as by 65 of the world's major airlines. Price of the recommended unit is $12.95; write the Sure Pure Co., Inc., Ringoes, New Jersey for details.

CONTAMINATED FOOD. Spoiled food can be dangerous! Never use a can of food that has become bulged or has been punctured.

CUTTING TOOL ACCIDENTS. To prevent becoming injured from sharp-edged instruments such as axes, machetes, hunting knives, and camp saws, you should have leather or canvas guards covering the cutting edge. Also, throw away your old-fashioned can opener. This article can and does cause more puncture and cut wounds than any other piece of kitchen equipment. It also leaves sharp, jagged edges on the cans which could cause further injuries.

Always take a good first-aid kit with you and know how to use it! Ask your doctor to make one up for you, or, at least, to suggest a list of essentials which you can purchase. Be sure to include codeine, sulpha, and several sleeping tablets, in addition to several sutures and metal clamps with which to close wounds if you do not care to use a needle and surgical thread.

If you haven't taken a first-aid course, take someone along with you who is an experienced first-aider!

ICE RESCUE

Safety officials of the American National Red Cross, working in cooperation with Police Departments, Education, Parks, and other organizations, have shown what skaters, ice-boaters, fishermen, hunters, and all who might be involved in ice accidents should do to rescue themselves or others. The Red Cross has demonstrated three major forms of ice rescue: Self-Rescue, Group-Rescue, and Equipment-Rescue. The Red Cross has also shown how a person should cross open ice, and demonstrated what a person alone should do if an accident occurs.

Simulated rescues were conducted with ladders, planks, ice crosses, ring-buoys, lines, mounted tires, and ice-boats. Spare tires mounted on car wheels have been used as life-buoys in emergency. A human chain was also formed to show how a group could save an ice accident victim.

Should you accidentally break through the ice, don't try to climb out! Extend both arms along the surface of the ice and then kick vigorously. This will help lift the body forward and on to solid ice—then *roll* to safety.

When attempting to rescue someone who has broken through the ice, *lie down flat and push* a plank, ladder, or rope to him. Don't stand up near the ice break, and never attempt a swimming rescue!

Always *keep simple rescue equipment at hand at ice skating sites* such as ponds, lakes, or streams; ropes, planks, ladders or buoys may be needed in an emergency and quick action is necessary.

CORRECT PROCEDURE FOR MOUNTAIN RESCUE

Suppose you are in charge of a mountain-climbing party or cross-country hiking party and a member of your group is taken seriously ill, is badly injured, or is accidently killed. Would you know what to do or how to proceed? Do you know advanced first-aid? Do you understand the proper action to take in securing experienced help to recover the body or remove the injured victim to the nearest medical care? If you don't, here is the action you should take.

IF YOU CAN HANDLE THE SITUATION. First, size up the situation quickly. *Render first-aid* to the injured as soon as they are reached. *Stop* and think over the whole situation, then get command of all the facts. *If* the person is dead, protect the body from the elements if possible. *If* you can handle the situation with your party and get the injured person to the nearest medical aid, fine.

IF OUTSIDE ASSISTANCE IS REQUIRED. If help is needed, do these things: *Make a list which shows:* (1) Number of persons injured; (2) the extent of the injuries; (3) exact location of accident; (4) time of accident; (5) notification to county coroner, if any fatalities, and if he wants the body removed to the trail head, or left at the scene until his arrival; (6) manpower, rations or food, and equipment at scene of accident; (7) name and address, and phone number if possible of the injured person (s); and (8) name of other party members.

Send For Help. (9) If help is indicated, send two messengers out, if possible, to insure that your message reaches the proper authorities. (Why two messengers? Because one might become lost on the way out or may meet with an accident in his hurry to obtain help.) Always leave someone with the injured person.

Mark the Route. Always mark the route on the way out. This will insure that the return rescue party will not lose time in reaching the hurt person. Hurry, but be careful so that you reach aid and do not become an accident victim yourself.

Telephone; Notify These Agencies, In This Order. (10) The District Ranger of the park or forest you are in; (11) the Mountain Rescue Team in the state in which the accident occurred; (12) Sheriff's office of the county; and (13) the State Police or Highway Patrol.

Tell Them: (14) Information listed above; (15) distance the injured or sick person is from road, trail, and how far off the trail; if a body of water is to be crossed, approximately how far across by boat; (16) if scene can be reached by helicopter; (17) type of terrain; (18) probable time to reach the scene of the accident; (19) equipment, rations and manpower required; (20) where you are phoning from, and where you will meet the rescue party;

(21) Stay on the phone until assured by responsible authorities that experienced assistance is on the way; (22) wait for the rescue party and guide them in if possible; (23) be sure to follow your back track so that the rescue party doesn't go astray;

(24) lay out signal panels, or be sure that radio calls are made on the radio time schedules being used by Air-Sea rescue or private planes assisting in the rescue; (25) take no chances while removing injured person; and (26) thank all agencies for their assistance.

Chapter 24

WILDERNESS FIRST-AID

FIRST-AID IF INJURIES DO OCCUR

(1) GIVE FIRST-AID for any injury or illness, however minor!

(2) For serious injuries give proper first-aid and get medical aid as soon as possible!

GENERAL DIRECTIONS

(1) Keep the injured person lying down in a comfortable position, his head level with his body, until you know whether or not the injury is serious.

(2) Look for serious bleeding, stoppage of breathing, poisoning, shock, wounds, burns, fractures, and dislocations. Be sure to find all injuries. *Remember,* (1) serious bleeding, (2) stoppage of breathing, and (3) poisoning, in that order, must be treated immediately, before anything else is done.

(3) Keep the injured person warm.

(4) Send someone to call a physician or an ambulance.

(5) Keep calm and do not be hurried into moving the injured person unless it is absolutely necessary.

(6) *Never* give water or other liquid to an unconscious person.

IMMEDIATE ACTION CASES

Some injuries must receive treatment at once. Delay in such cases can be serious.

SHOCK. Remember, any severely injured person will develop shock and treatment must start immediately without waiting for the symptoms of shock to develop. Symptoms of shock are pale face, breathing shallow and irregular, nausea, skin cool and moist, and pulse weak.

Treat shock as follows: (1) Conserve body heat by wrapping patient underneath and above. Do not apply external heat except in extremely cold weather. Patient should be made comfortable but not hot. (2) Keep patient lying down with his feet raised. (3) Fluids may be given by mouth unless patient has abdominal injury or is unconscious. Water, hot tea, coffee, milk, or broth may be given. *Note:* In cases of head or chest injury, or if face is flushed as in sunstroke, keep patient lying down but with head *higher* than feet.

WOUNDS WITH SEVERE BLEEDING. Treat severe bleeding as follows: (1) Use direct pressure on wound. Place thick layer of gauze on wound and apply firm pressure until bandage can be put on. Press with finger at appropriate arterial pressure point to help stop flow of blood. (2) If direct pressure

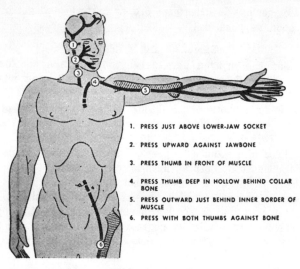

1. PRESS JUST ABOVE LOWER-JAW SOCKET
2. PRESS UPWARD AGAINST JAWBONE
3. PRESS THUMB IN FRONT OF MUSCLE
4. PRESS THUMB DEEP IN HOLLOW BEHIND COLLAR BONE
5. PRESS OUTWARD JUST BEHIND INNER BORDER OF MUSCLE
6. PRESS WITH BOTH THUMBS AGAINST BONE

PRESSURE POINTS.

is difficult to maintain and bleeding is from a limb, a tourniquet may be necessary. Apply tourniquet at limb tourniquet point. *Warning: A tourniquet is always a dangerous instrument and should not be used if bleeding can be checked readily otherwise.* Get the patient to a doctor as quickly as possible. Release of the tourniquet, when once applied, should be carried out only by a physician or by medical personnel. (3) Treat for shock.

SNAKE BITE. Any person bitten by a venomous snake will naturally be nervous and excited in spite of the fact that first-aid manuals caution the victim to remain calm—I know from my own personal experience! Kill the snake for later identification—also to keep from being struck again.

Here is the latest and most effective method for treating poison snake bite under field conditions:

(1) Have the victim lie down. This will help slow down the blood circulation and spread of the venom.

(2) Next tie a constricting bandage two or three inches above the bite on the leg (or arm). Another constricting band should be placed above the knee or elbow on the same limb. Tie just tight enough to retard the bloodflow in the surface veins, but not tight enough to cut off arterial flow. When the bandages are correctly applied and adjusted, there should be some oozing of blood and lymph fluid from the bite. If the limb turns white or blue in color, the constricting bandages are too tight. Both constrictors should be loosened every twenty minutes for two or three minutes each time.

(3) If medical aid is not available (very unlikely in the "back country"), sterilize a knife or razor blade by burning the blade with a match or flame from a cigarette lighter, and make shallow incisions over the fang marks. First paint the wounds with an antiseptic, and if you have a first-aid kit containing novocain, inject novocain under the skin near the fang puncture. Be sure that you sterilize the needle and clear it of all air bubbles.

(4) Normally the incisions should be no deeper than the fang penetration to reach most of the venom. The first aider must guard against the danger of severing nerves, tendons, or blood vessels. Most first-aid manuals recommend the cuts be no deeper than $\frac{1}{8}$ to $\frac{1}{4}$ inch. Experience has proven that simple line cuts (parallel with the limb involved) stimulate drainage more than the traditional X cuts. Of course, the length of the cuts will depend on the size area that the suction cups will cover. If too large you will not get suction.

(5) Suction should be applied and kept up continuously for the first two hours; thereafter for 8 to 24 hours except that the suction cups should be removed for 15 minutes each hour. Keep the wounds covered by moist, sterile, saline packs during this rest period. (You can boil the water to sterilize it). If you do not have suction cups, apply suction by mouth; be sure to spit out the material sucked from the fang mark. If ice is available from your camp icebox (or snow in higher elevations), make a "cold-pack" and place it on the wound during the rest period. This will assist in keeping the swelling down and slow the spread of the venom.

(6) If antivenin is available, it may be used in a quite serious case. Experience has proven that it requires from 40 to 120 cc's of antivenin, especially if a large snake such as a Texas or Florida diamondback has been stirred up and angrily strikes with a full sac of venom.

(7) Remember it is safer to over-treat than under-treat a poisonous snake bite! Get the victim to a doctor as quickly as possible—even if it is hours or even days later after you have had emergency first aid. You will need a physical checkup!

OVERCOME BY SMOKE, ASPHYXIATION, STOPPAGE OF BREATHING. (1) Start artificial respiration immediately. (2) Move patient into open or clear air. (3) Loosen clothing, and remove any obstructions to breathing in mouth. (4) Check for wounds. (5) Treat for shock.

Artificial Respiration. The most important thing to remember in giving artificial respiration is to *begin immediately.* Don't waste time moving the victim to the ideal location; don't wait for mechanical equipment. You may have learned the old prone pressure method or the more recent back pressure-arm lift or back pressure-hip lift methods. In these cases the victim was placed so as to be lying on his stomach. It has now been proved that the new exhaled air (mouth-to-mouth or mask-to-mouth) method is far better than any other. In this method the victim is placed so as to be lying on his back. It saves many lives and it is simpler to do. You should not worry about getting infected or waste time trying old methods. The possibility of infection is remote. Another important consideration in any method of artificial respiration is that the air passageway be open. If there is an obstruction, air cannot enter the lungs regardless of the method used. This passageway of an unconscious victim is usually blocked to some degree. There are three main causes for obstruction. The first is liquid, false teeth, or other foreign matter in the mouth or throat. The second is the relaxation of the jaw. The tongue is attached to the jaw so that it falls backward and blocks the throat. The third is the position of the neck. When the neck is bent forward so that the chin is down close to the chest, there is a tendency for the throat to become "kinked" and block the passageway. These can be overcome by placing the head in the position of an individual looking upwards while holding his lower jaw forward in a "sword swallowing position."

Technique Of Mouth-to-Mouth Method. Step 1. Turn the victim on his back. Step 2. Clean the mouth, nose, and throat. If the mouth, nose, and throat appear clean, start exhaled-air artificial respiration immediately. If foreign matter such as vomit or mucus is visible in the mouth, nose, and throat, wipe it away quickly with a cloth or by passing the index and middle fingers through the throat in a sweeping motion. Step 3. Place the victim's head in the sword swallowing position. The head must be placed as far back as possible so that the front of the neck is stretched.

Step 4. Hold the lower jaw up. Approach the victim's head from his left side. Insert the thumb of your left hand between the victim's teeth at the midline. Pull the lower jaw forcefully outward so that the lower teeth are farther forward than the upper teeth. Hold the jaw in this position as long as the victim

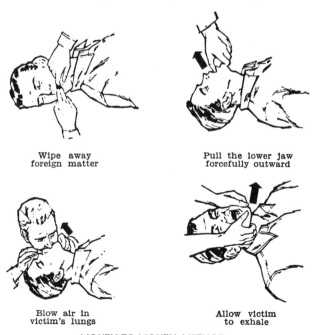

Wipe away
foreign matter

Pull the lower jaw
forcefully outward

Blow air in
victim's lungs

Allow victim
to exhale

MOUTH-TO-MOUTH METHOD.

is unconscious. A piece of cloth may be wrapped around the thumb to prevent injury by the victim's teeth. Step 5. Close the nose. Do this by compressing it between the thumb and fore-finger of the right hand.

Step 6. Blow air into the victim's lungs. Take a deep breath and cover the victim's open mouth with your open mouth with *airtight contact*. Blow rapidly until the chest rises. Blow force-fully into adults and gently into children. Step 7. Let air out of victim's lungs. After chest rises, quickly separate lip contact with the victim, and allow the victim to exhale by himself. If the chest did not rise when you blew in, improve the support of the victim's air passageway, and blow more forcefully. Repeat the inflations of the lungs 12 to 20 times per minute—continue rhythmically without interruption until the victim starts breath-ing or is pronounced dead. A smooth rhythm is desirable, but split-second timing is not essential.

Mask and Tube Method. Several devices, consisting of a short tube with a mask at one end to cover the victim's face, have been developed to increase efficiency and provide sanitation. One, the "venti-breather," has a valve to control inhalation and exhalation through slots in the tube. The rescuer breathes in one end of the tube. A mask at the other end covers the victim's nose and mouth, permitting air to be blown through the nose in case the lips are clamped shut. Venti-breather does away with steps 5 to 7.

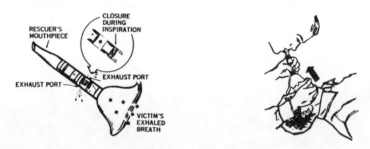

VENTI-BREATHER AND ITS USE.

EMERGENCY OXYGEN. "Lif-O-Gen" is now for sale and comes in a small cylinder, if an oxygen inhalant is indicated for emergency use. The cylinder weighs only 24 ounces with face mask and is priced at $6.95. Directions are simple. The oxygen is inhaled through the mouth or plastic mask furnished with each cylinder. To operate, press and inhale—release and exhale. *Caution:* Keep away from open flame or flammables. Do not smoke when using. "Lif-O-Gen" can be purchased at most drug stores. It would be an excellent practice to carry one aboard each pleasure boat or plane and for mountain climbers to have along at high elevation. This item may be secured direct from "Lif-O-Gen," 1445 City Line Avenue, Philadelphia 31, Pennsylvania.

FIRST-AID IF HEART STOPS.* A new technique for heart stoppage (cardiac arrest) is now being taught to fire, police, ambulance operators, rescue squads, and other first-aid men across the country. The technique was developed by W. B. Kouwenhoven, Ph. D., an electrical engineer, with assistance of staff members of Johns Hopkins University's School of Medicine. It is called "closed-chest massage." It should whenever possible, be used in conjunction with mouth-to-mouth resuscitation for best results—one person giving artificial respiration by the mouth-to-mouth method, the other person administering the chest-massage method. If you are alone with the victim when his heart stops, by all means start immediately with the "closed-chest" method since this will force some air into the lungs. If the victim's heart is beating but he has stopped breathing start mouth-to-mouth respiration.

This is how it works:

(1) Check for pulse first. It is easiest to detect in the throat on either side of the windpipe near the collarbone. If no pulse is apparent, start working at once. Don't waste seconds going for equipment or help for the great peril of any heart or breathing arrest is anoxia, i.e., lack of sufficient oxygen carried in the blood to feed the brain. The brain is the most sensitive tissue of the body, and the results of oxygen starvation become irreversible within a few minutes—usually about three—after respiration circulation is cut off. A victim who survives belated treatment thus faces the possibility of extensive brain damage.

(2) Lay the patient face up on a solid support such as the floor; a bed or couch is too flexible.

---

* "If A Heart Stops Beating—There's Help At Hand," *The Readers Digest*, November, 1960 (Condensed from Paul W. Kearney in *Today's Health*). Copyright 1960 by The Reader's Digest Association, Inc. Reprinted with permission.

(3) Tilt the head far back (if the head sags forward the patient may be asphyxiated while you work.)

(4) Kneel so you can use your weight in applying pressure. Place the heel of your right hand on the breastbone, with fingers spread and raised so pressure is only on the breastbone, not on the ribs.

(5) Place your left hand on top of the right and press vertically downward, firmly enough to depress the breastbone one to one-and-a-quarter inches. (With a child, use only one hand and relatively light pressure.) The chest of an adult, resistant when he is conscious, will be surprisingly flexible when he is unconscious.

(6) Release the pressure immediately, lifting the hands slightly; then repeat in cadence of 60 to 80 thrusts per minute, approximating normal heart action.

(7) The patient should be taken to the hospital as soon as possible even if apparently normal heart beat and respiration have resumed. Professional care will be needed.

(8) Continue the massage until you get professional medical aid to take over, or right into the emergency room of the hospital. Continue too, if possible, the mouth-to-mouth breathing, until someone arrives with a tank of oxygen to take over. If you are on your own and the victim shows no response, continue with your efforts until the patient responds or until rigor mortis sets in.

Medical men find it increasingly hard to say when a person is really dead beyond recall. Many of the old signs, like dilated eye pupils which won't contract under a bright light, are no longer considered valid.

HEART ATTACK. There are times out on the trail when one of your party may have a heart attack, or you may arrive at a hunting camp where a member has just suffered a heart attack. Symptoms: Symptoms include (but are not limited to) shortness of breath, chest pains, bluish color of the lips and about the finger nails, a chronic cough, and swelling of the ankles. Pain is most often located in the chest, particularly under the sternum or breastbone, and sometimes down the left arm, or into the head and neck. Sometimes the pain in the arm and shoulder is severe. At times pain in the upper abdomen, especially in a person of middle age or older, frequently reflects an acute heart attack. Indigestion manifested by nausea and vomiting is associated with heart attacks. In one type of attack, the patient insists on lying still in a position comfortable to him; such attacks usually subside shortly. In other cases the pain in the chest or abdomen may be so severe as to induce profuse sweating. The patient may insist on walking about rather than lying down.

If the victim has been under medical care, the first-aider should assist in administering prescribed medicine. If medical care hasn't been given previously, medical advice should be obtained at once if possible. In the meantime, defer transporting the patient. If he is faint, the lying down position is best. Raising the legs may be beneficial.

For shortness of breath, raise the head and chest of the patient to his most comfortable position. When pain is acute, the lying-down position again is best, but the pain may not permit such a position at first. Lying down entails less strain than the upright position.

A messenger should be sent to the nearest phone or radio so that medical advice may be obtained and a helicopter or other transportation sent for to remove the heart-attack victim to the nearest hospital.

In the meantime, the patient must have absolute rest and quiet. It is best not to show extreme concern, and to avoid naming or referring to the seizure as a heart attack. If oxygen is available from the small "Lif-O-Gen" cylinder that some facilities or parties have for emergency—use it.

Should a helicopter or rescue plane be unable to land close by, it will be necessary to transport the patient via an improvised stretcher. This can be done, in the absence of a better stretcher by using one made by cutting two poles approximately 8 feet long and about 1½ inches in diameter. Lay the poles about two feet apart and lace ropes or strips of blanket or canvas between, weaving them back and forth for a distance of five or six feet. Carefully place the patient on the stretcher in a sleeping bag or wrapped in blankets. The patient's body and weight will hold the poles apart.

It is extremely important that the victim stay recumbent during transportation. The patient will ride more comfortably if the two litter bearers walk "out of step." They must, of course, use care not to trip and fall. Easy does it!

SPECIAL CASES

Some injuries may not require remedial action at once, as do those discussed above under "Immediate Action Cases." Although the time element may not be critical, special care is needed.

BURNS. Shock and infection are the chief dangers from burns. First-aid duties are to relieve pain, prevent infection, and treat shock.

For burns of limited extent apply sterile petroleum ointment or burn ointment and cover with sterile gauze. Snow or ice packs will relieve pain.

Extensive burns are very serious—shock is always present. Remove loose clothing from the burned area. If clothing sticks to the burn, cut around it and leave for the doctor to remove. Apply burn ointment from your first-aid kit and bandage snugly. If you are out of ointment you may use salad or other oil. Or you may dip strips of clean cloth in a solution of three tablespoons of baking soda or Epsom salts in one quart of warm water and apply cloth to burned area. Keep the patient covered and warm.

BROKEN BONES OR DISLOCATION. *Remember:* If in doubt, treat as a fracture. Proper handling of a fracture is essential.

(1) Unless absolutely necessary, do not move the patient until the fracture has been immobilized by a splint. (2) Improvised splinting or immobilization material may be made from boards, wire, blankets, pillows, or folded coats. Pad the splint to make more comfortable. (3) A general rule is to make splint long enough to immobilize both the break and the joints above and below the break.

WOUNDS, BLEEDING NOT SEVERE. Treat as follows: (1) Keep the wound clean to prevent germs from entering. (2) If the wound must be cleaned, wash gently with plain soap. (3) Cover with sterile dressing and bandage snugly in place.

POISON, INTERNAL. For general first-aid, remember two practices: (1) *Dilute.* Give patient large amounts of fluid such as soapsuds, salt water, baking soda in water, lukewarm water, or warm mustard water. (2) *Wash Out.* Induce vomiting repeatedly. Continue diluting and washing out until fluid is as clear as when it was swallowed. Treat for shock.

SPRAINS. To treat a sprain: (1) Elevate the part. (2) Apply cold. (3) If the sprain is severe, have a doctor examine it.

PROLONGED EXPOSURE TO COLD. When a person is exposed to excessive cold for a long time he becomes numb, movement is difficult, and irresistible drowsiness overtakes him. He staggers, his eyesight fails, he falls, and he may become unconscious.

If breathing has stopped, begin artificial respiration. Bring the patient into a tent or cabin if one is available. Warm him as rapidly as possible by wrapping him in blankets or in sleeping bags. If a canvas bath tub or any other tub is available (unlikely in the back country), place him in a tub of warm (78 to 82 degrees F.) but *not hot* water. When he reacts, give him a hot drink. Dry him thoroughly as soon as he is revived enough to terminate the warm water treatment.

FOOD POISONING. Contaminated food can be a serious menace to health. The stomach should be well rinsed and washed out with several glasses of water in which a quarter-teaspoon of bicarbonate of soda per glass has been added. These should be drunk one after the other to cause vomiting. If vomiting doesn't occur, induce it by tickling the back of the throat with a finger. Administer two or three small paregoric tablets every 4 to 6 hours for as long as required to control any attendant diarrhea.

If vomiting continues and interferes with the paregoric treatment, place a quarter-grain morphine sulphate tablet under the tongue; if trouble continues, you may assume that the medication is not working; it may not have had time to reach the affected area through the blood stream or it may not have been sufficiently concentrated. In some cases chewing and swallowing small chips or pieces of ice will stop the spasm cycle if you are in snow or ice locations. Once the vomiting and diarrhea are under control, further treatment required may involve need for one of the sulphas. Two sulpha tablets may be given and repeated in 3 or 4 hours. If no improvement is noticed after several tries, change over to penicillin. Keep body fluids up by having the patient drink large amounts of water, tea, and milk if available. The patient's drinking water should be slightly salted to ward off dehydration.

DIGESTIVE UPSETS. Severe vomiting from digestive upsets can usually be relieved, by paregoric. This should also relieve any diarrhea involved.

FEVER AND INFECTIONS. For infections with fever, take one penicillin tablet orally 4 to 6 hours apart, 3 or 4 times a day.

PNEUMONIA AND VIRUS FLU. Give one penicillin tablet orally 3 or 4 times a day as directed by your physician. Continue until fever drops. After fever has declined and normal temperature prevails for 12 to 14 hours, cut dosage in half for several days.

It is dangerous to take antibiotics for prolonged periods, and without the supervision of a doctor. Do not use penicillin over 7 to 10 days. Have patient drink large amounts of water and diluted fruit juice. Be sure to keep patient warm and out of drafts. Keep him on a light diet for a few days. Do not allow him to travel until he is strong enough, and then take it easy.

INFECTIONS. In case of a bad knife or axe cut, half dosages of penicillin can be taken orally for several days. In the more serious accidents such as puncture wounds, gunshot wounds or a compound facture, full dosages are indicated.

Local infections should be opened and drained. Infections that extend over a wide area can be relieved by applying hot, wet compresses to localize them. Do not squeeze, and don't lance before the infection is well localized. It then may be opened with a sterilized lance or needle, and treated.

HEADACHES. A simple headache may be relieved if you happen to be in an area where snow can be obtained readily. Make an ice pack out of a towel or other material and apply to head and back of neck.

ABDOMINAL INJURY. In case of an injury to the abdomen where the intestines protrude, do not force them back in. Place a sterile wet salt pack over the wound. Salt water can be boiled to sterilize it, and the bandage can be made sterile by first backing or burning lightly with a match or holding it near a flame. Remove the patient by stretcher, if you must, from back country, but first try to get a helicopter and medical help.

PRECAUTIONS WITH GAME. Be sure all wild game like bear, wild boar, and javalina is well cooked before eating to avoid possibility of contracting trichinosis. Beware of tularemia that can be contracted through handling infected rodents, ground squirrels, hares, etc. This disease also is called "deer fly fever" and "rabbit fever." The flesh of infected animals can be eaten, however, in dire emergency if the meat is well cooked.

Rabies is an acute and deadly infection transmitted by the bite of infected animals. It is more or less endemic in the State of Alaska and parts of Canada, particularly in the fox population. Occasionally it is carried by wolves, dogs, and other carnivores. Medical treatment is a must if bitten by an infected animal.

ANTIDOTE. When a more specific antidote for poisoning is not known nor available, one made of two parts crumbled burnt toast, one part strong tea, and one part milk of magnesia may be beneficial.

WILDERNESS CAMP MEDICINE

Indians and primitive man found many herbs and plants which they used to relieve pain and heal wounds. These are too numerous to mention here.

COLD TREATMENT. In the past few years science has discovered that cold can be used in surgery and give relief from pain. Usually ice or snow can be found in the shady spots at higher elevations. Ice or snow packs will bring relief for headaches, insect bites and stings, and will reduce fevers and swelling in cases of sprains or broken limbs, and will retard bleeding. Apply a cold pack to the abdomen in a suspected case of appendicitis and get the victim to a doctor or hospital as soon as possible. *Never apply heat or give a laxative* to a person suspected of having appendicitis. Ice or cold packs are used in the treatment of poisonous snake and spider bites in conjunction with suction and antivenin injections. Cold retards the spread of poison and assists in breaking up its components. Some desert outdoorsmen carry a small cylinder of CO_2 or liquid air to use in case of snake bite. This freezes the bite area until the victim can reach a hospital. Severe vomiting can be stopped by swallowing small pieces of ice or small bites of snow. Toothache and swelling may be reduced by the cold method. A cold pack placed on top of a sterile compress covering a burn will remove the sting and pain of minor burns.

HEAT TREATMENT. Hot packs made from towels wrung out in hot water can be used to relieve stomach cramps and muscular pain. Hot rocks wrapped in a towel or other material may be used to keep an injured person warm. Place at feet and along body. Be certain not to burn a patient. *Never use heat in suspected case of appendicitis.* Infected limbs may be soaked in very hot water to reduce infection and swelling. Hot packs may be applied to infections on the body to secure relief. Half-hour immersion, repeated every two hours, is the best method.

BICARBONATE OF SODA. A sour or acid stomach may be relieved by drinking a teaspoonful of bicarbonate of soda in a glass of warm water.

Packs of wet bicarbonate of soda will relieve insect stings and bites and will also remove and relieve the itch and pain of poison oak, poison ivy, nettles, and poison sumac. Wet soda packs will reduce the pain of minor burns.

MUSTARD. To induce vomiting when necessary to clean out the stomach, drink warm mustard water and put a finger down throat and tickle back of throat. A hot mustard poultice can be made to relieve backache and other pains. It will also help draw infection in cases of boils.

SUGAR PINE SUGAR. If a laxative is indicated and none can be found in camp, find a sugar pine tree and chew and eat the lumps of dried sugar sap found in the crevices of the bark or in hollows of a sugar pine stump. If you are in a region where you can find and brew cascara bark and berries, it will serve the same pupose. (This is an old Indian remedy.)

SALT. For burns, use three tablespoonfuls of salt to one quart of water. (Be sure to sterilize solution.) Soak a clean cloth in the solution and bind very snugly. Keep air out.

GREASE. Bacon grease or cooking oil may be used to soften hard saddle sores on animals. Bicarbonate of soda will assist in healing soft sores if healing powder is not available.

VINEGAR. Applying vinegar will assist in removing the pain of insect stings and bites.

MISCELLANEOUS. A mixture of salt and baking soda is excellent for brushing teeth when tooth paste or powder is not available. A 50-50 mixture is best.

Hot drinks are beneficial in cases of weakness.

FIRST-AID TRAINING. Whenever you go into wilderness country where you will be away for days or weeks from quick medical aid, there should be at least one person in the party who is well versed in advanced first-aid. This person should also know how to administer a few drugs in an emergency.

Before venturing on a trek of this magnitude, you should consult your family physician and have a physical check-up. Check with your dentist also. Get advice on the types of first-aid material and drugs to take along and of course instructions on how to use them for various illness that might be contracted on the trip. Be sure that you get a prescription for the necessary drugs.

Here is a list of medical supplies and equipment for a 4-man trek into wilderness country for a period of two or more weeks. The advanced first-aid member of the party should be taught definitive medical procedures as how to clean, sew up, clip, or tape-close a common laceration. Evacuation of patient to qualified medical care should be undertaken as soon as possible.

Recommended: Revised edition, 1955 *The Ship's Medicine Chest and First Aid at Sea,* by the U. S. Public Health Service. Write for it to the Superintendent of Documents, U. S. Government Printing Office, Washington 25, D. C.

MEDICAL SUPPLIES DESIRABLE

6—Codeine sulphate tablets, ½ grain, for pain.

50—Aspirin or Bufferin tablets, 5 grain, for headaches and joint pains.

12—Gantrimycin (Roche) tablets, size as recommended by physician. Use 2 to 5 tablets every six hours for infection or pneumonia, and for those allergic to penicillin.

1—Zinc oxide ointment 2 oz. tube to protect nose and face from sunburn.

7—pHisoHex 5 oz. squeeze-bottle, or bar of Ivory soap for cleansing hands and wounds with copious washings.

1—Bismuth and paregoric, 2 oz. For diarrhea, 1-tablespoon after each bowel movement until patient is back to normal.

1—Tr. Merthiolate, 1-1000, 1 oz. bottle for wound disinfectant.

1—Butyn eye ointment ¼ oz. For painful eye dressing must be worn at least 8 hours after last administration. Helps to relieve pain caused by snow blindness and other inflammation.

1—Cod liver oil-vasoline ointment, 50-50, 1 oz. tube. Excellent for burns.

1—Elixir of terpin hydrate with codeine, 2 oz. For nagging cough. 1 to 2 teaspoons at bedtime.
50—Halazone tablets for purifying water.
50—Bursalina iodine tablets for purifying water.
1—Earache medicine, ¼ oz. Use 2 or 3 drops on a pledget of cotton and insert into ear.
1—Oil of cloves, ½ oz. For toothache.
54—Sterilized "Q" Tips, or swabs for applying disinfectant to wounds.
1—First-aid kit (16 unit). Add laxative and Vitamins B Complex and C in high potency. To replenish body needs drained through a severe accident or illness.
1—Metal fever thermometer (non-breakable type).
1—Rubberized wide-mouthed ice pack-bag. For headache and to reduce swellings.
1—Rubberized hot-water bag (chemical bags may be substituted). For shock.
1—Snake-bite kit (suction type). Two kits, 10 cc each, syringe type, if in bad snake country.
2—Wire malleable splints.
12—Safety pins.
1—Spool of silk ligature thread.
1—Pair of dressing forceps, or bandage scissors.

Chapter 25

SURVIVAL

WATER SURVIVAL

MILLIONS OF people are turning to water sports each year—fishing, swimming, water-skiing, surfboarding, boat racing, and camp cruising. The steady increase in popularity of water sports has also taken an unnecessary toll of lives of outdoor people. For first aid *when artificial respiration measures* are needed, *see the preceding chapter.*

"DROWNPROOFING." There is no need for the over 7,000 fatalities annually caused by drowning, if people will just take time and learn a simple method that will enable them to survive accidents of this type. A non-swimmer or an injured person with a broken arm or other injuries can remain afloat for hours, or even reach shore at a speed of about one mile per hour. In fact, some years ago a man fell overboard when his ship was many miles at sea. He was able to stay afloat for several days and nights before he was spotted and picked up by a passing vessel.

Drownproofing* is being taught to thousands of students every year.

HOW "DROWNPROOFING" WORKS.

Float Stroke. (1) Take a breath and immediately lay your head forward in the water until your chin is on your chest. Relax your entire body, letting your hands dangle. If you're fat, you may find your buttocks swinging upward. Exhale a little air through your nose and you will return to the vertical position. Rest, just "hanging" in the water. A few inches of the back of your head will protrude above the surface.

(2) After a few seconds, but *before* you need air, leisurely cross your arms in front of your head, forearms together. Raise one knee toward your chest, then extend the foot forward. Simultaneously, extend the other foot behind you. Move easily and smoothly so that you remain vertical, head lolling.

---

* Worked out by Fred R. Lanoue, professor of physical education and head swimming coach at Georgia Institute of Technology. See Joseph P. Blank, "Nobody Needs to Drown," *Everywoman's Family Circle,* June, 1960.

FLOAT STROKE.

(3) Raise your head quickly but smoothly, stopping with your chin still in the water. As you raise your head, exhale through your nose, beginning while your face is under water and continuing as it emerges.

(4) Finish exhaling; open your mouth to inhale. To keep your mouth above water while you inhale, gently sweep your palms outward and step downward on the water with both feet. Don't move too vigorously or you will pop your shoulders out of the water. You don't need a 100-percent change of air; experiment to learn just how much you must have.

(5) Having inhaled, close your mouth, and drop your head toward your knees. Relax, go limp, in the same position as in step 1. If you tend to sink a few feet below the surface, it is because you have failed to drop your arms after putting your head in the water. When you need another breath, swing smoothly into steps 2, 3, 4 and 5 again. If your chest feels tight under water, either you are resting too long or you are not exhaling deeply enough. Adjust these factors through repeated practice.

Swimming Stroke. (1) Take a breath and sink vertically. As your head goes under, push down gently with your hands to arrest any tendency to sink too deep.

(2) Tip your head forward to the face-down position. Bring

SWIMMING STROKE.

your hands to your forehead and open-scissor your legs with the rear foot raised as high as possible. This will begin to swing your body into a horizontal position.

(3) Extend your arms forward and toward the surface, hands together. The moment they are extended full length, give a scissors kick with your legs.

(4) As your feet come together from the kick, slowly sweep your arms outward and back, finishing the stroke with your hands at your thighs. Make the movement *easily*.

(5) As you glide forward and upward, keep your body relaxed and your hands at your thighs, and begin to exhale through your nose.

(6) When you're ready for a fresh breath (don't wait until you *need* it), begin returning to the vertical position by bowing your back, bringing both knees toward your chest, and raising your hands toward your head. Continue exhaling through this and step 7.

(7) Continue swinging toward the vertical by extending one leg in front of you and bringing the other knee up to it. Cross your arms in front of your head, forearms together, palms out.

(8) Now you are ready to go for more air. Open-scissor your legs to propel yourself upward, and begin raising your head. Don't try to raise your head until your trunk is vertical.

(9) To keep your head up while inhaling through your mouth, gently sweep your palms outward and downward and smoothly bring your feet together. If you get a little water in your mouth, spurt it out under water between pursed lips.*

The main thing to remember is not to panic and to try and remain as relaxed as you possibly can and follow your drown-proof training.

SURVIVAL IN COLD AND SNOW

The problems facing a survivor in areas of heavy snow and extreme cold are among the most hazardous and severe with which man can come in contact.

SHELTER AND WARMTH ARE THE FIRST NEEDS.

Hunters seeking the elusive polar bear or the great brown bear can find their quarry only in places where the cold is

---

* Joseph P. Blank, "Nobody Needs to Drown," *Everywoman's Family Circle*, June, 1960.

intense. Mountain climbers may find that a sudden storm in the higher elevations has suddenly placed their lives in peril. To survive in such areas for any length of time, man must be able to find or to build a shelter and to kill or trap game. His immediate problem is to find shelter and warmth, for if he is unable to maintain his body heat, he will perish from the extreme cold.

In recent years, more and more sportsmen have been making hunting and camping trips to Alaska and Northern Canada. Although such trips usually involve the services of an experienced guide or outfitter, the hazards confronting those who become separated from their party should never be underestimated. The hunter in such cold weather areas should prepare for the bitter cold with special clothing, equipment, and food. He will find that low temperature and the "windchill" effect of a strong wind will both add to the cold danger. One of the windiest places is in the Aleutian Islands off Alaska, where the terrible "williwaw" wind has been known to exceed 150 miles per hour.

However, even in the continental United States, cold and snow can sometimes threaten survival. Temperatures recorded in several of our states, such as in Montana, Colorado, Wyoming, and parts of the Dakotas, have sometimes in blizzard conditions, approached the cold of the polar regions. Even in New England the cold is sometimes intense, especially on the slopes of Mount Washington, New Hampshire where wind gusts have reached almost 250 miles per hour.

Visitors to the Arctic must be prepared to cope with the effects of cold, frost, ice, and wind. Summer is the time of heavy fogs, especially in the coastal areas. The fog may last for weeks at a time, making plane and helicopter rescue practically impossible. Ice fog and white-outs in the winter are similar to sea or coastal fogs, in that they cut visibility to zero. Ice fog, unlike other fog, consists of very fine ice crystals.

THE WILL TO LIVE. It has been claimed that man cannot live in the extreme cold of the polar regions, yet the Eskimo has been able to exist there throughout the years. Men have had their ships frozen in, cracked by ice and sunk beneath the ice pack. It took some of them months to fight their way back to civilization. Some died en route, but others with a will to live survived their terrible ordeal.

One tale out of the north tells about an expedition that lost its ship to the ice. Members of the expedition hauled one of the ship's small boats southward for days over the ice pack so that they could cross the open stretches of water they encountered. However, the small boat became unseaworthy from dragging it over the rough terrain and it had to be abandoned. A most discouraging fact became evident one night when they were able to get a star-shot and discovered that after trekking southward all day, they were actually farther north than when they had started out in the morning. The ice floe was drifting north faster than they could travel south over the rough ice ridges. Finally, they became separated one night when the ice pack they were camped on split up into smaller floes and floated away from each other. Several men in one party made the Alaskan coast, where they were found by a search party. The sole survivor in the other group finally landed months later on the Siberian coast with no clothes left on him but the tattered remains of his long-handled wool underwear. The point is that some of these men survived their terrible experience because they had that certain something—the will to live.

COLD WEATHER EQUIPMENT AND KNOW-HOW. Modern man should at least have a basic knowledge of cold weather survival if he is likely to find himself in an area of extreme cold.

Keep Your Clothing Dry. One point that must be emphasized for those that anticipate going into extremely cold regions is that no matter how much polar knowledge or experience one may have, if his clothing somehow becomes wet, he may slowly freeze to death in sub-zero temperatures. If he should be so unfortunate as to accidentally fall into open water, he could be dead within a short time if he isn't fished out, dried out, and warmed up in a very few minutes. Some don't even survive when promptly rescued, due to cold-shock that is always present in an accident of this type. If he isn't cared for properly, the victim usually goes into deep traumatic shock and dies. Many seamen died of cold-shock in the last two wars when they were washed overboard in the north Atlantic, or when their ships were torpedoed and sunk.

Improvised Shelter. Cold, not lack of food and water, is the most critical factor in frigid areas. Any person stranded in arctic conditions and temperatures must have a basic knowledge of how to supplement the protection given by the clothing he may have on at the time he finds himself in a survival predicament; and he must take advantage of, and make the best use of any material that he may be able to salvage from his surroundings until a rescue plane or helicopter or other help arrives. He can conserve his body heat by building a snow cave or house, igloo, or some type of shelter. He must by all means keep in mind that he mustn't exert himself so that he perspires, and thereby causes his clothing to dampen and then freeze. If he happens to be in a timbered area, he can build a bough shelter and keep warm with a wood fire. Due to inclement or uncertain flying weather conditions, it might be days before he is found by a search party.

Under survival conditions you must have a basic knowledge of how to find or improvise emergency shelter. Winter, the most severe season, presents the greatest shelter problem. The snow-cave is a comfortable and practical shelter when properly constructed along snow-house principles with a low tunnel entrance, raised sleeping platform, domed roof, and roof ventilation. Any steep snow slope is suitable for constructing a snow-cave.

The snow-house or igloo is built with snow blocks. Firm, wind-pressed snow is necessary for its construction. If the snow is not compressed by the elements, it must be pressed and compacted by stamping down on it with snowshoes or skis before it can be cut into building blocks. Blocks should be 18 to 20 inches high, 30 to 36 inches wide, and 8 to 10 inches thick. Towards the top the blocks should be thinner; 6 inches and then 4 inches when finishing the dome or top.

Distress Signals. If fortunate to be near timber, he should build up three large brush piles about fifty yards apart in a triangle shape to be used as a fire signal on hearing or sighting a search plane. If in tundra country, he will have to stamp out a call for aid in the snow. It is best to wall up one side of the signal so that any light may throw a shadow on one side, and make the signal word stand out more sharply.

FINDING FOOD. *Game.* Nearly every living animal and bird leaves the high Arctic during the long winter, or hibernates until spring. Caribou and musk ox migrate to the sub-arctic where they can dig for nutritious lichens. The lemmings burrow under the snow. A few rock ptarmigan do winter in the Arctic along with the arctic fox, and a few polar bear come out and roam around briefly. There is more animal and bird life than is generally known in the far north, such as several species of birds, ducks, arctic hare, fox, wolverine, wolf, ermine, weasels, ground squirrels, voles, lemmings, caribou, and musk ox.

Along the coast, the Indians and Eskimos catch seal, whale, walrus, and fish.

Edible Vegetation. Most Eskimos are meat eaters; however, those tribes living in western Alaska, Labrador, and southwest Greenland do use some plants and berries. There is also more plant life in the Arctic than is realized by the layman. Among the berries are mountain cranberries, bilberries, and crow-berries. The natives seem to favor the sweet salmon berries found throughout the Northwest.

The usual vegetables eaten by west Alaskan Eskimos are the leaves and flowering axils of marsh fleabane, coltsfoot, the root tubers of the Eskimo potato, vetch, and the flowering stems of rose root. A number of fern weeds are also used as pot herbs. Several species of seaweeds grow along the rocky coastal areas of the Arctic, and many are edible, nourishing, and full of minerals that are beneficial to good health.

Scurvy. Odd as it may seem, the Eskimo manages to live and survive on a straight diet of meat, and still avoid scurvy. Scurvy is not restricted to the far north, since seamen have suffered from it throughout the years, but anyone having a steady diet of salt-cured meats is likely to incur it. Numerous tragedies in the early whaling days linked scurvy with the Arctic.

Many years ago, trappers and miners prevented scurvy by eating the leaves of sorrel and scurvy grass. Natives of Russia and others overcame the scourge by drinking reindeer blood. In this modern age, man has overcome this disease by using vitamins.

CHECK LIST OF MINIMUM ARCTIC SURVIVAL EQUIPMENT:

(1) Axe.
(2) Ammunition.
(3) Arctic sleeping bag, double Eiderdown, mummy style.

(4) Boots, insulated Sno-paks, or Mukluks, native style.
(5) Compass, declination, adjustable with sighting line.
(6) Can, leak-proof, with spout, one-gallon size.
(7) Dark glasses (to prevent snow-blindness).
(8) Felt inner shoe soles.
(9) Firearms.*
(10) Flares, six red signal type.
(11) Flint and steel for fire starting.
(12) Insulated two-piece underwear.
(13) Magnifying glass for starting fires.
(14) Knife, BSA type with leather punch, screwdriver, and can opener.
(15) Matches, waterproof type.
(16) Match case, waterproof type.
(17) Map of area flying or hunting in (topographic).
(18) Mirror, steel, for signaling.
(19) Mittens, inner mittens wool, outer mittens waterproof.
(20) Snowshoes or skis (two ski poles).
(21) Stick, anti-fog, for glasses.
(22) Shovel and saw, Arctic survival type (aluminum shovel with ice saw).
(23) Stove, Primus type, gasoline or alcohol fuel.
(24) Socks, lightweight wool, inners, heavy wool outers ½ size larger.
(25) Tent, two-man Army Arctic type with air vents.
(26) Parka, knee length, full zipper in front, hood edge Wolverine trim.
(27) Pants, smooth weave, windproof, water-repellent.
(28) Pemmican or emergency rations and vitamins.
(29) Rucksack.
(30) Fish hooks.

WARNING. Watch out for frost bite. Do not rub. Thaw out by warming the affected part with your hands. Thaw hands by putting inside against body. Move and work slowly to conserve energy; and keep from perspiring, keep clothing dry and prevent freezing! Wear snow goggles to prevent snow blindness. Salvage all usable material from your wrecked ship or plane that will assist in your survival. You are lucky if you had time to radio your last position or were able to salvage a workable radio.

Various types of snow shelters and woodcraft are shown in chapter 8. For full details on all types of survival, see the Navy's handbook, *How to Survive on Land and Sea*, U. S. Naval Institute, Annapolis, Maryland.

---

* Auxiliary rifles: The Stoeger Arms Corporation catalog for 1962 lists the ArmaLite Model AR-7 as the civilian development of the AR-15 Air Force Survival rifle. The AR-7 will float; it is made in .22 Long Rifle caliber, and weighs only 2¾ pounds.

DESERT SURVIVAL

The deserts of North America can be as cruel and terrible as any other desert when one's life is at stake in a survival situation.

TEMPERATURE RANGES. Temperatures range from one extreme to another, sometimes very abruptly. Death Valley National Monument, a part of the great American Mojave Desert, lies east of the vast Sierra Nevada range in California and Nevada. A considerable contrast in elevation is found in this region; Mount Whitney rises to an elevation of 14,495 feet, the second highest point in the United States, while the lowest elevation in the western hemisphere is forty-five miles due east in Death Valley, at Bad Waters, and is 282 feet below sea level.

The Mojave Desert is the second hottest desert in the world, with an official maximum temperature of 134 degrees, with the Sahara only .4 degrees warmer.

THE DESERT CAN BE DANGEROUS. With the modern fast mode of transportation, more people are getting into unpleasant situations in the desert than ever before, by becoming lost, hurt, or running out of water and gasoline for their car. When they face a life or death situation in the desert, often they do not know what to do, or how to do it.

More and more rock-hounds, miners, prospectors, uranium hunters, and desert campers are hitting the desert trails by power wagons, jeeps, burros, helicopters, planes, and the family bus. Some are out mostly to enjoy the wild flowers in the spring, while others go into the most remote areas to hunt or prospect for riches. Some don't use good judgment and as a result get into serious survival difficulties.

Cars and jeeps have broken down in distant sections of the desert, and stock have drifted off at times, leaving their master stranded far from help. Occasionally a plane or helicopter will crash or have to make a forced landing in some out-of-the-way place, so it is necessary that a person entering the desert have a basic knowledge of how to survive, should the need ever arise.

Deserts are vast areas with few places of habitation, or places where water and supplies may be obtained; yet, deserts can be beautiful in the spring, and kind to those "in the know."

but cruel to those who do not heed warnings! As an old prospector once said, "You will soon learn the three S's of the desert: *everything either sticks, stings, or stinks!*" The old boy was right, in a manner of speaking, since the spring flowers are sweet and fragrant, the shrub's smell is pungent, the cactus sticks, and the scorpion and other insects sting if one doesn't use good "burro sense."

YOU CAN SURVIVE, IF—. Many persons mistakenly believe that deserts are uninhabitable places where plants, animals, and man cannot exist. This is untrue, for there is food to be found, plants and roots that can be eaten, and desert animals to be trapped or snared. Water or moisture may be obtained from certain cacti, and water holes found if one knows the signs to look for; in other words, if one has a knowledge of desert lore.

In northern deserts, temperatures are not so extreme, and a person can travel farther and go longer without water than one can in the southern arid regions where travel is difficult and dangerous in the hot sunlight.

Water. Finding water is a *"must"* if one is forced to hike out on his own. You can forego food for a considerable length of time, but not water. Willows and cottonwoods usually mark the permanent water sources, with desert willows, mesquite, paloverde, and tesota lining the drier waterbeds.

Game. Larger animals roam the northern deserts, such as elk, mule deer, and antelope. Cotton tail and jack rabbits, desert fox, coyotes, ground squirrels, desert woodrats, and gophers are abundant in some sections. Various species of snakes, lizards, and horned toads are also found. Quail, sage hen, and many other species of bird life are present.

In the southern deserts of the Southwest, a greater variety of game may be encountered. Mexican mule deer in Arizona, and the smaller burro deer are found along the Colorado River. Wild horses and burros, and a few wild cattle range these waste lands. One would need a rifle to secure these fast-moving animals. The coyote, fox, and red wolf are found here. Brush and jack rabbits are plentiful, and wild pigs (the Mexican javelina) are found in certain areas. Snakes and lizards are abundant and not too unpleasant to eat when roasted. Desert quail and dove are encountered near springs and wells in the early morning and evening. Fish are caught in the Colorado River along its full length. Roasted grasshoppers are tasty, if you are hungry enough!

Edible Plants. Plant life can be obtained in both northern and southern American deserts. In the northern part, purslane, filaree, saltbush, amaranth, lamb's quarters, Russian thistle, mustards, and many fresh green plants can be prepared and cooked like spinach. Beware of those plants that have a milky sap, unless you are certain that they are safe. A diet of this roughage is quite a change from man's regular food, and may cause one to have diarrhea for several days until his system becomes acclimated to this drastic change in food habits. The plants contain minerals and vitamins, and eaten with roast rabbit, snake, lizards, or other meat one has been able to club, snare, or catch, should give him strength to reach some point of civilization.

In the southern deserts, roots, the young shoots of cacti, hog potato, desert thorn cacti, and spiderworts, the flower and soft parts of yuccas, agaves, and fruits of hackberry and strawberry may be eaten.

Saguara, organ pipe, and prickly pear are edible when the thorns are scraped off. Most tree fruits can be eaten, and so can seeds of most grasses. In the higher desert elevations, one can secure the nuts of the piñon pine, which are very nutritious.

DON'T PANIC. There is little reason for anyone to starve or die of thirst if he will not panic. If he will just stop and think his predicament over, he can usually plan a way out to save himself.

It cannot be overemphasized that good equipment can make survival easier. It might be mentioned here that a lone survivor with a will to live, and with none or a very few personal items such as a knife, cigarette lighter, etc., can still survive successfully if he is not badly hurt or ill. Even a few seriously injured survivors from plane accidents have been rescued and survived their ordeal because they used good judgment at the time and wanted to live.

WHAT TO DO IN CERTAIN DESERT SURVIVAL SITUATIONS.

Example No. 1. You have a forced landing while flying across a remote section of desert terrain, or your car or jeep has broken down, and you are unable to restart the motor or repair it.

(a) Best plan is to stay with the plane or vehicle! Why? Because no doubt you filed a flight plan at the airport (if you didn't you should have, without question!), or left word at a ranger station or sheriff's sub-station as you drove through, saying where you were going and when you expected to return. Whether you stay with the car or plane will be a matter of judgment, depending on the situation at the time. If injured, it's always best to stay at the scene of the accident.

(b) An air and land search will be instituted by officials when you fail to return after a certain time has elapsed. This can start any time after twenty-four to forty-eight hours after your "zero" hour. The reason for this waiting period is to give you time to come in on your own, as most do, and also gives the authorities time to check up on you and get organized properly before they begin to search for you, if you don't appear during the waiting period.

(c) A plane or land vehicle can be seen from the air more clearly than a person, due to the difference in size. Time after time, a plane that has been forced down or a disabled vehicle has been located quickly, but the occupants have left the scene and become lost, or have gotten themselves into other difficulties. This means that the search must continue, adding to the length of the search and more expense to the taxpayer, with continued worry for those waiting at home.

(d) If you happen to have an Army survival kit or one of the new civilian survival kits with you, you used good judgment, indeed, because it may have happened that you got into a survival situation on your first day out, and hadn't planned to check in for a week. This could mean that you would have eight or nine days to wait before a search would be instituted for you, unless you are able to signal some passing plane or some individual, such as a prospector passing through, who happens to spot your predicament.

(e) The next step is to build a wind break or shelter from a parachute, or canvas tarpaulin from a car or pack-outfit.

This will provide some comfort from wind and the direct rays of the sun.

(f) For a distress signal, gather brush and any available fuel and build three large brush piles in a triangle about fifty yards apart to be lighted at night, or when a plane is heard. If you use the brush piles in the daytime as a smoke signal, be sure to pile green shrubbery on top to cause a dense smoke column.

(g) Normally there should be enough water left in a vehicle radiator to last through the situation, unless the motor is air cooled, or the water has been contaminated by antifreeze. Desert alkali water can be rendered harmless and nearly palatable by leaching it through sand or soil that isn't saturated with salt. Water may also be obtained from the barrel cactus.

Example No. 2. If it is a case of hiking out to civilization under your own power, you are in a more serious predicament!

(a) One cannot conceive of anyone traveling by plane or other means into, or over a desert, or remote back-country, without having a good map of the region along with him at the time. Therefore, he should have some idea by the course he has been traveling, and from the sun, as to which direction is north. All there is to it is to check your dead reckoning, and your map, and you should have a rough idea how far and which way you will have to travel or hike to a road, railroad, or place of habitation. Now comes the real planning in figuring out the shortest and easiest route to take. Once this is done and you have started, you are committed to getting out afoot. An appraisal should be made of what equipment is salvageable from the vehicle or plane that can be used to advantage, such as maps, compass, canteen, knife, matches, wire for making traps and snares, steel mirror for signaling, sun helmet or other head covering, and a container to carry this equipment in. (Maybe you are fortunate and carry a survival kit in your plane.) Include your first-aid kit, and any water or food.

(b) If you happen to be a lost hunter after desert sheep or wild pigs, or if you're a camper, or prospector, you will have the equipment you happen to have on your person, and you'll have to take it from there! At least a hunter will have a skinning knife, rifle, and possibly a compass, map, matches, and a few other things of survival use, so he is probably better off than others.

(c) It will be of prime importance to travel at night and early morning if caught out in the summer time. In cooler weather, one can make better time in daylight. Be extra cautious when traveling at night and be alert for rattlesnakes, for this is their feeding period when they are looking for rodents and other food.

(d) Those hardy persons packing into the desert with saddle and pack stock should be extra careful that their animals do not stray off and leave them afoot while the stock heads for the home corral. This can sometimes mean a walk out, if the missing stock cannot be located within a reasonable length of time. If you are left afoot, you will have all the necessary food and equipment at hand, but it also means that you will have to pack all necessities to get you out—on your own back. It should be quite easy to backtrack your trail, if wind hasn't caused sand to obliterate the horse tracks.

(e) Remember that it can be as much as 20 to 30 degrees cooler if you can get off the hot ground and into the shade of a bush. By digging down into the ground in a shady spot for a depth of 16 to 20 inches it will be very much cooler.

COASTAL SURVIVAL

People who may become lost, whether hunters, fishermen, travelers, or even survivors from a shipwreck or ditched plane, will find a greater variety and quantity of food stuff in a coastal area than in other types of country.

BASIC SURVIVAL TECHNIQUES. Of course, you should have a knowledge of basic survival techniques and be able to apply them along with a little "beachcomber" sense, and thereby survive in more comfort than others forced to survive in, for instance, a jungle or the Arctic. Your chances of being spotted on an open beach are greater than in a wooded area.

Survival conditions would of course be radically different, should the incident not occur in a temperate area but instead in a tropical or in arctic seashore regions. If the survival situation occurs in a polar area, you should select a safe campsite and construct an adequate shelter before looking for water and food. However, if you are in a tropical zone, look first for fresh water and a food supply, before building a shelter, since cold and wind will not be a deciding factor.

SEASHORE FOODS. One can find a considerable amount of sea food along the shore if he knows how to go about it. Even if the area is completely uninhabited, there are various types of clams, mussels, scallops, oysters, shrimp, lobsters, crab, fish, and edible seaweed that may be obtained with ease. The above-mentioned food can be secured by searching the beach areas at low tide. The dark of night, with the aid of a homemade torch or a flashlight, is the time to find lobsters and some types of fish.

Vegetation near most coast lines is varied and plentiful, and it should be used to supplement the diet. Caution should be used to select plants that you know, or that resemble vegetation with which you are familiar. Avoid plants that have a milky sap or whose sap is bitter or has a soapy taste.

If you have any doubt about the safety of eating a wild plant, test it by eating an amount about the size of half a walnut. Then wait six or eight hours, and if no diarrhea, cramps, or nausea occur, it is safe to eat a reasonable amount.

Cooking. Some plants are not edible until they have been cooked by boiling, or have been baked. Many wild plants that are poisonous when raw become edible and safe to eat when cooked. Boiling and changing the water several times removes most of the bitterness out of really bitter plants.

(1) Flowers of all plants are edible either raw or cooked.

(2) Most fruits, nuts, and berries are edible, but beware of baneberry, for it is poisonous!

(3) Cook nuts by roasting or boiling them. They can be ground between two rocks to make flour.

(4) You can use plant greens cooked like spinach, or raw for salad; however, they do not provide much nourishment, but do contain minerals, and supply bulk and roughage.

(5) The underside of plants and roots, shoots, tubers, and root stalks contains the greatest nutritive value of the plant.

(6) Cook all underground plant parts by boiling, roasting, or baking.

Fuel. Driftwood is usually plentiful for cooking and keeping one warm around the campfire. Be sure not to set your fire in driftwood—make it in a safe place, or an inshore wind may cause the fire to jump into inland brush and forest, and thereby cause an uncontrolled forest fire that may sweep many miles inland.

BIOLOGICAL HAZARDS. When wading, bathing, or swimming along a rocky shore in shallow waters of reefs, be sure to protect your feet from rock bruises, coral, shell scratches, and cuts of this type—for they are difficult to heal, and infection sets in readily. Be especially alert for the stings of anemone and Portuguese men-of-war!

It is essential that you take good care of your feet, for they may be the only means of reaching a place of habitation, in case you have to walk out.

SIGNAL FIRES. Build up three large piles of brush about fifty yards apart, and have plenty of green boughs or grass stacked nearby so that you can make plenty of smoke, should a plane or search ship be sighted. It is best to locate the brush piles to form a triangle. In this manner, the smoke will normally show up from the air as three distinct columns—the universal S-O-S!

Appendix I
ADDRESSES OF OUTFITTERS

Large mail order firms such as Sears, Roebuck and Company, and Montgomery Ward and Company carry all types of camping equipment, fishing tackle, and gear; firearms and ammunition; outdoor clothing of all types for men and women, including the small fry; and boating and marine supplies. Sears and Roebuck also handles Marine and other types of insurance, and are in the Automobile Club business. Both of these companies maintain retail outlets in most towns.

The following is a partial list of other outfitters:

Abercrombie, David T., Co., 97 Chambers St., New York 7, N. Y.

Abercrombie & Fitch: Madison Avenue at 45th St., New York 17, N. Y., 9 North Wabash Street, Chicago 2, Ill., and 220 Post St., San Francisco 8, Calif.

Ames-Harris-Neville Co., 2800 17th St., San Francisco, Calif.

Boy Scouts of America, National Supply Division: New Brunswick, N. J.; 231 South Green St., Chicago 7, Ill.; and 485 Brannan St., San Francisco 7, Calif.

Girl Scouts of U. S. A., National Equipment Service: 155 East 44th St., New York 17, N. Y.; 1824 Washington Ave., St. Louis 3, Mo.; 770 Mission St., San Francisco 3, Calif.

Canadian Alpine Equipment Co., 1315 14th St. N. W., Calgary, Alberta, Canada.

Charles Brun's Ski Shop, 616 Pennsylvania Ave., Washington 3, D. C.

Camp & Trail Outfitters, Light Weight Camp Equipment, 112 Chambers St., New York 17, N. Y.

Dave Cook's Sporting Goods Co., 1603A Larimer St., Denver 1, Colo.

L. L. Bean, Inc., (Camping, Hunting & Fishing), Freeport, Me.

American Thermos Product Co., Norwich, Conn.

Gateway Sporting Goods Co., 1321 Main St., Kansas City 5, Mo.

I. Goldberg's (One of the largest Camp and Marine Supply Outfitters) 429 Market St., Philadelphia 6, Pa.

Corcoran, Inc., Stoughton, Mass.

Dolt Hut, Mountain Equipment, 2241 Sawtelle Blvd., West Los Angeles 64, Calif.

Gerry, Inc., Light Weight Camping and Mountain Climbing Equipment, Boulder, Colo.

Don Gleason's, Hunting, Fishing and Camping Equipment, 9 Pearl St., Northampton, Mass.

Holubar, Camping Equipment, 1215 Grandview Ave., Boulder, Colo.

Klein's Sporting Goods, 227 W. Washington St., Chicago 6, Ill.

Norm Thompson, Outfitter, 1805 N. W. Thurman, Portland 9, Ore.

Laacke and Joy Co., Camping and Mountain Climbing Equipment, 1433 North Water St., Milwaukee 2, Wisc.

Morsan Tents, Camping, Hunting & Fishing Equipment (One of the World's largest tent selections), 10-15 50th Ave., Long Island City 1, N. Y.

Trailwise (Ski Hut) Light Weight Camping and Mountaineering Equipment, 1615 University Ave., Berkeley 3, Calif.

Thomas Black & Sons, Inc., Camping Equipment, Ogdensburg, N. Y.

Mountaineering Supply, 897 St. David's Lane, Schenectady, N. Y.

Palley's Surplus, 2263 East Vernon Ave., Los Angeles 58, Calif.

Recreation Equipment Inc. (Light Weight Camping Equip.), 523 Pike St., Seattle 1, Wash.

Warshal's Sporting Goods, First Street and Madison, Seattle 1, Wash.

The Trading Post, 3336 M St., Washington 4, D. C.

Note: Advertisements in OUTDOOR magazines carry the names and addresses of many fine outfitters and equipment supply houses. Most Sporting Goods Stores carry besides hunting, fishing and camping gear; outdoor clothing for the whole family.

Appendix II
BIBLIOGRAPHY

A Climber's Guide to the Interior Ranges of British Columbia, American Alpine Club, New York, New York.

Adventures in Good Eating, Duncan Hines Institute, 408 E. State St., Ithaca, N. Y.

Air-Sea Bulletin, Air-Sea Rescue Agency. U.S. Coast Guard, Washington 25, D. C.

American Merchant Seaman's Manual, Cornell and Hoffman. Cornell Maritime Press, New York. 1942.

Animals of the Southwest Desert, Olin and Cannon. Southwest Monuments Association, Box 1562 S, Gila Pueblo, Globe, Arizona.

Arctic Manual, V. Stefansson. The Macmillan Company, 1944.

Ashley Book of Knots, Clifford W. Ashley. Doubleday, Doran Company, New York.

Axe Manual of Peter McLaren, Peter McLaren. Fayette R. Plumb, Incorporated, Philadelphia, Pennsylvania.

Bears In My Kitchen, Margaret Merrill. McGraw-Hill, New York.

Be Expert With Map and Compass, Bjorn Kjellstrom. American Orienteering Service, New York.

Belaying the Leader, Sierra Club, 220 Bush Street, San Francisco, California.

Better Camping Magazine, Kalmbach Publishing Co., 1027 N. 7th St., Milwaukee, 3, Wisconsin.

Bike Ways, Godfrey Frankel. Sterling Publishing Company, New York.

Boating Guide, W. N. Wallace. New York Herald Tribune, 230 West 41st Street, New York 36, New York.

Boating Magazine, Fawcett Publications, Inc., Greenwich, Connecticut.

Boats—Do It Yourself. Douglas Fir Plywood Association, Tacoma 2, Washington (Also ask for catalog of *Plywood Boat Plans.*)

Campground Atlas, Alpine Geographical Press, Champaign, Illinois.

Campground Guide for Tent and Trailer Tourists, Robert O. Klotz. Campgrounds Unlimited, Blue Rapids, Kansas.

Camping, Forest Service, U. S. Department of Agriculture, Washington, D. C.

Camping and Woodcraft, Horace Kephart. The Macmillan Company, New York.

Camping Family's Guide to Campsites, S. C. Hammond and Co., Maplewood, New Jersey.

Camping Guide, Harle Publications, Inc., 1250 Camden Ave., S. W., Canton, Ohio.

Camping Maps, U. S. A. Box 862, Upper Montclair, New Jersey.

Charts of the Great Lakes. U. S. Lake Survey, 630 Federal Building, Detroit, Michigan.

Climber's Guide to the Cascades and Olympic Mountains, Fred Beckey. The American Alpine Club, Washington.

Climber's Guide to the High Sierra, A, Sierra Club, San Francisco, California.

Climber's Guide to the Teton Range, A, Sierra Club, San Francisco, California.

Cruise Tips for Skippers, C. L. Lovejoy. The New York Times, 229 West 43rd Street, New York.

Dangerous Marine Animals That Bite, Sting, and Are Non-Edible, Bruce W. Halstead. Cornell Maritime Press, Cambridge, Massachusetts.

"Diet Problems of Mountaineers in the Himalaya," Dr. G. A. J. Teasdale. *Himalayan Journal,* Volume XI, 1939.

Equipment and Technique for Camping On Snow, Bester Robinson, Sierra Club Bulletin, San Francisco, California. 1937-1941.

Explorer's Manual. Boy Scouts of America, New Brunswick, N. J.

Experts Book of Boating, The, Ruth Brindze, Prentice-Hall Inc., Englewood Cliffs, New Jersey.

Family Boating, Fawcett Books, Greenwich, Connecticut.

Family Camping, Duluth Publishing Co., 1025 Race St., Philadelphia, Penna.

Family Camping and Places to Camp in the North Central States, George T. Wilson. A. Laake Company, Milwaukee, Wisconsin.

First Aid Textbook, Corrected and Revised. American Red Cross. Philadelphia, Pennsylvania.

Folders On Individual Reservoirs. Corps of Engineers, U. S. Department of Army, Washington, D. C.

Going Light With Backpack or Burro, David R. Brower, Editor. Sierra Club, San Francisco, California. 1958.

Golden Book of Camping and Campcrafts, The, Gordon Lynn. Golden Press, New York.

Gourmet Guide to Good Eating, Simon and Schuster, New York.

Guide To The John Muir Trail and the High Sierra Region, Walter A. Starr, Jr. Sierra Club, San Francisco. 1953.

Handbook of American Mountaineering. Kenneth A. Henderson, Boston, Massachusetts. 1942.

Handbook of Auto Camping and Motorists' Guide to Public Campgrounds, George and Iris Wells. Harper and Brothers, New York.

Handbook of Knots, Raoul Graumont. Cornell Maritime Press, New York.

Handbook On Wilderness Travel, George and Iris Wells. Harper and Brothers, New York.

Handbook On Mountain Skiing, Colonel George Bilgeri. Chadwick Press, London, England.

Hikers' Handbook, Douglas Leechman. W. W. Norton and Company, New York.

Hiking, Camping, and Mountaineering, Roland C. Geist. Harper and Brothers, New York.

Horses, Hitches and Rocky Trails, Joe Back. Alan Swallow, publisher, Denver 10, Colorado.

Hotel Redbook, American Hotel Association, 221 W. 57th St., New York.

How to Abandon Ship, Richard P. and J. J. Banigan. Cornell Maritime Press, New York.

How to Fish the Pacific Coast. Lane Publishing Company, Menlo Park, California.

How to Go Live In The Woods on $10 A Week, Bradford Angier, The Stackpole Company, Harrisburg, Pennsylvania.

How to Survive on Land and Sea. U. S. Naval Institute, Annapolis, Maryland.

Junior Book of Camping and Woodcraft, Bernard S. Mason. The Ronald Press Company, New York.

Living Off The Country, Bradford Angier. The Stackpole Company, Harrisburg, Pennsylvania.

Lodging for a Night, Duncan Hines Institute, 408 E. State St., Ithaca, N. Y.

Manual of Ski-Mountaineering, National Ski Association of America, University of California, Berkeley, California.

Map and Aerial Photography Reading, The Stackpole Company (formerly published by The Military Service Publishing Company), Harrisburg, Pennsylvania.

Map of The Olympic Mountains, George Martin and Richard Pargeter. Olympic College, Bremerton, Washington.

Meteorology Workbook, Peter E. Kraght. Cornell Maritime Press, New York.

Military Ski Manual, Frank Harper. The Stackpole Company, Harrisburg, Pennsylvania.

Motel Blue Book, National Hotel Publishing Co., 179 W. Washington St., Chicago 2, Ill.

Modern Camping Guide, George D. Martin. D. Appleton, Century Company, New York.

Mountaineering in Rocky Mountain National Park, U. S. Printing Office, Washington, D. C.

National Forest Vacations. Forest Service, U. S. Department of Agriculture, Washington, D. C.

National Park System, Eastern United States, The (map), *National Park System, Western United States, The* (map). National Park Service, U. S. Department of Interior, Washington, D. C.

National Parks, Historic Sites, and National Monuments, PL-35. Government Printing Office, Washington, D. C.

New Horizons USA, Simon and Schuster, New York.

New Way of The Wilderness, The, Calvin Rutstrum. The Macmillan Company, New York.

On Your Own, S. A. Graham and E. C. O'Roke. Lund Press, Minneapolis, Minnesota.

On Your Own In The Wilderness, Whelen and Angier. The Stackpole Company, Harrisburg, Pennsylvania.

Outboard Boating. The Outboard Boating Club of America, 307 North Michigan Avenue, Chicago, Illinois.

Outboard Boating Handbook, Fawcett Books, Greenwich, Connecticut.

Outdoor Cooking, Ora, Rose, and Bob Brown. New York.

Outdoor Sports Manual, Popular Mechanics Co., 200 East Ontario St., Chicago, Illinois.

Outdoor Tips With Aluminum Foil, Bates, Aluminum Company of America, Pittsburgh, Pennsylvania.

Outdoorsman's Cook Book, Arthur H. Carhart. The Macmillan Company.

Pacific Crest Trails, Joseph Hazard, Superior Publishing Company, Box 2190, Seattle 11, Washington.

"Parachuting of Expedition Supplies, The," *Geographical Review,* 1942.

Pilot Rules. U. S. Coast Guard. (See local district office.)

Piloting Seamanship and Small Boat Handling, Charles F. Chapman. Motor Boating, 517 Madison Avenue, New York.

Poisonous Dwellers of the Desert, Dodge. Southwestern Monuments Association, Box 1652 S, Gila Pueblo, Globe, Arizona.

Radio Amateur's Handbook. American Radio Relay League, West Hartford, Connecticut.

Reclamation's Recreational Opportunities. Bureau of Reclamation, U. S. Department of Interior, Washington, D. C.

Recreational Areas of the United States (map and folder). This Week Magazine, P. O. Box 239, Radio City Station, New York.

SAC Land Survival Guide Book. Director Administrative Services, Headquarters, U. S. Air Force, Washington 25, D. C.

Scout Field Book. Boy Scouts of America, New Brunswick, New Jersey.

Shelters, Shacks and Shanties, Daniel C. Beard. Charles Scribner and Sons, New York.

Ship's Medicine Chest and First Aid at Sea, U.S. Public Health Service, Superintendent of Documents, Government Printing Office, Washington 25, D. C.

Skiing, Forest Service, U. S. Department of Agriculture, Washington, D. C.

Ski Mountaineering, The Sierra Club, 1050 Mills Tower, 220 Bush St., San Francisco, California.

Ski Safety. American Red Cross, Doubleday and Company, Incorporated, Garden City, New York.

Ski Safety and First Aid, Lawrence M. Thompson. Washington.

Snow Structures and Ski Fields. Lane Publishing Company, Menlo Park, California.

Sportsman's Guide, The, Charles B. Roth. Prentice-Hall, Incorporated, New York.

Sportsman's Handbook, Science and Mechanics Publishing Co., 450 E. Ohio St., Chicago, Illinois.

Sunset Ideas for Family Camping. Lane Publishing Company, Menlo Park, California.

Sunset Western Campsite Directory. National Recreation Association, 8 West Eighth Street, New York.

Tent Camper's Guide (New England and New York), Outdoor Publishers, Rocky Hill, Connecticut.

The Camper's Bible, Bill Riviere. Doubleday & Company, Garden City, New York.

The Complete Book of Camping, Miracle and Decker. Harper and Bros., New York, New York.

Tide Tables—Current Tables and Current Charts. U. S. Coast and Geodetic Survey, Washington, D. C.

"Transportation of the Injured in Snow Rescue," Milton Hildbrand. *Western Ski Annual,* 1940-41.

United States Coastal Charts and Inland Waters. U. S. Coast and Geodetic Survey, Washington, D. C.

U. S. Weather Bureau, Cloud Forms. Government Printing Office, Washington, D. C.

Vacation Campgrounds, Southeastern Edition; Vacation Campgrounds, Northeastern Edition, Charles and Kay Hultquist. Vacation Campgrounds; Box 265, Maryville, Tennessee.

Weather Forecasting, George S. Bliss. U. S. Department of Commerce, Washington 25, D. C. (25 cents)

Weather Handbook, Lou Williams. Girl Scouts, Incorporated. New York.

Western Campsite Directory, Lane Publishing Co., Menlo Park, California.

Western Outdoors, Western Outdoors Publishing Corp., 540 W. 19th St., Costa Mesa, California.

Wilderness, Forest Service, U. S. Department of Agriculture, Washington, D. C.

Wilderness Cookery, Bradford Angier, The Stackpole Company, Harrisburg, Pennsylvania.

Wilderness Trails. Boy Scouts of America, 2 Park Avenue, New York.

Wildwood Wisdom, Ellsworth Jaeger. The Macmillan Company, New York.

Your Own Book of Campcraft, Catherine T. Hammet. Pocket Books, Incorporated, Rockefeller Center, New York.

INDEX

A

Accidents, 132, 342, 345, 349; (See also First-Aid)
Advance planning, 8
Advantages, hiking, 202; mobile camper/hiker, 81
Ailments, camping, 342; horses, etc., 333-336
Air mattresses, 190, 211
Air mattresses, sizes, 190
Alaska, 40, 41, 68-71
  Alaska highway, 69
  Fishing, 70
  Free information sources, 71, 72
  Haines-Skagway-Juneau ferry, 70
  Hunting, 70
  Licenses, hunting, fishing, 71
  Railroads, 69
  Skiing, 71
  State Ferry system, 69
Alaska, Alaska highway
  Accommodations, 66
  Camping equipment for, 65
  Car, trailer precautions, 64, 65
  Entering Canada, 67, 68
  Fishing, 66, 67
  Hunting, 66
  Routes to, 62, 63
  Travel seasons, 63, 64
Altitude, cooking time increases, 192
Aluminum foil, in cooking, 252
Animal pests, 106
Anti-fog sticks, 196
Antifreeze, 7
Apache, tent trailer, 113
Appalachian Trail, 206, 207
Area classifications, Forest Service, 237
Areas, outdoor recreation, trends, 81
Army
  Arctic explorer tents, steps to erect, 92, 93
  Blanket fold, saddling, 313
  Compass, 283
  Frame-Pack, 195
Arrival time, planning, 102
Attack, heart, 356
Automobile
  Camping, 80, 86
  Clubs, 115
  In cold, 7

Packing sequence, 117, 118
Standard disabled car distress signal, 133
Avalanches, 197
Axemanship, 274
Axes
  Safety check list, 277
  Tightening loose heads, 275
  Types, 275, 276
Azimuth, back, 289

B

Back packing, 211
Bears, 107
Belt as tape measure, 308
"Be prepared," 341
Bergan-Meis pack, 195
Birdlife, listing by locales, 119-121
Bird watching, 118-121
Bivouac sheet, 186
Blankets as sleeping bag, 231
Blisters, 343
Boats and boating, 138-164
Boat
  Cruise, camping check list, 149
  Launching check list, 142, 143
  Motor buyer's check list, 141
  Operator's check list, 143, 144
  Precautions, 143
  Trailering check list, 141, 142
  Canoes
    Carrying, 157, 158
    Landing and embarking, 158
    Portaging, 159
  Desirable Gov't marine publications, lists, 144, 145
  Folboting, 161-164
Boots, how to break in, 208
Boundary Water Canoe Area, 50-58, 237
  Arrowhead Trail, 54
  Campsites, 57
  Echo Trail, 57
  Fernberg Trail, 57
  Gunflint Trail, 54, 57
  Isabella Area, 57
  Sawbill Trail, 54, 57
  State H'y No. 1, 35 Area, 57
  Virginia-Tower Area, 57
Breakfasts, 260
Building igloo or snowhouse, 370

Building summer homes on Gov't land, 237
Burns, 344, 358; sun and wind, 343
Burros, 230

C

Cabin owner's safety check list, 241
Cabin, cottage style tents, steps to erect, 92
Camp bread, 254
Camp cots, merits of, 99
Campfire
  Control, 242
  How to start, 243
  Permit, 242
  Rules for, 246-251
  Types of fire lays, 245
  Association, 7
  Campsites, Boundary Waters Canoe Area, 57
Camping
  Equipment, winter, 182
  Fire lays, 245
  Popularity of, 1
  Seasons, 7
  (See also Where to go)
  Two-way radio in, 165-176
  Varieties, 1
  With family dog, 109-112
  With special vehicles, 80
  Women and children in, 3
Camp knives, 277
Camp medicine, 361
  Bicarbonate of soda, 362
  Cold treatment, 361
  Emergencies, First-aid (See also Emergencies), 349
  First-aid training desirable, 363
  Grease, 362
  Heat treatment, 362
  Illnesses, 361
  Medical supplies, 363, 364
  Mustard, 362
  Salt, 362
  Sugar pine sugar, 362
  Vinegar, 362
Camp saws, 277
Campsite check list, 105, 106; selection, 102, 341
Canada, 47, 61, 62
  Regulations, entry, 67, 68
Canoe
  Camping check list, 59
  Choosing, 155

Handling, 155, 158
In Quetico-Superior country, 50-58
Load, how packed, 153
Motor with, 153
Safety check list, 159, 160
Safety precautions, 159
(See also Boats and boating)
Strokes, 156
Trip safety precautions, 57
Trips, outfitting, 54, 58
Canopy over camp table, 87
Canyoneering, 59
Cascade Crest Trail, 204
Catalogs, camping items, 114
Care of stock, 320, 330-336
Carrying axe, proper way, 276
Cave exploring, 135, 136
CB radio
  Canada, Mexico, 175
  Channels, 173
  Converter, 172
  Crystals and range, 169
  Equipment uses, 173
  In campiny, 165-176
  Interference, 172
  Regulation, 167-168
"Chain," in measuring, 308
Check lists
  Arctic survival equipment, 371
  Automobile, 132
  Automobile camping, 127
  Axe safety, 277
  Balky outboard motor, 149, 150
  Before leaving home, 131
  Belongings, 132
  Boat cruise camping, 149
  Boat launching, 142
  Boat operator's, 143, 144
  Boat trailering, 141, 142
  Cabin owner's, 241
  Campsite, 105, 106
  Canoe camping, 59
  Canoe safety, 159, 160
  Care of stock, 336, 337
  Citizen-Bander's, 175, 176
  Compass, 290
  Desert trips, 179, 180
  Equipment, knapsack trip, 215
  Equipment, winter camping, 200
  For boat motor buyer, 141
  For boat operator in water skiing, 146
  For pleasure boat buyer, 140, 141

(Check lists—Continued)
  Handling sled dogs, 339
  House trailer, 129
  Knapsack, individual, 214
  Pack animal equipment, 321
  Pack outfit equipment, 231
  Scuba diving, 147
  Skiing, 200
  Skin diving, 148
  Snow snoozer's, 191
  Swimming, 145
  Theft prevention, boat, motor, 151
  Winter apparel, 184
  Winter camping, 200, 201
Children, safety precautions, 342
Citizen-Bander's check list, 175, 176
Claiming campsites, practices, 103
Claims (See Mining claim)
Climbing mountains (See Mountain Travel)
"Closed chest massage," 355
Clothing
  In camp, 1
  Need for dry in survival, 369
  Quetico-Superior country, 56
  Summer mountain travel, 210
  Winter camping, 183, 184
Cold weather survival, 367-372
Compass
  Back azimuth, 289
  Checklist, 290
  Examples, 288, 291, 292, 293
  Gunstock, 294
  History, 280
  Kinds, 280, 282, 295
  Reading angles, 287
  Use, 282, 287, 290, 294
Cooking
  Effect, altitude, 192
  Fruit in foil, 257
  High altitudes, 267
  Kit for hiker, 213
  Kits, snow camping, 193
  Meats and vegetables, 253
  Outdoor recipes, 253
  Without utensils, 258
Cooling tent with fly, 97
Copperhead snake, 135
Coral snake, 135
Costs
  Camping outfit, 116
  Canoe trips, outfitting, 58
  Coach bodies, 83

  Pack train trips, 229
  Renting pack animals, 229, 230
  While traveling, 130
Cottonmouth snake, 135
Covering gear, plastic sheets, 98
Cutting tool accidents, 345

D

Dangers, carbon monoxide, 96
Davis Summit pack, 194
Declinations, magnetic, 284, 285
Dehydrated foods, 215, 266
Desert
  Animals and plant life, 177
  Camping in, 177
  Driving precautions, 179
  Emergency water, 374, 377
  Maps needed, 178
  Pack trips, watch stock, 378
  Survival, 373-378
  Travel, best times, 178, 179
  Trips, planning, 178
Desert Crest Trail, 205
Determining directions, 286
Diarrhea, 359, 360
Dining flies, tarps, to erect, 93, 94
Direction finding
  Compass, 286
  North star, 306
  Shadow method, 302, 303, 304
  Watch and sun, 303
  Without compass or map, 301
Distress signals, survival, 370, 377
Dogs
  Emergency treatment, poisoning, porcupines, 111, 112
  Feeding on trail, 338
  In camping, 109-112
  Regulations applicable in camping, 110, 111
  Sled, 338
Dog food, for trail, 338
Dog sleds, 199
Dog teams, 198-200
Dri-Lite foods, 267, 270
Drinking water, 344
  From snow, 191
  Obtaining in desert, 374
  Preserving, 87
Driving economically, tips, 131
"Drownproofing," to float, 365
Dry ice, 86
Dry well for ice, 87
Duty-free, purchase amounts, 77

E

Elevations, campgrounds, 6
Emergency
  Accidents, etc., 349
  First-aid, 349
  Rations, suppliers, 270, 271
  Repair kit, snow camping, 196
  Shelters, 187, 189
  Treatment of dogs, porcupines or
    poisoning, 111, 112
Equipment
  Lists (See Check lists)
  Motor camper, 86
  Where to get, 114
Expenses, camping (See Costs)
Explorer tents, steps to erect, 92

F

Facilities, National Forests, 6
Falcon automobile, 81, 83
Falling through ice, 346
Family camping, 78
Field offices, Forest Service, 15
Fire dangers, tent materials, 101,
  193
Fire lays, 245
Fire permits, 8
Fire precautions, 125
First-aid, 349
  Abdominal injury, 360
  Artificial respiration, 352
    Mask and Tube, 354
    Mouth-to-mouth, 353
  Bleeding, 350, 358
  Broken bones, etc., 358
  Burns, 343, 358
  Digestive upsets, 360
  Emergencies, 349
  Fever and infections, 360
  Food poisoning, 359
  Headaches, 360
  Heart attack, 356
  If heart stops, 355
  Immediate action cases, 349
  Infections, 360
  Kit, snow camping, 196
  Oxygen, emergency, 354, 355
  Pneumonia and virus flu, 360
  Poison, internal, 358
  Precautions with game, 361
  Prolonged exposure to cold, 359
  Shock, 349
  Snake bite, 350
  Sprains, 359

Unconsciousness from smoke, 352
First-aid training, 363
Floating, water survival, 365
Fly, 95
Folbots, Folboting (See Boats and
  boating)
Folding tent trailer outfits, 113
Food
  Back-pack trip, 213
  Camping, 260
  Coastal survival, 379
  Contaminated, 345
  Dehydrated, 265
  Finding for survival, 370, 374,
    375
  Foil cooking, 252
  For stock, pack trips, 331
  Lists, 261-263
  Menus (See also Recipes)
  Menus, 261, 262, 269
  Recipes, outdoor cooking, 253
    (See also Recipes)
  Selection for snow camping, 192
  Storage in camp, 262
  Suppliers, dry foods, 270, 271
Foot care, hiking trips, 208
Forest rangers, 232
Forests (See National Forests)
"Freeze cans," 86
"Freeze-dry" foods, 266
Frost bite, treatment, 372

G

Game laws, to get information, 41
Gas mileage, improving, 131
Geological Survey maps, 297
Getting ready to camp, 5
Glasses, sun, 196
Gloves, foil cooking, 253
Greenbriar station wagon, 81
Guards, cutting tools, 345
Guides, canoe trips, 57

H

Halazone tablets, 160, 344
Hammock, in camp, 99
Handling sled dogs, check list, 339
Hawaii, to get information, 42
Hazards, camping, 340-346
Heart cases, first-aid, 356
Heat-tabs, 193
Heating tents, 95, 96
Heilite, tent trailer, 113
Help, obtaining, 347
High altitude cooking, 267

"Hiker's spot pack" trip, 230
Hiking-pack trips, 229, 230
Hiking, rates of speed best, 209
Hiking trails
    Appalachian Trail, 206, 207
    Cascade Crest, 204
    Desert Crest, 205
    John Muir, 205, 213
    Lava Crest, 205
    Oregon Skyline, 204
    Pacific Crest, 203-206
    Sierra Crest, 205
Hitches and knots, 322-328
Horse, buying, 337
Horse, mounting, etc., 315
Horse shoeing, 331
House trailer, 113, 114
    Bodies, 83
    Check list, 129
How long until sunset, 311, 312
How to
    Conduct ice rescue, 346
    Erect dining flies, tarps, 93, 94
    Erect tents, 91-94 (See also in-
        dividual tent styles)
    Hike, 208
    Lay campfire, 245
    Make sleeping bag from blankets,
        231
    Pack knapsack, 213
    Purify water, 344
    Sharpen axes, 275
    Stake mining claim, 299
    Travel in mountains (See Moun-
        tain travel)
    Treat snake bite, 350
    Waterproof tent, 101, 102

I

"Ice cans," making, 87
Ice rescue, 346
Ice, treating snake bite, 351
Illnesses, 361 (Also see Camp medi-
    cine)
Imperial gallon, 65
Indian method paddling, 155, 156,
    157
Insurance policies, check, 8

J

Jeep, 80
John Muir Trail, 205
Jungle hammock, 91

K

Kamp-Pack foods, 267, 268
Kelty pack, 194
Knapsack packing, 213
Knapsacks, 211
Knapsack stove, 213
Knives, camp and outdoor, 277
Knots and hitches, 322
Kyack, 8, 318

L

Lake Superior Loop, 49, 50
Lashings, 329
Lava Crest Trail, 205
Leaks, checking tent, 101
Lean-to, 185, 186
Lean-to or Baker tents, steps to
    erect, 93
Leupold and Stevens, 283, 288
"Lif-O-Gen." (oxygen), 354, 355
Loose axe heads, 275
Lost person, what to do, 127
Lunches, 260

M

Magnetic north, 284
Maps
    Compass bearing from, 287
    Geological Survey, 116, 297
    Orienting, 287, 301
    Quetico-Superior country, 55
    Reading, 296
    Scale, 296
Marble compass, 283
Measuring
    Height, trees, etc., 310, 311
    Time until sunset, 311, 312
    Width of stream, etc., 309, 310
Medicine, camp, 361
Menus, 261, 262, 268, 269
Meridians, declinations, 284, 285
Mexico, 72-77
    Car permits, 75
    Description, 72, 73
    Fishing, 76
    Hunting, 75
    Information, 48, 72
    Licenses, hunting, fishing, 75, 76
    Regulations, entry, 73
    Traffic, 74
    Trailering, 74
Microbus, Volkswagen, 81
Mining claim, how to stake, 299
"Mission 66," program, 240
Mobile camping outfits, 81-83

Mother Lode country, 2
Motor camping, 81, 86, 87
Motor vehicles on trails, 80
Mountain climbing (See Mountain
   travel)
Mountain driving, 135
Mountain rescue, 346
Mountain sickness, 342
Mountain travel, 217
   Balance climbing, 220
   Belaying, 222
   Climbing, 217
   Combination climbing holds, 222
   Main climbing holds, 221
   On grassy slopes, 219
   On hard ground, 218
   On scree slopes, 219
   On steep slopes, 220
   On talus slopes, 219
   Rappeling, 225
   Rope climbing, 222, 224
   Rope signals, 225
   Safety, 220, 226
   Walking, 217
"Multiple use," principle, 235

N

National Forests
   Allegheny, 32
   Angeles, 26
   Angelina, 37
   Apache, 20
   Apalachicola, 34
   Arapaho, 18
   Ashley, 24
   Beaverhead, 16
   Bienville, 35
   Bighorn, 19
   Bitterroot, 16
   Black Hills, 19
   Boise, 22
   Bridger, 25
   Cache, 24
   Caribou, 23
   Carson, 21
   Challis, 23
   Chattahoochee, 35
   Chequamegon, 40
   Cherokee, 37
   Chippewa, 39
   Chugach, 40
   Cibola, 21
   Clark, 39
   Clearwater, 15
   Cleveland, 26

Coconino, 20
Coeur D'Alene, 15
Colville, 17
Conecuh, 34
Coronado, 20
Croatan, 36
Cumberland, 32
Custer, 16
Davy Crockett, 37
Deerlodge, 16
Delta, 35
Deschutes, 29
De Soto, 36
Dixie, 24
Eldorado, 26
Fishlake, 24
Flathead, 16
Francis Marion, 37
Fremont, 29
Gallatin, 16
George Washington, 33
Gifford Pinchot, 31
Gila, 22
Grand Mesa-Uncompahgre, 18
Green Mountain, 32
Gunnison, 18
Helena, 17
Hiawatha, 39
Holly Springs, 36
Homochitto, 36
Hoosier, 38
Humboldt, 23
Huron, 38
Inyo, 26
Jefferson, 33
Kaibab, 21
Kaniksu, 15
Kisatchie, 35
Klamath, 27
Kootenai, 17
Lassen, 27
Lewis and Clark, 17
Lincoln, 22
Lolo, 17
Los Padres, 27
Malheur, 29
Manistee, 39
Mark Twain, 40
Medicine Bow, 19
Mendocino, 27
Modoc, 27
Monongahela, 33
Monti-La Sal, 24
Mount Baker, 31
Mount Hood, 29

(National Forests—Continued)
Nantahala, 36
Nebraska, 19
Nezperce, 15
Nicolet, 40
North Tongass, 41
Ocala, 34
Ochoco, 29
Oconee, 35
Okanogan, 31
Olympic, 31
Osceola, 35
Ottawa, 38
Ouachita, 34
Ozark-St. Francis, 34
Payette, 23
Pike, 18
Pisgah, 36
Plumas, 27
Prescott, 21
Rio Grande, 18
Rogue River, 29
Roosevelt, 18
Routt, 18
Sabine, 37
Salmon, 23
Sam Houston, 38
San Bernardino, 27
San Isabel, 18
San Juan, 19
Santa Fe, 22
Sawtooth, 23
Sequoia, 28
Shasta-Trinity, 28
Shawnee, 38
Shoshone, 20
Sierra, 28
Siskiyou, 30
Sitgreaves, 21
Siuslaw, 30
Six Rivers, 28
Snoqualmie, 31
South Tongass, 41
Stanislaus, 28
St. Joe, 15
Sumter, 37
Superior, 39
Tahoe, 28
Talladega, 34
Targhee, 23
Teton, 25
Toiyabe, 24
Tombigbee, 36
Tonto, 21

Tuskegee, 34
Uinta, 25
Umatilla, 30
Umpqua, 30
Uwharrie, 36
Wallowa-Whitman, 30
Wasatch, 25
Wayne, 40
Wenatchee, 31
White Mountain, 32
White River, 19
William B. Bankhead, 33
Williamette, 30
Winema, 30
National Forest campgrounds, 6
National Forests, information, 15
National Parks, information, 9
National Parks
Acadia, 9
Big Bend, 9
Bryce Canyon, 10
Carlsbad Caverns, 10
Crater Lake, 10
Everglades, 10
Glacier, 10
Grand Canyon, 10
Grand Teton, 10
Great Smoky Mountains, 11
Haleakala, 11
Hawaii, 11
Hot Springs, 11
Isle Royale, 11
Kings Canyon, 11
Lassen Volcanic, 12
Mammoth Cave, 12
Mesa Verde, 12
Mount McKinley, 12
Mount Rainier, 12
Olympic, 13
Petrified Forest, 13
Platt, 13
Rocky Mountain, 13
Sequoia, 13
Shenandoah, 14
Virgin Islands, 14
Wind Cave, 14
Yellowstone, 14
Yosemite, 14
Zion, 14
National Park campgrounds, 6
National Park regions, 9
Need for prudence, 340
Nimrod tent trailer, 113
North star, locating, 306

O

"Operations Multiple Use," 240
Oregon Skyline Trail, 204
Organizations, camping, 7
Orienting maps, 287, 301
Outboard motor check list, 149, 150
Outboard motors, canoe uses, 153
Outfitters, river or canyoneering trips, 59-61
Overload springs, needed, 86
Owendoff, 303
Oxygen, emergency, 354, 355

P

Pacific Crest Trail, 203-206
Pacing, in measuring, 308
Pack animals
   Ailments, 333
   Average day's travel, 320
   Care of, 320, 330, 378
   Feeding, 330, 331
   Knowing peculiarities, 330
   Leading, 319
   Load limits, 320
   Saddles, 316, 317, 318
   Saddling and loading, 316
Packers, arrangements with, 228
Pack outfit equipment check list, 231
Packs, for hiking, 211
Paddling canoe, 155
"Para-Wing," 98
Park animals, 108
Park rangers, 232
Parks (See National Parks)
Pathfinding with maps, 296
"Pigs-in-a-blanket," 255
Planning
   Advance, 8
   Back-packing trip, 208
   Desert camping trips, 178
   Trail hiking trips, 207, 208
   Trip, 115
   Trips, places to visit (See Where to go)
Plastic sheets, uses, 98
Pleasure boat buyer's check list, 140, 141
Plywood shelves, station wagons, 85
Poison ivy and poison oak, 134
Poisonous snakes, 135
Porcupines, 106, 107
Potomac-Appalachian Trail Club, 115

Precautions
   Cutting tools, 345
   Driving coach bodies, 83
   For dog in camping, 109-112
   Handling dry ice, 86
   Ice rescue, 346
   Overloading station wagon, 86
Preparing dehydrated foods, 266
Preserving ice, 86
Primitive Areas, 237
Professional packer, status, 229
Puerto Rico, to get information, 46
Pup tents, steps to erect, 94
Purifying water, how to, 344

Q

Quetico-Superior, 50
Quetico-Superior country
   Best seasons, 54
   Campsites, 56, 57
   Canoe outfitting, 58
   Clothing needed, 56
   Description, 50-52
   Equipment needed, 55, 56
   Guides, 57
   Maps, 55
   Points of entry, 54, 55
   Wildlife, 52-54

R

Radio communication, camping, 165-176
Ranger naturalist, 232
Rappeling (See Mountain travel)
Rattlesnake, 135
Reading angles, 287
Recipes, outdoor, 253
Recipes
   Bean stew, squawman's, 255
   Biscuits, Canadian, 254
   Biscuits, High Sierra, 254
   Bread, camp, 254
   Bread, dessert, 256
   Bread, fry pan, 254
   Bread, miner's sourdough, 254
   Clam chowder, fishermen's, 255
   Clam paddies, Alpine, 255
   Coffee, camp, 253
   Coffee, cowboy, 254
   Corn beef casserole, hunter's, 256
   Cornbread, camp, 255
   Erbswurst, Alpine, 257
   Fish, fishermen's fry, 255
   Franks, hiker's, 255
   Fruit, foil cooked, 257

(Recipes—Continued)
Hash, ranger's, 256
Hash, sheepherder's, 256
Meat pie, packer's, 256
Mulligan, cowboy's, 256
Mush, mule skinner's, 255
Paddies, Salmon River, 255
Pancakes, trail, 254
Pemmican, Alaska, 257
Pigs-In-A-Blanket, 255
Pinole, commando, 257
Potatoes, camper's delight, 255
Potatoes, canoeist mashed, 256
Potatoes, mountaineer's hash
    brown's, 255
Rice-A-Roni, ranger's delight, 256
Rice pudding, shepherd's, 257
Soup, woodsmen's creamed po-
    tato, 255
Stew, last camp, 256
Stickobob, hiker's, 257
Tamale pie, hunter's, 256
Tea, northwoods, 254
Tea, Sierra, 254
Toast, mountaineer's 257
Toast, pioneer, 257
Refuse, disposition in camp, 259
Regulations, pack trips, 227
Remedies, etc., 361
Renting burros, pack stock, 230
Renting camping gear, 108
Rescue procedure, mountains, 346
Rivers and canyoneering, 59
"Roman pace," 307, 308
Rubber balls, fastening plastic, 98
Rucksacks, 193
Rugs, camp uses, 101
Rules, using compass, 289

S

Saddle horse, buying, 337
Saddling horse, 313, 314
Safety (See also Check lists)
Avalanches, 197
Axe, check list, 277
Axes, 277
Boating, 143
Canoe, 159
Check list, cabin owner's, 241
Children, 341
Choosing campsites, 104, 341
Contaminated food, 345
Desert trips, 180, 181
Disabled car distress signal, 133
Driving truck-coach vehicles, 83

Gas cylinders, 342
Ice rescue, 346
Mountain driving, 135
Points reviewed, 340-346
Precautions, cutting tools, 345
Purifying water, 344
Station wagon, 86
Tents, 96, 101, 104, 193
Saws, camp, 277
Scale, maps, 296
Scuba diving check list, 147
Scurvy, 371
Seasons, camping, 7
Selecting campsites, 104, 105
Semi-self-contained vehicles, 81-83
Separate tents, uses, 94
"Shadow-tip" method, finding direc-
    tion, 303, 305
"Shadow tip" method, telling time,
    305
Shelter, improvised, 370
Shelters, winter camping, 185
Shoeing stock, pack trip, 331
Sickness, etc., 342
Sierra Crest Trail, 205
Sighting, with compass, 287
Silva compasses, 281, 283, 284, 295
Size tent, how to estimate, 88
Skin diving check list, 148
Skiing check list, 200
Skis, 196
Climbers, 197
Poles, 196
Waxes, 197
Skunk, 106
Sled dogs, 198, 338
Sleds (dog), 199
Sleeping bags, 187, 210
Sleeping bags, double-bed, 189
Sleeping bags from blankets, 231
Sleeping bag liners, 188
"Slip-on" camping units, 83
Snake bite, CO_2 in treating, 361
Snake bite, treating, 350
Snares, 273, 274
Snow, as drinking water, 191
Snow blindness, 343
Snow camping, dog teams, 198-200
Snowshoes, 197
Snow snoozer's check list, 191
Soapy dishes, health hazard, 344
Socks, hiking, 209
Sod cloth, tents, 90
"Special Use Permit," 227
Spelunking, 135, 136

"Spot pack" trips, 230
Staking mining claim, 299
State Park campgrounds, 6
Station wagons
  Camping, 84-86
  Combinations possible, 84
  Extra large, 85
  Tents and shrouds, 84
  2-door vs 4-door, 86
Stirrup length, 315
Stock (see Pack Animals)
Stove
  Fuel, snow camping, 193
  Knapsack model, 213
  Pipe, mounting in tent, 95
  Primus, 193
  Snow camping use, 193
Stretching travel dollars, 131
Suction, for snake bite, 351
Summer homes on Gov't land, 237-240
Suppers, 260
Suppliers, dry foods, 271
Supply lists, temporary camp, 262, 263, 264
Survival
  Along coasts, 378-380
    Food, 379
    Hazards, 380
  Cold weather, 367
    Food, 370
    Equipment check list, 371
    Improvised shelter, 370
  Desert, 373
    Principles, 374
    Water
  Ice accidents, 346
  Signal fires, 380
  Water, 365-367
"Swamp-buggy," 80
Swimming check lists, 145

T

Tarpaulins, uses, 96, 97
Taylor compass, 283
Teams, dog, 198-200
Technique, mountain travel, climbing, 217
Ten tips for travelers, 133
Tents
  Back-pack trip, 210
  Checking over new, 101
  Choosing, 90
  Features, 94, 95

Fly, 95, 96
High altitude, 88, 89, 185
High-walled, 90
How to erect, 91-94
Inflammable materials, 101
Pegging in sand, 104
Poorly ventilated, 94
Sizes and types, 88
Stoves, 95
Testing trips, 116
Trailers, 87, 112
Umbrella, 88, 90, 94
Using with station wagons, 84
Wall, 90
Waterproofing, 101
Theft prevention, boat, motor, 151
Tips for tent campers, 94
Toilet facilities, 100
"Tote-Goat," 80, 83
Trailer
  Campgrounds, 6
  Camping, 112
  Coach bodies, "slip-on," 83
Trail guides, 214
Trails, hiking (See Hiking trails)
Trans-Canada highway, 61
Travel information, to get, 41
Travel, mountainous terrain (See Mountain travel)
Travel Top, Greenbriar vehicle, 82
Trip planning, 115
Treating illness
  Accidents and illnesses, 342-364
  Camp medicine, 361
  First-aid, 349
Treatment, horses, etc., 333-336
Trees, how to cut, 276

U

Umbrella tent, steps to erect, 91
Upset boats, 144
Used foil, disposition in camp, 259

V

Vacation homes on Gov't land, 237
"Vapor lock," treatment of, 114
Virgin Islands, 46
Visits, Canada, Mexico, purchase amounts duty-free, 77
Visklamp, 98

W

Wall tents, steps to erect, 92
Watch and sun, directions, 303

Water
  Filter, 345
  Finding in desert, 374
  Ice rescue, 346
  Moccasin (Cottonmouth) snake, 135
  Purifying, 344
  Safe, 344
  Survival, 365
Watering stock, 330
Waterproofing tents, 101
Water skiing, boat operator check list, 146
Weather, 121
  Signs for outdoorsmen, 123
  Wind-barometer indications, 122, 123
What to do if lost, 127
Where to get
  Alaska, Alaska highway information, 71, 72
  Camping equipment, 114
  Catalogs, 114
  CB radio information, 175
  Hiking trail information, 207
  Information, Forests, 15
  Information, game laws, 41
  Information, Parks, 9

River or canyoneering outfitter information, 59-61
  Travel information, 41
Where to go
  Alaska, Alaska highway, 62-72
  Canada, 62, 67
  Lake Superior Loop, 49, 50
  Mexico, 72-77
  Quetico-Superior country, 50-58
  Trans-Canada highway, 61
Why we camp, 78
Wild Areas, 237
Wilderness Areas, 237
Wilderness skills desirable, 272
Will to live, 368
Windbreaks, canvas, 87
Window screens, station wagons, 84
Winter apparel check list, 184
Winter camping equipment, 182
Winter camping, equipment check list, 200
Wood, best kinds for campfire, 242
Wrapping food, 252

Y

Yosemite, 5
Your camp tent, 87